Brenden Kennelly

Oct 90.

KU-620-967

Electoral Laws
and Their
Political Consequences

This is the first volume of a series on Representation.
Series Editor: Bernard Grofman

Electoral Laws and Their Political Consequences

Edited by

Bernard Grofman
University of California, Irvine

and

Arend Lijphart
University of California, San Diego

AGATHON PRESS, INC.
New York

© 1986 Agathon Press, Inc.
111 Eighth Avenue
New York, NY 10011

All Rights Reserved

No portion of this book may be reproduced by any
process, stored in a retrieval system, or transmitted
in any form, or by any means, without the express
written permission of the publisher.

Printed in the United States

Library of Congress Cataloging-in-Publication Data
Main entry under title:

Electoral laws and their political consequences.

  Bibliography: p.
  Includes index.
  1. Elections—Addresses, essays, lectures.
2. Voting—Addresses, essays, lectures. 3. Election
law—Addresses, essays, lectures. 4. Comparative
government—Addresses, essays, lectures.
I. Grofman, Bernard. II. Lijphart, Arend.
JF1001.E395 1985   324.6   85–15609
ISBN 0-87586-064-8 (cloth)
ISBN 0-87586-074-5 (paper)

Contents

Part I.
The Effect of Election Type on Political Competition

Part II.
Evaluating the Impact of Electoral Laws:
Proportional and Semiproportional Systems
Case Studies

Part III.
Evaluating the Impact of Electoral Laws:
Plurality Systems

Part IV.
Redistricting

Acknowledgments

Earlier versions of two of the papers in this volume were presented at the panel on "Electoral Engineering" at the 1982 Annual Meeting of the American Political Science Association in Chicago, and earlier versions of two others were given at the panel on "Electoral Laws and Their Political Consequences" at the August 1982 Meeting of the International Political Science Association in Rio de Janeiro. We are indebted to the American Political Science Association for permission to excerpt from William Riker's article, "Two-Party Systems and Duverger's Law: An Essay on the History of Political Science" [*American Political Science Review* 76 (December 1982), 753–766]; and to the *California Journal* for permission to reprint the maps of California Congressional districts which appear in Gordon Baker's article. We are indebted to the School of Social Sciences, University of California, Irvine, for a small seed grant to plan this volume, and to the National Science Foundation's Political Science Program and the Guggenheim Foundation, respectively, for research support while working on this volume. Invaluable assistance has been provided to the editors by Sue Pursche, Dorothy Gormick, George Ferrington, Nguyen Ngo, and the staff of the Word Processing Center, School of Social Sciences, UCI. Final editing on this volume took place while Ms. Pursche was a Fellow at the Center for Advanced Study in the Behavioral Sciences, Stanford.

List of Tables and Figures

Tables *found on page*

Tables *(continued)* *found on page*

Figures

About the Editors

Bernard Grofman is Professor of Political Science and Social Psychology, School of Social Sciences, University of California, Irvine. He is a specialist in mathematical models of collective decision making, with over three dozen published articles on topics such as jury verdict choice, reapportionment and voter turnout, and coalition formation models. During the past two years he has been involved in eleven states as an expert witness in redistricting litigation or as a court-appointed reapportionment expert. He is coeditor of *Representation and Redistricting Issues, Choosing an Election System,* and *Information Pooling and Group Decision Making.*

Arend Lijphart is Professor of Political Science, University of California, San Diego. His field of specialization is comparative politics, with a special interest in Western democratic states and the relationship between election rules and party systems. He is the author of four books: *The Trauma of Decolonization: The Dutch and West New Guinea; The Politics of Accommodation: Pluralism and Democracy in the Netherlands; Democracy in Plural Societies: A Comparative Exploration;* and *Democracies: Patterns of Majoritarian and Consensus Government in Twenty-One Countries;* as well as numerous articles in leading international journals on democratic theory and comparative electoral politics.

About the Contributors

Gordon E. Baker is Professor of Political Science, University of California, Santa Barbara. His major research interests have centered on reapportionment and representation. He is author of three books: *Rural versus Urban Political Power; State Constitutions: Reapportionment;* and *The Reapportionment Revolution;* as well as numerous articles and chapters in books. In 1973 he served as consultant to special masters charged by the California Supreme Court with the redistricting of the state's legislative and congressional districts.

Carol A. Cassel is Associate Professor of Political Science, University of Alabama. She has published articles in the areas of political participation, public opinion, and voting behavior. Her recent papers (including an article in the *American Journal of Political Science*) deal with research methodology; e.g., issues in measurement and model specification.

Maurice Duverger is Professor of Political Science at the Sorbonne, University of Paris I. He is the author of *Political Parties: Their Organization and Activity in the Modern State* (first published in French in 1951 and first published in English translation in 1954) and of many other books and articles in comparative public law and comparative politics.

Richard L. Engstrom is Professor of Political Science, University of New Orleans. His fields of specialization are urban and minority politics, with a special interest in the issue of racial vote dilution. He has published articles in the *American Political Science Review, American Journal of Political Science, Journal of Politics,* and other leading journals, and has served as an expert witness in numerous vote dilution cases.

Peter C. Fishburn is a member of the Mathematics and Statistics Research center of Bell Laboratories, Murray Hill, N.J. His research interests focus on individual and societal decision making and on discrete mathematics. He is the author of five books, including *Utility Theory for Decision Making, The Theory of Social Choice,* and *The Foundations of Expected Utility,* and coauthor with Steven Brams of *Approval Voting.* His numerous articles have been published in technical journals in the fields of mathematics, economics, statistics, political science, and operations research, and he serves on several editorial boards.

Graham Gudgin is a Senior Research Officer, Department of Applied Economics, University of Cambridge. He is currently working on macro-economic models and theory. His other interests are in regional growth and in forecasting regional labor market conditions. He has a strong interest in politics, and it was this interest which led to the book with Peter Taylor, *Seats Votes and the Spatial Organization of Elections.* Other books include *Industrial Locational Processes, Unequal Growth,* and *Non-Production Activities in the UK Manufacturing Industry.*

R. J. Johnston is Professor of Geography, University of Sheffield, U.K. His main interests are in electoral, political, and urban studies, and he is the author of several books in these areas, including *Political, Electoral and Spatial Systems, Geography of Elections* (with P. J. Taylor), and *City and Society.* He was an expert witness in a recent case challenging the decision of the Boundary Commission for England.

Richard S. Katz is Professor of Political Science, Johns Hopkins University. His principle research is on electoral systems and political behavior in Western Europe and the United States. He is the author of *A Theory of Parties and Electoral Systems* and of numerous articles that have appeared in leading European and American journals. He is also interested in public broadcasting and government support of the arts.

William R. Keech is Professor of Political Science, University of North Carolina, Chapel Hill. His research and teaching interests are in the theory and practice of representative government and in the politics of macro-economic policy. He is author of *The Impact of Negro Voting* and coauthor of *The Party's Choice.* In addition to articles on the United States, he has written on Soviet and on Swiss politics.

Rafael Lopez Pintor is Tenure Professor of Sociology, Universidad Autonoma, Madrid. He has a doctoral degree in law from the University of Madrid and a Ph.D. from the University of North Carolina. He has been Director General of the Center for Sociological Research in Madrid from 1979 to 1983. Most of his research work has dealt with Spain and Latin America in the areas of public opinion and electoral behavior as well as organizations. His latest book, *La Opinion Publica Espanola del Franquismo a la Democracia* (Madrid: CIS, 1982) deals with opinion trends and mass political behavior from the late Franco regime of the 1960s to the eve of the Socialist electoral landslide.

Peter Mair is Lecturer in Government, University of Manchester. His fields of specialization include political parties, party systems, and electoral studies, and he has published a number of articles in various political science journals on Irish politics and West European politics. He is coeditor of *Western European Party Systems: Continuity and Change.*

Michael D. McDonald is Assistant Professor of Political Science, University of New Orleans. His fields of specialization are legislative processes and elections. He has written articles on election systems and electoral behavior that have appeared in the leading political science journals.

William H. Riker is Wilson Professor of Political Science, University of Rochester. His books include *Liberalism Against Populism: A Confrontation Between the Theory of Democracy and the Theory of Social Choice; An Introduction to Positive Political Theory* (with Peter Ordeshook); *The Theory of Political Coalitions; Federalism;* and *Democracy in the United States.* His current work concerns a formal theory of heresthetic (political manipulation) and rhetoric.

Giovanni Sartori is Albert Schweitzer Professor in the Humanities, Columbia University, New York City. His fields of interest are political theory, comparative politics, and social science methodology. His major works are *Democratic Theory; Parties and Party Systems: A Framework for Analysis;* and *La Politica: Logica e Metodo in Scienze Sociali.* Among the volumes he has edited, the most recent one is *Social Science Concepts: A Systematic Analysis.*

Howard A. Scarrow is Professor of Political Science, State University of New York, Stony Brook, where he has taught since 1963. He is a specialist on comparative electoral politics and is author or coauthor of five books (including *Canada Votes* and *Parties, Elections and Representation in the State of New York*) and numerous articles in major political science journals, including *Journal of Politics, World Politics,* and *Comparative Politics.*

Yasunori Sone is Associate Professor of Political Science, Keio University, Tokyo. His research interests include the study of decision-making rules and various aspects of Japanese democracy, especially electoral politics and the electoral system. He is the author of *Political Economy of Decision-Making* and the coeditor of *Japanese Politics in the World Perspective* (with N. Tomita) and *Contemporary Democratic Theories* (with R. Shiratori and M. Nakano). He has also written many articles in professional journals and chapters in multi-authored volumes.

Peter J. Taylor is Senior Lecturer of Geography, University of Newcastle upon Tyne. His field of specialization is political geography with particular reference to electoral studies and the role of the state in the world economy. He is editor of *Political Geography Quarterly*. He has published many articles in geographic and politics journals on electoral and political geography. He is joint author of *Geography of Elections* (with R. J. Johnston), *Seats Votes and the Spatial Organization of Elections* (with G. Gudgin), and *Section and Party* (with J. C. Archer); and joint editor of *Political Studies from Spatial Perspectives* (with A. D. Burnett).

Leon Weaver is Professor, School of Criminal Justice, College of Social Science, Michigan State University. His discipline is political science. His specializations are security systems, personnel administration, and comparative election systems and behavior. His experiences as a practitioner include elective local offices; service on a charter drafting commission grappling with electoral-system issues, serving as a consultant to a court adjudicating such issues, and membership on the Freedom House mission to observe and report on elections in Zimbabwe-Rhodesia. He has a special interest in electoral politics in societies plagued by violence or other high levels of social conflict.

J.F.H. (Jack) Wright is President of the Proportional Representation Society of Australia. His professional work has involved the study of electoral methods for many years. He is the author of *Mirror of the Nation's Mind—Australia's Electoral Experiments*, a study of the use of preferential and other electoral methods in Australia, and of several papers relating to electoral procedures.

Introduction

Bernard Grofman and Arend Lijphart

The aim of this book is to provide an overview of recent research on electoral laws and their political consequences by scholars who have helped shape the field. After several decades of virtual neglect (except for Douglas Rae's seminal work), the comparative study of electoral systems is undergoing a lively revival. In the past five years, over a dozen books on electoral systems have been written by scholars from many nations and from many disciplines (see reviews of a number of these in Lijphart, 1984a). Political geography, long moribund, is undergoing a remarkable renaissance (see reviews in Grofman, 1982d; Taylor, Gudgin, and Johnston, this volume). Social choice theorists have begun to link axiomatic criteria for representative systems to practical political issues in choosing an election system (see especially Brams and Fishburn, 1983, 1984a, 1984b; Fishburn, this volume). In the United States, sparked in large part by the efforts of the section on Representation and Electoral Systems of the American Political Science Association, the history of American electoral experimentation with proportional representation, weighted voting, and limited voting is being rediscovered (see Grofman 1982a; Weaver, this volume).

This renewed scholarly attention to the study of electoral systems is long overdue. The late Stein Rokkan wrote as recently as 1968, "Given the crucial importance of the organization of legitimate elections in the development of the mass democracies of the twentieth century, it is indeed astounding to discover how little serious effort has been invested in the comparative study of the wealth of information available" (Rokkan, 1968, p. 17). The long past neglect of electoral systems by social scientists is especially surprising since election rules not only have important effects on other elements of the political system, especially the party system, but also offer a practical instrument for political engineers who want to make changes in the political system. Indeed, Sartori aptly characterizes electoral systems as "the most specific manipulative instrument of politics" (1968b, p. 273).

No single volume can do justice to the range of issues which ought to be dealt with in a complete study of the political consequences of electoral laws. For example, the independent variables analyzed by Rae (e.g., ballot structure, election type, number of representatives to be elected from each district, and total number of representatives in the legislature) are only a partial inventory of those that can have a critical impact, and the principal dependent variables he considers (proportionality of party representation and creation of legislative majorities), while among the most important elements of a proper analysis of electoral laws and their political consequences, omit a large number of relevant concerns. In particular, in addition to

1. Electoral formulas [e.g., proportional representation (PR) vs. majoritarian systems; for alternative typologies see Rae, 1967, 1971; Grofman, 1975]
2. Ballot structure (e.g., nominal vs. ordinal)
3. District magnitude (number of seats)
4. Size of legislature
5. Number of candidates/parties

we should consider (cf. Fishburn, 1983):

1. Suffrage and registration requirements
2. Ease of voter access to the electoral process (e.g., availability of bilingual ballots, polling hours, number and location of polling stations, and enforcement of voter rights against intimidation)[1]
3. Ease of party/candidate access to the political process (e.g., candidate eligibility requirements, signature-gathering rules, nominating fees, party-slating procedures, and bans on "antisystem" parties)
4. Structure of political competition (e.g., partisan vs. nonpartisan ballots and availability of intraparty preference voting)
5. Special features of ballot format (e.g., office block vs. party check-

off, machine vs. paper ballot, open versus secret, and sequencing rules for candidate/party ballot position)

6. Special features for transforming votes into outcomes (e.g., the U.S. electoral college and electoral thresholds in PR systems)
7. Districting procedures (e.g., rules which constrain districts to satisfy equal population guidelines or compactness norms, or to provide representation of ethnic or other communities of interest)
8. Campaign financing rules (limits on donations and spending, nonconfidentiality of information on donors, and provisions for public financing)
9. Campaign timing rules (e.g., fixed vs. variable interval elections and length of term in office)
10. Other features of campaigning (e.g., rules on media access, rules prohibiting "unfair" advertising, rules on sites where campaigning is forbidden, and restrictions on the period during which a campaign can be conducted)
11. Number and type of offices which are subject to electoral choice (e.g., appointive vs. elective vs. administrative mechanisms for various policy domains, number of different elections voters are expected to participate in annually, and regularity of election dates)
12. Degree of "bundling" of elections (e.g., sequencing of dates for local, state, and national elections and for executive and legislative elections; and regularity of election dates)
13. Mechanisms for voter intervention (e.g., initiative, referendum, and recall)

Similarly, while the degree of seats-votes proportionality and facilitation of majority legislative control are among the most important political consequences of electoral laws, also relevant are (1) the effects on ideological polarization of the electorate; (2) the structure of party organization; (3) intraparty versus interparty competition; (4) regional and national integration; (5) the interaction of political and economic "cycles"; (6) voter participation and sense of voter efficacy; (7) incentives to strategic voting; (8) perceived regime legitimacy; and (9) representation of racial, ethnic, and other group interests.

Since we could not cover all the variables and issues enumerated above, our selection of topics has been guided by three principles. First, we commissioned review essays on topics where there is a substantial body of research which could usefully be summarized and which may not be well-known to specialists in comparative election systems. Thus Engstrom and McDonald write on the effects of at-large elections on minority representation; Cassel writes on nonpartisan elections; Weaver considers PR in the United States; Taylor, Gudgin, and Johnston take up political geography; and Fishburn reviews social choice approaches. Second, we commissioned articles on various electoral institutions which are not well researched, as a spur to further work. Included are Lijphart, Lopez-Pintor, and Sone on limited voting in Spain and Japan; Lijphart on proportionality by non-PR methods; Scarrow on ballot format and cross-endorsement in plurality systems in the United States; Katz on intraparty preference voting; and Keech on the length and renewability of electoral terms. Finally, we sought to avoid duplication of the literature surveys in such excellent compilations as Butler, Penniman, and Ranney (1981), Cadart (1983), and Bogdanor and Butler (1983).

Effects of Election Type on Political Competition

We are especially pleased to begin this volume with a set of three complementary essays on one of the most important issues in the analysis of the effects of electoral laws: the relationship between type of electoral system (e.g., simple plurality, plurality with double ballot, and various forms of proportional representation) and the number of political parties contesting elections. All three articles take as their starting point the formulation in Duverger (1951a) that the plurality system favors the two-party system, commonly referred to as "Duverger's law," while PR methods and the double-ballot system favor multipartyism, referred to as "Duverger's hypothesis."

The first of these chapters is by William Riker, "Duverger's Law Revisited."[2] After discussing the ambiguities in Duverger's original formulation concerning the deterministic or probabilistic nature of the claimed relationships, Riker reviews evidence unfavorable to both Duverger's hypothesis and Duverger's law and then seeks to reformulate the latter so as to be able to account for the apparent counterexamples of Canada and India. His proposed modifications focus on a distinction between localized versus national two-party competition, on the one hand, and the presence or absence of a party capable of regularly commanding a majority against any probable *single* opponent, on the other. Riker then goes on to discuss the rationally grounded motivations for voter and party leaders which could explain the empirical fit of Duverger's law.

Sartori's chapter, "The Influence of Electoral Systems: Faulty Laws or Faulty Method?" deals with the scientific status of assertions about the link between election type and party number. After first clarifying

Duverger's own original formulation of his laws, Sartori goes on to question their imprecision as to causality, determinism, and variable operationalization. This analysis leads him to grave skepticism about the possibility of their empirical verification, at least in the form initially stated. Sartori then reviews two proposed modifications of Duverger, those of Rae (1971) and Riker (1982a, excerpted in this volume), and finds neither author's attempt to reformulate Duverger to be satisfactory.

Sartori asserts that PR does not multiply the number of political parties. In particular, "whenever the introduction of PR happens to be followed by the surge of new relevant parties, we are not really pointing at the *effects* of PR, but at the *side effects* resulting from the removal of preexisting obstacles." On the other hand, "a plurality system cannot provide by itself a nationwide two-party format, but . . . it will help *maintain* an already existing one." Sartori's analysis of the effects of election type hinges upon the geographic distribution of partisan support and upon the presence of a structured party system. Sartori goes on to relate election type (ideological or other) and party polarization (defined as the distance between the most distant relevant parties) to the nature of the system of party competition that can be expected to emerge. He concludes by referring to necessary and sufficient factors that he feels contribute to a two-party format, as well as two other laws about the reductive or maintaining effect of election type on party number.

The third chapter in this volume is by Maurice Duverger. In "'Duverger's Law': Forty Years Later," Duverger traces the history of his own work, beginning with its earliest formulation in 1946, and then, responding to his critics, considers the presently available evidence on the tendencies he pointed to in *Political Parties* (1951a). Duverger reminds his readers that he has long recognized that

> the relationship between electoral rules and party systems is not mechanical and automatic: A particular electoral regime does not necessarily produce a particular party system; it merely exerts pressure in the direction of this system; it is a force which acts among several other forces, some of which tend in the opposite direction.

Duverger points to specific social and cultural features (as well as electoral features) which can help explain the tendencies of Ireland, Austria, and Germany to a two-party system despite their use of forms of proportional representation. He concludes his essay with a very preliminary but nonetheless suggestive discussion of the structural factors which may lead to "bipolar multipartyism," a multiparty system where political conflict is shaped by two opposing blocs.

Richard S. Katz's essay, "Intraparty Preference Voting," calls attention to an important and too often neglected feature of electoral systems, the available mechanism for within-party choice of candidates. As Katz reminds us, "all candidates of a single party are not alike." Moreover, a party leader or supporter "might prefer the representatives of a particular area, interest, or faction to be proportionately stronger within the party even at the expense of overall party strength." Thus, in systems with partisan elections, we may think that electoral competition takes place on at least two levels: between party and within party—with interdependencies between those two types of competition. For example, "voters may exert an indirect influence on party-nominating decisions by demonstrating a differential willingness to support the party based on the identity of its candidates."

Katz identifies the diverse mechanisms for intraparty preference voting in fifteen election systems, including ones using list PR, STV (the single-transferable vote), and plurality. Among the party list systems, Katz identifies a wide range of options. At one extreme, in some party list systems the order of elections is determined solely by the preference votes cast for individual candidates. In several systems the special features of panachage and cumulation permit an unusual degree of voter flexibility. At the other extreme are systems in which the party list order prevails unless changed by a very large number of voters. Among plurality systems there are also a wide range of options ranging from challenge primaries, where only candidates who receive a minimum level of support in their own party's caucus or convention can challenge the decision, to blanket primaries, where all the candidates for each office are listed together regardless of party. Using recent elections from each of his fifteen polities, Katz identifies the effects of within-party and between-party competition on the re-election success of incumbents, and looks at the relationship between incumbent reelection success and election type and at the implications of his findings for party unity.

The concluding chapter in this section, William R. Keech's short essay on the length and renewability of electoral terms, is intended to stimulate interest in another important, but neglected, topic. Keech begins by noting that "those who see elections as a positive good and an effective guide for the behavior of public officials are likely to favor frequent elections and unlimited renewability of electoral terms. Those who see elections as necessary evils which interfere with the deliberations of statesmen tend to favor infrequent elections and limits on the possibility of reelection." Beginning with a discussion of the arguments advanced in *The Federalist Papers*, Keech then turns to recent statistically sophisticated models of the interaction between election timing and the timing of economic policies intended to be politically advantageous to incumbent politicians, and goes on to consider the implications of variable rather than fixed election terms. While Keech's analysis is intended to be only preliminary, based on models which dramatically simplify reality, this line of research has potentially important policy implications; for instance, for the desirability of imposing limits on reelection such as these in the Twenty-second Amendment to the U.S. Constitution (which limited presidents to two terms).

Proportional and Semiproportional Systems

Section II contains five chapters which are case studies or comparative analyses of proportional and semiproportional systems. Included are essays on list PR formulas, the limited vote, and mechanisms for PR-like representation by non-PR methods, such as separate ethnic lists.

Arend Lijphart's brief but comprehensive essay, "Proportionality by Non-PR Methods: Ethnic Representation in Belgium, Cyprus, Lebanon, New Zealand, West Germany, and Zimbabwe," which begins this section, discusses the use of quotas, ethnically designated election districts or election rolls, and other special election features whose aim is to provide enhanced religious or ethnic representation. His examples offer a comparative analysis of several little-known systems. Lijphart considers the advantages and disadvantages of PR versus non-PR methods, with a conclusion largely favorable to the former. For example, he notes that even if the ethnic groups entitled to special modes of representation are specified, it may still be difficult to determine ethnic identification, especially in multiracial societies. Moreover, "the very principle of officially registering individuals according to ethnicity may be controversial or even completely unacceptable to many citizens," although this problem can be mitigated by making ethnic registration optional or by permitting voters a choice of slates, or by using geographic concentrations of ethnically identifiable voters to determine districts.

Jack F. Wright's essay "Australian Experience with Majority-Preferential and Quota-Preferential Systems," reviews in detail the relatively little-studied Australian use of the single-transferable vote (STV) (referred to by Wright as the quota-preferential method or, also following

Australian usage, the Hare-Clark system) and of majority-preferential voting (commonly known as the alternative vote). Australia pioneered the use of an early form of STV in the state of Tasmania in 1896, and the use of majority preferential voting in the state of Queensland in 1892. STV was adopted for the Australian Federal Senate in 1946. Australia's national electorate of over 8 million voters is the largest to make use of STV. Tasmania's experience with STV, employed with only minor changes since 1896, is the longest continuous example of the use of STV for legislative elections.

Wright's description of seats-votes outcomes under majority-preferential voting shows that it is closer to plurality and majoritarian methods than to PR or semiproportional methods. On the other hand, Wright points out that the use of STV in Tasmania (and for the Australian Federal Senate) has led to effective proportional representation of voter preferences and has not led to a fragmentation of the party system.

Leon Weaver's comprehensive overview of "The Rise, Decline, and Resurrection of Proportional Representation in Local Governments in the United States," discusses the adoption of STV in municipal elections in nearly two dozen U.S. cities in the first part of the century and the reasons for the abolition of PR in all but one of those cities by the mid 1960s. Weaver shows that "one of the important reasons for the abandonments was the opposition of party organizations and their leaders." Rather than affected by the issues which have preoccupied political scientists (e.g., the merits of seats-votes proportionality vs. the demerits of factionalism and immobilisme), in the United States, Weaver shows that STV rose (and then fell) with the ability of the various political actors who felt they were advantaged or disadvantaged by STV, to rouse voters on their behalf or against their opponents. Weaver also emphasizes that rumors of the end of STV in the United States have been exaggerated. It remains alive and well in Cambridge municipal elections and (since 1971) in New York City school board elections.

In seeking to derive lessons from the United States use of STV in local nonpartisan elections, Weaver makes the general point that the potential political consequences of any change in electional laws must be understood in the context of the political system in which it is embedded. Weaver also shows that many of the claims made about the political effects of STV in the United States have failed to disentangle STV from other structural features which were often adopted simultaneously with it, such as the council/city manager system. It does appear, however, that STV had a significant effect on styles of personal campaigning.

The third chapter in this section—by Arend Lijphart, Rafael Lopez-Pintor, and Yasunori Sone, "The Limited Vote and the Single-Non-transferable Vote: Lessons from the Japanese and Spanish Examples"—a tricontinental collaboration, again deals with election data which has been rather neglected, in this case data on limited voting (and its polar case, the single-nontransferable vote, SNTV) drawn from national elections in Spain and Japan. Limited voting (like cumulative voting) can be characterized as a semiproportional system; that is, it combines some of the features of both plurality and PR. The limited vote uses multimember districts in which each voter has fewer votes than there are seats at stake in the district. Lijphart, Lopez-Pintor, and Sone characterize the limited vote as "both the most important kind of semiproportional system and the most straightforward and logical compromise between the plurality and PR principles." Under the SNTV system (used in Japan's lower house since 1900), voters in 3-, 4-, and 5-member districts have 1 vote each. In Spain's Senate since 1977 the basic arrangement is that voters in 4-member districts have 3 votes each. Lijphart, Lopez-Pintor, and Sone analyze the theoretical proportionality features of the limited vote as a function of district magnitude and of the number of votes each voter is entitled to cast, and then analyze recent elections in the two countries. They find that, as expected, in terms of the matchup of vote share and seat share, the limited vote is "intermediate" between PR and non-PR systems but leans more toward the plurality end. They also find that, because a party which overestimates its strength and nominates "too many" candidates will be severely penalized by electoral setbacks, most parties (especially the larger ones which are likely to suffer the greatest disadvantage from miscalculation) are conservative in how many candidates they nominate.

Lijphart's concluding chapter in this section, "Degrees of Proportionality of Proportional Representation Formulas," deals with the proportionality of six standard PR formulas. He finds the largest remainder formula the most proportional, and the Imperiali highest average formula the least so. Further, he unifies (and corrects) earlier work on this topic.

Plurality and Pluralitylike Systems

Section III of our volume deals with plurality and pluralitylike systems. It begins with a comprehensive and integrative review essay by the three authors whose works have spearheaded the recent renaissance in political geography in Britain: Peter J. Taylor, Graham Gudgin, and R. J. Johnston, "The Geography of Representation: A Review of Recent Findings." The starting point of the research they review is the study of elections as it represents the interaction between two spatial distributions: the pattern of voters and the network of constituency boundaries. Taylor, Gudgin, and Johnston inventory findings on seats-votes relationships for single-member plurality elections. Key variables which enter these analyses are district size; the number, average magnitude, and partisan homogeneity of the clusters of partisan concentration of voter support; and the geographic pattern of clustering (spatial autocorrelation). This research provides important new insights into issues such as the likely empirical realism of the "cube law" of electoral representation, the proportionality of representation for third parties, and the relative power of political parties.

Peter Fishburn's essay, "Social Choice and Pluralitylike Electoral Systems," discusses a literature whose relevance to the analysis of comparative election systems has only recently been recognized by political scientists (see esp. Riker, 1982b). Fishburn focuses on the effects of electoral systems on matters such as candidate strategy (especially ideological positioning), voter behavior (e.g., the incentives to vote for candidates whom the voter prefers but who have little or no chance of election), the accuracy with which voter preferences are represented, and the structure of within-party competition. Election systems analyzed by Fishburn include simple plurality, plurality with runoff (the double-ballot system), double plurality (not to be confused with the double-ballot system; double plurality gives each voter exactly two votes, but, as in simple plurality, the candidate with the most votes wins), and approval voting (a new method permitting voters to vote for each candidate whom they regard as "satisfactory" for them, rather than merely voting for their first choice).[3]

The essay by Richard L. Engstrom and Michael D. McDonald, "The Effect of At-Large versus District Elections on Racial Representation in U.S. Municipalities," deals with a topic which has become increasingly important in the past two decades—the opportunities for racial and linguistic minorities to obtain representatives of their choice in single-member district systems as compared to at-large (multimember district) elections held under a plurality (or plurality with runoff) rule. Engstrom and McDonald focus on U.S. municipal elections, and begin by reviewing the history of local election practices in the United States, finding an early twentieth-century wave of "reform" which led to the adoption of at-large systems and then a more recent trend (also labeled "reform") away from at-large elections and back to single-member districts. This new reform has been motivated by the argument that multimember plurality elections (with their winner-take-all nature) tend to submerge minority voting strength.

Engstrom and McDonald conclude that the electoral format has a major impact on the number of black elected officials: "In cities in which all of the members of the council are elected from districts, the relationship between the black population and the black membership on the council is virtually proportional. . . . If at-large elections are used, however, blacks can be expected to be underrepresented." Engstrom and McDonald also look at the modifying effects of features (e.g., socioeconomic variables, political context, size of black population, and geographic region) which might be expected to affect the relationship between election type and the proportionality of minority representation. Their careful review of the literature shows that the dilutive effect of at-large elections on minority representation in U.S. municipalities persists even when other factors are controlled. They conclude with a discussion of the rather inconclusive data testing the hypothesis that municipal responsiveness to black concerns increases as the level of black city council representation increases.

Carol A. Cassel's chapter, "The Nonpartisan Ballot in the United States," complements the Engstrom and McDonald chapter which precedes it, since at-large elections and nonpartisan ballots were two of three elements of the tripod on which the municipal reform movement of the early twentieth century rested (the third element being the professional city manager). As Cassel points out, early reformers saw nonpartisan elections as a critical tool to "limit the power of corrupt party machines, insulate local elections from the influence of state and national party politics, facilitate more efficient and business-like administration of local government, and encourage recruitment of superior candidates." As with at-large elections, one generation's reforms may become the next generation's errors that must be corrected. Although there is no current crusade for the reform of partisan city politics comparable to that now calling for a return to single-member districts, post-World War II scholarship has suggested that nonpartisan elections have a number of undesirable properties; for instance, it has been claimed that they tend to be "issueless in nature, that incumbents are advantaged and less accountable to the public in nonpartisan systems, that nonpartisan bodies lack collective responsibility, and that channels for recruitment to higher office are restricted by nonpartisanship."

Cassel's essay offers a thorough and balanced treatment of the available empirical evidence examining the alleged pros and cons of nonpartisan elections. Her intriguing conclusion is that "neither the reformist nor the revisionist theory of nonpartisan municipal elections is generally supported by empirical studies. The differences between partisan and nonpartisan systems appear to be less than both the proponents and critics of nonpartisanship argue," although "there are some discernible and measurable differences."

Howard Scarrow's two brief essays touch upon structural features of U.S. election systems which have been relatively little researched: ballot format and cross-endorsement/cross-filing procedures. His first essay reviews the strong evidence supporting the claim that the office-block ballot increases the incidence of split-ticket voting as compared to the party-column ballot. Scarrow, however, calls attention to some important and customarily neglected distinctions between office-block arrangements which facilitate straight-party voting (e.g., all of a party's candidates being located on a single horizontal row) and those which do not. Scarrow concludes this essay with an examination of the literature on ballot position and election success.

Scarrow's second essay is on cross-endorsement (a practice in which a candidate may run as the nominee of more than one party) and on cross-filing (in which a candidate may simultaneously seek the endorsement of more than one party) and compares and contrasts the effects of these two practices. He also notes that in both cross-filing and cross-endorsement, however, usually a candidate's name will appear more than once on the ballot; thus *both* practices may be contrasted with the related phenomenon of electoral alliances in European multiparty systems, in which the candidate's name will appear but once. Scarrow attributes to the state of New York's peculiar cross-endorsement rules the growth of a five-party system in that state, despite a single-member district plurality system. This essay thus provides an instance where analysis of state and local election systems in the United States may suggest modifications of generalizations (about election system and number of parties) based on studies of national parliaments.

Redistricting

The fourth and final section of this volume deals with redistricting issues. The lead chapter in this section, by Gordon E. Baker, looks at "Whatever Happened to the U.S. Reapportionment Revolution?" In the 1960s federal courts stepped in as guarantors, first of periodic reapportionment and then of "one-person, one-vote" standards for state and federal redistricting. Baker points out that adherence to the standard of "one person, one vote" was achieved in a remarkably record time after judicial intervention, despite the fact that population discrepancies across districts were (in 1960) widespread and extreme. The reform ideas which drove political scientists (and others) to demand reapportionment were the desire for fair and effective representation, and, in particular, the need to end the chronic underrepresentation of urban (and more liberal) interests. Among the consequences of the reapportionment revolution discussed by Baker are gains for the Democratic party in state legislatures outside the South, a shift of Republican strength from rural to suburban districts, and an apparent reduced likelihood of divided party control at the state level—although direct policy consequences appear to have been very limited and remain hard to measure. However, although it achieved some of the earlier aims of reformers, the reapportionment revolution has left as yet largely unsettled a number of fundamental issues—including the problems posed by multimember elections and partisan gerrymandering. Indeed, in Baker's view, "by 1969 the Supreme Court had paradoxically encouraged the potential for widespread gerrymandering by developing a single-minded quest for mathematical [population] equality."

R. J. Johnston's chapter, "Constituency Redistribution in Britain: Recent Issues," provides us information on which to base a comparative analysis of the U.S. and British redistricting experience. Johnston points out that a mismatch between partisan vote share and partisan legislative seat share can occur both intentionally and unintentionally. He argues convincingly that the moves in Great Britain (beginning in the 1940s) to ensure equality in constituency population and to take the decision-making responsibility regarding boundary delimitation out of the hands of politicians, have ensured a "fair" procedure but do not necessarily ensure a "fair" result—although he does assert that "it is unlikely that a neutral procedure will perpetrate a major gerrymander. In Great Britain, as in the United States there has been debate over the importance of "representation of place" (i.e., counties and boroughs) relative to "representation of people," and these issues have gone to the courts; however, in Britain (unlike the United States) judicial intervention has not really taken place, and exact numerical standards have not been laid down.

Our concluding essay by Peter Mair, "Districting Choices Under the Single-Transferable Vote in Ireland," shows that reapportionment is not an issue exclusive to single-member districting. Mair first reviews the operations of STV in Ireland and then discusses its accessibility to partisan manipulation, particularly that which is achieved through variations in district magnitude (number of seats to be filled per district). Mair also calls attention to the extent to which STV's multimember districts are subject to "intraparty bailiwicking," an arrangement in which party voters in different areas within the same multimember district are instructed to place different candidates at the top of their preference ordering.

Mair concludes that there is considerable potential for partisan political gerrymandering under STV in the Irish system because of the feasibility of altering district magnitude and the ability to predict probable election results. Mair makes the important point that "while in theory proportionality should increase as constituencies become larger . . ., smaller districts will not necessarily favor larger parties. Rather, depending upon its *precise* vote, a large party may prefer a 4-seat to a 3-seat constituency or a 5-seat to a 4-seat constituency." His analysis of redistricting under STV provides a nice counterpoint to the earlier chapters in this section, which deal with redistricting in plurality systems.

Conclusions

Compared to even as recently as a decade ago, we know a great deal about the political consequences of electoral laws, and the scope of study has been considerably broadened. Until quite recently, the literature on the political consequences of electoral laws has, in our view, too often been marred by the following:

1. An unnecessary divorce between Americanists and comparativists, in which the former study the United States, treating it as sui generis, while the latter focus on political institutions in Western Europe and other industrialized nations, with only an occasional mention of data from the United States;
2. An unnecessary divorce between the work on formal models of social choice and the study of comparative election systems, with each group of scholars writing largely in ignorance of the work of the other group;
3. A similar unnecessary ignorance by political scientists of the highly sophisticated and highly relevant work being done by political geographers;
4. A view of the domain of study which is too narrowly focused on

the issues of seats-votes relationships such as those so elegantly analyzed in Rae's *Political Consequences of Electoral Laws* (1967, 1971).

As noted, that situation, happily, now appears to be changing rather dramatically. We are optimistic that this renewed scholarly interest in electoral institutions will continue and that it marks a permanent recognition of the fact that institutions can constrain and structure political choices in a fundamental way.

Notes

1. No analysis of elections can be complete without at least mention of the degree of honesty of the political process (e.g., existence of ballot-stuffing and voter intimidation).
2. Riker's chapter is excerpted, with revisions, from his 1982 article in *APSR* (see Riker, 1982a). We first heard this paper as it was delivered at the International Political Science Association Meeting in Rio de Janeiro in August 1982, and it helped convince us that the present volume was a feasible project. Thus it is appropriate that Riker's essay should be the lead chapter.
3. Approval voting has been proposed by Brams and Fishburn (1983) as a way of improving the traditional (single-member district election) methods used in presidential and other U.S. primaries.

PART I

The Effect of Election Type on Political Competition

CHAPTER 1

Duverger's Law Revisited

William H. Riker

The Law and the Hypothesis

Duverger's law, in his own formulation, is the proposition, "The simple-majority single-ballot system favors the two-party system." He described this sentence by saying, "Of all the hypotheses . . . in this book, this approaches . . . perhaps . . . a true sociological law" (Duverger, 1963, p. 217). Related to this sentence is another, which, however, Duverger did not elevate to lawlike status. "The simple-majority system with second-ballot and proportional representation favor multipartyism" (Duverger, 1963, p. 239). I will refer to the first proposition as "the law" and to the second proposition as "the hypothesis." These propositions distinguish among three kinds of electoral systems which, although far from a complete list of the systems in current use, are the only ones used widely enough to admit the observation of their relationship with the number of political parties:

1. Plurality voting (rather misleadingly called the simple majority, single-ballot system by Duverger), in which the unique winner is the candidate with the most votes. With two candidates or less, the

---

This chapter is excerpted and revised from the author's paper, "The Two-Party System and Duverger's Law: An Essay on the History of Political Science," *APSR,* 76 (December 1982): 753–766.

winner has a simple majority of the votes cast. With three or more candidates, the winner may have only a plurality.

2. Runoff majority voting among three or more candidates with two ballots, in which, at the first ballot, the winners are the two candidates with the largest and second largest number of votes, respectively, and, at the second ballot between exactly these two, the winner is the candidate with a simple majority. Coupled with the two-ballot system (also known as the double-ballot system) are various alternative vote methods in which counting, rather than voting, occurs twice, using the same definition of winning as in the two-ballot system.

3. Proportional representation, in which the winners are those candidates who obtain some quota of votes, usually $(v/(s + 1))$ or $[(v/(s + 1)) + 1]$, where v is the number of votes cast and s is the number of winners to be selected. Since $s > 1$, some winners must have less than a plurality.

Though it is easy to clarify Duverger's terminology, it is not at all easy to straighten out the ambiguity in his statement of the relationship between electoral systems and the number of parties. Is plurality voting a necessary condition of the two-party system or a sufficient condition or both or neither? The claim that the relationship is "a sociological law" suggests causality or a necessary and sufficient condition, while the use of "favors" suggests that the relationship is at best probabilistic, not deterministic. I suspect the formulation was deliberately ambiguous because the author was not himself entirely certain of what he wanted to claim. Just what the claim *ought* to be is not immediately obvious, so I leave the question of the relationship to be settled in the course of my survey of the present state of knowledge about the law.

The Formulation of the Law

Duverger's ideas first appeared in print in 1951, but, as is usually the case with scientific laws, similar propositions had already been widely discussed and reformulated with some increasing degree of sophistication.[1] Indeed, related propositions appeared in popular discussion almost as soon as methods other than plurality voting were proposed or adopted for legislative elections in which large numbers of people were expected to vote.

Political parties, whatever their other functions of an ideological or programmatic nature, serve to organize elections. (For a recent elaboration, see Katz, 1980.) Politicians and candidates with some common interests—perhaps only a common desire to win or perhaps also a common ideology or a common identification with a group—appeal to voters under a common banner and thereby generate political parties. Since one motive for the common appeal is the desire to win, it is not surprising that the constitutional definitions of winning have an effect on the parties thereby generated. If winning is defined as receiving the most votes; that is, as a plurality, then one might reasonably expect a two-party system owing to the necessity under this definition of maximizing votes. Since the best way, in the long run, to get the most votes is to get more than half, each of two parties might be expected to structure a coalition in the hope, *before the election*, of getting a majority. Alternatively, if winning is defined as receiving over half the votes at a runoff election, candidates do not necessarily have to maximize votes at the initial election—the candidate who comes in second initially may have enough to win in the end. And if winning is defined as the achievement of some number of votes less than half (as is necessarily the case under proportional representation), then the necessity of maximizing disappears entirely. In short, when the accepted definition of winning forces candidates to maximize votes in order to win (as in plurality systems), they have strong motives to create a two-party system; but when winning does not require them to maximize votes (as in runoff and proportional systems), then the motive for two parties is absent.

The twin conditions of a large electorate and proposals for methods other than plurality voting were met in Europe in the latter half of the nineteenth century, but general public discussion on the subject did not appear until the 1850s. In 1856 Denmark, which then had a small electorate, adopted a form of proportional representation for over half the members of its unicameral legislature; about the same time Lord John Russell's unsuccessful reform bills provided for what the British called three-cornered constituencies, a rudimentary form of representation of minorities based on each voter having two votes in a three-member constituency. In 1859 Hare in *The Election of Representatives*, set forth an elaborate method of proportional representation, the single-transferable vote; and in 1861 Mill popularized it in *Considerations on Representative Government*, which contained a philosophical justification of Hare's method. Mill believed Parliament should contain "not just the two great parties alone," but representatives of "every minority . . . consisting of a sufficiently large number" (Mill, 1910, p. 263), which number he defined precisely as the number of voters divided by the number of seats. Mill argued that the Hare method would bring about this result, so from the very beginning of the discussion there was some dim appreciation of Duverger's hypothesis, though not necessarily of Duverger's law. The appreciation was quite dim, however, because in the parliamentary debate on cumulative voting in 1867 Mill expressed himself in a way that clearly indicates that he thought proportional representation would not upset the two great parties:

> The right honorable gentleman said one thing that perfectly amazed me. He said that . . . it was wrong that the representation of any community should represent it only in a single aspect, should represent only one interest—only its Tory or Liberal opinion; and he added that, at present, this was not the case, but that such a state of things would be produced by the adoption of this proposal. I apprehend that then, even more than now, each party would desire to be represented . . . by those men who would be most acceptable to the general body of the constituencies fully as much, if not more, than they do now (Hansard, 1867, pp. 1103–1104).

Clearly Mill expected that the proposed system would produce Tory free traders, Tory corn law supporters, and so forth, without upsetting the two-party system.[2] About the same degree of appreciation was shared by the opponents of change. Disraeli, for example, when speaking in the same debate against cumulative voting (which was, however, adopted in the form of the "limited vote" or two votes per voter in three-member constituencies), said,

> I have always been of the opinion with respect to this cumulative voting and other schemes having for their object to represent minorities, that they are admirable schemes for bringing crochetty men into this House—an inconvenience which we have hitherto avoided, although it appears that we now have some few exceptions to the general state of things [N.B.: Mill then sat on the other side of the House]; but I do not think we ought to legislate to increase the number of specimens (Hansard, 1867; p. 1112).

Quite recently Duff Spafford sent me what he and I believe is the earliest known explicit statement of the law. Henry Droop, an English barrister, advocate of proportional representation and inventor of the Droop quota, wrote in 1869 about plurality voting:

> Each elector has practically only a choice between two candidates or sets of candidates. As success depends upon obtaining a majority of the aggregate votes of all the electors, an election is usually reduced to a contest between the two most popular candidates or sets of candidates. Even if other candidates go to the poll, the electors usually find out that their votes will be

thrown away, unless given in favour of one or other of the parties between whom the election really lies.

Droop was apparently influenced by an observation in an address by Ernest Naville, president of the Geneva Association for Reform, which Droop translated as follows: "When the majority alone [i.e., Naville meant "by the plurality rule"] chooses the representatives of all, the electors inevitably group themselves into two camps because, to arrive at representation, it is necessary to obtain the majority." Naville did not apparently believe that this force was sufficient for the two party system, and Droop's position in 1869 is ambiguous. But by 1881, he was prepared to argue: "these phenomena [i.e., two-party systems] I cannot explain by any theory of a natural division between opposing tendencies of thought, and the only explanation which seems to me to account for them is that the two opposing parties into which we find politicians divided in each of these countries [United Kingdom, United States, and so forth] *have been formed and are kept together by majority voting.*" (Emphasis added; Droop means, of course, plurality voting.)

This is the earliest explicit statement of Duverger's law that I have seen. By 1901 it was a commonplace definition. In the controversy over proportional representation for the new Australian constitution. The Ashworths set up their problem thus:

> The claim that every section of the people is entitled to representation appears . . . so just that it seems intolerable that a method should have been used . . . which excludes the minority. . . . But in view of the adage that it is the excellence of old institutions which preserves them, it is surely a rash conclusion that the present method of election has no compensating merit. We believe there is such a merit—namely, that *the present method of election has developed the party system* [emphasis in original; the party system referred to is, of course, dual]. Once this truth is grasped, it is quite evident that the Hare system would be absolutely destructive to party government. . . . The object of this book is to suggest a reform, which possesses the advantages of both methods and the disadvantages of neither (Ashworth and Ashworth, 1900, pp. vii–viii).

Needless to say, the Ashworths failed to achieve this goal, but they do deserve credit for their clear enunciation of both Duverger's law and Duverger's hypothesis.

The Acceptance of the Law

In the previous section I reported a gradual development culminat-

ing in a clear and unambiguous statement of both Duverger's propositions twenty years after Hare and seventy years before Duverger. In
the succeeding half century scholarly support became quite general so
that it was indeed reasonable for Duverger to call one of them a law.
The general theme of this development is that of an initial skepticism,
followed by increasing acquiescence.

A. Lawrence Lowell, whose books on comparative politics dominated the field at the turn of the century, thought that the two-party
system was essential for effective parliamentary government. He attributed this system in Great Britain to the historical experience of the
English people, but he also thought that the absence of it in France
was owing to the majority system and to the second ballot (Lowell,
1896). Thus, in effect, he accepted Duverger's hypothesis but not
Duverger's law. Other prominent scholars of that period were less
clear. Ostrogorski, for example, was so eager to do away with political
parties by his own pet reforms that he never quite diagnosed the
causes of structural features of parties (Ostrogorski, 1908, vol. 2, p.
705). Practical publicists, excited by the controversy over proportional
representation, which was considered or adopted in most European
countries between 1900 and 1925, tended to favor proportional representation if they belonged to parties without a majority, and to oppose
it if they belonged to parties with the majority or close to it. Implicitly,
therefore, they behaved as if they agreed with Duverger's law. One
author who explicitly stated this belief was MacDonald, later a Labour
prime minister, who wrote frequently against proportional representation and clearly explained the forces involved in Duverger's law
(MacDonald, 1909, p. 137). As a Socialist, he thought the plurality
system was good discipline for new Socialist parties like the Labour
party; and, furthermore, when his party won, he wanted it to win the
whole thing—his Majesty's Government—not just a chance at a coalition. On the other hand, most minority publicists were not so frank;
and, when they favored proportional representation, they typically
denied Duverger's hypothesis (on the effect of proportional representation) and pointed out that countries without proportional representation often did not have two-party systems. (For an example, I quote
Williams. "In France, Italy, and Germany, there are more parties than
with us [Great Britain]. . . . But this is not the result of proportional
representation" (Williams, 1918, p. 68.) Conversely, those opposed to
proportional representation were not quite sure. The authors of the
Report of the Royal Commission on Electoral Systems remarked in
puzzlement, "It is asserted by some that small parties would spring
up like mushrooms when the repressive influence of the majority

[they meant plurality] method was removed; by others that the two-party system would survive any change of mechanism whatever" (Royal Commission on Electoral Systems, 1910, p. 31).

Two strands of intellectual development removed the doubts. One was the spread of dissatisfaction in the 1930s with proportional representation; the other was an increased scholarly examination of the origins of the two-party system that characterized the successful American polity. Since the dissatisfaction with proportional representation relates to Duverger's hypothesis (that proportional representation caused multiple parties, the lesser of Duverger's two propositions), I will skip over most of that debate, which was especially aimed at identifying the reasons for the initial successes of the German National Socialist party. An excellent example of the effect of that experience is observable in the two editions of a Fabian Society tract by Finer, a prominent student of comparative politics. In the initial edition (Finer, 1924) he criticized proportional representation in much the same way as had MacDonald fifteen years earlier; that is, as a system that confused responsibility. In the second edition (Finer, 1935), however, he added a postscript in which he blamed proportional representation in Italy and Germany for increasing the number of political parties. Then he attributed the weakness of executives and the instability of governments to the multiplicity of parties and he explained the rise of Mussolini and Hitler as a reaction. "People become so distracted by fumbling governments, that they will acquiesce in any sort of dictatorship . . ." (Finer, 1935, p. 16). Hermens's *Democracy or Anarchy: A Study of Proportional Representation* (1941) constitutes the most elaborate indictment of this electoral system for its encouragement of national socialism and, though not published until 1941, its evidence had been widely circulated for several years before that. While many now recognize that Finer and Hermens had made too facile an attribution and inference, still they were frequently uttered; and the collection of evidence on this subject by Hermens and others (e.g., Mellen, 1943) had, I believe, a significant persuasive effect in support of Duverger's hypothesis.

The scholarly study of the two-party system tended to increase the evidence for, and scholarly certainty about, Duverger's law. Holcombe, a prominent American political scientist in the first half of the century, affirmed Duverger's law as early as 1910: "The tendency under the system of plurality elections toward the establishment of the two-party system is . . . almost irresistible" (Holcombe, 1910). Although as late as 1919, Monro, in a popular textbook, attributed the two-party system to the "practical capacity of the Anglo-Saxon race"

(Monro, 1919, p. 329), and although authors of other popular text-books of the next decade (e.g., Merriam, Ogg, and Sait) avoided the subject entirely, still by 1933 the notion was well established that plurality voting for executives generated the American two-party system. MacMahon argued that "centrifugal tendencies [i.e., for many factions] have been offset by the fact that in the face of the necessity of choosing a single candidate the alternatives open to electorates have been sharply narrowed" (MacMahon, 1938). This example of presidential and gubernatorial elections proved extraordinarily convincing and, within a decade, the more general form of Duverger's law was enshrined in popular American textbooks. Thus Friedrich observed that the "single-member district with plurality elections . . . forces the electorate to make up its mind between two clear-cut alternatives" (Friedrich, 1937, p. 290), and Schattschneider wrote that the "single-member-district-system-plus-plurality-elections . . . discriminate *moderately* [emphasis in original] against the second party; but against the third, fourth, and fifth parties the force of this tendency is multiplied to the point of extinguishing their chances of winning seats altogether (Schattschneider, 1942, p. 75), a force that thereby guarantees exactly two parties. Key (1949) even applied the idea of the law to the superficially one-party system of the states of the old Confederacy, observing that, where primary elections in the one main party were conducted with the plurality rule, there was bifactionalism and, where conducted with the runoff majority rule, there was multifactionalism. Key was, however, uncertain about the effect because he also thought that the main force for bifactionalism probably was the existence of a serious Republican opposition.

Scholarly acceptance of both Duverger's law and Duverger's hypothesis was, therefore, quite general by the time he uttered them. Duverger's own contribution was twofold: (1) He sharply distinguished the law and the hypothesis, which had often previously been mistakenly interpreted as duals of each other. (Since plurality and proportional systems are only two out of many, the absence of one does imply the presence of the other.) (2) He collected and systematically arranged a large amount of historical evidence in support of both sentences so that their full significance was apparent.

The Testing of the Hypothesis

I start with Duverger's hypothesis (that proportional representation and majority systems favor multiparty systems). Clearly Duverger himself was uneasy about it, did not call it a law, and asserted it only as a probabilistic association, not a deterministic one.

The earliest attack on the hypothesis was, however, entirely misdirected. Grumm (1958) asserted that the causal direction in the hypothesis was reversed, that proportional representation did not cause multiparty systems but rather that multiparty systems caused proportional representation. His evidence was that five continental governments that adopted proportional representation had more than two parties when they did so. Presumably they acted to preserve the balance among existing parties. But all those governments had, at the time of adoption, either majority systems (i.e., second ballot) or a history of earlier proportional representation or no experience with democracy. Since Duverger coupled the majority system with proportional representation as a cause of multiple parties as, indeed, had Lowell (1896) and Holcombe (1910), it is entirely to be expected from the hypothesis that multiparty systems occur in the five countries at the time they actually occurred; that is, before proportional representation. So Grumm's evidence supports rather than refutes the hypothesis.

Incidentally, the few European countries that changed from plurality to proportional representation also changed from a two-party system to a multiple party system (Polyzoides, 1927).

Entirely apart from Grumm's error, however, there are numerous counterexamples to Duverger's hypothesis. For a long time Australia has had the alternative vote, which can be interpreted either as a rudimentary form of the Hare system or as a version of the majority system. Its parties have indeed increased from two to three, and there the number has stabilized. If the hypothesis were true, however, the number should continue to increase. It has not, and, indeed, the third party is effectively an appendage of one of the two main parties. Austria has maintained both proportional representation and a two-party system since the end of the Second World War. There is no apparent feature of the electoral system that accounts for this fact, so it seems a true counterexample. Despite partial proportional representation, Germany has, since 1945, developed a system with two major parties and a small third party allied continually with the same major party. This is not a good counterexample, however, because the proportional system also has a plurality feature intended by its authors to minimize the number of parties in excess of two. Finally, Ireland provides a devastating counterexample. Despite the use of the Hare system, its parties have decreased sharply in number since a high point in 1927 when there were seven parties plus fourteen independents. In 1969 there were three parties, one of them very small, and one independent. This result was substantially reproduced in 1973 and 1977, in which year one party obtained an absolute majority of the votes. Not unreasonably, one student of Irish elections, who initially seemed to accept Duverger's hypothesis (O'Leary, 1961), has now specifically rejected it (O'Leary, 1979, pp. 112–113). Katz (1980) tried to discount the force of this counterexample by calling the Hare system a modified form of the plurality rule (p. 40, because voting is for individual candidates, not parties) and by predicting then (p. 61), from Duverger's hypothesis, that there should be a greater number of Irish parties than in Britain (with the unmodified plurality rule) and fewer than in Italy (with the party list system of proportional representation). This is, however, too easy a way out. The Hare system is indubitably proportional, and it lacks entirely the main feature of the plurality rule, namely, the force encouraging parties to maximize votes.

Since these four counterexamples appear to have nothing in common, it seems impossible to save the hypothesis by modifying it. And that is the lesson to be learned from Rae's more general analysis of the cases. He has shown very neatly that, for the development of a successful new party, proportional representation is neither a necessary condition (see, for example, the British Labour party in a plurality system) nor a sufficient condition (see the absence of successful third parties in Austria). Instead Rae (1971, pp. 151–158) offered a list of seven variables, one of which is the presence of proportional representation, that may be associated with successful new parties. Altogether Rae made an extremely strong case that the hypothesis, at least as it related to proportional representation, cannot be more than a probabilistic association.

The empirical evidence is not so conclusive in the case of the two-ballot majority. No one, aside from Duverger, has devoted much attention to party systems associated with this rule. Most continental governments used it before they adopted proportional representation, and, as has already been remarked, Lowell (1896) and later some advocates of proportional representation (e.g., Williams, 1918) believed that the multiparty system developed as a rational political response to this rule. Canon (1978) conducted the most impressive test of the relationship. He was inspired mainly by Key's (1949) uncertainty about the application of the hypothesis to the multifactionalism in southern states. Canon used as data the presence of bifactionalism or multifactionalism from 1932 to 1977 in the Democratic gubernatorial primaries in sixteen southern and border states. Ten of these states use the runoff primary with a majority required for nomination at either the first or second ballot. The other six use the plurality method with just one primary. While factionalism is not easy to measure, still a reasonable index of it showed in fairly close approximation of Duverger's hypothesis, that factionalism in all but one of the plurality primary states was lower—often much lower—than in all the runoff primary states. For the one anomaly, West Virginia, the index was only slightly higher. Furthermore, the percentage of the primary vote for the top candidate (and for the top two candidates) was much greater in the plurality states than in the runoff states, which is exactly what one would expect if the two-ballot system encourages multifactionalism. Still, longitudinal averages cover up significant deviations. Canon also noted that Alabama, a runoff state, has in the last decade developed something close to bifactionalism, while West Virginia, a plurality state, still had fairly evident multifactionalism in the earlier part of his period. Since these two exceptions are not fully explained at present, the case is strengthened that Duverger's hypothesis is no more than a probabilistic association.

This is, I believe, what a theoretical interpretation, in terms of rational choices by politicians, would suggest. The rational choice theory, standing implicitly behind the hypothesis, is that proportional representation and the second-ballot runoff both offer politicians an incentive for the formation of new parties and do not give them any disincentive. The incentive is that these systems sometimes, given particular configurations of potential coalitions, permit new parties (and heretofore excluded politicians) to get a bit of political influence with relatively few votes. That is, in these systems a new party does not have to get the most votes to win, merely some indefinite number less than the most. Under proportional representation, the candidate or list with the second most votes can almost always win seats and sometimes so can candidates with even fewer votes. Indeed the purpose of the system is to encourage this result. In the runoff majority system a candidate with the second most votes initially can ultimately win provided the supporters of eliminated candidates vote for the runner-up at the second ballot. Hence, if a group of politicians can see a chance to come in second, third, etc., it is often worthwhile to form a new party.

In the plurality system, on the other hand, this positive incentive is turned into a disincentive because it is rare for the prospective builders of a new party to predict that they may come in first past the post. This then constitutes a real disincentive because the leaders of the new party are likely to be regarded as politically irrelevant. This disincentive is absent from proportional representation and runoff systems, however, because even leaders of failed parties are welcome in expanded coalitions of continuing parties. Neither feature of this incentive system is strong enough to permit one to say that these electoral systems, for certain, favor multiple parties. The incentive is weak because it operates only when people want to form new parties for other reasons. Surely there are, however, many configurations of potential coalitions, configurations lasting through many elections, that do not render it likely that new parties will come in second (probably the case in Austria) or even third (probably the case in Ireland). Similarly the absence of a disincentive for new parties within the system of proportional representation itself is not very important. While the existence of proportional representation prohibits the direct use of the disincentive inherent in plurality voting, there are other kinds of efficacious disincentives that can be combined with proportional representation, as has been done in Germany and perhaps Austria. So the incentive is not sufficient and the disincentive is not necessary. Hence the hypothesis cannot be deterministically valid, although doubtless there is a fairly strong probabilistic association between, on the one hand, proportional representation or runoff elections and, on the other hand, the multiparty system.

The Testing of the Law

We can, therefore, regard Duverger's hypothesis in its deterministic form as abandoned (though still useful for practical life) and proceed to the more interesting question of Duverger's law (relating plurality elections and two-party systems). The difficulties with the law are less formidable. There are indeed counterexamples, but not, I believe, definitive ones, so that the law may possibly survive with appropriate revisions. If we can also fit it to an adequate theory, it may even be persuasive.

The two most pressing counterexamples to Duverger's law are in Canada and India where, despite plurality elections, there are more than two parties. In Rae's study of 121 elections in 20 countries, 30 elections were conducted under plurality rules and 7 of these—all in Canada—resulted in more than 10% of the votes for a third party. Rae explained the Canadian deviation as owing to the fact that geographically local parties survive as the main parties in some provinces, while being third parties nationally. Doubtless this situation derives from the extreme decentralization of Canadian government wherein the chance of provincial control is of itself enough to motivate political action.

On the basis of the Canadian exception, Rae reformulated Duverger's law from the theory that "the simple-majority, single-ballot system favors the two-party system," to "plurality formulae are always associated with two-party competition except where strong local minority parties exist" (Rae, 1971, p. 95). Rae commented that his revision produced a "much less dramatic proposition" (Rae, 1971, p. 96) although when he came to write about the long-range effects of plurality formulas, he concluded by reaffirming Duverger's proposition. After noting the Canadian exception, Rae said, "Insofar as the electoral law exerts a controlling pressure, the single-member district is likely to press the system toward two-party competition" (Rae, 1971, p. 143) which is almost exactly Duverger's sentence, with the verb structure "likely to press the system toward" rather than "favors."

The reason Rae fell into this logical trap of both denying and then affirming Duverger's law is that he, like Duverger himself, could not decide whether the law was deterministic or probabilistic. So Rae's restatement of it is deterministic, but his actual use of it is probabilistic. I suspect the reason for his ambivalence is his belief that the revised deterministic law was "less dramatic" and less useful. But attaching conditions to a law is, to my mind, unexceptionable. The elementary form of the law of demand is that "demand curves do not slope positively," but to state this law accurately, one must say, "Holding other prices, income, and tastes constant, demand curves do not slope positively," perhaps less "dramatic"—if drama is what one wants from science—but certainly more useful because it is more accurate. Similarly Rae's revision involves greater accuracy and greater utility.

The Indian counterexample is more difficult to deal with. India began plurality elections about the same time Duverger formulated his law, and only once has something approaching a two-party election been held. Congress, the party of Nehru, his daughter, Indira Gandhi, and his grandson, Rajiv Gandhi, has been dominant most of the thirty years since 1951, even though Congress candidates have never obtained as much as 50% of the vote. Because of the large number of candidates in many constituencies, a genuine multiparty system, Congress has usually translated an electoral minority into a majority of legislative seats. It is an interesting puzzle why the numerous minor parties do not disappear or consolidate. They have decreased in number since 1951, but there are still at least four or five significant parties. One wonders why it is taking so long for Duverger's law to work.

Two types of explanations have been offered for the delay. Weiner (1957, pp. 223, 262–264) argued that the minor parties were social groups providing emotional satisfaction to activists, entirely apart from the goal of winning elections. Since, presumably, activists maximize the pleasures of membership rather than the rewards of office, it is not to be expected, in Weiner's theory, that they reduce the number of political parties other than accidentally. While I think Weiner was on the right track in looking at the motivation of politicians rather than of voters, it was a serious mistake to lump all politicians together. Certainly the leaders of the main parties besides Congress behave as if they are intensely motivated by the chance of office. To attribute to them a group loyalty that prevents them from doing what is necessary to win is to describe them as truly irrational men. I suspect, however, that they are just as rational as Western politicians, and so I reject Weiner's explanation, except as it applies to very small and politically irrelevant parties.

On another occasion (Riker, 1976), I have offered a different kind of explanation. Because Congress, the largest party, includes the median, so I believe, of the voters arranged on an ideological spectrum, Congress has, most of the time, been the second choice of many voters on both its right and its left. Hence, it has probably been a Condorcet winner most of the time, although it has never obtained an absolute majority.[3] Congress has been clearly defeated only when the opposition has been so consumed with intense popular hatred of Mrs. Gandhi or with intense elite lust for ministerial office that politicians and voters alike could put aside their ideological tastes and act as if they ordered their preferences with Congress at the bottom of the list. When they have done so, they have defeated Congress in both state and national elections. Then, typically, coalitions of each end against the middle (like Janata in 1977–1979) have dissolved and Congress has won again, presumably as the Condorcet choice. With these thoughts in mind, I constructed a model in which, with rational participants who wished to maximize political satisfaction (i.e., for office and ideological tastes), a multiparty equilibrium was consistent with plurality elections (Riker, 1976). The essence of this model was that some party in the multiparty system was regularly a Condorcet winner. Utilizing this feature, it is possible to revise Duverger's law further, incorporating Rae's revision, to account for both the apparent exceptions (Canada and India).

In my revision the law reads,

> Plurality election rules bring about and maintain two-party competition, except in countries where third parties nationally are continually one of two parties locally and except for countries where one party among several is almost always the Condorcet winner in elections.

Note that this formulation is deterministic—an attempt to avoid the ambiguity of Duverger and Rae. The law asserts that the plurality rule is, with the exceptions noted, a sufficient condition for a two-party system. It is not, however, an assertion of a causal relation inasmuch as the plurality rule clearly is not a necessary condition (vide, Austria).

The Theory of Sophisticated Voting

The foregoing reformulation is entirely consistent with our knowledge of the empirical world, accounting both for the long history of two-party competition in Anglo-American countries with plurality voting, and for the apparent exceptions like Social Credit in Canada, the Irish in Britain in the nineteenth century, the multiparty grouping around Congress in India, and the few third parties in the United States that have survived more than one election. But the law itself is entirely empirical, the record of observations. It explains nothing and tells us nothing about why it works.

Duverger offered two theoretical reasons for the plurality rule to destroy third parties: (1) a "mechanical effect" of underrepresenting losing parties and (2) a "psychological factor" of voters not wishing to waste their votes on losers. Both these reasons derive (implicitly) from a view of both politicians and voters as rational actors; that is, expected utility maximizers. The mechanical effect gives politicians an incentive to abandon parties that win even less than they might be expected to. The psychological factor gives voters, observing wasted votes and even votes that, being wasted, indirectly contribute to the victory of least liked parties, an incentive to vote for their second choices. If both these propositions are correct, they can be combined, as they were by Duverger, into a theoretical explanation of the operation of the law.

The existence of the mechanical effect was disputed by Grumm (1958) on the basis of a modest bit of evidence. But Rae (1971, pp. 88–92) showed definitively by an empirical comparison that plurality rules gave a greater relative advantage to large parties over small ones than did proportional representation rules. Sprague (1980) carried Rae's analysis quite a bit further by calculating precisely how much plurality systems are biased against third parties. A fair or unbiased system is, of course, one in which, regardless of the size of a party's vote, it gets the same proportion of seats in a legislature as it gets proportion of votes. In nearly all systems parties with a small proportion of votes get an even smaller proportion of seats (a negative bias), and parties with a larger proportion of votes get an even larger proportion of seats (a positive bias). Building on Tufte (1973), Sprague defined an exactly unbiased threshold point, B, of the proportion of the vote through which a party would pass, as its vote increased, from suffering a negative bias to enjoying a positive bias. Using Rae's data, Sprague calculated B for plurality systems to be 0.32 and for proportional systems to be 0.12. That is, third parties in proportional systems get a fair or positively biased proportion of seats if they get one eighth or more of the vote, while in plurality systems they get a fair shake only if they get one third or more of the vote. This comparison quite vividly reveals how Duverger's "mechanical effect" is such a severe discouragement to the formation of third parties. There seems to be little question that this effect in plurality systems enters the calculations of potential organizers of third parties, helping to dissuade them from the effort.

The main dispute is, therefore, about the validity of the "psychological factor," which Downs bluntly described thus:

> A rational voter first decides what party he believes will benefit him most; then he tries to estimate whether this party has any chance of winning. He does this because his vote should be expended as part of a selection process, not as an expression of preference. Hence even if he prefers party A, he is "wasting" his vote on A if it has no chance of winning because very few other voters prefer it to B or C. The relevant choice in this case is between B and C. Since a vote for A is not useful in the actual process of selection, casting it is irrational (Downs, 1957, p. 48).

What Downs describes has come to be called sophisticated voting, whereby the voter takes account of anticipated votes by others and then votes so as to bring about the best *realizable* outcome for himself, regardless of whether or not his vote is sincere (i.e., for his most preferred alternative).

In the election of single executives, sophisticated voting, if it occurs, always works against third parties. (Indeed, early statements of Duverger's law in the United States, e.g., by MacMahon, 1933, emphasized the special importance of the elected executive in bringing the "psychological factor" into play.) In the election of members of a legislature, however, which of the several parties is weakened by sophisticated voting depends on conditions in the constituency. If the third party nationally is the weakest locally, then sophisticated voting by its supporters weakens it. If, however, the third party nationally is one of the two larger parties locally, then sophisticated voting by supporters of the weakest party (i.e., one of the two larger parties nationally) strengthens the third party. This latter effect is probably what has kept the British Liberal party and some Canadian third parties alive. But by reason of the fact that these third parties remain third parties, the main force of sophisticated voting must work against third parties.

Given the great importance of sophisticated voting in the explanation of why Duverger's law works, one very important question then is: Does sophisticated voting occur? Or, are ordinary voters clever enough and bold enough to vote against their true tastes?

Shively (1970) made the first attempt to discover sophisticated voting. He interpreted Duverger's law (rather too broadly, I think) as the sentence: "Where the likelihood that a party can win . . . is low, voters are less likely to continue voting for it, or, . . . to begin voting for it." For a test, he created an index of the likelihood of winning and regressed the change of a party's proportion of the vote in two consecutive elections on this index. He expected a positive association (i.e., low likelihood linked with decline in share of votes) but got a negative one. This led him to further statistical manipulation and to a reinterpretation which he believed supported the law, though only weakly. Hence he concluded that the psychological factor had "a trivial impact on election outcomes."

Given the empirical strength of Duverger's law at the institutional level, these results from electoral data were, to say the least, perplexing. Since, however, Shively's form of the hypothesis and his method were far too gross to study the truly relevant behavior, other scientists have looked more precisely at voters' desertion from third parties. They have found a relatively large amount of sophisticated voting in four polities (Britain, Canada, Germany, and the United States), which I here report case by case.

Britain

Spafford (1972) observed that Shively's hypothesis involved no discrimination between situations in which sophisticated voting would or would not be efficient. But, in fact, one would expect more sophisticated voting as the chance increases to affect the outcome between one's second and third preferences. That is, if the race is close between the major parties, then third-party supporters are more likely to desert their party at the polls. Spafford tested this for 104 constituencies with Liberal candidates in both the 1964 and 1966 elections and found a highly significant, positive association between the Liberal share of the vote in 1966 and the share of the vote of the winning party in 1964. For example, lower Liberal shares went with lower shares for the winning party in the previous election, which means that, with a greater chance to influence the outcome, more Liberals deserted. Clearly sophisticated voting occurred.

Lemieux (1977) elaborated on this analysis by comparing, for all seats Liberals contested and for each pair of elections from 1959 to 1970, the effect of the Liberal vote in all constituencies with its effect in marginal constituencies (i.e., those in which the margin between Conservative and Labour was less than 15%). Categorizing constituencies according to the Liberal strategy (to contest in both elections, or the second only, or the first only), he found in 5 of the 9 possible cases that the Liberals had a significant effect on the Conservative share of the vote when considering *all* the constituencies in the category. For these 5 cases, considering just the marginal constituencies, the Liberals' effect was also significant but of the *opposite sign* and just about the *same absolute size*, which means that, for the marginal seats, the incentive for the Liberals to desert their party is extremely great. Lemieux (1977, p. 177) remarked, and I agree, that these results indicate a large amount of sophisticated voting.

Cain (1978), in still a third study of third-party voters in Britain, examined the matter two ways: using election results and survey responses, both from 1970. Since the results from the latter confirm results from the former, we have yet another confirmation of the existence and significance of sophisticated voting. First, Cain regressed third-party vote shares in constituencies on Closeness (i.e., the difference between major party shares) and on Abstention, a new variable in these discussions. His hypotheses were that (1) a positive association between Closeness and third-party share (as the race between the major parties becomes indeterminate—that is, a smaller difference between the major parties—the third-party vote would also decrease) and (2) a negative association between Abstention and third-party share (as the proportion of nonvoters increases, the proportion of third-party votes decreases). The theory was strongly confirmed: Both coefficients were the right sign and highly significant (Cain, 1978, p. 645).

Given this promising discovery in macro-analysis, he then turned to survey responses for micro-analysis. Relative to individual decisions, expected utility theory holds that the choice of the individual is a function of the utility, U, of the several outcomes, i, where outcome i is a victory for party i, $i = 1,2,3$, times the probability, P_i, that the voter can bring about these outcomes. Cain estimated the probabilities from data about actual outcomes in respondents' constituencies and from the utilities from survey responses. Then he regressed the vote of those who voted sincerely (for their first choice) and the vote of those who voted sophisticatedly (for their second choice) on expected utility, degree of political participation, and intensity of first preference. He found that the coefficient for expected utility was in the right direction for both categories of voters and statistically significant for sophisticated voters. That is, sincere voters had $P_1U_1 > P_2U_2$, while sophisticated voters had the reverse. Furthermore, the closer that sophisticated voters judged their first and second choices to be, the more likely they were to vote sophisticatedly, which fact greatly strengthens the inference that the voters were in fact consciously sophisticated (Cain, 1978, pp. 650–651).

Germany

In elections for the Bundestag, voters cast two ballots simultaneously, one for a candidate to be chosen by the plurality rule in single-member districts (*Erststimme*) and the other for a party list to be awarded seats by proportional representation in a statewide multi-member district (*Zweitstimme*). Each party then gets its plurality-won seats plus the number of seats won by the proportional rule less the number of plurality-won seats. If sophisticated voting occurs, one would expect that the two major parties would get more *Erststimmen* (votes in plurality elections where voting for small parties is "wasteful") than *Zweitstimmen* (votes in proportional elections, where every vote for a small party can count) and vice versa for small parties. Fisher (1974) found this to be exactly and universally the case: In every state in every election, 1961–1972, Christian Democrats and Social Democrats had fewer *Zweitstimmen* than *Erststimmen*, while every minor party had more. The typical shift was 1% to 2% for the large parties and, in 1972, up to 5% for the Free Democrats, then the only surviving minor party. More to the point, one would expect the shift to be especially large for minor parties, and this was exactly what Fisher found. In 1961, 1965, and 1969, the Free Democrats lost between 13% and 38% of its *Zweitstimmen* when their voters cast the *Erststimmen*, while the major parties never lost as much as 7%. This provides an estimate of sophisticated voting for supporters of Free Democrats: between 1/10 and 2/5.

Canada

Black (1978, 1980) also used survey data to study individual decisions. Using preference orders from survey data and probabilities of affecting outcomes from actual outcomes in constituencies, for one test he categorized voters into (1) those for whom it would be advantageous to vote sophisticatedly and (2) those for whom it would not be. For data from elections in 1968 and 1972, about 37% and 62% of the former (advantaged) and only 10% of the latter (not advantaged) actually did so. For another test, he categorized voters into marginal (i.e., small preference for first-over-second choice) and nonmarginal (large preference). The marginal voters were found to be much more likely to vote sophisticatedly than the nonmarginal; and for those marginals for whom sophisticated voting was advantageous, actual voting for the second choice ranged between 50% and 100%. These two tests were repeated and confirmed in elaborate regression equations. Altogether they indicate a remarkable amount of sophisticated voting.

United States

The 1968 presidential election with a third-party candidate and national survey data about preference orders allowed Bensel and Sanders (1979) to estimate the proportion of sophisticated voting in that election. Comparing those for whom sophisticated voting was advantageous (mostly Wallace supporters) with those for whom it was not, they found that the 12% of the advantaged voted sophisticatedly, while only 4% of the not-advantaged did. Since the electoral college breaks up the national electorate into 50 parts, with different information about probable outcomes in each one, this allowed them to compare voters' calculations. If voting is sophisticated, it should be the case that, where Wallace was strong (i.e., had more chance to carry the state), his supporters would be more likely to vote sincerely than where he was weak. The effect was striking: In strong Wallace states only 4% voted sophisticatedly, while 17% did elsewhere.

The Problem of Sophisticated Behavior

The foregoing evidence renders it undeniable that a large amount of sophisticated voting occurs—mostly to the disadvantage of the third parties nationally—so that the force of Duverger's psychological factor must be considerable. It seems initially appropriate and attractive, therefore, to construct a theory to explain Duverger's law out of the theory of rational choice. Nevertheless, we cannot do so blithely. In the first place, not everyone votes sophisticatedly, although the evidence collected here suggests that most people who "should" do so by reason of the expected utility calculus probably do so actually. It is a bit difficult, however, to build a theory on behavior that is not certainly universal. Even if it is universal, however, there remains a serious and unresolved paradox in the argument, which is that the expected utility calculus of voting may itself be irrational.

In Downs's statement of the theory, which I cited previously, it is said that the rational voter should expend his vote "as part of the selection process," not as "an expression of preference." Yet this statement may be indefensible because, as Downs pointed out himself (1957, pp. 36–50, 260–276) and as Ordeshook and I have elaborated (Riker and Ordeshook, 1968), it may be impossible for an individual to influence the selection process. One interpretation of influence is the chance to make a tie or to break a tie that occurs in the absence of the individual's vote. This chance is, of course, extremely unlikely in most elections in the modern state. Under this definition, it is objectively the case that one cannot expect to contribute much to the decision process. If so, the rational action may be simply to express a preference.

Ferejohn and Fiorina (1974, 1975) have suggested that individuals calculate, not their chance of influence, but merely their satisfaction, minimizing thereby the maximum regret they would feel if an undesired candidate won. The debate over the relative merits of minimax regret and expected utility is extensive (Beck, 1975; Mayer and Good, 1975). While the bulk of the evidence about the way people behave now seems to favor expected utility (Aldrich, 1976; Cain, 1978; Black, 1978), still the fact that the minimax regret interpretation can be put forward plausibly suggests that some people may be interested merely in utility, not expected utility.

If the chance to influence is negligible, then energy spent on a calculus and sophisticated voting is a waste and irrational, while voting merely to express a preference may be entirely rational. Meehl (1977), facing this problem squarely, has insisted that the "wasted vote" argument is at best meaningless and at worst a fraud. Voters' motivation is rational, he argued, only in terms of their sense of moral obligation. This obligation cannot involve a means-end calculation—for that is meaningless when votes are not influential—but must instead respond to a moral imperative. He acknowledged that moral imperatives might also lack meaning, in which case all justifications of voting are irrational. But if only the morally motivated vote is rational, then it is impossible to waste a vote (or to behave irrationally) by voting simply for one's first preference.

Granting some persuasiveness to Meehl's argument, the theoretical underpinning of Duverger's law is surely weak if behavior in accord with the psychological factor of individual voters' calculation of expected utility is itself irrational. It seems necessary, therefore, to find some new, or at least additional, theoretical explanation of why Duverger's law works.

The direction one must go, I believe, is to turn attention away from the expected utility calculus of the individual voter and to the expected utility calculus of the politician and other more substantial participants in the system. The groups and individuals who buy access and the politicians who buy a future do have substantial interests, and it is their actions to maximize expected utility that have the effect of maintaining the two-party system under plurality voting.

One especially interesting feature of politics under plurality rules is that minor parties regularly appear. The reason is, I believe, that, quite reasonably, not all voters vote sophisticatedly. Instead they are willing, like Meehl himself, to support a program that appeals to their ideological taste. Potential politicians are in turn often willing to experiment with, and invest in, new programs and platforms to form a possible winning venture. Since some of these win locally, they can remain in the system for a long time. And in the United States there is the additional attraction to politicians in that we have a two-ballot majority system (rather than a plurality system) at the electoral college level. This fact encourages third parties because their leaders may convince themselves that they have a chance to throw the election into the House of Representatives (Bensel and Sanders, 1979). Coupling the interest of potential leaders with the sincere behavior of many voters, one understands why there is an almost constant supply of third parties.

The interesting question about such parties is not why they begin, but why they fail. The answer is, I believe, that donors and leaders disappear. A donor buys future influence and access, and many donors are willing to buy from any party that has a chance to win. (In the United States, at least, many donors give to *both* parties.) But as rational purchasers they are not likely to donate to a party that has a slim chance of winning. And in a plurality system most third parties have only that chance, because plurality rules give large parties a large relative advantage over small parties (Rae, 1971, pp. 88–92; Sprague, 1980). Similarly a potential leader buys a career. And as a rational purchaser he has no interest in a party that may lose throughout his lifetime. So the answer to the question of failure is that third parties are rejected in the rational calculus of expected utility by, especially, leaders, though also in the calculus by many simple voters. Any adequate theory to subsume Duverger's law must, I believe, begin there, which is a task for scholars in the next decade.

Conclusions

This history of Duverger's law has shown that it first passed through a forty-year period in which writers struggled to enunciate it, and then through another half century of clarification until Duverger asserted it as a law. In the last thirty years, it has been examined with increasing scientific sophistication in three principal ways. First, it has been examined empirically. Counterexamples have been analyzed, and the law has been revised to subsume them. Second, it has been examined theoretically. A theory of the behavioral forces involved has been enunciated and revised. From the first enunciation by Droop, the law has been implicitly embedded in a rational choice theory about the behavior of politicians and voters. This theory has been rendered more and more explicit, especially in the last two decades, so that recent empirical work consciously invokes the rational choice model. Finally, it has been examined as a source of hypotheses. Propositions inferred from it have been tested; for example, the inquiry about sophisticated voting was undertaken because, if the law is valid and if the theory is appropriate, something like sophisticated voting must occur.

Of course, there is much yet to be done. If the theory is revised along the lines I have suggested, conditions to cover the counterexamples will doubtless be clarified and simplified. And there are more polities to examine. Nigeria adopted plurality voting, although recently, and regrettably, it has again become a military dictatorship. Assuming, however, a democratic future, its experience with or without a two-party system will be another test of the law.

Although we are only part way along in this history, it still seems to me that the law is much more defensible than when the Ashworths uttered it eighty years ago. Many—perhaps most—political scientists who specialize in the study of political parties now accept the law.[4,5]

Notes

1. It is customary to call the law by Duverger's name, not because he had much to do with developing it, but rather because he was the first to dare to claim that it was, in fact, a law. The memorial honors, therefore, a trait of character, as much as a scientific breakthrough.
2. Leys (1959) has said that Mill understood Duverger's law, although what Leys and I have discussed relates to the effect of proportional representation (Duverger's hy-

pothesis), not to the effect of plurality voting (Duverger's law). In any event, Leys's remark is highly anachronistic. To say that Mill understood Duverger's law is like saying that the child with burned fingers understands the chemical principles of combustion.

3. A Concorcet winner is a candidate who can beat any other in a pairwise contest. Such a winner, even with only a plurality, is surely in a stronger position than a plurality winner who would be beaten in pairwise contests because supporters of candidates from other parties would combine to defeat him. In the Indian case Congress has probably been a Condorcet winner. That is, it probably would have been able to defeat rightists in a pairwise contest because leftists would vote for Congress rather than rightists; and, similarly, it would have been able to defeat leftists in a pairwise contest because rightists would vote for Congress rather than leftists.

4. See, for example, Katz, 1980, who, however, thought it applied particularly at the local level.

5. Still, not all political scientists are convinced it is valid—and that is exactly as it should be, for skepticism about supposed truths is the heart of science. Still, nearly everyone would agree, I believe, that there has been accumulation of knowledge.

CHAPTER 2

The Influence of Electoral Systems: Faulty Laws or Faulty Method?

Giovanni Sartori

In much of the philosophy of science literature, "laws," that is, causal-type generalizations expressed in lawlike form that withstand falsification, are displayed as the hallmark of science—if no laws, then no science. Curiously, however, the more political science claimed, from the fifties onward, scientific status, the less it pursued the search for "laws." Even so, we do have cases in the realm of politics in which it would seem that lawlike generalizations are manageable and relatively easy to formulate. One such case is the "Duverger laws" concerning the influence of electoral systems on the number of parties.[1] But for some three decades the profession's concern has been to dismiss them—rather than giving them another and better try. In this essay we shall use Duverger's laws and the ensuing discussion as a case study that sheds light on the paradoxical vagaries of a science "without laws," a science seeking scientific recognition and yet neglecting lawlike generalizations.

Duverger's Formulation

The first law of Duverger reads: "The majority [plurality] single-ballot system tends to party dualism." The second law reads: "The second-ballot [majority] system and proportional representation tend to multipartyism."[2] Let us not quibble on why Duverger does not call his lawlike propositions "laws" and leave this matter by saying that he doubtlessly conceives them as such.[3] And let due acknowledgment be made of the fact that a first attempt is hardly ever conclusive, that its value is primarily a pioneering value. Yet the weakness of Duverger's treatment remains striking.

In the first place, Duverger assumes that a causal relation can be warranted by a correlation; that is to say, he never gives the impression of perceiving the difference between "cause of" and "associated with." In the second place, and more importantly, a law (causal generalization) is verifiable if, and only if, the cause and the effect are clearly specified, whereas the effect of Duverger's first law (party dualism) is as hazy as can be, and the effect of his second law (multipartyism) also suffers from excessive imprecision. That Duverger's "dualism" is an accordionlike notion has been noted many times and need not be stressed again here. It suffices to recall that a number of countries (e.g., Australia, Canada, Western Germany, Italy) are declared at one point "dualistic" or "bipartisan" and at other points, respectively, three-party, four-party, six-party, and eight-party (Duverger, 1954a, pp. 240, 241, 253, 276). The laws posit an effect on the *number* of parties; yet Duverger never abides by any consistent counting rule. At times he counts all the parties at their face value; at other times he dismisses some parties as local, half-parties, presumably ephemeral (in the long run), or minor disturbances. In sum: since the effect of the assumed causal factor is never pinned down, Duverger can all too easily tailor his evidence as being a confirming one. Even so, his laws remain crippled by exceptions that Duverger confronts on a sheer ad hoc basis.

In the third place, his second law is both ambiguous and puzzling. Not only is it preceded by lengthy disclaimers concerning the difficulty of defining its alleged effect, that is, "multipartyism" (Duverger, 1954a, pp. 258–259), but it is defended on the basis of a distinction between "the technical notion of multipartyism" and the "ordinary notion of multiplication" (1954a, p. 276). So, what does the law say: that proportional representation, or PR (I shall set aside the double ballot system) "coincides" with more than two parties, or that it multiplies them? In the first case we have no law. However, it is in fact the case that Duverger (since he does have a causal relationship in mind) does insist very much on the "more parties" effect—if only a limited and not necessarily immediate one—of PR. He asserts over and over again that "the multiplying effect of PR is undeniable" (1954a, pp. 279, 281, 282). So, Duverger does hypothesize, here, a law; but a most puzzling one. After all, a system of proportional representation is required to represent *in proportion*. That is to say, PR is supposed to mirror, to reflect. In what way is this a "multiplying"?

I shall revert to this puzzle below. For the time being the point is that both the methodological and substantive feeblenesses of the laws of Duverger are patent and easily demonstrated. Is this a good or sufficient reason for giving up? Is it difficult to do better? In due course I propose to show that it is easy. The fact remains that until recently a crushing majority of authors have been content with showing that Duverger was wrong—often on wrong grounds.[4] The mood of the discipline for some thirty years is well represented, it seems to me, by the suggestion of Eckstein and Apter (1963, p. 253) that perhaps "electoral systems only express the deeper determinants of society." A suggestion that is hardly furthered when the conclusion of an inquiry is that "the relationship between electoral system [and] party system . . . are not such as can be summed up in scientific laws" (Bogdanor, 1983, p. 261).

The notable, single exception to the aforesaid mood is the one of Douglas Rae (1971). However, if the problem is (as Riker, 1982a, appropriately suggests) the "accumulation of knowledge" and, if so, whether there has been a buildup upon the Duverger beginning, then Rae can hardly be said to belong to such a cumulative process.

Douglas Rae and William Riker

Rae does deal with Duverger. Duverger's first law (concisely reformulated: "plurality formulae cause two-party systems") is, as formulated, rejected (Rae, 1971, pp. 92–96, 180), while Duverger's second law is broken down into so many "propositions" and variables (Rae, 1971, especially pp. 148–176) that here I am at a loss to tell whether any thread between Duverger and Rae can be said to remain. However that may be, the methodological approach of Rae is entirely different from the one of Duverger—and it is here that the "accumulation" entirely breaks down. Duverger has causal "laws" in mind; Rae never uses the word cause (except to reject it) and very deliberately speaks of "propositions" that assert, in turn, a wide gamut of linkages ("tends to," but also "associates with"; "almost always," but also "often"). Duverger was parsimonious, even excessively. Rae formulates, antiparsimoniously, no less than seven "similarity propositions," thirteen "differential propositions," plus two corollaries, for a total of 22 propositions (Rae, 1971, pp. 179–182). A major difference bears also on how the effects of the causal factors are conceived.

Duverger looks at concrete systems (even though he is unable to specify them), while Rae makes a special effort to avoid reference to concrete systems. Most of the time his effects are expressed in terms of "fractionalization." The one concrete system that Rae confronts as such is "two-party competition," but his definition of such a state of affairs is in percentages: two-party systems are "those in which the first party holds less than 70% of the legislative seats, and the first two parties together hold at least 90% of the seats" (Rae, 1971, p. 93).[5] Now, if Duverger is to be criticized because laws must declare effects that are specific enough to allow testing, the same criticism applies even more to Rae's propositions.[6]

All in all, it cannot be said that Rae builds upon Duverger: he attends to an entirely different thing. This is confirmed, it seems to me, by the fact that Rae's work has been widely acclaimed and utilized for its statistics (the measure of fractionalization) while disregarded, despite its title, on the "consequences of electoral laws." In this latter respect Rae has neither been disconfirmed nor put to use. The nomothetic attempt of Duverger has thus remained for another decade a neglected nonissue.

The one author, then, who unquestionably attends to a cumulative improvement upon Duverger's premises is Riker (1982a; see also, chapter 1). Riker gives up on Duverger's second law, the one on the effects of PR. He writes: "it seems impossible to save the hypothesis by modifying it," and "Rae made an extremely strong case that the hypothesis . . . cannot be more than a probabilistic association" (1982a, p. 759). Since Riker reaches very much the same negative conclusion as regards the effects of the double ballot system, he actually attends only to Duverger's first law, the one on the effects of plurality systems. Riker deals first with Rae's revision: "plurality formulae are always associated with two-party competition except where strong local minority parties exist" (Rae, 1971, p. 95; Riker, 1982a, p. 760). Riker's criticism is twofold. Methodologically Rae is charged with falling into the "logical trap of both denying and then affirming Duverger's law," and this because Rae, like Duverger, "could not decide whether the law was deterministic or probabilistic" (Riker, 1982a, p. 760). The second criticism is factual: India uses a plurality system and yet cannot be accounted for in Rae's revision. In order to incorporate the Indian exception, Riker proposes a new formulation:

> Plurality election rules bring about and maintain two-party competition except in countries where (1) third parties nationally are continually one of two parties locally, and (2) one party among several is almost always the Condorcet winner in elections. (Ibid., p. 761)

So, with Riker one of Duverger's laws or hypotheses is abandoned (and this amounts to half of all Duverger), and we are simply left with a second try (after the one of Rae) at Duverger's first law. Have we moved forward? I doubt it. First, what is the gain in substituting "party dualism" (Duverger) with "two-party competition"? Neither Rae nor Riker explain this shift, which substitutes one obscurity with another. If two-party competition implies, literally, that only two parties actually compete in straight contests (i.e., the absence of three- or four-cornered races), we almost run out of cases. If it implies other characteristics, they should be stated, and they are not. Second, Riker specifies "bring about and maintain," a specification that Duverger does not enter into his law, and yet a difference that he well perceives in his discussion (Duverger, 1954a, pp. 276–286). "Bring about" imputes a genetic or developmental influence; "maintain" is a lesser and far more easily testable influence. Plurality systems *alone* cannot (as we shall see) bring about anything, whereas it is plausible that they alone can maintain whatever happens to be already in place. Hence, two such very different influences can hardly be subsumed under the same law. Third, Riker's first clause ("third parties nationally are continually one of two parties locally") makes a good point in the worst possible way—circularly. Fourth, and more importantly than all the rest, Riker's second clause (the Condorcet winner) is not, as stated, an *explanans* but an *explanandum*—the thing to be explained.

Here Riker is in fact entering a "new law" concerning Condorcet winners into his revision of Duverger's first law. But he makes no attempt at even showing that Condorcet winners materialize wherever his definition applies. He simply applies the notion to India and assumes that the Indian exception is thus incorporated within the law. Methodologically this is unacceptable. A Condorcet winner is defined as "a candidate that can beat any other in a pairwise contest," and the concept is exemplified as follows: the Indian Congress party presumably defeats "rightists . . . because leftists would vote for Congress rather than rightists, and similarly . . . rightists would vote for Congress rather than leftists" (1982a, p. 761). Now, any party format above two is amenable to the notion of pairwise contests. Thus England should or might display a Condorcet winner but instead has long displayed (in the perfectly fitting instance of the Liberal party) a *Condorcet loser* that does not profit from its in-between positioning between rightists and leftists but is instead caught in a middle squeeze. Australia and New Zealand provide similar counterinstances, that is, in between third parties which perform even more poorly than the English Liberals and may thus be called Condorcet-crushed.[7] So, why does a Condorcet winner win? Under what conditions is a Condorcet configuration conducive to the Indian-type predominant party system (Sartori, 1976, pp. 192–201) rather than to two-partyism? Unless this question is answered, we are simply left with saying that two-party-ism does not materialize when something goes wrong (eventually in Condorcet's name). If so, Riker's law turns out to be more objection-able and even feebler than the one of Duverger.

A final point needs to be surveyed. Riker appraises his revision of Duverger's law as follows: "Note that this formulation is *determinis-tic*—an attempt to avoid the ambiguity of Duverger and Rae. The law asserts that, *with the exceptions noted,* the plurality rule is a sufficient condition for a two-party system. *It is not,* however, an assertion of *a causal relation,* inasmuch as the plurality rule clearly is *not a necessary condition* (vide, Austria)" (1982a, p. 761, my italics). I confess that I cannot make head or tail of all of this. What is a "deterministic law" that does not even assert a "causal relation"? In turn, why is it that failing a "necessary condition," and yet having a "sufficient condi-tion," we do not have a "causal relation"? Why does a necessary condi-tion (i.e., a condition stated negatively) establish a causal link, whereas a sufficient condition (a condition that *suffices* to produce an effect) does not? Let it be added that throughout his article Riker builds much of his case on the distinction between "deterministic" and "probabilistic" laws. That this distinction does not carry as much weight as its propounders believe is a point to which I shall come shortly. At the moment it bears stressing that Riker opts for a "deter-ministic law" while asserting at the same time that a number of "ex-ceptions" have to be noted. How can that be if a law is not probabilis-tic but deterministic? Perhaps here Riker does not do justice to himself, for he does in fact attempt (albeit unsuccessfully) to incorpo-rate the exceptions into his law. Even so, it is striking that his own summation should put the matter as it does.

When all is said, we are brought back to the question: why are we not doing better? Is it because human behavior is lawless to the extent of defying any and all attempts at construing "laws"? Or is it because our methodological legs are atrophied? My sense is that the latter is the case. While the political science profession has made, in the last thirty years or so, impressive progress in research techniques and statistical processing, it has, if anything, regressed in the logical method that prefaces and conditions technical sophistication. In the case in point, "laws" can hardly be formulated unless we are clear-headed as to how they relate to causal analysis, condition analysis, the notion of probability, and, conclusively, as to how they are cor-rectly confirmed or disconfirmed. A somewhat long detour into meth-odological premises is thus unavoidable.

Conditions, Laws, Exceptions

A scientific law may be defined as a generalization endowed with *explanatory power* that detects a regularity. To be sure, a law stands so long as it is not falsified and must be formulated in ways that permit empirical testing, i.e., confirmation or disconfirmation. Pure and simple "statistical laws" (such as: 52.5% of all newborn children are females) do quantify well-confirmed regularities or frequencies, but they have no explanatory power and therefore do not qualify as being "laws." As for the "explanatory power" requirement, the rule of thumb is this: the explanatory power is greater, the more a law definitely and clearly asserts cause-effect relationships. No matter whether causal language is avoided, if a law does not assume some kind of causal direction, some kind of causal imputation, then its explanatory power is either feeble or must be supplied by a supporting background theory. The bottom line is that a law is required to assert more than a regularity and cannot consist of a mere generalization.[8]

The crucial question is: can social science laws, laws that apply to behavioral regularities, be *deterministic*? The logical notion of determinism is straightforward. Causally stated, it postulates that given the cause C, the effect E is also given: it will necessarily and invariably follow. This means that, given the cause, its effect is already known, i.e., predictable with certainty. The laws of physics are deterministic,[9] but the laws that apply to human beings cannot be. Behavioral laws cannot assume that given a cause C the effect E is certain, that it will always and necessarily follow. Does this imply that social science laws are, must be and can only be, *probabilistic*? If the notion of probability is understood technically—in its mathematical and statistical meanings—the reply is no; the standard, even if appropriate, is impossibly high. Hence, "probabilistic" must be understood, far more often than not, in the ordinary meaning of the word, namely, that social science laws hypothesize "likely" outcomes or "frequent" effects. So far, so good—except that a law that is called probabilistic in the ordinary meaning of the word may not be a law at all. For example, in ten instances a law is confirmed while in five instances it is disconfirmed. A ratio of ten to five does point to a greater likelihood of one outcome over others; yet nobody would claim on such grounds that a "probabilistic law" is upheld.

Little is clarified and nothing solved, then, by saying that our laws are probabilistic. Unless this notion is endowed with mathematical power—as is seldom the case with explanatory laws (as defined)—we are simply left with a qualification ex adverso: our laws are not deterministic. In short, "probabilistic" may delude rather than help. If so, where do we turn? When mathematics does not help, classical logic still does. Instead of playing with the word probabilistic, the far less miraculous and (alas) far more difficult course is to engage in *condition analysis*, that is, the mode of analysis based on the notions of necessary and sufficient conditions. John Stuart Mill went as far as defining "cause" as "sufficient condition(s)." He was wrong on the point—but was on the right track. All the necessary and sufficient conditions for an event to occur may be present, and yet nothing happens. Condition analysis is not quite causal analysis: in the latter, "cause" is a triggering factor, whereas in the former no triggering factor is assumed. A discourse on conditions is analytic; a causal discourse is synthetic. But while Mill went too far in his assimilation, he was giving the social scientist a suggestion that still awaits adequate implementation.

To be sure, social scientists make abundant reference to conditions that are often specified as necessary and/or sufficient. Nonetheless, it is apparent that most social scientists have no clear grasp of such notions. A condition is *necessary* when it asserts: *sine qua non*—not without it. The implication is that necessary conditions establish the conditions of applicability, that is, whether a causal generalization applies or does not apply. A condition is *sufficient* when it asserts: on this condition alone a specified consequence can follow. That much we all know. But the intricacies seemingly escape us.

As regards necessary conditions, the first caveat is that the necessary conditions may be numerous, and this implies that in our actual proceedings the conditions of applicability of a law are hardly ever—at least at the outset—fully enumerated and adequately specified. As regards sufficient conditions, the crucial caveat is that *a* sufficient condition is not *the* exclusive condition, and this entails that a same effect can be produced by other sufficient conditions. Thus E may occur even when SC_1 (sufficient condition one) is absent, and this because the same effect is produced by SC_2 (sufficient condition two). If so, SC_1 is not rejected, but SC_2 (and so forth) must be included in the analysis as another, additional and independent sufficient condition.

It is generally assumed that necessary conditions have less explanatory value than do sufficient conditions, and that the latter class of conditions is the more difficult one to spell out. I wonder. For one, necessary conditions are cumulative. If we discover ten necessary conditions, they are *all* necessary. Conversely, sufficient conditions are discrete: *each one suffices*. Sufficient conditions are more powerful (logically and otherwise) than necessary conditions if, and only if, we are permitted to say: this sufficient condition is the *only one*. But this we can seldom say. In fact we generally refer to *a* condition that suffices, that is, to a condition that lacks exclusiveness (that obtains substitutes).

In order to appreciate how the above affects our substantive proceedings, let me take, as an illustration, the way in which Rae handles the first law of Duverger, reformulated as follows: "Plurality formulae cause two-party systems." According to Rae "this proposition implies that plurality formulae are a necessary and sufficient condition for two-party competition. If this is correct, all two-party systems will be associated with plurality formulae, and all plurality formulae will be associated with two-party systems. By the same logic, no other formulae will be associated with two-party competition, and two-party systems will never exist beside formulae other than plurality types" (Rae, 1971, p. 93). I submit that this is not so. The test proposed by Rae assumes a deterministic law, whose correct formulation would have to be: plurality formulae are the *one and only* necessary and the *one and only* sufficient condition. It is only under these restrictions that two-party systems will "never exist" without plurality elections. The ulterior implication is that anything less than a perfect positive correlation suffices to falsify the law. The test, here, is not the strength of the association but whether any single exception is found. If found, a deterministic law is *eo ipso* rejected. But let us restate the law as a behavioral (nondeterministic) regularity, as follows: plurality formulae are *only one of* the sufficient conditions. This formulation no longer implies that two-partyism will "never exist" in the absence of plurality elections. If so, and only if so, the law admits a correlational testing (how relatively strong is the positive association) and for exceptions that need not imply its rejection.

Resuming our thread, it is apparent that in less simple cases than Duverger's the intricacies of a logically correct condition analysis may turn out to be bewildering and, perhaps, unworthy of their cost. We may thus have recourse to a different categorization of conditions, namely, to conditions that are *facilitating* or, conversely, *obstructive*. To be sure, the other construct (necessary and/or sufficient conditions) is to be preferred whenever possible; but in order to get anywhere we often have to settle for the looser categorization. The objection might be that the notions of facilitating versus obstructive conditions lack logical status and therefore that we are now landing at a looseness that no longer meets scientific standards. I take the view, however, that if the appropriate test conditions for "facilitating" and "obstructive" are entered, we still have a heuristic tool which is better than no tool at all.

At this stage of the argument it becomes important to note that "laws" in the social sciences are in fact of many kinds. Statistical laws and also grand historical laws à la Comte or à la Marx (philosophy of history laws) aside, one broad category of laws may be identified as "tendency laws" (e.g., the ones of Mosca and Pareto); whereas other laws affirm a direct relation (the greater . . . the greater) or, instead, an inverse relation (the greater . . . the lesser).[10] The crucial difference among laws is, however, whether they predict *single events* or not. The law of gravity applies to *all* falling bodies (the general class of such events) and to *each* body that falls. Social science laws seldom share this beautiful combination of properties. But the laws on the influence of electoral systems (cause) upon the number of parties (effect) do: they apply—when disturbances are smoothed out—to all and each electoral event(s). If found, they would thus predict single events. Can such laws be found? Before attempting to do so, a last methodological caveat is in order.

A law that predicts single events is ill tested by frequencies and correlation coefficients. Putting it the other way around, statistical testing is appropriate and decisive for laws that apply to classes of events but has only subsidiary value when a law is assumed to predict discrete single outcomes. Hence the crucial notion is, in the case at hand, the one of *exception*. In Rae's correlational testing of Duverger's first law, his finding is that "of . . . 107 cases, 89.7% fall into the predicted categories of association"; and Rae comments that this "suggests a relationship which is somewhat weaker than the term 'sociological law' might lead one to expect, but is, nevertheless, a strong association" (1971, p. 94). The association is indeed an amazingly strong one; but I do not think that it can legitimately help us decide whether we have a law and whether it is weak or not. Thus it is Rae's instinct (rather than his methodology) that immediately and correctly leads him to probe the matter on the basis of the "exceptional cases." The question remains how exceptions are to be handled.

I have noted that exceptions are lethal only for a deterministic law. But even for a social science law exceptions always pose a puzzle. The puzzle can be disposed of in either one of two ways: by entering a necessary condition that restricts the applicability of the law (and, if so, the exception no longer subsists), or by incorporating the exception(s) into a reformulation of the law that subsumes them. Since this is how I propose, in fact, to proceed, the two strategies will be explained in due course. Assume, however, that neither strategy works, that exceptions remain. It is only at this residual point, I submit, that ad hoc considerations offer grounds for claiming that a law holds despite such and such exceptions.

Heads and Tails

Reverting from the method to the real world, I am compelled by brevity to confine my attention to: (1) plurality single-member districts and, (2) PR multimember districts.[11] In the first case we have a one-member sized constituency in which the winner takes all. In the second case we have a more-than-one member sized constituency that roughly translates the votes into seats in proportion. One element is, then, the magnitude of the constituency (measured by the number of candidates it elects); the other element is the method or formula according to which votes are translated into seats. The plurality formula (the-first-past-the-post system) disregards proportions and represents, in principle, the very negation of proportionalism. The proportional formulas display, however, very diverse degrees of proportional correspondence between votes and seats, ranging from highly impure (disproportional) to pure (exactly proportional) fits.[12]

The noteworthy point is this: the size of the constituency affects the proportionality of PR more than do the various mathematical translation formulas (Sainte-Laguë, highest average, largest remainder, etc.).[13] Hence, PR can be technically (mathematically) pure and constituency-wise impure. In this regard the rule of thumb is that the smaller the district the lesser the proportionality and, conversely, the larger the district the greater the proportionality.[14] Since it is in fact the case that across the world we do find district magnitudes that go without discontinuities from 2 to 30 (or somewhere in that vicinity), we have here a truly continuous continuum expressed in, and measured by, natural numbers.[15] The rationale that goes to support the aforesaid rule of thumb is that small districts are, by the same token, more numerous districts. This multiplies, in turn, the occasions of vote losing, that is, the below-quota waste of votes: a waste that disproportionately penalizes the minor parties—to be sure, under the proviso that remainders (the lost votes) are not carried forward from the constituencies to a national pool.

Let us immediately confront the central query, namely: are electoral systems causal factors of consequence, and, if so, can their impact (effect) be stated under the form of lawlike rules that are both predictive (of single events) and verifiable? The direct effect (influence) of electoral systems clearly is on the voter; but if they affect the voter, it may be cogently assumed that electoral systems also, albeit indirectly and derivatively, affect (shape) the party system as a whole. Nonetheless, the two influences are analytically and empirically distinct. The voter is influenced where he votes, that is, in the local context of his constituency. The party system under consideration is, instead, an aggregate, nationwide outcome.

In order to expedite the discussion, let me preface it by asserting without proof (the proofs will emerge along the way) that the effect of the electoral system on the voter (the direct influence) can either be *constraining* or *unconstraining*. If it is utterly unconstraining, we have no cause to pursue the matter: the electoral system has no effect – and that is that. Conversely, if the effect is, in some respect and to varying degrees, *manipulative* in the primary sense of being constraining and/ or restraining, then we do have a case. On this premise, an electoral system that unquestionably exerts a manipulative influence will be classified as being a *strong* electoral system. Conversely, if an electoral system exerts no such influence or exerts it only minimally, I propose to class it as a *feeble* electoral system. The dichotomy simply defines the clear-cut cases that cluster in the vicinity of the ends of a continuum. It allows, therefore, for other cases to fall in between and to be assigned (ordinally) to a cluster of *strong-feeble* electoral systems.

Since no one has ever denied, to my knowledge, that plurality (let alone majority) voting does condition – constrain and restrain – the behavior of the voter, I shall assign without further ado the plurality formula to the class of the strong electoral systems. But where do PR systems belong? Contrary to a still widespread opinion to the contrary, the greater the proportionality of PR, the lesser its impact. At the limit, a pure PR system is a no-effect system. However, most PR systems are impure. Some are indeed strongly disrepresentative, as when access to representation is barred by an exclusion clause or when one or more of the major parties are allotted a premium.[16] In other cases PR systems are rendered disproportional by the small size of the constituency. And then, of course, over- and underrepresentation may result from the methods that translate votes into seats. Both the disrepresentative and the low-proportional PR systems can thus be assigned to the "mixed class" of strong-feeble electoral systems. But more on PR later. We must first dwell on the single-member plurality formula, that is, on the case that eminently illustrates the class of the strong electoral systems.

As I was saying, nobody has ever denied that the plurality formula conditions the voter. It will also be conceded, I trust, that the manipulative conditioning in question is a *constraining-restraining effect*. This means that the voter's choice (unless he prefers to waste his vote) is concretely restricted, very often, to the front-runners. Hence, the plurality single-member district system does indeed "manufacture" and contrive, constituency by constituency, two-party competition. But if the voter is restrained (vis-à-vis his first and unfettered preferences), a reductive effect on the total number of national parties by no means necessarily follows. The restraining effect on the voter is not the same as a *reductive effect* on the number of parties that compose the overall system. Hence it cannot simply be that the plurality formula "tends to produce" a two-party system. The reason for this, let it be repeated and emphasized, is straightforward: the voter is restrained where he votes. Therefore, no electoral system can reduce the number of relevant parties to two at the national level, unless the same two parties happen to be the relevant contestants in all the constituencies. The question thus becomes: under what conditions does a political system pass from local bipartyism to national bipartyism? Since the effect of the electoral system is a *constituency effect*, it is clearly the case that a necessary condition is missing and that we must search for at least another factor or variable. And the missing variable is the party system itself.

The point that has largely escaped recognition is, then, that the effects of electoral systems cannot be assessed without assessing at the same time the manipulative properties of the party system *as such*. For party systems, too, condition the voter and can be divided—just like electoral systems—into strong or feeble party systems, depending on whether they are, qua systems, structured or unstructured. The question turns on what we mean by *structured system* and, consequently, on the conditions that are conducive to a structured system of parties.

So long as the voter is personality-oriented, so long as he merely votes for a person, parties remain labels of little, if any, consequence. Hence, as long as these conditions prevail, the party system is not structured. A moment comes, however, when allegiance is given to the party more than to the personages, that is, when the voter relates to abstract party images. At this moment it is no longer the individual leader that "elects" the party, but the party that elects (puts in office) the individual. As the process develops, it is the party system that becomes perceived as a natural *system of channelment* of the political society. And when the electorate takes for granted a given set of political routes and alternatives very much as drivers take for granted a given system of highways, then the party system has reached the stage of structural consolidation qua system (Sartori, 1976, pp. 21–23, 41, 244).

How a structured party system comes about genetically is a very intricate matter that cannot be discussed here (see Sartori, 1968a, pp. 288–297). It will suffice to note that the voter cannot identify himself with an abstract party image as long as the image is not provided, that is to say, as long as he is confronted with mere parties of notabilities. By the same token, and concurrently, the voter cannot perceive the party as an abstract entity unless he acquires a capacity for abstraction, and this implies, in turn, literacy. Under conditions of widespread illiteracy the structural consolidation of a party system can hardly occur. Concretely and simply put, we "see" a structured party system when the organizational mass party (Sartori, 1968a, pp. 292–293) displaces and largely replaces the parties of notables.

The point at issue can now be restated as follows: plurality systems have no influence (beyond the district) until the party system becomes structured in coincidence with, or in reaction to, the appearance of mass parties. The important implication is that we have long been misled, in this connection, by citing evidence that bears no proof. The authors who deny the reductive effects of plurality systems almost invariably make reference to unstructured party systems, thereby challenging a "law" in situations in which the law does not apply.[17]

A most important head, or tail, has yet to be addressed. Thus far we have adequately specified the cause (electoral systems), but we have not adequately specified the *final,* if indirect, effect. The final effect is assumed to be—in Duverger's version, and still in much of the common wisdom—either a reduction or a multiplication of the total *number* of parties. If so, it is imperative that we establish *how to count* the parties. This requirement has not been met by Duverger nor, at least for the purpose at hand, by Rae. This leaves us with "laws" that defy the very testing to which they are being subjected. I am thus left to abide by the counting rules that I have proposed elsewhere (Sartori, 1976, pp. 121–125; Sani and Sartori, 1983, p. 320). It should be understood, therefore, that my forthcoming references to two-, three-, four-, five-, and more-than-five party systems apply to *relevant parties* as defined by my counting rules, that is, to the parties which are given (by my criteria) *systemic relevance.*

Bearing this general proviso in mind, let us revert to whether and to what extent plurality systems have a *reductive effect* on the total (systemic) number of parties. In this case, how should the predicted effect be specified? Duverger's "party dualism" is far too ambiguous and will not do. The same applies, I have already suggested, to Rae's statistical definition of two-partyism and even more to his notion (and/or measures) of defractionalization. So, which concrete systems are two-party systems? By which criteria are the controversial cases (especially Canada and Australia) included or excluded? The consensus among scholars also excludes from the two-party type the German Federal Republic and Ireland, even though they do not differ, in terms of format, from England and Australia. The problem thus is: are two-party systems defined by their format (the sheer number of parties), or by their mechanics, by their functional characteristics? (Sartori, 1976, pp. 185–192.)

It is clearly the case that the specimen cannot be identified only on the basis of its format.[18] Going beyond the sheer format, a two-party system may be characterized by three traits: (1) over time two parties recurrently and largely outdistance all the others, in such a way that (2) each of them is in a position to compete for the absolute majority of seats and may thus reasonably expect to alternate in power; and (3) each of them governs, when in government, alone. On this definition, however, Australia and Canada still do not qualify. In order to include the two countries, as the *consensus scholarum* seemingly demands, the second and third characterizations must be relaxed as follows: the winner who fails to attain a majority of seats opts for minority single-party government instead of yielding to coalition government (Canada), and a standing coalescence of two parties (as the one among the Australian Country and Liberal parties) is considered equivalent to, and counted as, one party.[19] The list of two-party systems now includes—in decreasing order of approximation to the ideal format—the United States, Malta, New Zealand, Austria, England, Australia, and Canada.[20]

The preceding discussion permits the following stipulation: a two-party *format* denotes *two relevant parties* each of which governs alone (regardless of third parties). A definite listing also has the merit of exactly sorting out the flagrant exceptions. India abides by plurality and yet is not, under whatever definition, a two-party system. Conversely, Austria abides by PR and yet has long displayed a two-party structuring (let alone a two-party mechanics between 1966 and 1983). Unless these exceptions are settled, it is doubtful that we have "laws."

The Effects of Electoral Systems

By assuming, as I have done so far, that electoral systems generally have a reductive effect, it looks as if the alleged "multiplying effect" of PR is being ruled out by definition, and by definition alone. It behooves me to show that this is not so. The logical point is this: since PR is supposed to mirror "in proportion," how can it multiply? What strange kind of mirror is that? I submit that the multiplying effect of PR is an optical illusion prompted by the historical sequencing of electoral systems. The first PR country was Belgium (1899), followed by Sweden (1907). Elsewhere PR generally appeared in the wake of World War I, and in the older European countries of the time PR was invariably preceded by plurality or, more often, by double-ballot formulas that equally displayed plurality-type restraining effects.[21] Let it also be noted that the introduction of PR was often accompanied by enfranchisements, by the entry into politics of hitherto excluded lower-class voters who generally sought new parties, "their own" parties. Thus, when PR was introduced it did result in a roundabout *removal of obstacles:* previous voters were allowed a greater freedom of expressing their first preferences, and new voters the very freedom of voting. So, when we say that PR multiplies the number of parties, we forget to complete the sentence by saying: with respect to a state of affairs in which the number of parties was kept small by small electorates (the exclusion of the have-nots) and/or reduced by "strong" electoral formulas. And if this qualification is entered, then the optical illusion disappears.

The correct argument is, thus, that whenever the introduction of PR happens to be followed by the surge of new relevant parties, we are not really pointing at the *effects* of PR but at the *side effects* resulting from the removal of preexisting obstacles. Had the historical sequencing been from PR to plurality, it would hardly have occurred to us that PR "causes" party system fragmentation or greater fractionalization. Certainly, the more PR exactly mirrors, the less it penalizes and obstructs the surge of new parties or the splitting of existing parties. But freedom to surge is no more the cause of surging than freedom to eat is the cause of eating. PR as such may be said (with some stretching) to cause "obstacle removal" but cannot be said to "cause multiplication."

To recapitulate, pure PR is a *no-effect* electoral system. Conversely, PR affects the party system to the extent that it is *nonproportional,* and this on a variety of counts: the relatively small size of the constituencies, clauses of exclusion, majority premiums, and, lastly, disproportional translations of the votes into seats. It follows from this that whenever PR obtains manipulative effects, these effects are restrictive, not multiplicative. Hence, the influence of PR merely represents an enfeeblement of the same influence that is exerted by the majority-plurality systems.

The road is clear, I trust, for the constructive part of my assignment. Let me first try my hand at a set of rules stated in somewhat descriptive terms:

Rule 1. A plurality system cannot produce by itself a nationwide two-party format (as defined), but under all circumstances it will help *maintain* an already existing one. Hence, whenever a two-party format is established, a plurality system exerts a brakelike influence and obtains a freezing effect.

Rule 2. A plurality system will *produce,* in the long run, a two-party format (not the eternalization of the same parties, however) under two conditions: first, when the party system is structured and, second, if the electorate which is refractory to whatever pressure of the electoral system happens to be dispersed in below-plurality proportions throughout the constituencies.

Rule 3. Conversely, a two-party format is *impossible*—under whatever electoral system—if racial, linguistic, ideologically alienated, single-issue, or otherwise incoercible minorities (which cannot be represented by two major mass parties) are concentrated in above-plurality proportions in particular constituencies or geographical pockets. If so, the effect of a plurality system will only be reductive vis-à-vis the third parties which do not represent incoercible minorities.

Rule 4. Finally, PR systems also obtain *reductive effects*—though to a less and less predictable extent—in proportion to their nonproportionality; and particularly whenever they apply to small-sized constituencies, establish a threshold of representation, or attribute a premium. Under these conditions PR, too, will eliminate the lesser parties whose electorate is dispersed throughout the constituencies; but even a highly impure PR will not eliminate the small parties that dispose of concentrated above-quota strongholds.

It will be noted that my rules largely hinge upon the distribution of electorates. The distribution of partisan allegiances is a historical given, however, only prior to the advent of a structured party system. Since my rules apply after the stage of local fragmentation of politics—under the condition that national mass parties are established—I am concerned only with that distribution of allegiances which remains unaffected by the structural consolidation. Hence my emphasis is on whether or not incoercible *above plurality* or, as the case may be, *above quotient* minorities happen to be geographically concentrated or dispersed.

It should also be noted that rule 2 already suffices to exclude India from consideration (that is, as an exception), because India does not satisfy the condition of being a structured party system.[22] Rule 3 applies nicely to the Canadian case, that is, it accounts for the fact that Canada displays, despite plurality, a three–four party format (counteracted, however, by its mechanics). Rule 3 is also well confirmed by the experience of Sri Lanka between 1948 and 1977: for at the 1977 last election all the minor parties, except for the regionally concentrated, ethnic Tamil parties, had disappeared.[23] On the other hand, rule 4 applies nicely to Ireland and Japan (with small 3-to-5 member constituencies)[24] and also helps explain (on account of the exclusion clause) the format of the German Federal Republic.[25] The patterns displayed by Turkey and Greece since the late forties reflect a wide array of threshold and disrepresentative devices and also fall under the jurisdiction of rule 4.

The next step is to relate the *formats* predicted by the foregoing four rules to *systemic characteristics*, that is, to distinctive types of party systems. From the typology that I have developed at length elsewhere (Sartori, 1976, pp. 125–216, 273–293), let me derive three major systemic patterns: (1) *two-party mechanics*, i.e., bipolar single-party alternation in government; (2) *moderate multipartyism*, i.e., bipolar shifts among coalition governments; (3) *polarized multipartyism*, i.e., systems characterized by multipolar competition, unipolar center-located coalitions with peripheral turnover, and antisystem parties. In this typology the decisive variable is systemic *polarization*, defined as the distance (ideological or other) between the most-distant relevant parties.[26] The question now is: will the format be followed by the expected, corresponding mechanics (functional properties)? Given structural consolidation (necessary condition) and polarization as the intervening and, to some extent, dependent variable, I hypothesize as follows:

Hypothesis 1. When the single-member plurality formula produces a two-party format (rules 1 and 2), the format will in turn produce a two-party mechanics if, and only if, the polarization of the polity is low. With high polarization, two-party mechanics breaks down. However, since a two-party mechanics implies centripetal competition, it tends to lessen, rather than heighten, systemic polarization.

Hypothesis 2. Assuming a below-quota dispersion of the incoercible minorities (if any), impure PR formulas are likely to allow for one–two additional parties above the two-party format, that is, three–four parties. This format will in turn engender the mechanics of moderate multipartyism if, and only if, the polity does not display high polarization. However, since moderate multipartyism still is bipolar-converging (centripetal competition), it will not tend to increase systemic polarization.

Hypothesis 3. Relatively pure or pure PR systems easily allow for a five-to-seven party format. Even so, under conditions of medium-low

TABLE 2.1. Combined Influences of Party and Electoral Systems

Party Systems	Electoral Systems	
	Strong	Feeble
Strong (structured)	(I) Reductive Effect of Electoral System	(II) Countervailing-Blocking Effect of Party System
Feeble (unstructured)	(III) Restraining-Reductive Constituency Effect	(IV) No Influence

polarization, the coalitional mechanics of moderate multipartyism is not impeded. However, under conditions of high polarization the format will display the mechanical characteristics of polarized multipartyism, thereby including a multipolar competition that eventually heightens systemic polarization.

The above is so condensed as to be only of suggestive value—and I shall have to leave it at that.[27] For I have yet to complete the argument. Thus far the independent (causal) variable has been the electoral system. But we already know that another independent variable has to be accounted for: *the party system qua system of channelment.* Let us attend, then, to assessing the case in its entirety.

Just like electoral systems, party systems can be trichotomized, with regard to their manipulative impact, into strong, strong-feeble, and feeble. However, in order to avoid lengthy complexities I shall proceed dichotomously, thus obtaining a matrix with four cells, that is, four possible combinations: (I) strong electoral system and strong party system, (II) feeble electoral system and strong party system, (III) strong electoral system and feeble party system, and (IV) feeble electoral system and feeble party system. Since the dichotomous reduction squeezes out the "strong-feeble" category, it should be understood that the "strong electoral systems" include not only, as is obvious, the plurality formula but also the strongly impure PR formulas (in substance, all the cases covered by my preceding rules). Conversely, the "feeble electoral systems" refer to the relatively pure to pure PR formulas (mathematically and districtwise). The overall interdependencies between the electoral system, on the one hand, and the party system, on the other hand, are shown in Table 2.1.

Combination I requires no further explanation. All the two-party systems singled out earlier (except Austria and Malta) fall here, thus confirming the predicted *reductive effect*. India, on the other hand, falls into Combination III and, therefore, does not represent an exception: no "Condorcet winner" is required to dispose of the case.

Combination II indicates that, when PR (even feeble PR) encounters a structured party system, the voter is still *restrained*, though not by the electoral system but by the potency of party channelment. In this case, then, the electoral system is counteracted by the party system: we have, I say, a *blocking* or a *countervailing effect*. That is the same as saying that here the causal factor, the independent variable, is the party system. Combination II not only explains why the introduction of PR may not be followed by "more parties," but also allows for a two-party format under PR, vide not only Austria but also Malta (single transferable vote). The combination in question disposes, then, of the exceptions: two-partyism without plurality. The general argument is this: a particularly strong structuring of the party system replaces (as sufficient condition two) the manipulative impact of a strong electoral system (sufficient condition one).

Combination III indicates that, when a strong electoral system encounters an unstructured party system, the effect is only a *constituency effect*, and specifically a restraining effect on the voter that translates itself into a reductive effect on the constituency parties. Here, then, the electoral system cannot produce reductive effects on the national scale. Still, the constituency impact remains, thereby discouraging fickleness and encouraging two-man races at the district level. The combination illustrates the state of affairs in much of continental Europe until or around World War I.[28] One may also suggest that here we have the optimal waiting and/or facilitating condition for the development of structured party systems of the bipolar kind (two-party mechanics and moderate multipartyism), and an obstructive condition as regards the development of extreme and polarized multipartyism.

Combination IV indicates *no influence*, meaning that, when relatively pure PR is combined with structurelessness, neither the electoral nor the party systems intervene in the political process with a manipulative impact of their own. Here the general point is (as we know) that the more we approach pure PR, and the more electoral or related obstacles are removed, the less whatever party system happens to exist is "caused" by the electoral system. Much of Latin America, on account of the intermittence of its party experience, i.e., of the repeated interruptions (detrimental to consolidation) caused by military seizures, comes close to falling into this cluster. And the combination conveys that the newborn countries that start with PR have set for themselves the least favorable conditions for overcoming party atomization and for attaining structural consolidation.[29]

The Laws: Another Try

We are now ready for rules that qualify as being laws because they are formulated in terms of necessary and sufficient conditions (as underpinned earlier). Since the electoral system is the causal factor under investigation, the electoral system is assumed to be *a sufficient condition* and, more precisely, the pertinent, albeit *not the exclusive* sufficient condition. As for the *necessary conditions*, our inquiry has found two such conditions, namely: (1) *systemic structuring* (of the party system), as opposed to structurelessness; (2) sizeable above-plurality concentrations or, with PR, sizeable above-quota concentrations, as opposed to below-plurality or below-quota distributions (of the first preferences of the voters) hereinafter abridged as *cross-constituency dispersion*. On these premises the *laws* that I venture to propose are as follows:

1. Given systemic structuring and cross-constituency dispersion (as joint necessary conditions), *plurality systems* cause (are a sufficient condition of) a two-party format.
1.1. Alternatively, a particularly strong systemic structuring is, alone, the necessary substitutive sufficient condition for causing a two-party format.
2. Given systemic structuring but failing cross-constituency dispersion, *plurality systems* cause (are a sufficient condition of) the elimination of below-plurality parties but cannot eliminate, and thus permit, as many parties above two as are permitted by sizeable above-plurality concentrations.
3. Given systemic structuring, *proportional representation* obtains a reductive effect caused (as a sufficient condition) by its nonproportionality. Hence, the greater the impurity of PR, the higher the entry costs for the smaller parties, and the stronger the reductive effect; and, conversely, the lesser the impurity, the feebler the reductive effect.
3.1. Alternatively, a particularly strong systemic structuring is alone the necessary and sufficient condition for maintaining whatever party format preexisted the introduction of PR.
4. Failing systemic structuring and assuming pure PR, that is, an

equal cost of entry for all, the number of parties is free to become as large as the quota permits.

The above numbering system may cause some confusion. How many laws do we have? At most, four, since laws 1.1 and 3.1 simply allow for the incorporation and/or dismissal of apparent exceptions under the proviso: varying the condition, the same effect may follow, because one sufficient condition is substituted by another. In fact, the "true" laws (if true) are three, since law 4 has explanatory but not causal power: it simply establishes where the effects of electoral systems end. So, the requirement of parsimony is surely met. On the other hand, the wording of my laws may appear somewhat cumbersome. This is so because they are deliberately and somewhat pedantically cast—as required by the demonstration that I have been pursuing—in causal language. Even so, it seems to me that my laws are straightforward enough. The objection might be, however, that they are too abstract and not specific enough. Not so, provided that they are read—as they are supposed to be read—in conjunction with the four rules set forth earlier. In particular, the specifics of law 1 are given in rules 1 and 2; the specifics of law 2 are provided by rule 3; and the specifics of law 3 are supplied by rule 4.

In order to pursue the exercise all the way, the last question is: can we be as parsimonious as Duverger? The reply is yes, provided that we replace the neatness and logical force of necessary and sufficient conditions with the laxity of *facilitating* versus *obstructive* conditions. If so, we are left with mere *tendency laws* that are not necessarily disconfirmed by exceptions and are sufficiently confirmed by occurring "far more often than not." Under these relaxations we can indeed settle almost everything with just two very simple laws, namely:

Tendency law 1: Plurality formulas facilitate (are facilitating conditions of) a two-party format and, conversely, obstruct (are an obstructive condition of) multipartyism.

Tendency law 2: PR formulas facilitate multipartyism and are, conversely, hardly conducive to two-partyism.

The above—had it been understood rightly—is just about all that Duverger said. Unfortunately, neither Duverger nor his commentators have ever come to grips with the methodological underpinnings of lawlike generalizations. The study of politics and of society is replete with causal-type generalizations that could easily be formulated as tendency laws, which might, in turn, be amenable to a relatively precise condition analysis. Had this route been pursued, I submit that we would dispose today of explanatory laws that would indeed attest to the cumulative growth of a scientifically respectable knowledge.

NOTES

1. They are formulated first in Duverger et al. (1950) and then reproduced in Duverger (1951a). My references are to the second 1954 French edition of *Les Partis Politiques* (Duverger, 1954a). The English translation of Barbara and Robert North (Duverger, 1963) is not used because it is, on key points, imprecise and even misleading.

2. Stated, respectively, in Duverger (1954a), pp. 247 and 269. The English translation (Duverger, 1963, p. 217) of the first law renders *tend aux* as "favors" and truly mistranslates *dualisme des partis* with "two party systems." It is permissible and appropriate, instead, to render Duverger's *majoritaire* as "plurality system," for it is clear that he means "relative majority" (plurality), not absolute majority. It is worth adding in passing that Duverger provides his own best (more analytic) formulation of his "formulas" as follows: (1) PR tends to a system of multiple, rigid and independent parties; (2) the majority second ballot system [tends to] a system of multiple, flexible [*souples*] and independent parties; (3) the majority [plurality] single ballot system [tends to] party dualism (Duverger, 1950, p. 13).

3. Riker (1982a, p. 758) asserts that Duverger "distinguished sharply between the law [the first one] and the hypothesis, which previously had often been misleadingly interpreted as duals of each other." But it is Riker, I fear, who is misled by the Norths' translation, for Duverger never says "hypothesis"; his general term, if any, is *schemas*, and he does indeed treat his "schemes" as duals (see, e.g., Duverger 1954a; p. 269). The only reason that sustains Duverger's claim that his first scheme is "the closest to a true sociological law" (1954a, p. 247) is a counterfactual one: "nowhere in the world has PR produced or maintained a bipartisan system" (1954a, p. 276). Since he was in fact wrong (Austria was PR and two party), we are left to note that no other difference subsists, in Duverger's actual proceedings, between the two schemes. He is just as assertive with regard to PR as he is with regard to plurality: "it is a sure thing that PR always coincides with multipartyism" (Duverger, 1954a, p. 276, and similarly, pp. 279, 281, 283). The "sharp distinction" that sustains much of Riker's argument is nowhere to be found; if anything, Duverger has more trouble in explaining away the exceptions to his first scheme (law) than to the second one.

4. The two representative and largely accepted contrary views have been the ones of Grumm and Mackenzie. The first author concluded, very much beside the point, that "PR is a result rather than a cause of the party system" (Grumm, 1958, p. 375); the second argued that comparatively tested generalizations are impossible to achieve (Mackenzie, 1957).

5. While Rae's cutoff points are adroitly doctored ex post to the returns of the systems that are generally considered two-party, Rae's defining criteria address discrete occurrences, not countries (over time political systems). If so, they should include Turkey in 1957 (first party 69.9; first two parties 98.6), Germany in 1976 (first party 49.0; first two parties 92.1), and Greece in 1981 (first two parties 95.6). Had Rae decided for 89% as his cumulative cutoff point (why not?), then another two-party

occurrence would be Germany in 1980 (total 89.4). In Venezuela, in 1973 the first two parties added up to 88.3, a close next. The point is that Rae already knows, on other unstated criteria, which countries are the two-party ones to which his testing applies.

6. See Sartori (1976, pp. 307–315), where I contend that Rae's index of fractionalization does not afford cutting points for identifying and classifying concrete systems with respect to distinctive systemic properties.

7. Reference is made to the Australian Democratic Labor Party and to the Australian Democrats (neither of whom have even won a single seat), and to New Zealand's Social Credit League (that occasionally wins one or, once, two seats).

8. For example, the statement that all swans are white is not a law; it simply establishes, if true, a defining characteristic. If so, a black swan would not be a swan. Since black swans do exist, the correct generalization is: most swans are white. But both the false and the true generalizations lack explanatory value.

9. The contention that physics too is "indeterministic" is immaterial, for it does not bridge by an inch the gap that separates the strictly mathematical "probability" that applies to the laws of nature from the nonmathematical or poorly mathematical probability nominally predicated of social science laws.

10. An example of direct ratio is Durkheim's law on suicide: the greater the anomie, the greater the frequency of suicides. The distinctions are not rigorous. For example, Michel's law is formulated both as a tendency law (oligarchy always tends to replace democracy), and as an inverse relation (the greater the organization, the lesser the democracy).

11. What is true for plurality (relative majority) formulas is even more true for majority (above 50%) formulas. Note also that plurality-majority formulas can be applied to multimember constituencies (e.g., Turkey in the fifties, where a plurality criterion applied to a list voting in multimember districts). However, the obverse cannot be: PR cannot apply to a single-member district.

12. Rose (1983, pp. 40–41) makes the point that "the difference in proportionality between the median election under proportional representation and plurality systems is very limited: 7%;" and his evidence (in Table 8, p. 26) indicates, furthermore, that some plurality countries display greater proportionality than some PR countries. The point is repeated in Rose (1984, pp. 74–75 and Table 7.1) where the difference in proportionality becomes 8%. But I fail to see how his statistics warrants his point. Rose discounts the very effects of the electoral system, namely, the fact that under plurality systems the voter is restrained and parties are eliminated. When we look at the returns, the distortions have already occurred. And the difference that Rose minimizes reappears at nonroutine elections, such as the British one of 1983, when the Alliance obtained 3.5% of the seats with 25.4% of the vote (each of its seats cost 400,000 votes, as against a cost of 40,000 for Labour).

13. This was first stressed by Hogan (1945, p. 13): "the decisive point in P.R. is the size of the constituencies." I made it over and over again (Sartori, 1968a, pp. 276, 279, 283, 291), but it was not until Rae's work that it became acknowledged, even though it remains to date underplayed. As for the exact appreciation of the under- or over-representative effects of the various mathematical translation formulae, see esp. Lijphart, this volume.

14. Countries with relatively small constituency average (rounded) size are: Ireland and Japan (4), Greece (5), Spain (6), Austria and Belgium (7). At the other extreme, Israel and the Netherlands, respectively, elect 120 and 150 members in a single, nationwide constituency.

15. This must be qualified by noting that the relationship, "the larger the constituency, the greater the proportionality," is curvilinear: as the district magnitude grows, the proportionality increases at decreasing rates. This entails that at some point the mathematical translation formula begins to carry more weight than the district size. Even so, Rae (1971, p. 163) calculates that "in the case of one district and two hundred seats, a party with a vote share of about 0.005 would be sure of winning a seat." Another caveat is that the average (and even the median) district magnitude can be a very misleading measure unless the dispersion is controlled. Fisichella's (1982, pp. 251–252) index of variability attributes the smallest dispersion (0.81) to Ireland, where the constituency size ranges between 3 and 5 members, and the widest dispersion (11.77) to Argentina, whose constituencies range from a 2-member to a 50-member size.

16. Aside from having an equally strong manipulative potential, denial of access and bonus giving obviously are entirely different devices. The threshold of exclusion can be as low as 3%; the German *Sperrklausel* is at 5%; and Turkey adopted, for its 1983 elections, a national 10% minimum vote barrier. As for the premium device, its most extreme form is probably the one devised in Paraguay, where two-thirds of the seats are allocated to the winning (plurality) party, thus leaving only one-third to a PR allocation among the remaining parties. Greece adopted, at one point in time, a similar device. Greece also displays, throughout its highly mobile electoral history, a sequel of above-10% exclusion barriers.

17. Interestingly, Duverger (1954a, pp. 250, 253) himself, in citing the cases of Sweden (before 1911) and Denmark (before 1920) as deviations from his first law, notes that Sweden was characterized at the time by the absence of true parties. But the insight is left at that.

18. This is even less the case if the format is established, in turn, by counting all the parties that hold at least one seat in parliament. Under this criterion (which includes the systemically "irrelevant" parties) Austria has displayed from 1945 to 1983 a 3–4 party format; New Zealand has been in 1966, 1978, and 1981 three-party; Canada often has 4 parties, arrived at 5 in 1968, 1972, and 1974, and at 6 parties in 1965; and England (in 1979) displayed as many as 10 parties. Since Australia is anomalous, we would thus be left with about two countries.

19. The Australian anomaly is facilitated by an electoral system for the Lower House (the alternative vote in single-member constituencies) that allows, in practice, the cumulation of the Liberal and Country party votes. The alternative vote system redistributes the preferences until a candidate obtains an absolute majority, and should not be confused, therefore, with the single transferable vote, which is a PR system.

20. On the sheer basis of its format, South Africa (a predominant party system in terms of mechanics) should also be included. Sri Lanka has come very close to qualifying for inclusion (see n. 23 below). Turkey (1946–60 and in 1983), Venezuela since 1973, Greece since 1974, are additional, possible candidates; but I would keep them on a waiting list on account of insufficient longevity and other uncertainties. Spain has displayed between 1976 and 1982 enormous electoral oscillations that seemingly attest to a still ongoing process of party system structuring. On the other hand, I deliberately exclude Uruguay (the 1973–83 military seizure aside), and even more Colombia, as being facade two-party arrangements that fail to meet even the relaxed defining characteristics.

21. It is difficult to generalize about double-ballot formulas, for they did and can cover a wide variety of very different arrangements: single-member but also multimember

constituencies; run-off restricted to the two front-runners (and therefore without alliance negotiations) or, instead, left entirely open to trade-offs. (For a survey see Fisichella, 1982, pp. 254–55, 263–66, 274–85.) Even so, in the 19th and early 20th century instances the double ballot generally did exert (at least, on a constituency basis) disrepresentative and restraining manipulative effects.

22. That is to say that by all standards the Indian party system is still feebly structured and might at most be classified as "semistructured" on account of the fact that only one of its parties, the Congress party (founded in 1885 and thus, long prior to independence, *the* party of non-Moslem Indians), has attained the degree of structural consolidation attainable in a country in which illiteracy still looms as large as it does across more than 700 million inhabitants. Even so, "personality politics" still predominates, as attested by the massive swings of the late 70s: the dramatic downslide of the Congress party in 1977 (down to 28% of the seats, from a previous 68%) followed by another landslide victory in 1980. India certainly attests, on the other hand, to what a plurality system impedes. Were India to switch to PR, it is a safe conjecture that it would quickly become one of the most fragmented, if not atomized, of all known party systems.

23. More exactly, in Sri Lanka the nonethnic minor parties and the independents fell from 26 seats obtained in 1960 to 2 seats in 1970 and in 1977; while the two Marxist parties (Communists and LLSP) fell from the 25 seats still obtained in 1970 to no seats in 1977. Unfortunately for our purposes, the new 1978 constitution drops the plurality system and endorses PR. But new elections under the new system have not occurred to date.

24. Here, however, the size of the constituency is not the only factor at play. Ireland employs the single transferable vote system, and Japan the limited vote (one vote for constituencies that return 3 to 5 members).

25. The fact that the FRG displays a fairly exact proportion between votes and seats does not detract from the fact that its parties are reduced by the 5% hurdle.

26. To be sure, this represents a strong simplification of my typology. Concerning "polarization," see esp. Sani and Sartori (1983) for how the concept is defined, measured, and fares with the comparative evidence.

27. Other, and better known, correspondences and implications bear on how plurality and PR systems, respectively, affect governability and the very principle of representation. As I have put it, "representational systems belong to two main patterns. . . . The English type sacrifices the representativeness of parliament to the need of efficient government, while the French type sacrifices efficient government to the representativeness of parliament. . . . We cannot build a representational system that maximizes at one and the same time the function of functioning and the function of mirroring" (Sartori, 1968b, p. 469). The quotation shows, I submit, that Nohlen's (1984a, pp. 84–87) point that "electoral systems should be classified and evaluated according to the principles of representation" is not as "new" (nor unknown to me) as he claims. I am also unable to grasp why my distinction between strong and feeble electoral systems rests on "normative premises," or why their effects (my topic) should not assume, as an appropriate parameter, a "no-effect situation."

28. This assumes (n. 21 above) that the kinds of double-ballot that actually preceded PR did in fact exert (contrary to Duverger's generalization) a restraining, pluralitylike impact on the voter.

29. This section, including Table 2.1, largely repeats, with minor modifications, Sartori (1968a, pp. 278–287). My text was drafted in 1966 and seemingly attests — in Riker's genealogical perspective — to a failed cumulation.

CHAPTER 3

Duverger's Law: Forty Years Later

Maurice Duverger

My theory of electoral systems, conceived after the Second World War, has never been completely neglected since then, but it became dormant until about 1975. Now our Sleeping Beauty has indeed revived! This chapter provides the opportunity to take a fresh look at it in the light of the evolution of Western parties during its hibernation. My aim is not to defend at all costs hypotheses that I never presented as definitive, but to correct their interpretation and to restate them on the basis of what we have learned in the past forty years. In this chapter my emphasis will not be so much on what confirms these hypotheses but rather on what appears to contradict and could lead to weaken or even disconfirm them.

Errors of Interpretation

Certain errors of interpretation have resulted from my own tentative and imprecise formulations. An example is the alleged difference between "Duverger's law" on the plurality rule's tendency to create and maintain two-party systems and the "hypotheses" concerning the tendency toward multipartism of proportional representation and the two-ballot majority system, Riker's (1982a; see also, chapter 1) analysis of this distinction is the most recent instance. In 1951, I did say in *Political Parties* that the former was "the closest to a sociological law among all the generalizations suggested in this book," but this remark did not have the significance that was later attributed to it. It simply reflected my cautious attitude which was a reaction to the criticisms of the propositions that I first stated in 1945 at a conference at the University of Bordeaux (Duverger, 1946a, 1946b), where I presented the consequences of the three electoral systems as a "threefold sociological law." I already discarded this expression in the paper presented at the 1950 Congress of the International Political Science Association which merely mentioned "three formulas" (Duverger et al., 1950, p. 13). But later I used it again in the first edition of my handbook *Droit Constitutionel et Institutions Politiques* which propounds "three sociological laws defining merely basic tendencies that interact with national and social factors" in terms which have hardly changed since then.

> (1) Proportional representation tends to lead to the formation of many independent parties, . . . (2) the two-ballot majority system tends to lead to the formation of many parties that are allied with each other, . . . (3) the plurality rule tends to produce a two-party system (Duverger, 1955, p. 113).

In the more recent editions, the second law is formulated as follows: "The two-ballot majority system tends to produce multipartism tempered by alliances."

All sociological laws remain more vulnerable than natural science laws, but the latter, too, are no more than interpretations of objects and relationships instead of relevations of their essence. The so-called hard sciences are more resistant—but not immune—to the erosion of time than are the soft sciences. In the realm of human relations and social structures, the empirical regularities are less precise and more fragile. Riker's analysis confirms that the link between two-party systems and plurality voting has been observed and verified for a longer time than the others. The evidence that I have collected myself also shows that it is more firmly established than the relationships between multipartism and the other electoral systems. To my mind, however, this entails only a difference of degree between the two categories and not a difference in kind. All of the following observations vindicate this point of view.

Other errors of interpretation are less the author's than the readers' fault. For instance, many commentators ignore the exact terms used in my propositions. Each states merely that a particular electoral system "tends" to lead to a particular party system, thus emphasizing that the former does not necessarily produce the latter. In 1945 I had argued in more absolute terms that a particular electoral system would "lead" to a particular party system. From 1950 on, I have used "tend to lead" instead of "lead," and the context has clearly underlined that the electoral system is only one of the causal elements (Duverger et al., 1950, p. 13). In 1955 I specified that "it is certain that the party system of a country is in the first place a reflection of national traditions and social forces. The influence of the electoral system can be counterbalanced by these basic factors" (Duverger, p. 115). In 1960 I added, "The relationship between electoral rules and party systems is not mechanical and automatic: A particular electoral regime does not necessarily produce a particular party system; it merely exerts pressure in the direction of this system; it is a force which acts among several other forces, some of which tend in the opposite direction" (Duverger, p. 40).

Moreover, the term *multipartism* has often been misinterpreted, in spite of the clarity and precision found in *Political Parties* where I condemn "the confusion between the notion of multipartism as I have defined it in this book (a system having more than two parties) and the current notion of multiplication, implying an increase in the number of parties existing at the time of the introduction of PR. It is possible that such an increase will not occur" (Duverger, 1951a, p. 338; 1954c, p. 245). A few pages later, I emphasized that "the multiplying effect of PR . . . is generally limited," mainly influencing the appearance of small groups. I concluded, "On the whole, PR maintains virtually without change the party system existing at the time of its adoption" (Duverger, 1951a, pp. 344, 346; 1954c, pp. 251, 252). In doing so, it saves the center groupings which generally prevent the formation of stable majorities.

The analysis of British elections provides a striking illustration of the concept of multipartism that is the basis for the sociological laws in question. With PR *none* of the general elections from 1930 until today would have allowed one of the two large parties to win by itself more than half of the seats in the House of Commons. With plurality, *all* elections during the same period allowed this to happen *with one exception:* the election of February 1974, which was soon followed by a new election in October of the same year that reestablished a parliamentary majority. However, this does not prove that PR would have substantially altered the number of parties in Great Britain. The examples of the German Federal Republic and Austria suggest the opposite.

Tendencies Toward a Two-Party System In Spite of PR

Both West Germany and Austria have two large parties and one small party, like the United Kingdom. They also tend toward a two-party system although they use PR. Ireland approximates the Austrian and English cases, but not as clearly. It is true that, in two of these three countries, PR has unusual features. In Germany each voter has two votes, one for half of the seats to be filled by plurality in single-member districts, the other to elect the second half of the seats by PR in each *land*, in such a way that the total number of seats won by each party corresponds with the percentage of the "second votes" for the party lists. The result is mathematically very close to traditional PR provided that the district seats may be retained in any case, which may increase a party's seat proportion, and that no party with less than 5% of the list votes or 3 district seats is entitled to any list seats.

Politically, this combination of the English system and PR exerts pressure toward a two-party system as a result of the first vote, which influences the citizens in how to cast their second vote. A few voters transfer their Socialist or Christian Democratic choice in the plurality vote to the Liberals in the list vote, but their number remains quite small. It is sufficient to give the Liberals the role of an arbiter, but not to dispel their image of being merely an addition to the two large parties which the first vote establishes as the essential actors. On the other hand, the 5% threshold bars the very small groups that are favored by pure PR.

The Irish single-transferable vote (STV) seems to conform to traditional PR in spite of the objections that are sometimes raised against this conclusion. Butler (1981, p. 21) has nevertheless shown that it may yield strange results; for instance, Fianna Fail (a party created in 1926 and which nowadays dominates the island's political life) won 51.7% of the seats with 45.7% of the votes in 1969, but only 47.6% of the seats with 46.2% of the votes in 1973. I shall not deal with Katz's (1980, p. 40) arguments which appear to apply to the Australian alternative vote rather than to STV; Riker's (1982a, pp. 758–759) refutation seems convincing.

We must remember, however, that the Irish districts are very small, with only 3 to 5 seats each. This normally deprives of representation any party which does not gain 20% to 25% of the votes, as Butler correctly points out on the basis of the excellent analysis by Rae (1967, pp. 116–117). We should not forget either that the president of Ireland is chosen in a nationwide direct election, which leads to the polarization of the citizens around the two large parties, in spite of the alternative vote that is used for this purpose. This factor also operates in Austria with even greater force: The president is elected by the citizens according to a majority system in which the second round is limited to the two top candidates in the first round, and hence to a contest between Socialists and Christian Democrats.

These special traits of the Irish, Austrian, and German electoral systems help to explain a certain tendency to a two-party system in spite of the opposite tendency provided by PR. But they do not constitute the essential factor in these anomalies. Remember that my 1955 formulation of the sociological laws specified that they "define merely basic tendencies that interact with national and social factors," that a country's party system is first of all a reflection of the latter, and that the electoral system is usually only an accelerator or a brake.

Typical in this respect is Austria, where the two large parties are deeply rooted in the country's history, where they are not only political organizations but complex entities linked with trade unions, cooperatives, economic enterprises, and with intellectual, sports, social, and even religious associations. In some districts, the number of members of a party is greater than its voters because the privacy of the voting booth allows the voters to reveal sentiments that cannot be expressed publicly. Citizens are induced to become members and pay dues in each of the two large parties in order to have the best chances in everyday life. Compared with these two fundamental institutions, the small Liberal party plays a paltry role. It represents a marginal position, a refusal to integrate into the rigid mechanism of a cumbersome and sometimes sclerotic system—exactly like its British counterpart.

The German Liberals present the same character, although they function in a country with a very different political tradition. The tendency toward a two-party system was already present in interwar Austria, but it was absent in Weimar Germany, where multipartism flourished. The Socialists and the Center party (predecessors to today's CDU-CSU) were flanked on the left by the world's second largest Communist party, after that of the Soviet Union, and on the right by reactionary and fascist movements from which the Nazi party emerged with the help of PR. The 1945 defeat removed these two wings from German parliamentary politics. The "brown" wing was destroyed in the defeat of the Third Reich, which deprived the extreme right of its legitimacy and credibility. The partition of the country and the Russian occupation of East Germany destroyed the "red" wing, or, more accurately, drove it back inside the territory of the German Democratic Republic. The examples of the Italian Christian Democrats and of the French MRP further helped the emergence of the CDU-CSU by providing a model of respectability that could win the victors' seal of approval for the vanquished. The 5% threshold did the rest by preventing the success of small groups.

In Ireland, the two-party tendency is directly related to the struggle for independence and unification. It explains the influence of the national hero Eamon de Valera and of the organizations led by him. The first, Sinn Fein, fought the English in 1917 and monopolized the Dublin Parliament established in 1921. De Valera resigned from it in 1926 in order to create the new party, Fianna Fail. Its present main rival, Fine Gael, was founded in 1933 on the theme of a unified Ireland; that is, the integration of Ulster into the Republic. In order to counterbalance the strength of Fianna Fail, it has to ally itself with the Labour party, the country's oldest organization that was created by the labor unions in 1912. Since 1932, Fianna Fail has won the absolute majority in 6 out of 17 legislatures; the coalition of Fine Gael and Labour has twice won an absolute majority. The other legislatures have been dependent on very small parties.

Ireland remains farther away from a two-party system than do Austria and West Germany. I examine it here only in order to respond to Riker (1982a, pp. 758–759), who regards Ireland as one of the deviant cases in terms of the sociological law concerning the effects of PR. In the past half century, the Dublin Parliament has never been composed exclusively of Fianna Fail, Fine Gael, and Labour. There has always been at least one other small party and most often several other parties. These outsiders frequently occupy more than 10% of the seats; for instance, in the legislatures elected in 1932, 1933, 1943, 1944, 1948, 1951, and 1957. Moreover, the number of very small groups has tended to increase. Reduced to one or two from 1932 to 1944, it increased to three from 1944 to 1957, four in 1957, 1961, and 1977, six in 1981, and again four in February 1982. The tendency of PR to favor small parties operates here, as expected.

Likewise its tendency to prevent stable majorities manifests itself, although the domination of Fianna Fail often succeeds in overcoming it. Of this party's six absolute majorities, the first three were won in the first 15 years of the past half century with only one brief legislative term between them (1933, 1938, and 1944). The last three occurred in the next 35 years with two or three nonmajoritarian legislatures in between. Since 1973 the growth of Fine Gael has been noteworthy. It received more than 38% of the seats in 1973, sufficient for a majority of its alliance with Labour. The same situation recurred in 1982 after three successive elections in less than a year and a half (June 1981, February 1982, and November 1982).

Thus, Irish politics since 1932 has known three different periods. First, Fianna Fail governed alone for 16 years with parliamentary majorities or near-majorities (1932–1948), and it maintained itself in power twice by dissolving parliament quickly after elections with unclear results. In the next 21 years, legislatures without majority were the rule, except for 1957–1961 when Fianna Fail could again rule by itself; in the other legislatures, external support was necessary—and sometimes very easy to obtain; for instance, when only one additional vote was sufficient in the years after 1965. A new majority phase appeared from 1969 on, characterized by an alternation between Fianna Fail victories (1969 and 1977) and those of the Fine Gael-Labour coalition (1973 and 1982), the last of which occurred after the three dissolutions just mentioned.

Hence the mechanism of alternation is weaker in Ireland than in Great Britain. In the half century from 1932 to 1983 (and even beyond 1983 because the new legislatures can last until 1987 and 1988, respectively), the London Parliament has only once experienced the absence of a majority requiring a quick dissolution: in 1974. In Dublin this rescue operation has had to be used five times—in 1932, 1937, 1943, 1981, and 1982—and the 1948, 1951, and 1954 legislatures had to be dissolved at the end of three years; that is, after only three fifths of their mandates. Because the Irish have followed the British parliamentary model, they have been able to obtain better results from these dissolutions than have the other countries with PR, where dissolution has not been an effective method for creating majorities except in very exceptional cases. The small size of the electoral districts is also helpful because it corrects the effects of PR.

West Germany and especially Austria control the effects of PR much better. In the former, the elimination of small parties is mainly the result of the 5% threshold. In the latter this threshold does not exist, but since 1945 no other group has been able to obtain representation than the Socialists, Christian Democrats, Liberals, and, until 1959, the Communists. The Communists have disappeared since then, and the decline of the Liberals, from 11.7% of the vote in 1949 to 5.4% today, has made one-party majorities possible, from 1966 to 1970 in favor of the Christian Democrats, and from 1971 to 1983 in favor of the Socialists. This phase of a British-style two-party system lasted 17 years except for the Socialist-Liberal coalition in 1970–1971, which was formed again after the 1983 elections. During the 17 years preceding this majoritarian phase (1947–1966), the Vienna government was a grand coalition between the two main parties. Catholics and Socialists equally divided the costs and the spoils of power, in particular the civil service appointments; this was the famous *Proporz,* which entailed both a profound consensus and a rigid immobilism.

Majoritarianism has therefore characterized Austrian politics almost half of the time since the Second World War in spite of PR. But it would have prevailed during the entire period with the plurality rule: Neither the Communists nor the Liberals would have had representatives in Parliament, and a parliamentary system of the English type would have operated without interruption. The traditional power of the Catholic and Socialist parties has partly limited the consequences of PR. The popularity of Chancellor Kreisky was undoubtedly another important reason for the maintenance of the Socialist majority from 1971 to 1983. To his compatriots he again presented the paternal image that had been lost with the departure of Emperor Franz Joseph. In the German Federal Republic the Adenauer symbol was equally efficacious. It probably explains why the CDU-CSU obtained the absolute majority of both votes and seats in 1957. In all other legislatures a coalition was necessary. In this sense, the Bundestag in Bonn is not as close to the English model as is the Vienna legislature after 1966.

The role of the Liberal party makes the Bundestag even more deviant. In contrast with the powerless Liberals in Britain, their pivotal power controls the formation of a government; their initiative, instead of that of the voters, is decisive. After another victory of the rightist coalition in the 1965 elections, the Liberals left their partner 13 months later—prompting the formation of the grand coalition that united the Christian Democrats and the Socialists for three years. At the end of this transition, the Liberals moved from the right to the left and joined the Socialists. After governing together for 13 years, the Liberals turned against the Socialists in 1982 in the same way that they had treated the Christian Democrats in 1966, but in a more brutal fashion— suddenly swinging from left to right. The voters followed reluctantly in the general elections held after this reversal of alliances. Nothing can be imagined that is farther removed from a two-party system than this strategy; it approximates that of the Radical party in the interwar period of the French Third Republic or that of the small center parties in Italy today. It is clearly a strategy of multipartism.

A Three-Party System in Great Britain?

In the 1981–1983 period, Britain seems to have provided a symmetrical counterexample to the ones just examined. While West Germany, Austria, and Ireland have appeared to move toward a two-party system under PR, Britain has appeared to tend toward multipartism in a plurality system. After the formation of the Social Democratic party by dissident Labourites and its alliance with the Liberal party, this centrist coalition was given 40% of the intended votes in the public opinion polls prior to the Falkland Islands war, placing it ahead of the Conservatives and Labour. If these intentions had been actually carried out in general elections, the Social Democratic-Liberal alliance would have won a parliamentary majority and would have governed the country during at least one legislative term.

This rise of the third party was by no means fortuitous, because it came as the extension of the Liberals' rebirth and steady growth. Starting with 9% of the votes in 1945, they reached their lowest point, 2.5%, in 1951. After a subsequent slow growth they reached 11.5% in 1964, fell again to 7.4% in 1970, but rose to 19.3% in February 1974. In the elections 9 months later, due to the absence of a majority in the February election and a dissolution of the House of Commons, the Liberals lost only 1 point, maintaining their strength at 18.3%. In 1979, they suffered from the left-right polarization that benefited the Conservatives, who gained 8 points—4.5% from the Liberals and 2.5% from Labour. But the pitiless law of the plurality system has always crushed the third party's parliamentary representation. Even with 19.3% of the votes in February 1974, it only won 14 of the 635 seats, or 2.2%. The alliance with the Social Democrats could reverse the situation if the alliance should succeed in overtaking Labour. It won only 24.6% of the votes in 1983, with 27.6% going to Labour. Nevertheless, the difference has become so insignificant that such a performance is no longer impossible.

It would have been accomplished in the case of elections in 1981 in accordance with the public opinion polls: a party, unknown two years earlier, seizing power with a single stroke. That this situation would have occurred to the advantage of a center organization evidently contradicts one of the propositions concerning the consequences of the plurality system. Wasn't Great Britain described in *Political Parties* as a "country in which precisely the electoral system prevents the formation of a center party" (Duverger, 1951a, p. 508; 1954b, p. 488)? This contradiction permits me to clarify the nature of the theoretical models defined after the Second World War. They are based both on empirical observation and on the logic of how rational actors behave. In the last few years, the second basis has been upset by the aberrant behavior of the English Conservatives and Labourites.

That the plurality system accelerates the elimination of center parties, whereas PR preserves them, is neither disputable nor disputed: The June 9, 1983, election confirms this tendency in Great Britain in spite of all high hopes and premature calculations. To say that the Social Democratic-Liberal alliance would have won a majority if there had been general elections in 1981 is to confuse opinion polls with real elections—which no serious political scientist can accept. The theory of electoral systems appeared to be proven wrong by illusions engendered by opinion surveys, but it has ultimately been corroborated by the real mechanism of the legislative elections of 1983 and of earlier years as well. The plurality system has operated exactly in line with the relevant sociological law. It has systematically crushed the third party. It is impossible to imagine how the system could work differently in future elections.

With its 24.6% of the votes, the alliance of Social Democrats and Liberals surpassed by 1 point the level of the Liberal party in 1929; that is, in the period in which it was in the process of collapsing, precisely because of the effect of being thrown into last place. How could it now emerge from this position when it was not even able to convert its 1981 promise into an electoral success in 1983? The Falkland Islands war was not the only cause of this failure: The inability of the new coalition to define a plausible program made it lose an audience that had already grown tired of the political discourse of its neighbors. In the end, the rhetoric of the outsider turned out to be just as disappointing as that of the old insiders. How can a center organization become a large party when it proves incapable of defining a center program? Its success in 1981 came from those voters who were antagonized by the exaggerations of the Conservative and Labour parties. In order for the moderates in the two camps to come together to form a governing majority, they had to overcome the contradictions between the center-right, which merely tries to promote an open conservatism, and a center-left, which seeks to introduce realistic reforms.

The 1981 surveys revealed the many defections prompted by the rigidity of the two large parties that had forgotten the plurality system's fundamental rule: In order to win, the Conservatives and Labour must obtain the support of the floating voters who are prevented by the electoral system from voting for the center. Their votes are wasted if cast for the Liberals but decisive according to whether they lean to the right or the left. Most Frenchmen think of the English system in terms of "two blocs" that divide the country and that rigidly maintain its opposing interests. Nothing is farther from the truth. The two-party system destroys the center at the organizational level, but it presses toward the center at the level of policy and practice. Victory is generally determined by the voters in the middle, who lean to one side or the other depending on the political situation and on the behavior of the parties. Each party naturally tends to appeal to them while avoiding excessive promises. In doing so, the party hardly risks losing its extremists, who have no other possibility than to vote for it or to abstain. This English system can never be governed *by* the center, but it always tends to be governed *in* the center.

A party that forgets this rule risks disaster; it will soon be replaced by its rival. The Labour party experienced this in 1979 after a very unpopular strike, forcefully applied by the labor unions controlling the party organization. When the two big adversaries go too far in their moderation and end up resembling each other too much, the Liberals serve as an outlet for the dissatisfied voters and supply some new ideas. This dissatisfaction may sometimes also be expressed through different parties; for instance, the regional nationalists in February 1974 when neither Labour nor the Conservatives won an absolute majority—but everything returned to normal after the dissolution 9 months later.

A completely different situation arose in 1981 when the voters' discontent was not based on an excess of moderation of the large parties that had applied the rules of the system too well, but on the fact that both parties had forgotten these rules—a very rare event in the history of the United Kingdom. Faced by a Labour party that had become inflexible as a result of the excessive demands of the unions that increasingly controlled it, the Conservatives adopted an openly reactionary policy stimulated by Mrs. Thatcher. The frustrated moderates in both camps found themselves ready to support a third force. This was the mechanism that gave rise to the alliance between Social Democrats and Liberals and that carried it ahead of all of the parties in the 1981 polls. It was unable to stay in first place because it failed to present a program and a leader that appeared capable of governing the country in the contemporary crisis of the Western world.

No one can predict whether it will overcome this handicap in the next legislative elections which should normally take place in 1987 or 1988. The Labour party's disarray, the fact that it has sunk below its 1922 level of 29.5% of the votes, and the slight difference (3 points) that now separates it from the Alliance would justify some optimism for the latter if it were not in full disarray itself after its election defeat. In any case, neither its hypothetical score in 1981 nor its actual score in 1983 are really in conflict with the sociological law relating the two-party system to the plurality method of election.

The situation in 1981 was the result of an incredible error on the part of the two big parties. Since the Conservatives leaned too far to the right under Mrs. Thatcher and Labour too far to the left under Michael

Foot, the moderates in the two camps found themselves abandoned and ready to follow a party that would take them out of the electoral ghetto. But they were left in the ghetto once again when the weakness and contradictions of the leaders of the centrist Alliance proved that the Alliance was equally unable to satisfy those who were disposed to support its cause. A large number of them were drawn back to the Conservatives by the Churchillian image of the Iron Lady. Hence the pitiless iron law of the plurality system crushed the third party once again in the usual fashion.

Bipolar Multipartism

The transformation of the French political parties presents one of the most interesting problems of the last 30 years in the framework of the theory of electoral systems.[1] In the Third Republic (1975–1940), the two-ballot majority system coincided with a multiparty system tempered by electoral alliances that fell apart again in Parliament. They were coalitions of individual politicians instead of alliances between parties, although they evolved in the latter direction in the interwar era. Nevertheless, the right-wing Cartel, victorious in 1924 and 1932, and the Popular Front of 1936 had to make place for majorities of the center allied with the right in 1926, 1934, and 1938 without the voters being consulted at all! Between 1875 and 1914, the voters succeeded only twice in installing a majority based on the electoral outcome: in 1876 and 1914. For the rest everything depended on the game of the notables who were loosely organized in parties that had neither activists nor discipline.

In the Fourth Republic (1946–1958), PR preserved this multipartism, weakened the alliances even more, and oriented them toward the center. Formerly they behaved in a bipolar style with "republicans" and "reactionaries," "anticlericals" and "clericals," right and left opposing each other, albeit without firm and precise boundaries between them. After the postwar national union government, first led by General Charles de Gaulle, the Communists and Gaullists were excluded from the majority formed by the center parties—Socialists, Christian Democrats, and the traditional right. Within this majority, the pendulum swung to one side or the other according to the leanings of the Socialists. The voters were not even aware that their choices were disregarded by the parties, because these choices did not exist any longer. No legislative election yielded a clear majority because PR did not permit it. It only allowed modifications in the way the cards were dealt to the different parties, each of which then played the game as it saw fit. The system's unpopularity produced by these political practices explains its fragility, which was fully revealed when the weak government leaders yielded to a rebellion in Algiers that was more or less supported by certain army units.

The Fifth Republic reestablished the two-ballot majority system, which makes interesting comparisons with the pre-1939 period possible. On the whole, the results confirm the law of this electoral system which, as just quoted, "tends to produce multipartism tempered by alliances." However, the number of parties has declined considerably from 10 parliamentary groups in 1958 to 4 in 1978. This is an extraordinary development especially because it took place without any civil war or foreign intervention, in contrast with the change in Germany from 1933 to 1945. But it stays within the limits of the theory since it is still a variant of *multipartism*—a term that designates any system consisting of more than two parties, not counting the tiny parliamentary groupings that are unable to prevent one of the two big parties from gaining an absolute majority.

It remains to be explained why the same electoral system coincided with a dozen parties in the Third Republic but ended up with only four in the Fifth Republic. It should be pointed out first that the difference is magnified by the different rules and practices under the two regimes. Before 1940, the formation of parliamentary groups was completely free, and some of them consisted of only a few personalities and did not amount to genuine parties. Since 1958, a parliamentary group must number at least thirty members, which forces the small groups to combine. This is one of the reasons that led to the formation of the UDF (Union for French Democracy) in 1978. Another factor has to do with what one may call the nationalization of the parties. Before the Second World War, their central organizations were weak, except for the Socialists and Communists. The others had more or less strong local roots but only very loose organizations at the level of the entire country. This entailed a natural fractionalization of closely related political tendencies according to personal affinities and political strategies. The development of radio and television over the last 25 years has tended to make party propaganda more uniform over the whole national territory and to concentrate it around the leaders— transformed into the stars of the electoral spectacle. They can succeed only with the support of a large organization. A party's size has become an important element in its capacity to collect votes—hence the tendency toward larger parties.

Furthermore, the nationalization of the parties is closely linked with the direct popular election of the president, which has transformed the political regime. From 1962 on it has become the decisive moment in French political life, in which the citizens make their most important choice of who will govern them. In the preceding 4 years, de Gaulle had already made the office of head of state into the nation's real leader. In 1962 he proposed that the president be elected directly by the voters, and he announced that he would resign if this proposal, rejected by the deputies, would also be rejected by the people. The purpose of the referendum was not just to decide on the constitutional reform; it was also its first application. By their overwhelming "yes" vote, the citizens kept General de Gaulle in the Elysée Palace. And in the legislative elections a month later, they gave him the means to control the National Assembly: For the first time in its history France had a disciplined parliamentary majority.

This majority lasted 19 years under the successive rule of de Gaulle, Georges Pompidou, and Valerie Giscard d'Estaing. At first it consisted of a strong party created by de Gaulle (the Union for the New Republic, which later became known as UDR and RPR) in alliance with a small group of the traditional right. The centrists gradually drew closer to each other and formed a large Giscardist organization with a confederal structure under the name of UDF. Together these two parties represented half of the country. The other half was then forced to unite in the same way in order to form a counterbalance. The Socialists and Communists had already formed a coalition for the second ballot of the 1962 legislative elections, before they agreed on a common program in 1972, and supported the candidacy of François Mitterrand in the first round of the 1974 presidential election. Thus a "fourfold bipolarity" developed—four large parties allied in two blocs. Each party nominated a candidate for the presidency in the 1981 election, which was won by Mitterrand. A month later, the French voters gave him the majority necessary for governing the country, as they had done for de Gaulle in 1962.

The combination of the two-ballot majority system of legislative elections with the popular election of the president has thus yielded four large parties in two opposing coalitions. Forming a coalition for the second ballot was necessary in order to elect deputies: This lesson was learned quickly by the left, which saw that its initial division led to utter defeat. With the same percentage of votes (36%), it obtained more than 22% of the seats in 1962 but less than 9% in 1958. The amalgamation of small groups into large parties is required for the credibility of the presidential candidates and for the organization of their campaigns; thus the various elements of the traditional right, the Christian Democrats, and the moderate Radicals and other centrists formed the UDF. The discipline of the alliances is made necessary by the system of government that is based on a president who is also the head of a parliamentary majority obedient to him. His challenger must secure the same docility from the opposition in order to be regarded as a serious rival.

The French example suggests the formulation of a type of party system—bipolar multipartisan—which did not occur to me 30 years ago, when bipolarity still coincided more or less with the two-party system. The autonomy of the four parties that share the seats in the National Assembly in Paris is very strong. The ideology of the RPR is much closer to that of the UDF than the ideology of the Socialist party is to that of the Communists. But the leadership struggles on the right take the place of the doctrinal battles that split the left. The rivalry between Jacques Chirac and d'Estaing is just as implacable as that between Mitterrand and Georges Marchais. Each of the coalitions is also very strong in spite of the intensity of their internal battles. This type of alliance develops a discipline that is just as firm as that of the British parties. The bipolar system yields majorities that are as cohesive and stable as those produced by the two-party system.

In France, the bipolar system is clearly the combined product of the two-ballot electoral systems, used in the legislative and presidential elections. But another factor seems to play a role, too: the fact that one of the poles acquired sufficiently strong roots and discipline to give it the opportunity to take power and to keep it. The majority formed around General de Gaulle and maintained by Pompidou forced the left to unite as strongly as the right in order to be able to replace it. Once the two coalitions are in place, each has an incentive to preserve its unity in order to make its weight felt vis-à-vis the other. When the direct election of the president and the constraints of the second ballot in the legislative elections are combined with the rivalry of two poles of virtually equal strength, a bipolar system becomes highly probable.

Such a bipolar system may also appear in the absence of these factors—in a parliamentary system based on PR. The Swedish example is interesting in this respect: The Social Democratic party gained a dominant position in 1936 that kept it in power for 40 years with or without the support of the very small Communist party. Faced by this bloc, the three so-called bourgeois parties (Conservatives, Liberals, and Agrarians) necessarily had to form a coalition as a counterbalance. Their alliance won a victory in 1976, but it gradually broke up again; and the Socialists were thus able to get their absolute majority back. A bipolar system under PR is naturally fragile. Moreover, it may only manifest itself when a party succeeds in attracting almost half of the popular votes. The others are then forced to unite in order to reestablish an equilibrium. When two coalitions confront each other, PR gives each of their members too much freedom to solidify them into a bipolar system of the French type.

However, the propositions concerning bipolar multipartism are neither sociological laws nor even hypotheses: They are merely suggestions that are based on too few observations to justify firm conclusions.

Notes

1. Here I summarize a part of the analysis presented in my book *La République des Citoyens* (Duverger, 1982). It is essentially devoted to the Fifth Republic, but it also makes comparisons with the Third and Fourth republics; the latter is described in chapter 2, "La République des Deputés" (pp. 39–56).

CHAPTER 4

Intraparty Preference Voting

Richard S. Katz

When people think about the outcome of a parliamentary election, they most often refer to the result with respect to the parties. Did the Democrats gain or lose seats in the House? Does the Christian Democratic coalition have enough seats to remain in office? Although concern also has been expressed, especially in the United States, for equitable representation of geographic units or for the voting strength of racial, ethnic, or economic groups, concern with the political consequences of electoral laws similarly has been directed primarily at the consequences for the parliamentary strength of the parties. Indeed, the centrality of this concern underlies Rae's very definition of electoral laws as "those which govern the processes by which electoral preferences are articulated as votes and by which those votes are translated into distributions of governmental authority (typically parliamentary seats) *among the competing political parties*" (emphasis added; Rae, 1971, p. 14).

This definition is satisfactory only if one assumes that parties are totally cohesive and in total agreement internally, so that their candidates and prospective candidates may be regarded as interchangeable, and only if one looks at the election solely from the perspective of an outsider. Neither of these perspectives is fully adequate, however.

As the internal controversies that rage in the British Labour party, in the Japanese Liberal Democratic party, or in the Italian Christian Democracy attest, all candidates of a single party are not alike. Turnover within a party's parliamentary delegation can lead to major changes in policy or leadership even while the party's numerical strength remains unchanged. Which particular members of a party are elected may be as important in the short run – and even more important in the long run – as their total number in determining the real outcome of an election. Factionalized parties are particularly prone to shifts in leadership or policy as the legislative strength of the factions changes, but even where the current leaders are unlikely to be deposed, secular changes in the composition of a party's parliamentary delegation are likely to have an impact on his thinking and on the party's general policy, and certainly will be relevant when, in the normal course of events, a new leader must be chosen or new issues addressed.

Which individuals are elected is also of obvious relevance to the candidates themselves. While the "average" candidate may be better off when his party is gaining seats, and worse off when the party is losing seats, this is not necessarily the case for each individual candidate. Except where made unavoidable by institutional arrangements, election results are rarely unidirectional. While a party is gaining strength in one area, it may be losing strength in another; while some incumbents are being defeated, newcomers of the same party may be elected for the first time (Katz, 1980, pp. 70–73). A candidate might prefer the representatives of a particular area, interest, or faction to be proportionately stronger within the party, even at the expense of overall party strength. Certainly candidates may value their own electoral success over that of the party as a whole. Indeed, a candidate's personal interests may be advanced most when he is winning but when the rest of the party is doing badly.

Similarly, although partisanship may be an important determiner of vote, this does not mean that voters must be blind to differences within the parties, nor must the ties that bind voters to a particular party be ideological, organizational, or sociological rather than personal. Charismatic appeal, friendship, or clientelistic considerations may lead a voter to support a party because it is the party of a particular politician. Even in supporting the party *qua* party, some voters will recognize the divisions within it and prefer one current rather than another. Voters may think of themselves as supporting an individual or subgroup in addition to, or rather than, the party as a whole, and may care which candidates are elected as well as how well their party does in overall numerical terms.

Intraparty Preference Voting Systems

In general terms, then, all elections may have important intraparty consequences as well as consequences for the balance of power among parties. In some systems, however, while there may be intense competition for nomination, the intraparty contest is resolved within each party's organization before the formal election and so is not directly a concern of electoral law. In single-member constituencies, for example, each party, as a private organization, may put forth only one candidate without any institutionalized consultation with the electorate at large. When the voters are consulted, at the general election, they must accept the party's candidate if they wish to vote for that party at all. Proportional representation (PR) systems achieve the same effect where each party's share of the parliamentary mandates is assigned to its candidates in strict accordance with the previously prepared order of its list. In either case, voters may exert an indirect influence on party nominating decisions by demonstrating a differential willingness to support the party based on the identity of its candidates, but this can only establish a "band of tolerance" rather than direct control.

The majority of democratic electoral systems, however, allow those voting for a party to determine, or at least under some circumstances to influence, the identity of the particular candidates to be elected from among those the party has nominated. In the United States, the direct primary takes even the nominating decision away from the party and gives it to the voters at large, while in other systems the voters' choice is limited to those who have secured the party's preliminary approval. Nonetheless, in such systems the number of candidates nominated usually far exceeds the number the party can hope to elect; and since parties will often attempt to minimize the disruptiveness of internal conflicts by nominating adherents of all subgroups (Obler, 1973), this choice may give the voters far more substantial control over parliamentary personnel than is afforded by parties anticipating the reactions of their supporters in making nominations.

The tendency to think of election results in purely partisan terms has meant that very little research has been done on questions relating to intraparty preference voting. While some of the standard works on electoral laws briefly discuss the possibility of preference voting, they do so only in the sketchiest terms. Scholars working on the politics of individual countries have sometimes commented on the importance, or unimportance, of preference voting within their own systems, but these discussions are rarely of any length.[1] Moreover, the attention that has been devoted to the subject of intraparty preference voting has been focused primarily on the questions of how many preference votes are cast and by whom, rather than on the difference they do or do not make (e.g., Allum, 1964). One result is that for many systems it is difficult even to find out if intraparty preference voting exists. Given this gap in the literature, a discussion of the mechanics of preferential voting systems is a necessary preliminary to consideration of their effects.

List PR Systems

The most straightforward system of preferential voting combines an intraparty vote with a list system of PR. The intraparty vote may be separate from, and additional to, the party vote, or the party vote may be simply the total of individual votes cast for affiliated candidates. In the former case, the preference vote will be optional, while in the latter case the expression of an intraparty preference is an inescapable part of voting.

Finland provides an example of a system in which voters cannot avoid expressing an intraparty choice. Candidates for the Finnish parliament nominally stand as individuals who have formed electoral alliances. The voter chooses one candidate by writing his identifying number in the appropriate place on the ballot. The voter may alternatively write in the name of any qualified person rather than the identifying number of a nominated candidate. In the latter case, the vote is counted as support for the candidate but is not added to the total for his electoral alliance. In determining the outcome, candidates are first ordered within each alliance in accordance with their individual votes. The total vote for each alliance is next computed, and seats are apportioned among the alliances using the d'Hondt method of PR, with the first candidate on the reordered alliance list given a comparison number equal to the total vote for the alliance, the second candidate given a comparison number equal to one half that total, and so forth (Tornudd, 1968).

The separate and optional preference vote is illustrated by elections of the Italian Chamber of Deputies. Each voter first chooses a party from among those presenting lists in his constituency. After this choice, the voter may additionally indicate in a special section of the ballot the names or identifying numbers of up to three or four (depending on the total number of deputies to be returned from that constituency) of the candidates on that party's list for that constituency. Mandates are assigned to each party in proportion to its list vote, but the order in which particular candidates are declared elected from within each list is determined by their individual preference vote totals; the party's original list order is consulted only in the event of ties.

The Finnish and Italian systems give the voters the greatest control over the choice of individual representatives among the systems based on list PR; order of election is determined solely by the preference votes explicitly cast for particular candidates. While the party's list order may indicate an organizational preference to which some voters may defer, it has no formal effect on the outcome (Katz and Bardi, 1980; pp. 108–109). Other systems, however, allow the party greater control.

The Greek electoral system is quite similar to the Italian. Each voter optionally may support either one or two candidates in addition to voting for a list. Seats are assigned to each list in proportion to the list votes and to candidates from each list in the order of their personal votes. Significantly different from the Italian system, however, is a provision giving priority of election to party leaders and to former prime ministers.[2]

Luxembourg uses a system of proportional representation with panachage and cumulation. Each voter is given as many votes as there are seats to be filled from his constituency. These votes may be given to candidates from more than one list (panachage), and two votes may be given to the same individual (cumulation). Seats are divided among the party lists in proportion to the total number of votes received by the candidates included on them, and among the candidates of each list in order of the votes they received personally. The voter may simply cast a party ballot, in which case each candidate on the party's list is awarded one personal vote.

Switzerland uses the same system for those cantons entitled to send more than one representative to the National Council except that the original party lists themselves may involve cumulation. Thus the party can select some candidates who will receive two personal votes instead of one for every party ballot cast. If a party chose to do so, it could therefore give a tremendous advantage to some candidates. At least in recent elections, however, most Swiss parties either have avoided cumulation or else have listed all of their candidates twice.

Each Danish constituency is divided into two to ten nominating districts. The parties each nominate one individual for every district, although the same individual may be nominated in more than one district. A party then can organize its list in any of three ways. The first is simultaneous list ordering. Here the voter may cast his ballot either for the party or for one individual from its list. Individual votes are counted with party votes to determine how many seats each party will win in each constituency, and then party votes are shared among the candidates in proportion to their individual votes to determine the order in which candidates are elected. This system may be combined with either of the others by simultaneously nominating a group of candidates in only some of the nominating districts within a constituency. With simultaneous list ordering, only those preference votes explicitly cast for individual candidates contribute to deciding the order of election. Secondly, the party may have its nominee in each district listed first on the ballot in that district with all others following in alphabetical order. In this case, party votes are counted as personal votes for the party's nominee in the district in which they were cast. Candidates nominated in the districts in which their parties receive large numbers of party votes are thus advantaged. For the sake of consistency with previous work in English (Pedersen, 1966), this ballot format will be identified as the "usual," although it is now relatively uncommon. Finally, the party may submit an ordered list for the whole constituency, although the nominee for each nominating district still appears first on the ballot in that district and party votes are counted as personal votes for that candidate. Under this system, a quota is computed, and all candidates with at least that many personal votes are declared elected. If this does not produce enough winners, the surplus votes of those elected are transferred to other candidates according to a complex formula which modestly favors those placed at the top of the party list.

A Belgian voter may choose to support either a party or a particular individual from its list. Both party and individual votes are totaled to determine the number of seats won by each list. Any candidates with more personal votes than the electoral quota computed by dividing their lists' total vote by one more than the number of seats awarded to it in their constituencies are declared elected. Uncast personal votes are counted as votes for the first candidate on the party list until he reaches the quota, after which they go to the second candidate, and so forth. Thus unless a number of voters equal to half of the quota all cast personal votes for the same candidate, the party list order prevails. The Dutch system essentially works in the same way with two exceptions. First, the number of seats won by each party is not augmented in the denominator of the electoral quota. Second, list votes are marked on the ballot as preference votes for the first candidate on the list with the effect that if he receives more explicitly cast preference votes than are required, this surplus is also transferred to other candidates.

In Austria, Norway, and Sweden, voters may modify the order of the lists submitted by their parties. All three systems are similar to the

Belgian and Dutch models, however, in that simple party votes are counted as preference votes for the party list in the order submitted. Austrian candidates from each list are elected according to the number of "points" they receive. The candidate ranked first is awarded as many points as there are candidates on the list, the candidate ranked second one less, and so forth. In Norway, the candidate with the most first-place votes is elected first; the remaining candidate with the most first- and second-place votes combined is elected second; and so forth. Within each Swedish list, up to the number of seats awarded to it, if a candidate is placed first by at least half the list's supporters, he is elected; if two candidates get the first- and second-place votes of two thirds of the list's supporters, they are both elected; if three candidates receive the top three preferences of three fourths of the list's supporters, they are all elected, and so forth. If the first candidates at any point fail to reach the required vote, the unelected candidate with the most preference votes is elected. In all these cases, the party order prevails unless changed by an inordinately large number of voters. This was also the case with the PR system of the Fourth French Republic under which the party list order prevailed unless explicitly changed in a concerted fashion by half of the party's voters (Campbell, 1965).

Single-Transferable Vote

Ireland and Malta use the single-transferable vote (STV) system.[3] Candidates are elected from multimember constituencies. The voter ranks all (or as many as he desires) of the candidates in order of preference. A quota is computed equal to the smallest number of votes each of the number of candidates to be elected could receive while denying that number of votes to any other candidate. Any candidate receiving at least that number of first-preference votes is declared elected, and any surplus votes are transferred to other candidates in proportion to the second preferences expressed by those voters. If no candidate reaches the quota, the candidate with the fewest votes is eliminated, and those ballots are transferred to the next candidate indicated on them. This process is repeated until the required number of candidates have reached the quota, or all but that number have been eliminated (Chubb, 1970, Appendix E). Parties often nominate more candidates than they can elect, and to the extent that this occurs, the voters determine which particular candidates will be elected by determining the order in which they reach the quota.

Plurality Systems

Among the industrial democracies using single-member plurality election, only the United States allows an intraparty preference vote. This is accomplished through the use of the direct primary.[4] Because some questions of electoral law are subject to state jurisdiction, primaries differ in the degree to which they allow party voters to challenge the decisions of the regular organization, to make the original nomination decisions themselves, or turn the party nomination decision over to any voters who care to participate, even within the confines of elections to the House of Representatives.

The most restrictive systems are the challenge primaries, in which the initial nomination is made by a party committee or convention but can be challenged by candidates defeated at this level. In some cases, only candidates who received a minimum level of support in the initial stage can challenge the decision; for example, Connecticut requires 20% of the vote at the nominating convention for a primary challenge. While a primary ultimately can decide the party's nominee, it is a contest between an "official" candidate and a challenger. Somewhat less restrictive is the simple closed primary. In this case, a primary election is held whenever more than one candidate seeks a party's nomination for the same office. Any voter who is enrolled in the party may participate, and the primary makes the final nomination decision. The open primary is even less restrictive in that voters need not choose a party until they reach the polls. The least restrictive is the blanket primary. All the candidates for each office are listed together regardless of party; thus a voter can support a Democrat for one office and a Republican for another. The top vote-getter from each party is nominated and competes in the general election. Finally, Louisiana uses a system that is sometimes called a blanket primary but is really a two-stage majority system. Candidates of all parties appear together on the "primary" ballot. If a candidate receives an absolute majority of the votes, he is declared elected; otherwise a general election runoff is held between the top two candidates, irrespective of party.

Finally, the Japanese use a system of single-nontransferable voting. Candidates are returned from multimember constituencies, but each voter can choose only one candidate. If, for example, three members are to be elected from a particular constituency, then the three who have the most votes win regardless of their parties and regardless of the total numbers of votes received by other candidates of their or other parties. As with STV, to the extent that a party nominates more candidates than it elects, the voters make the final selection. This system also has the perverse effect, however, that a party can be seriously hurt if one of its candidates is *too* popular. For example, in a 5-seat constituency a party with 67% of the vote would win 3 seats in any fairly proportional system and reasonably could win as many as 4 seats under the Japanese system. (It is, in fact, possible that a party with 67% of the vote would win all 5 seats.) If, however, one of its candidates had 35% of the vote while four others shared the other 32% equally, those four might all lose to four candidates of other parties who shared the remaining 33% of the vote equally.

Impact

The consequences of intraparty preference voting are more difficult to assess than are the consequences of most other aspects of electoral law. For example, in comparing PR with plurality election, one is comparing two different ways of aggregating the same type of preferences, although the dubious assumption that the actual preferences expressed are themselves independent of the way in which they will be counted is required for the simplest numerical comparisons.[5] With intraparty preference voting, on the other hand, the question is whether allowing a particular kind of preference to be expressed at all makes a difference.

The most important characteristic distinguishing among preference voting systems concerns the preference votes not explicitly cast for any particular candidate. In some systems (Finland, Ireland, Japan, and Malta) this is not a problem; it is impossible to vote at all without expressing a relative preference among a party's candidates. In other systems (Italy, Luxembourg, and the United States) the casting of an intraparty preference vote is optional, but only those votes that are cast contribute to the determination of which candidates are elected. The remaining systems allow the parties to place some candidates in a privileged position, usually by counting the preference votes of those who make no explicit choice (i.e., cast a simple party ballot) as if they had cast preference votes for the party's list in the order submitted.

One indication of the possible impact of these differences is given by the information in Table 4.1. This table shows the minimum number of voters whose concerted support for a single candidate would be required in order to elect that individual rather than a candidate of the party's choice, defined here to be those candidates who would be elected if no explicit preference votes were cast, assuming all other voters cast simple party ballots. These numbers thus are analogous to

TABLE 4.1. Minimum Numbers of Voters Required to Alter Order of Election of Parliamentary Candidates

	Number of Voters
Austria	$\dfrac{v}{c+1}$
Belgium[a]	$\dfrac{v}{2(e+1)}$
Denmark	
Simultaneous list[b]	1
Party or usual list	$\dfrac{v_e - v_{e+1}}{2}$
Finland[b]	1
Greece[c]	1
Ireland[b,d]	0
Italy	1
Japan[e]	—
Luxembourg[b]	1
Malta[b,d]	0
Netherlands	$\dfrac{v}{2e}$
Norway	$\dfrac{v}{2}$
Sweden	$\dfrac{v}{e+1}$
Switzerland[f]	$\dfrac{v}{3}$
United States[b,g]	1

Note. v is the total number of votes cast for a party in a given constituency; e, the number of members it elects in that constituency; and c, the number of members it presents.

[a]Can be less if a number of voters greater than the electoral quota cast preference votes for a single highly ranked candidate.

[b]There is no official list order; only explicitly cast preference votes influence the outcome.

[c]Assuming the party wins more seats than it has candidates favored by the electoral law (i.e., party leaders and former prime ministers).

[d]Minimum number of first-preference votes required for ultimate election.

TABLE 4.1. (*Continued*)

^ePreference votes entirely determine the order of election, but because these are insepa-
rable from party votes, the minimum number of votes required for election in a constituency electing k representatives is 1 more than the number of votes received by the
$k + 1$th candidate, regardless of party.

^fAssuming cumulation for e candidates on the official list, otherwise, 1.

^gNumber of votes required to win a primary election.

Rae et al.'s (1971) "threshold of exclusion" for parties. In this table, v is
the total number of votes cast for a party in a given constituency, e is
the number of members it elects in that constitutency, and c is the
number of candidates it presents. (For Denmark, v_i is the number of
votes cast for the party in the ith nominating district ranked in order
of that party's voting strength in the constituency.)

By far the most restrictive preference voting system is that used in
Norway. Since in filling the jth seat the top j preference votes expressed by each voter are counted, the preference voting system operates as a multimember plurality election. Thus, unless half of a party's
voters move the same candidate up on their ballots, the party's list
order will prevail.

The preference voting system in Austria is effectively the Borda
count. As such, the outcome is not independent of irrelevant alternatives (Arrow, 1963, pp. 26–27, 94–95), and the minimum number of
voters required to elect a candidate who would otherwise have been
defeated depends both on the candidate's initial list position and on
the number of candidates ranked below him. To reverse the order of
two candidates requires that $v/(c + 1)$ voters put the lower-ranked candidate first on their ballots while deleting the higher-ranked candidate
altogether. Thus $v/(c + 1)$ voters can replace the eth candidate with the
$e + 1$th. Since Austrian lists may include more than 70 candidates, it is
theoretically possible for a very small percentage of the voters to effect
the outcome. On the other hand, if the voters wish to replace a candidate ranked more highly on the party list, or to favor a candidate other
than the one in the $e + 1$th position, many more votes would be required, with half the party's total vote as the limiting case.

The minimum numbers of votes required to elect candidates in Sweden, Belgium, and the Netherlands all depend on the actual number
of mandates secured by the parties in their constituencies. In Sweden,
if $v/(e + 1)$ voters fail to include one of their party's top e candidates
among the top e names on their ballots, they can prevent the automatic election of the party's top candidates. If they have additionally

ranked the same individual first on their ballots, that will be adequate to insure his election. In Belgium and the Netherlands, the requirement to prevent the automatic election of the top candidates on a party's list is that a number of voters equal at least to half the district electoral quota [$v/2(e + 1)$ in Belgium; $v/2e$ in the Netherlands] vote for some other candidate. In this case, after the party votes have been distributed to the highly ranked candidates, this individual will still have more preference votes than the last of the party's privileged candidates.

Along with the Austrian system, the Danish "usual" and "party-list" ballot forms allow the parties to give different candidates different degrees of advantage, rather than simply advantaging one group of candidates relative to another for any fixed value of e. With these ballot forms, were all voters to cast simple party votes, then the e candidates from the e nominating districts in which the party polled the most votes would be elected. Since it is relatively easy to predict on the basis of population and previous election results in which districts the party will do well, the party can, by nominating its preferred candidates in the districts in which it expects to do well, give them an advantage. The size of the smallest such advantage is then $v_e - v_{e+1}$, and the minimum number of voters required to upset this advantage would be half that difference, provided they were all in the nominating district of the eth candidate and all decided to vote for the $e + 1$th candidate instead.

If a Swiss party listed twice the names of exactly as many candidates as it could elect in each canton, those candidates would have an advantage almost as great as that enjoyed by candidates at the top of Norwegian party lists. To replace one of those candidates with another candidate from the party list would require the action of $v/3$ voters; if they all cumulated two votes for one candidate while all deleting the name of the same favored candidate from the party list, they could just replace that candidate with their own among those elected. Along with the possibility open to Danish parties of adopting a simultaneous list ordering, the Swiss system is the only one of those discussed here that allows the party the *option* of favoring some candidates. Parties in Austria, Belgium, the Netherlands, Norway, and Sweden must have ordered lists and so must favor some candidates; those in the remaining countries cannot, except informally and with the exception of the priority given Greek party leaders and former premiers, favor particular candidates. In fact, Swiss party lists rarely involve official cumulation.

In the remaining systems, all candidates of a party in a single constituency compete on an equal footing, at least so far as the formal counting of votes is concerned. In Greece and Italy, although parties submit ordered lists and although the party list order may be taken as a cue by its supporters so that a high-list position increases the likelihood of receiving personal preference votes, the orders have no bearing on the translation of votes into a list of winners. In Finland, Ireland, Japan, Luxembourg, Malta, and the United States, parties do not submit ordered lists at all. Indeed, while Finnish and Luxembourgeois candidates are tied to party lists, candidates in the other systems compete as individuals, even though their party affiliations may be listed on the ballot. Thus in those countries in which it is possible to cast a simple party ballot (Finland, Greece, Italy, and Luxembourg, as well as in Switzerland without official cumulation and Denmark with simultaneous list ordering), if everyone else did so, the personal preference vote of a single voter would be enough to determine the election of a candidate. Similarly, if only a single voter cast his ballot in an American primary, that individual would determine his party's nominee. If one considers only first-preference votes, it would be possible for an Irish or Maltese candidate to be elected on the basis of transfers from other candidates while having started with no personal votes at all. Only in Japan, among the systems in which candidates must compete on an equal footing, are more votes required, but these are not so much intraparty preference votes as they are interparty votes.

Another approach to the question of impact is to look at the relative importance of the preference vote as a source of interelection turnover of parliamentary personnel. From the point of view of an outsider, is intraparty voting significant in the process of renewal of a party's parliamentary delegation, so that trends in its ideological or social composition might ultimately be traced to the voters? From the point of view of a member of parliament, is intraparty competition an important factor in determining whether or not he will be reelected?

Data bearing on these questions are presented in Table 4.2, which shows for each country the outcome of one general election with regard to members of parliament chosen in the previous general election. In simple terms, each member of parliament must be reelected (column 1), defeated (columns 2–4), or not be considered a candidate (column 5) at the next election. Those who are defeated can lose in either of two ways. On one hand, their party can lose strength so that it no longer wins sufficient mandates to allow all the incumbent members standing to be reelected. If no nonincumbent on a party's list was elected in a given constituency, then all defeats of incumbents on the list were regarded as "partisan defeats" (column 2). On the other

TABLE 4.2. Sources of Interelection Turnover Among Parliamentary Parties

	Elections	Reelected (1)	Partisan Defeat (2)	Intrapartisan Defeat		Not Candidate (5)
				List Order (3)	Preference Vote (4)	
Belgium	1977–78	79.8	5.6	2.8	0	11.7
Denmark	1977–79					
Simultaneous list		64.6	3.1	0	6.9	25.4
Party/usual list		46.5	11.6	2.3	2.3	37.2
Finland	1970–72	60.0	6.0	0	14.0	20.0
Greece	1974–77	55.6	14.2	0	17.0	13.2
Ireland	1969–73	82.0	7.9	0	2.9	7.2
Italy	1972–76	55.3	6.0	0	7.8	30.7
Japan	1972–76	70.7	8.6	0	9.0	11.7
Luxembourg	1974–79	55.9	5.1	0	8.5	30.5
Malta	1976–81	67.7	0	0	20.0	12.3
Netherlands	1981–82	80.5	10.1	3.4	0	6.0
Norway	1977–81	79.2	3.1	0	0	17.6
Switzerland	1975–79	68.9	3.6	0	3.1	24.4
United States	1978–80	80.2	6.0	0	1.8	9.7

hand, if a new member is elected in a constituency, then the defeat of an incumbent cannot be regarded as purely a partisan matter; instead, intraparty processes must have played a significant role. If at least one nonincumbent was elected in a constituency, then all defeats of incumbents of the same party were regarded as "intrapartisan defeats." These, in turn, may be the result of list order (column 3), if the new candidates were given a more favorable list position than the incumbents who were defeated, or of the intraparty preference vote per se (column 4).

The first observation which flows from these data is that the principal source of turnover in the parliaments of these countries is the failure of incumbent members to stand for reelection. Among those who do stand, however, intraparty processes (list ordering and preference voting) are slightly more important as sources of turnover than is interparty competition; more incumbents lost to members of their own parties than lost to members of other parties. Moreover, the importance of the threshold for influencing the order of election is apparent. Among those countries with thresholds greater than one, only in Denmark with the "usual" list format were there any intrapartisan defeats attributable to preference voting; and in the one Danish case in which a member was defeated by a new candidate with a more advantageous district, the actual advantage conferred was only 132 votes. Indeed, the candidate with the most advantageous district came in third.

Among those systems in which the preference vote entirely determines the order of election, there is no apparent relationship between the interparty electoral system and the proportion of members of Parliament who suffer intrapartisan defeats. While the second-highest proportion of intrapartisan defeats is found in a list PR system,[6] so too is the third lowest. On the other hand, while the American system ranks lowest in intrapartisan defeats, the Japanese multimember plurality system ranks fourth, and the Maltese STV system ranks first.

There is, however, a substantial relationship between the proportion of intrapartisan defeats and constituency magnitude as indicated by the average number of mandates per constituency, as shown graphically in Figure 4.1. There is only one substantial outlier among the PR systems, the point corresponding to Greece. This discrepancy from the norm can be explained in two ways. First, the newly reestablished Greek democracy was in an obvious state of flux between 1974 and 1977, as evidenced by an unusually high rate of parliamentary replacement overall. Second, the average constituency magnitude reflected in the figure is deceptively low. Unlike most PR systems, in which there

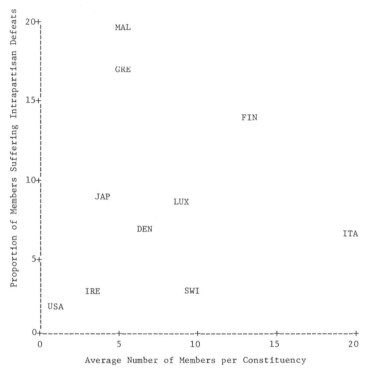

FIG. 4.1. Proportion of members suffering intrapartisan defeats and average number of members per constituency.

tends to be some clustering of constituencies around the average size, the Greek system combines the two very large constituencies of Athens and its suburbs, a few moderate-sized constituencies, and a large number of very small constituencies, including seven electing two members and three electing a single member. The bulk of the intrapartisan defeats occurred in the larger constituencies.

Although the data are not tabulated here, a similar result was found within each country. Intrapartisan defeats are most important within the parties electing more members in each constituency. The reason is twofold. When a party has fewer members in a constituency, each seat represents a larger proportion of its total representation. Thus, there is less of a chance that some nonincumbent will be elected, meaning that the defeat of any incumbent will be partisan rather than intrapartisan; in the limiting case, if a party loses its only seat in a constituency, the loss of its incumbent member, if he is a candidate, must be partisan. Furthermore, the more members elected from a constituency, the smaller the proportion of the party vote each one requires in order to win, and the smaller the gap between the last candidate elected and the strongest candidate defeated. If one consequence of large district PR is to make each party's share of the parliamentary seats more secure, another consequence when it is coupled with intraparty preference voting is to make individual members less secure.

Finally, it must be observed that what has been said here may seriously underestimate the importance of preference voting. The failure to stand for reelection has many causes. Death and retirement take their toll; some members of parliament may move on to more attractive offices; others may be denied renomination for a variety of reasons. Certainly if the American experience is in any way generalizable, however, some may also retire because they sense that if they were candidates for reelection they would lose, and it may be an intrapartisan rather than a partisan defeat that they fear. Moreover, unless a party loses its entire representation in a constituency, preference voting is not irrelevant to partisan losses. In these cases, the fact that some incumbents lose is the result of interparty processes, but the particular incumbents who are not reelected are still determined by preference voting.

Party Unity

While the effects of preference voting on turnover may be of great importance to the politicians whose careers are placed in jeopardy (or advanced), for the analyst this is only an intermediate step leading to the effect of preference voting on the character of political parties. Whether or not cohesion is the "natural" state of a political party, effective intraparty preference voting creates a powerful incentive to disunity.

Where preference voting is important, a candidate cannot rely solely on his party for election. Rather, he must at some point distinguish himself from other candidates of the same party in order to compete for preference votes. This requires the development of an independent base of support within, or in addition to, the regular party apparatus. This undermines party unity in two ways. First, because the candidate does not owe his election only to the party, he has less reason to be loyal to it once elected. Moreover, an independent campaign organization gives a politician the wherewithal credibly to buck party discipline. Second, in building an independent campaign base, a candidate will incur debts, make compromises, and develop loyalties different from those of other candidates of the same party.

The specific character of candidates' campaign bases, and subsequently of their parties, depends largely on the size of constituencies and the distribution of mobilizable resources. In single-member American constituencies, for example, candidates for the House of Representatives traditionally have built their own organizations from resources mobilized within their constituencies (Kingdon, 1968; Leuthold, 1968). There are few rewards or punishments that party leaders can offer, and one result has been extremely fragmented parties, perhaps best seen as no more than conglomerates of candidates' private organizations. A potential consequence of the rise of national political action committees as important sources of campaign support might be to increase factional development *within* each party.

With multimember constituencies, Irish (Sacks, 1970) and Japanese (Curtis, 1971) candidates establish personal bailiwicks. Each candidate concentrates his campaign in, and receives the majority of the preference votes from, a restricted area within the constituency. In Ireland, few other resources are necessary for a successful campaign, but in Japan, where substantial financial resources are also necessary, this combines with the centralized nature of the Japanese economy to form one of the essential bases of factionalism within the Liberal Democratic party (Thayer, 1969). The situation in Italy is quite similar to that in Japan, except that with much larger constituencies, division into clear bailiwicks is impossible. All of the significant non-Communist parties are factionalized, and the factions are clearly connected to groups able to mobilize campaign resources (Gilsdorf, 1970; Spreafico and Cazzola, 1970).

On the other side, one can conclude simply with a speculation. Although there is substantial evidence that preference voting is associated with intraparty disunity, it is not clear that abolishing an established system of preference voting would make parties more cohesive. Instead, it may be the case that, by allowing contentious factions to compete within the party, preference voting makes complete rupture less likely. As with most questions concerning preference voting, research is just beginning.

Notes

1. For example, Mackenzie (1958) and Butler et al. (1981) each devote only a few paragraphs to the subject of intraparty choice, while Rae (1971) ignores the question altogether. Birke (1961), however, considers the problem at greater length.
2. In late 1982, legislation was under consideration in Greece to abolish preference voting.

3. This system also is used to elect the Australian Senate. These elections, however, are not considered here.
4. American primaries differ from the "primaries" of some European parties in that they are public elections in which any qualified voter may participate without the approval of the party as an organization and without incurring any obligations, such as the payment of dues, to the party.
5. Simple analyses of the translation of votes to seats made under this assumption capture the element of the consequences of plurality election that Duverger calls the "mechanical factor" (Duverger, 1959; pp. 224–226). The "psychological factor," which leads voters to distort their preferences in response to the electoral system, is denied by this assumption.
6. These figures were all computed on a constituency by constituency basis. Because Maltese candidates may stand in two constituencies simultaneously, the figures reported here for Malta may overstate the actual level of intraparty turnover.

CHAPTER 5

Thinking about the Length and Renewability of Electoral Terms

William R. Keech

Arguments about the length and renewability of electoral terms are commonly rooted in beliefs about elections. Those who see elections as a positive good and as an effective guide for the behavior of public officials are likely to favor frequent elections and unlimited renewability of electoral terms. Those who see elections as necessary evils which interfere with the deliberations of statesmen tend to favor infrequent elections and limits on the possibility of reelection.

Contemporary political science cannot resolve these differences of belief and opinion. However, since Arrow's impossibility theorem (Arrow, 1951), the theoretical case that elections can assure desirable outcomes was dealt a blow from which it is unlikely ever to recover fully. Indeed, since then the argument that elections cause positive harm has become more common (see, for example, Brittan, 1975; Buchanan and Wagner, 1977; Nordhaus, 1975), though the case that they do so is far from resolved. This essay will present some evidence and arguments about term length and renewability growing largely out of literature on American politics, but relevant to a variety of settings, including parliamentary systems with variable term length.

There is relevant evidence that for better or worse elected officials' policy positions move closer to those of their constituents as election time approaches, which implies that shorter terms may be associated with more popular policies. (See Amacher and Boyes, 1978; Kuklinski, 1978; Jackson, 1974, chap. 5.) But the implications of these observations for the most desirable term length are also contingent on beliefs or assumptions about the quality of voters' judgments. If voters are wise, shorter terms may be desirable. If politicians are wiser than voters, longer terms may be preferable. What is needed is a theory which would relate the behavior of voters and elected officials to some conception of public well-being as mediated by term length. One of the richest sources of relevant ideas is still *The Federalist Papers.*

Madison argues in *Federalist* No. 52 that frequent elections are the only way to assure that governments have a common interest with the people and concludes that short terms are desirable for the House of Representatives. A modern development of this idea is offered by Amacher and Boyes (1978), who implicitly assume that voters make good choices and that public officials may not do so unless constrained by elections. They argue that the optimal term length is that which minimizes the sum of the decision costs (which rise with the frequency of elections) and external costs (which fall with the frequency of elections). In this view, elections are seen as a minimizer of undesirable policy which politicians might carry out if left unconstrained. The only reason not to have elections as often as possible is that decision costs would be prohibitive.

Just as the constitution it defended has different term lengths for different offices, *The Federalist* articulates other rationales for term lengths. For example, Hamilton defends a somewhat longer term for the president, because short terms lead to "feebleness and irresolution" and they do not provide resistance to the transient impulses prompted by those who flatter public prejudices and betray the public's interests (No. 71). Presumably the public is not invariably an infallible judge of its own interests.

Madison himself takes an approach to term length for the Senate which is quite different from his rationale for short terms in the House. In No. 63, he observes that some policies depend on "a succession of well-chosen and well-connected measures which have a gradual and perhaps unobserved operation," in contrast to policies which have immediately visible consequences. In such cases, longer terms may bring the period of accountability into line with the period in which policy-making has its consequences. Also, when effective policy-making demands sustained activity, longer terms may provide an opportunity for such activity.

The Federalist is thus a rich source of thinking on rationales for different term lengths, and it ably defends a Constitution which has three different term lengths for three elective institutions. The arguments are sketchy, however, and deserve elaboration in the sense that Amacher and Boyes elaborate the Madisonian rationale for short terms in the House. This essay summarizes some research which elaborates some features of the arguments for longer terms found in *The Federalist* essays on the president and the Senate.

A Model for Elaborating the Argument for Longer Terms

The central features of *The Federalist* argument for longer terms are that the public is not always a good judge of its interests (No. 71) and that some policies operate with delays and should not therefore be evaluated prematurely (No. 63). Nordhaus's model of "The Political Business Cycle" (Nordhaus, 1975) conceptualizes features of both of these issues in a form that lends itself to analysis of term length. Nordhaus's model distinguishes between a mathematical function that measures votes and a function that measures welfare, or public well-being. Both the vote and the welfare function depend on unemployment and inflation, which are seen as directly or indirectly under the control of an elected official. Thus in principle, a politician who maximizes votes may do so at the expense of welfare, and political goals may be at odds with maximum public well-being. This much is congruent with Hamilton's view that some politicians may flatter public prejudices at the expense of public interests.

Inflation and unemployment, the variables which determine votes and welfare, are related empirically in a separate dynamic model which has the effect that short-run vote maximizing can imply long-run welfare loss, and that a sustainable improvement in welfare may take a long time to achieve. Specifically, certain desirably low combinations of inflation and unemployment are achievable in the short run but not sustainable in the long run. Unemployment that is "too low" may have delayed inflationary consequences. Or alternatively, unemployment that is "too high" can make possible unsustainably low combinations of inflation and unemployment later on.

The essence of the model Nordhaus builds out of these features is that if voters support incumbents on the basis of the most recent experience of inflation and unemployment, and if these voters do not understand the implications of doing so, vote-maximizing politicians may manipulate the economy in ways that increase their votes at the expense of public well-being. These features are similar to Madison's rationale for longer terms for the Senate.

Nordhaus himself makes no inferences about term length, but this essay will report the results of analyses which use his model to do so. None of these analyses does full justice to the arguments presented in *Federalist* Nos. 63 and 71, but they do approximate those ideas, and, more importantly, they provide some intellectual leverage on optimal term length issues.

A First Cut: "It Depends"

Keech and Simon (1983) propose an abstract mathematical analysis of the original Nordhaus model, asking what term length brings the highest average welfare per year under the assumptions of the model. A main conclusion is that even for a world as simple as that conceptualized by Nordhaus, there is no generally valid answer to the question of the best term length. The optimal length depends on the parameters, or coefficients, of the equations in the mathematical model, such as that representing the length of the voters' memory.

For example, Keech and Simon (1983) show that the poorer the voters' memory, the shorter the optimal term length. The reason is that if voters' memories are poor enough and the term is long enough, a vote-maximizing politician might induce a recession early in a term, which voters would not remember at the next election. This early recession would facilitate an unsustainably low combination of inflation and unemployment for the end of the term. The forgetful voters would remember only the good times and give the incumbent more votes than he would receive if the whole term were weighted equally or if he had kept the economic variables at a sustainable, feasible combination. Shortening the term when voters' memories are bad has the effect of bringing more of the electoral period into the span of voters' memories, and therefore not permitting the incumbent to escape evaluation for hard times.

The Keech and Simon (1983) analysis is of limited practical application, but it is useful for making a general point. Even when rather bold assumptions are made about the motivations and capacities of elected officials in the context of one particular phase of policy-making, an unambiguous answer about term length is not forthcoming. Clearly there is no one best term length for all conditions. This much can be seen as a substantiation of the cumulative insights of *The Federalist*, which argued for three different term lengths. Furthermore, Keech and Simon also show that making the wrong choice may not be very costly. In particular, they found that when a complex parameter which is very sensitive to voters' memory is positive, there is little risk associated with a suboptimal term length, and term length makes very little difference for welfare. However, when it is negative, the wrong term length can lead to disastrous consequences for welfare if all of the assumptions of the model are maintained. In general we might say that it takes deeper belief in the model to conclude that term length is a critical issue than to conclude that it is of marginal importance.

A Second Cut: Implications of a More Realistic Model

Chappell and Keech (1983) elaborate and develop the analysis just discussed. They present a more complex model of the economy, which distinguishes between the policy instruments under the control of politicians and the policy outcomes which affect votes and welfare. This model of the economy is realistic enough that they can estimate empirical values of the parameters analogous to those which Keech and Simon considered unknown.

This article addresses the well-known proposal for a 6-year presidential term by comparing the welfare associated with two 6-year terms and that associated with three 4-year terms in a constant 12-year period. Analogously to the previous analysis, they evaluate a welfare function which measures the inflation and unemployment associated with vote maximizing in each term.

The analysis is based on a computer simulation of such activity under alternative assumptions about voter memories. The findings showed that under most circumstances 6-year terms were associated with more welfare (lower average values of inflation and unemployment) than 4-year terms. Even when voters' memories are good and when they evaluate the entire term with equal weights on all periods, term-by-term vote maximizing has welfare costs because it involves ignoring the inflationary costs for the period after the election, the next term. Six-year terms are better than 4 in this context because they imply fewer elections. Additional elections imply more incentives to achieve short-run gain with postponed costs.

Only when voters' memories are very poor (implying little recollection of the early part of the term) are 4-year terms preferable. The reason is the same as that reported in Keech and Simon, that shorter terms bring more of the electoral period into the range of voter memories.

A Third Cut: Variable Term Length

This discussion of the implications of the Nordhaus model is built on the assumption that electoral terms have fixed lengths, as in the American context. However, many parliamentary systems provide for term lengths that may vary in several ways.[1] For example, governments may choose to call an election before the maximum term has expired, as often happens in Britain. Alternatively, a minority government, or a government based on a fragile coalition of parties, may find that a censure vote brings an early election against the will of the government.

When a majority government can call an early election, it has in effect another control variable in addition to its control over the economy. If the economy reaches a premature electoral optimum before the maximum length of the term, the government can schedule the election during the optimal conditions rather than depending entirely on creating the conditions for the fixed election date.

When the time of election is out of the control of the government, as in the case of a minority government vulnerable to censure, the problem can be modeled as one of maximizing the expected vote, with the election date being considered a random variable with a known distribution. It can be shown that under such circumstances a politically induced business cycle will still exist, but with reduced amplitude and, of course, irregular phase. (See Ginsburgh and Michel, 1983; Lächler, 1982.)

Lächler (1982) models a case in which the opposition's potential control is imposed by an inequality constraint such that the government cannot allow conditions to fall below a certain level defined in terms of the voting function. If it does, the opposition censures the government, calling an election which the government will lose. Lächler shows that the government may be able to create a stable cycle in which it is repeatedly reelected or that it may lead into an inflationary spiral in which neither the government nor the opposition can be reelected, and the political structure may break down (Lächler, 1982, pp. 113–117).

From Modeling Back to the Real World

I have described modeling exercises that attempt to capture some of the features of *The Federalist Papers'* argument relating shortsightedness by voters and delayed consequences of policies to desirable term length. In order to relate these issues systematically and precisely, we have had to make numerous assumptions which have caricatured reality. The conclusions about optimal term length may be valid only to the extent that the assumptions are valid. But we can learn from the results of the modeling exercise even if we do not accept all the assumptions. There is intellectual leverage in the enterprise which does not depend on the validity of the assumptions.

For example, one of the most questionable assumptions we have made is that politicians repeatedly maximize votes in the present term (Wittman, 1983). Chappell and Keech show that a politician who maximizes *welfare* over three 4-year terms may receive more votes in the final 4-year term than a politician who maximizes votes in each of the same three terms. The reason is that vote maximizing in each term normally implies higher inflation in the next term, which in turn implies lower vote potential for vote maximizing in that next term. This is analogous to the situation modeled by Lächler in which an inflationary vote maximizing spiral may lead to system breakdown.

Thus the term-by-term vote maximizing behavior we have assumed for purposes of analysis may be self-defeating over several elections. If politicians understand this and take a long view, they may not maximize votes in each term at the expense of welfare unless they feel insecure about their chances of reelection.

In such a context, a public-spirited opposition to a minority parliamentary government might induce the government to keep its policies at a sustainable optimum by calling a new election whenever the government tried to maximize future votes with a politically induced business cycle. Furthermore, if the incentive for politicians to maximize welfare rather than votes derives from the hope and prospect of repeated reelection, nonrenewable terms should be counterproductive whatever their length. By implication, the 6-year term proposal should be divorced from the nonrenewability feature with which it is usually associated. This line of reasoning also implies that the Twenty-second Amendment to the U.S. Constitution, which limited presidents to a single reelection, was a mistake.

Acknowledgment. I would like to acknowledge the assistance of National Science Foundation grant no. SES 8006562.

Notes

1. The most imaginative argument about optimal term length may be that of Martin Krakowski (1975), who suggests that term length should vary with the quality of governmental economic performance. The worse things get, the closer the next election is scheduled. Similarly, improved performance buys more time in office.

PART II

Evaluating the Impact of Electoral Laws: Proportional and Semiproportional Systems Case Studies

Proportionality by Non-PR Methods: Ethnic Representation in Belgium, Cyprus, Lebanon, New Zealand, West Germany, and Zimbabwe

Arend Lijphart

T he principal aim of proportional representation (PR) is exactly what its name implies: the allocation of seats in representative bodies according to the number of votes received by political parties or by individual candidates. This is of special importance to minority parties or candidates who tend to be severely underrepresented or excluded by non-PR systems. However, electoral systems may contain special provisions for the representation of minorities, particularly ethnic minorities, *without* using, or *in addition to,* the normal PR methods. This chapter will focus on the attempts to achieve ethnic proportionality by non-PR methods. It will classify these electoral mechanisms, analyze their operation in six countries, and discuss their advantages and disadvantages. The minorities benefiting from these unusual provisions for ethnic representation are the Francophones in Belgium, the Turks in Cyprus, the Christians in Lebanon, the Maoris in New Zealand, the Danish speakers in the West German *Land* of Schleswig-Holstein, and the whites in Zimbabwe.

The Conventional Classification of Electoral Systems

The two most important dimensions of electoral systems are the electoral formula and the average district magnitude (Rae, 1971, pp. 19–39). Electoral formulas are usually classified into three broad categories: plurality and majority formulas, semiproportional formulas (such as the cumulative vote in Illinois from 1870 to 1980 and the single-nontransferable vote in Japan), and PR formulas. The average district magnitude is the average number of representatives elected per district. These two dimensions are related to each other. Plurality and majority formulas may be applied in both single-member districts and multimember districts, but for the election of national legislatures single-member districts are the rule. Semiproportional and PR formulas require multimember districts.

There are two types of PR formulas: list PR and the single-transferable vote. List PR formulas can be further classified according to the method used for the allocation of seats: d'Hondt, pure and modified Sainte-Laguë, largest remainders, and Imperiali (see chap. 10 in this volume). The special provisions for ethnic representation in the six countries discussed in this chapter do not fit any of these conventional PR categories.

Table 6.1 presents the basic characteristics of the electoral systems in our six countries in terms of the two major dimensions. Plurality and majority formulas are, or were, used in three countries: Cyprus, Lebanon, and New Zealand. Cyprus used the plurality formula for its first election as an independent republic in 1960, which was also the only national election held under normal circumstances. Lebanon used a French-style two-ballot system for the elections of 1943, 1947, and 1951; but the second ballot was abandoned, and the simple-plurality formula was adopted for all subsequent elections. New Zealand also briefly experimented with a two-ballot system in the elections of 1908 and 1911, but it has used plurality since then.

Belgium and West Germany fit the category of PR formulas, and both use the d'Hondt method for the allocation of seats. The Belgian PR system that will be discussed here is not the system used for the election of the national legislature but is the system adopted for the election of the 24 Belgian representatives in the European Parliament in 1979. The 1980 election in Zimbabwe was mainly a PR election: four fifths of the legislators were chosen by list PR, but one fifth were elected by plurality.

The fourth column of Table 6.1 gives the average district magnitudes in the different electoral systems for selected years. The average dis-

TABLE 6.1. Electoral Formulas and District Magnitudes of Six Electoral Systems

	Size of Legislature	Number of Districts	Number of Single-Member Districts	Average District Magnitude
Plurality				
Cyprus, 1960	50	12	1	4.2
Lebanon, 1953	44	33	22	1.3
1957	66	27	10	2.4
1960	99	26	1	3.8
New Zealand, 1946	80	80	80	1.0
1972	87	87	87	1.0
Two-Ballot System				
Lebanon, 1947	55	5	0	11.0
1951	77	9	0	8.6
Mixed PR-Plurality				
Zimbabwe, 1980	100	28	20	3.6
PR districts	80	8	0	10.0
Plurality districts	20	20	20	1.0
Proportional Representation				
Belgium, 1979[a]	24	2	0	12.0
West Germany, 1949	402	11	0	36.5
1980	497	1	0	497.0

[a]The Belgian system refers to the election of the 24 Belgian representatives to the European Parliament.

Source. Based on data in Craig and Mackie (1980, pp. 15–23); Crow (1962, p. 503); Gregory (1981, pp. 63–66); Mackie and Rose (1974, pp. 142–143); McRobie (1980, pp. 65–74); and Nohlen (1978, pp. 153–155).

trict magnitude is calculated by dividing the total membership of the legislature (in the Belgian case, the size of the delegation in the European Parliament) by the number of electoral districts; these two variables are also shown in the table. In addition, the third column presents the number of single-member districts used.[1]

When we examine the relationship between electoral formulas and district magnitudes in Table 6.1, one unusual feature should be noted: Two of the plurality and majority systems deviate from the general rule that these formulas are usually combined with single-member districts. The 1960 plurality election in Cyprus was conducted in districts with an average magnitude of 4.2; all except 1 of the 12 districts were multimember districts. Lebanon has experimented with a wide variety of districting arrangements. Its average district magnitude has ranged from a high of 11.0 in 1943 and 1947, to a low of 1.3 in 1953, when there were 22 single-member and 22 two-member districts. In 1957, 10 single-member districts remained, but from 1960 on almost all districts, 25 out of 26, have been multimember districts. The other countries follow the general rule: The New Zealand and Zimbabwe plurality elections take place in single-member districts, and the PR elections in Zimbabwe, Belgium, and Germany are conducted in multimember districts.

So far, therefore, we have been able to describe our six cases in terms of the conventional classification of electoral systems. What makes our cases unusual is the special provisions in their electoral laws for ethnic minority representation. Four methods of special ethnic representation can be distinguished: rigid nongeographic ethnic districts, optional ethnic districts, predetermined ethnically mixed slates, and special exemptions for ethnic minorities.

Nongeographic Districts

The simplest method of guaranteeing the representation of ethnic minorities is the institution of districts on the basis of ethnic criteria instead of, or in addition to, the more familiar geographic criteria. This requires the registration of voters on separate ethnic rolls. Because the term *district* usually has a geographic meaning, it is important to remember that *electoral* districts are not necessarily or exclusively geographic. Rae (1971, p. 19) describes electoral districts as "the units within which voting returns are translated into distributions of parliamentary seats. These districts are usually defined territorially, but may also be defined by population groups." We find the latter type of districts in Cyprus, New Zealand, and Zimbabwe.

In these three examples, the term *nongeographic* districts is an exaggeration because their districts are defined both in territorial and in ethnic terms. For instance, the 4 Maori single-member districts of New Zealand consist of the Maori voters in 4 different areas of the country: 3 districts are in the North Island, and the fourth includes part of the North Island, the entire South Island, and Stewart Island. All of the remaining non-Maori districts are also defined territorially but are much smaller in size (McRobie, 1980, pp. 67, 73). The mainly multimember districts of Cyprus were separate Greek and Turkish electorates in 6 geographic areas, resulting in a total of 12 electoral districts (see Table 6.2). In Zimbabwe, separate electoral registers were set up for whites (including Asians and Coloreds) and blacks. In the 1980

TABLE 6.2. District Magnitudes of Twelve Ethnic-Geographic Districts in Cyprus, 1960

Geographic Area	Greek Ethnic Districts	Turkish Ethnic Districts	Total
Nicosia	12	5	17
Famagusta	7	3	10
Limassol	7	2	9
Paphos	4	2	6
Larnaca	3	2	5
Kyrenia	2	1	3
Total	35	15	50

Source. Adapted from Nuscheler (1969, p. 1424).

election, blacks voted in 8 multimember districts by PR for 80 representatives, and whites voted in 20 single-member districts by plurality (Gregory, 1981).

Although ethnic districts based on separate voter registers constitute a simple and straightforward device for ethnic minority representation, it has two serious drawbacks. (1) Which ethnic groups will be officially recognized as deserving guaranteed representation? (2) How can all of the individual voters be assigned to these predetermined groups? Both problems arise from the fact that ethnically divided societies are usually not divided by completely clear-cut cleavages; some groups and individuals are likely not to fit any predetermined pattern.

The first problem may be illustrated by the case of Cyprus. During the negotiations about the constitution and the electoral law, the question of how to define membership in the Greek majority community and in the Turkish minority community and the question of how to deal with the other, much smaller, minorities such as the Armenians and Maronites were discussed with "extraordinary intensity," as Xydis (1973, pp. 490–492) reports. Xydis speculates that the Turkish Cypriots may have been "anxious to prevent any other minority in Cyprus from acquiring the status similar to that of the Turkish community, with all its political implications."

The second problem is that, once the ethnic groups have been determined, it may be difficult to assign individual voters to the ethnic districts. In addition, the very principle of officially registering individuals according to ethnicity may be controversial or even completely unacceptable to many citizens.

Optional Ethnic Districts

A solution to the second problem was found in New Zealand in 1975. The formerly rigid Maori electoral districts were made optional. "Maoris who wished to retain separate parliamentary representation could choose to register as electors on a Maori roll, while those who believed that this was no longer necessary could choose the general electoral roll" (McRobie, 1980, p. 74; 1978, pp. 274–275).

A similar solution was adopted for the election of the 24 Belgian representatives to the European Parliament in 1979. Two districts were established on the basis of both ethnic and geographic criteria: a Flemish district, comprising Flanders and the Flemings living in Brussels, with 13 representatives, and a French-speaking district, consisting of Wallonia and the Francophones in Brussels, with 11 representatives. In Flanders and Wallonia, the voters could vote for only Flemish and French-speaking candidates, respectively; but residents of Brussels received a ballot with both sets of candidates printed on it side by side, and they could use either the Flemings' or the French-speakers' part of the ballot without having to register on an ethnic basis (Neels, 1979, p. 246). Since ethnicity and geography largely coincide in Flanders and Wallonia, and since ethnic affiliation in Brussels was an individual, voluntary, and secret choice, no ethnic registration was required anywhere in the country.

It should be pointed out, of course, that neither the post-1975 New Zealand system nor the 1979 Belgian method solves the first problem of which ethnic groups should be recognized. In the Belgian case, the decision to establish only two ethnic districts and to add the small German-speaking minority in Eastern Belgium to the French-speaking district was a highly controversial one (Hearl, 1980, pp. 39–40).

Ethnically Proportional Slates

A different solution to the second problem has been found in Lebanon. It is usually referred to as the "list system"—not to be confused with the normal list PR formula—or the "single-college" system. One part of the Lebanese solution is to establish geographic districts with largely homogeneous populations. As Table 6.3 shows, the 1960 electoral law set up 10 districts of this kind electing about one fourth of the members of the Chamber of Deputies. In each of these districts, only members of the district's dominant sect can be candidates. For instance, in the mainly Greek Orthodox two-member district of Koura, only Greek Orthodox candidates are allowed to compete. The other 4 homogeneous Christian districts are reserved for Maronites. Similarly,

TABLE 6.3. Religiously Homogeneous and Heterogeneous Electoral Districts in Lebanon, 1960–1972

	Number of Districts	Number of Seats	Average Magnitude
Homogeneous Districts			
Christian	5	13	2.6
Moslem	5	11	2.2
Heterogeneous Districts			
Christian	3	16	5.3
Christian-Moslem	13	59	4.5
Total	26	99	3.8

Source. Adapted from Baaklini (1976, p. 146), and Smock and Smock (1975, p. 119).

there are 5 Moslem districts: 3 elect only Shia representatives, and 2 elect only members of the Sunni sect (Baaklini, 1976, pp. 146–147).

This method is comparable to the Belgian system for European Parliament elections as far as the areas of Flanders and Wallonia are concerned. Both systems make use of the fact that the heterogeneous countries do have some homogeneous areas; thus geographic districts are simultaneously ethnic districts. These cases may also be compared to the Canadian plurality single-member district system: Because the French-speaking minority tends to be geographically concentrated, most of the electoral districts are ethnically homogeneous, and French-speakers are represented in the House of Commons in rough proportionality to their share of the Canadian population.

The more important part of the Lebanese single-college system concerns the election of representatives in heterogeneous districts. Their average magnitude of 4.7 representatives per district is about twice that of the homogeneous districts. In a few of the heterogeneous districts, only members of different Christian sects can be elected, but in most of them there are both Christian and Moslem candidates (see Table 6.3). For instance, in the five-member Baabda district, three seats are reserved for Maronites, one for a Druze, and one for a Shia Moslem. The ballots normally contain two or more proportionally constituted "lists"—slates or tickets—as well as individual candidates. In the Baabda district, lists consist of three Maronite candidates, one Druze candidate, and one Shia candidate. Most voters tend to vote for one of these lists, but they may also select five candidates from different lists or from the independents as long as they do so according to the predetermined 3:1:1 sectarian ratio for the district (Baaklini, 1976, p. 147).

The sectarian composition of the entire Chamber of Deputies is therefore established in advance. Suleiman characterizes the Lebanese electoral system as *"preset* proportional representation . . . on a communal or religious basis" (Suleiman, 1967, p. 45, emphasis added). The total membership of the chamber has fluctuated between 44 and 99 (see Table 6.1), and the number of representatives from each sect has also gone up and down, but the overall ratio of 6 Christians to 5 Moslems—corresponding with the respective population shares in the 1932 census—has been maintained in every election since 1943 (Zuwiyya, 1972, pp. 5–9).

The advantage of the single-college system is that it does not require separate voter rolls. The only prerequisite is a determination of the sectarian composition of each district, based on either census data or estimates. Another advantage that is frequently cited is that of "minimizing interconfessional electoral competition and conflict, as well as enhancing the electoral chances of moderate candidates and working to the disadvantage of confessional chauvinists" (Smock and Smock, 1975, p. 120; see also Hudson, 1968, pp. 213–215). A theoretical weakness is that it violates the basic principle of representation: Being the representative of a certain group means not just belonging to that group but being chosen by the group. This also entails a serious practical drawback. As Rondot has pointed out, especially in the larger heterogeneous districts: "each elected person is above all the representative of members of communities [sects] other than his own. . . . To be elected as a deputy, a man must be a compromise candidate. The typical champions of each community run the risk . . . of being passed over in favor of tamer individuals" (Rondot, 1966, pp. 132–133). As a result, the deputies are not the true spokesmen for the sects, and the chamber has not been a very effective representative body.

Conclusions: Special Ethnic Representation Versus Normal PR

How do the special provisions for ethnic representation, rigid or optional ethnic districts and the single-college system, compare with the conventional forms of PR? If one wants proportional representation of ethnic groups, why not use normal PR? Normal PR requires neither ethnic registration nor the potentially invidious determination of which groups are entitled to special representation and which are not. A very high degree of proportionality, and hence the representation of even very small ethnic minorities, can be accomplished by PR if it is applied either nationwide (as in Israel and the Netherlands) or in smaller districts but with supplementary seats distributed at the national level in order to maximize proportionality (as in Denmark and Sweden), *and* if there is no high threshold aimed at barring small parties.

As far as threshold barriers are concerned, the West German electoral law, which sets a high threshold of 5% of the national vote, offers another example of a special provision for ethnic representation: The threshold "does not apply to parties representing national minorities" (Urwin, 1974, p. 137). The South Schleswig Voters League, representing the small Danish-speaking minority, took advantage of this exemption and won one seat in the 1949 Bundestag election. In Schleswig-Holstein, a similar exemption has enabled the party to be represented in the *Land* legislature since 1962 (Römer, 1980, p. 93). It should be noted that this special rule for ethnic representation is not so much a deviation from normal PR as it is an extension of the PR principle.

There are three valid reasons why non-PR methods for ethnic representation may be preferred to normal PR. First, if special provisions for ethnic representation are combined with the plurality formula, they may not affect the plurality formula's tendency to encourage a two-party system. The plurality formula does not guarantee a two-party system—as the Canadian and Nigerian multiparty systems attest—but PR is very likely to undermine an existing two-party system. In the case of New Zealand, for instance, the establishment of PR would probably result in a multiparty system and a break in the long-standing pattern of one-party majority cabinets.

The New Zealand electoral law also exemplifies the second advantage of special ethnic representation. Its single-member districts encourage a clear and close link between representative and represented. This advantage cannot be cited, however, for the Cypriot and Lebanese systems, both of which use mainly multimember districts, nor for Belgium and Zimbabwe, which are exclusively or mainly conventional multimember PR systems. Moreover, the German electoral law shows that single-member districts can be effectively combined with overall PR.

Third, it may be argued that the special provisions for ethnic representation tend to be more favorable to ethnic minorities than PR: They provide *overrepresentation* to minorities instead of merely proportional representation. Table 6.4 shows that this is indeed the usual pattern. The overrepresentation is particularly and deliberately strong in the cases of Cyprus and Zimbabwe. In Lebanon, the 6:5 ratio between Christians and Moslems was originally a proportional one. By the 1970s, however, the numerical balance had shifted in the Moslems'

TABLE 6.4. Ethnic Minority Over- or Underrepresentation in Six Electoral Systems

	Minority	Percent of Population	Percent of Seats	Percent Over-/ Under- Representation
Belgium, 1979	Francophones	38.6	45.8	+ 7.2
Cyprus, 1960	Turks	19.1	30.0	+ 10.9
Lebanon, 1972	Christians	45.5	54.5	+ 9.0
New Zealand, 1946	Maoris	5.8	5.0	− 0.8
1972	Maoris	7.9	4.6	− 3.3
West Germany, 1949	Danish speakers	0.3	0.2	− 0.1
Zimbabwe, 1980	Whites	4.2	20.0	+ 15.8

Source. The population percentages are based on the numbers of voters in the 1979 Belgian election (Craig and Mackie, 1980, p. 21); in the 1949 German election (Mackie and Rose, 1974, p. 162); on the 1960 census in Cyprus (Kyriakides, 1968, p. 1); on the 1945 and 1971 censuses in New Zealand (New Zealand Department of Statistics, 1981, p. 84); on official estimates for Zimbabwe in 1978 (Simson, 1979, p. 8); and on the author's estimates for Lebanon.

favor. Koury speaks of the "Christian minority" and the "Moslem majority" (Koury, 1976, p. 58). He also writes that, in the Moslems' self-image, they are a disadvantaged majority of as much as 60% of the population. This is almost certainly an exaggeration, and Table 6.4 merely assumes that the Moslems had a 6–5 majority over the Christians in the early 1970s instead of the other way around.

The only exceptions to the pattern of overrepresentation are Germany and New Zealand. In the 1949 Bundestag election, the South Schleswig Voters League received 0.25% of the seats with 0.32% of the vote, a nearly proportional result. For many years, the four Maori seats in New Zealand did not deviate much from proportionality. Table 6.4 shows that the Maoris were only slightly underrepresented in 1946, and Lipson could write that at that time they were "equitably represented on a numerical basis" (Lipson, 1948, p. 193). By the time of the 1972 election, when the Maori districts were still rigid ethnic districts, the Maoris were clearly underrepresented. Their share of the population had increased sharply while their seat share had declined: There were still 4 Maori seats, but the number of non-Maori seats went up from 76 to 83.

It should be pointed out, however, that minority overrepresentation is not incompatible with normal PR. This is exemplified by the Belgian system, which is mainly a conventional PR system. The German model of granting advantages to specially designated ethnic minority parties can also be adapted for the purposes of overrepresenting minorities; for instance, all votes cast for such minority parties could be given a double or any other specified weight.

In summary, there appears to be only one strong justification for special provisions for ethnic representation that are added to non-PR systems: the prevention of the weakening or destruction of an existing two-party system, which requires a plurality system instead of PR. In that case, single-member districts should be used, both because they give the advantage of close voter-representative contact and because plurality systems become increasingly disproportional as district magnitude increases (Blondel, 1969, pp. 191–193). If there is no two-party system to be supported, the plurality method is not necessary; in addition, if the special provisions entail multimember districts, normal PR is the more logical and flexible method for ensuring the right of minorities to be fairly represented.

Notes

1. The district magnitudes can be determined without difficulty in all cases, with the possible exception of Germany. The German electoral system is often described as a mixture of PR and plurality single-member districts. Counting all of the single-member districts as real districts, Rae (1971, p. 42) arrives at very low magnitudes for Germany: 1.6 in 1949 and 2.0 from 1957 on. However, the allocation of seats is decided almost entirely on the basis of PR in large multimember districts – the *Länder* in 1949 and 1953 and the entire country from the 1957 election on – and the very high average district magnitudes given in Table 6.1 are therefore the correct ones (Roberts, 1975, p. 208; Vogel et al., 1971, pp. 196–198).

CHAPTER 7

Australian Experience with Majority-Preferential and Quota-Preferential Systems

Jack F. H. Wright

Since the beginnings of self-government in Australia about 150 years ago, there has been a notable readiness to innovate in electoral procedures. The written secret ballot was used in public elections for the first time in the world in the state of Victoria in 1856, and developments such as the widening of the franchise to all adult males and then to all adults occurred in Australia earlier than in most countries. At present, the provisions for the maintenance of electoral rolls and for the recording and counting of votes are probably the best in the world. There has been considerable use of methods of election that have had very little use elsewhere.[1]

Party Structure

For many years, there have been three main parties in Australian federal politics which have retained their essential characteristics in spite of some name changes. The Liberal party resembles the British Conservative party rather than being in the traditional liberal mold. It presents itself as the political embodiment of the private enterprise philosophy. It is in virtually permanent coalition with the National party, formerly known as the National Country party, and before that, as the Country party. The Labour party, which evolved at about the same time as the Labour party in the United Kingdom, has traditionally been strongly associated with the trade union movement. Although its support is now more widely based, trade unions continue to provide funds and support.

Besides the National party, there have been at various times several other smaller parties, some of which have had considerable effects on Australian politics. The Democratic Labour party (DLP), which broke from the Australian Labour party in the mid-1950s, attracted considerable support, especially in Victoria and Queensland. Since 1977, a party known as the Australian Democrats has become an important force. The Democrats direct their appeal mainly to people concerned with consensus rather than with pursuing the policies of either of the major parties.

The Introduction of Preferential Systems

Since 1963, voting in all parliamentary elections has been preferential; that is, making use of a ballot on which voters order their preferences. The first legislation providing for preferential voting was in Queensland in 1892, and it applied in all states by 1936. In 1919, preferential voting was introduced for both houses of the federal Parliament.[2] In Queensland, plurality voting was reintroduced for state elections in 1944 but was again replaced by a majority-preferential system before the 1963 election.[3]

There has been limited use of multimember-district majority-preferential systems. The largest application was in elections of the federal Senate from 1919 to 1946. With six senators from each state, the system was designed to elect three senators from each state at each half-Senate election, senators having overlapping six-year terms. A similar system has been used in local-government elections in many districts in New South Wales.

A significantly different kind of preferential system was introduced in the state of Tasmania in 1896, when the state was divided into 29 electoral districts, 27 of them returning one member each, the other 2 being multimember districts based on the two main cities of the state. In these districts, a quota-preferential system of proportional representation, known locally as the Hare-Clark system, was used. The standard version of this system is commonly known as the single-transferable vote, or STV. In 1900, a system of 35 single-member districts was introduced; but in 1907, a bill providing for an improved version of the Hare-Clark system was passed. The House of Assembly was elected in 1909 from 5 districts, each returning 6 members. This system, with some changes, has continued in use to the present time. The most significant change was made in 1958, when the membership was increased to 35, with 7 elected from each district. This is the longest continuous application of STV for the election of any parliamentary body in the world.

A quota-preferential system was also applied in three elections of the Legislative Assembly of New South Wales in 1920, 1922, and 1925. It replaced a second-ballot system that had applied in elections of 1910, 1913, and 1917. In 1928, a quota-preferential method was introduced for local-government elections in the municipality of Armidale, in northern New South Wales; and in 1953, a quota-preferential system was introduced in all districts in New South Wales where three or more seats were filled in a single election. After a change of government, a majority-preferential system (the alternative vote) was used until 1976, when, after another change of government, proportional representation was again introduced and applies currently in most local-government areas in the state.

The majority-preferential system used for elections of the federal Senate was replaced after the 1946 election by a quota-preferential system similar in principle to the Hare-Clark system but differing in some important details. Half the seats in each state are filled at each regular (staggered) Senate election. With over 8 million votes, this is the world's largest application of a quota-preferential method in a public election.

The Legislative Council of New South Wales was elected indirectly from 1933 to 1976. After the 1976 election, the newly established Labor government introduced legislation for direct election of the Council; and, after considerable debate, a quota-preferential system similar to that used for the federal Senate was adopted.

In South Australia, where the Legislative Council had been the last parliamentary body other than the New South Wales Legislative Council elected on a restricted franchise, the introduction of full adult franchise in 1973 was accompanied by the adoption of a party-list system of proportional representation. This system was used in elections in 1975 and 1979 but was replaced in 1981 by a quota-preferential system practically identical with that used for the New South Wales Legislative Council. This system has so far been used in only one election, in November 1982.

The present situation is that the lower houses of New South Wales, Victoria, Queensland, South Australia, and Western Australia; the federal House of Representatives; and the Legislative Assembly of the Northern Territory are elected from single-member districts by major-ity-preferential methods. The upper houses (Legislative Councils) of Victoria and Western Australia are elected from two-member prov-inces with overlapping-term provisions so that in effect, a single-member-district system applies. The Legislative Council of Tasmania is elected from single-member districts by a majority-preferential method. The House of Assembly of Tasmania, the Legislative Coun-cils of New South Wales and South Australia, and the federal Senate are elected by quota-preferential methods. Thus, 10 of the 14 parlia-mentary bodies are elected by majority-preferential methods and 4 by quota-preferential methods.

The results of the numerous elections held with these preferential systems provide a significant amount of information on their perform-ance in full-scale use. In assessing the political consequences of their use, it is necessary to bear in mind that they have been applied in an environment with a tradition of Westminster-style Parliaments. At the same time, it is probable that the people who came to Australia in the late eighteenth and nineteenth centuries were more disposed to change than those they left behind.

Single-Member-District Preferential Systems

The single-member-district majority-preferential systems used in Australia were in general introduced to replace single-member-district plurality systems, which had often given results noticeably inconsis-tent with the views of the voters. Those promoting the introduction of preferential systems suggested that their use would result in a wider choice being available to the voters. In particular, it was suggested that parties with similar policies could nominate their own candidates without risk of helping the election of candidates of opposing parties, since votes for a candidate who did not receive many first preferences would be passed on to candidates shown as the next preference.

The introduction of preferential voting took place over a period in which significant changes in the structure of the political parties were proceeding. In particular, where at the beginning of the twentieth century the main differences were concerned with tariff protection, changes during the early years of the century led to a structure in which the Labour party and a coalition of conservative parties became the main political entities (Loveday et al., 1977, especially sections 8 and 9).

Some people in the Labour movement believe that preferential vot-ing was introduced specifically to reduce the chances of the election of

Labour candidates. This view is to some extent derived from the history of the introduction of preferential voting for House of Representatives elections (Graham, 1962). Early in 1918, a vacancy in the district of Swan, in Western Australia, was filled in a plurality by-election by a Labour candidate with 34.36% of the votes, the other three candidates all being anti-Labour. Legislation to provide for preferential voting was introduced by the Hughes Nationalist government before another by-election later in the same year in the Victorian district of Corangamite. In this case, with one Labour candidate and four non-Labour, the Labour candidate received 42.45% of the first preferences, but the seat was won by one of the other candidates after distribution of preferences.

Examination of the results of a large number of elections, both federal and state up to 1980 with majority-preferential systems in single-member-districts (Wright, 1980, pp. 57–84), has shown that these methods have commonly failed to provide representation corresponding with the views of the voters. Further evidence has been provided by more recent elections.

The normal pattern has been that each party contesting a seat has endorsed only one candidate. As primary elections are not held, the choice of candidates for endorsement is made by relatively small numbers of people within the parties. The details vary somewhat from party to party, but in no case do the voters play any significant part in the choice of candidates.

There have been very few cases where the proportions of seats won have closely corresponded to the votes for the various parties. The 1980 House of Representatives election was not unusual. The first preferences for the Liberal-National Country party coalition amounted to 46.29% and for the Labour party 45.15%. It has been estimated (Parliamentary Library, Australia, 1980, p. 11) that 50.2% of all who recorded formal votes preferred the coalition to the Labour party. But 74 candidates of the coalition parties and only 51 Labour candidates were elected. In 1983, the overrepresentation was reversed. Labour, with less than 50% of first preferences and an estimated 53.6% (Whitton, 1983) preferring it to the coalition, won 75 seats to 50 for the coalition.

In earlier elections, there have been cases where majorities of seats have been won by parties with only minority support from the voters. In the House of Representatives election of 1954, the Labour party received over 50% of first preferences, but the Liberal-Country party coalition won a majority of seats. In 1961 and 1969, Labor was estimated to have been preferred (Maley and Maley, 1980, p. 251) to the coalition by more than half the voters, but on each occasion it failed to win half the seats in the House. There have also been elections of state houses which have given results of this kind. An example is the election of the House of Assembly of South Australia in 1968, when Labour candidates received 51.98% of the first preferences but the party won only 19 of the 39 seats.

Senator Gietzelt (1981), then the Labour party's spokesman on electoral matters in the federal Parliament, argued that the single-member-district preferential system had demonstrated a bias against Labour over a considerable period. While the examples he quoted supported this case, there is also evidence that the same system can on occasions lead to overrepresentation of Labour. The election of the New South Wales Legislative Assembly in October 1981 gave the Labour party, with 55.71% of the first preferences, 69 of the 98 contested seats, or 70.41%. In April 1982, in the election of the Legislative Assembly of Victoria 49 of the 81 seats were won by the Labour party, which received 50.04% of the first preferences. In the federal House of Representatives election in March 1983, as just mentioned, Labour won 60% of the seats with less than 50% of the first preferences.

Results such as these suggest that a change of opinion by a relatively small number of voters could lead to a substantial change in the composition of an elected body. This is certainly borne out by the results of some Australian elections. A spectacular recent example was the election of the House of Representatives in 1975. The election took place after the dismissal of a Labour government by the governor-general, an action that has led to continuing disagreement among constitutional lawyers. The change in support for the parties since the previous election has been expressed in terms of the "two-party-preferred vote" (Maley and Maley, 1980, p. 251) as a fall of 7.4%, from 51.7% in 1974 to 44.3% in 1975, in support for Labour. This led to a loss of 30 seats by Labour, leaving it with only 36 seats to 91 held by the coalition. The election of 1983 provided another example. The increase in Labour representation in the House from 51 seats (40.8%) in 1980 to 75 seats (60.0%) in 1983 resulted from an increase of only 3.6% in the "two-party-preferred vote." The "landslide" phenomenon is, of course, well-known in plurality systems, and the Australian experience shows that it is certainly not eliminated by a change to preferential voting.

The possibility that placing electoral district boundaries can have a substantial effect on winning seats is widely recognized, and it is common for governments arranging for redistributions to be accused of gerrymandering. While variations in district population make discrepancies between voting support and winning seats more likely, redistributions based on more nearly uniform populations have not removed such discrepancies. In 1974, legislation providing for a limit of 10% on departures from state averages was passed by the federal Parliament. The first election after the subsequent redistribution was held in 1977. In terms of the representation of parties, the results were certainly inconsistent with the one-vote, one-value principle. The Liberal party, with fewer votes than the Labour party, won 67 seats while Labour won 38. The National Country party, with a quarter of the votes of the Labour party, won half as many seats. With a "two-party-preferred vote" (Maley and Maley, 1980, p. 251) of 54.6%, the Liberal-NCP coalition won 86 seats to Labour's 38. The 1981 election of the New South Wales Legislative Assembly, mentioned earlier, was held just after a redistribution with a 10% tolerance on differences across districts, and resulted in the Labour Party winning a disproportionately large number of seats.

Even with provision for preferential voting, it has been usual for a high proportion of seats to be won by candidates who have received absolute majorities of votes. In the 1980 House of Representatives election, for example, this was true in 85 of the 125 districts. There were only six districts in which a candidate who did not receive the largest number of first preferences was the one finally elected. It should not be assumed, however, that a different party would have won any of these seats with a plurality system. It is most unlikely that parties with similar policies would have competed against each other in a plurality election, the more probable arrangement being an agreement as to which districts each would contest. So far as the voters are concerned, the end result is probably the same, but the preferential system does allow voters to indicate first preferences for candidates other than those whom their votes finally help to elect.

In all Australian single-member-district electoral systems, many seats are regarded as "safe" for one party or another. The terms *safe, fairly safe,* and *marginal* have been defined (Parliamentary Library, Australia, 1980, p. 1) as follows:

Safe	swing of over 10% needed for loss
Fairly safe	swing of 6 to 10% needed
Marginal	swing of less than 6% needed

On this basis, the Legislative Research Service of the Parliamentary Library classified 54 districts as safe, 18 as fairly safe, and 53 as marginal after the 1980 House of Representatives election. This means that the membership of parliamentary bodies is determined largely by those who control preselection in safe districts, and that the decision as to which party forms the government is made in the relatively small number of marginal districts.

At times, the smaller parties have had a considerable influence on the political situation through their ability to affect the results in some districts. During the 1950s and 1960s, the Democratic Labour party, a breakaway from the Australian Labour party, received sufficient support to exert a considerable influence on the policies of the Liberal and Country parties. In exchange for their adoption of certain policies relating mainly to foreign affairs and to the allocation of public funds to nongovernment schools, it directed its followers to give their second preferences to coalition candidates. Although the DLP never won a seat under a single-member-district system, its influence was considerable in relation to its share of the votes.

More recently, the later preferences of voters for Australian Democrat candidates have been of critical importance in some closely contested elections. The party has not generally attempted to direct its supporters as to how they should mark preferences after those for its own candidates and the influence of Democrat voters has differed in different elections according to Democrat perceptions of the issues at the time of each election.

The basic characteristic of single-member-district preferential systems, as with plurality systems, is that only one group of voters in each electoral district can see the election of the candidate of their choice. It might be thought that the use of a preferential system would give improved voter satisfaction compared with plurality systems. The record of single-member-district preferential elections in Australia is that substantial numbers of voters, usually amounting to between 40% and 50% of the total number, do not see the election of the candidates they support. In 1980 46.51% voted for candidates who were not elected, and in 1983 the proportion was 44.77%.

Multimember-District Majority-Preferential Systems

The majority-preferential system used for elections of the federal Senate from 1919 to 1946 was normally applied in the election of three senators in each state on each occasion. In the first election in 1919, the Nationalist party won 18 of the 19 seats contested. It was not until 1925 that a party failed to win any seats, in that case Labour, with 45.03% of the votes. In 1934, Labour again failed to win any seats; but in 1943, with 55.09% of the first preferences, it won all of the 19 seats contested. The system failed in all 10 elections to give representation consistent with the views of the voters, and it was replaced before the 1949 election by a quota-preferential system of proportional representation.

Quota-Preferential Systems

The Hare-Clark system introduced for two districts in Tasmania in 1896 had some defects that were remedied in the version introduced for the whole state in 1907.[4] The improved method was used in 17 elections between 1909 and 1956 to elect 6 members from each of 5 districts, these being the same as those used to return 1 member each to the federal House of Representatives.[5] With a quota of 14.29%, it might be thought that independents or minor-party candidates would be elected in substantial numbers. In fact, in the 17 elections held on this basis, only 26 of the 510 seats filled were won by candidates outside the main parties. Agreement between party vote share and the numbers of seats won was consistently good, especially when it is recognized that 1 seat in a House of only 30 is 3.33% of the membership.

Since 1959, 7 members have been elected in each district.[6] In 4 of the 6 elections with the 7-member-district system, the result has been a clear majority of seats for one party: in 1964, 1972, and 1979, Labour; and in 1982, the Liberal party. In the elections of 1959 and 1969, neither party received the votes of a majority.[7] In 1959, Labour, with 44.51% of the first preferences, won 17 seats, and the Liberal party, with 41.06%, 16 seats. Labour was able to form the government with the support of two independents. In 1982 the Liberal party won 19 seats; while Labour, with a low vote of 36.86%, won 14 seats. Two candidates outside the main parties were elected, both strongly opposed to the construction of a controversial hydroelectric dam.

In Tasmania, the parties, having endorsed candidates, leave them free to conduct their own campaigns; and, in contrast to the practice in the other states, they do not issue "how-to-vote" recommendations. Candidates normally campaign for first preferences, and the voters have a major influence on the selection of the individuals who become members of the House, as well as determining the party numbers. Each major party usually endorses 7 and sometimes more candidates in each 7-member district. A voter has a choice between about 20 candidates, including those of both main parties, and (in recent years) the Australian Democrats, and usually some independents. With this range of choice, about 70% of voters have seen the election of their first-preference candidates; and another 20%, the election of other candidates early in their preference order. This freedom of choice has sometimes allowed new candidates of parties to replace long-standing members who have been judged less worthy of support by the voters.

With the relatively large numbers of candidates and a requirement for the marking of preferences for at least 7 candidates to make a vote valid, the preparation of incomplete ballots has not been high.[8] In recent years, this proportion has varied between roughly 3.5% and 5%. In the 1982 election, a new provision designed to reduce the effects of "donkey-voting"; that is, numbering the candidates in order of the appearance of their names on the ballot paper (or sometimes in reverse order), was used on a statewide basis for the first time. The ballot papers were printed so that the names of all candidates had approximately equal exposure in the favored positions on the papers. The voters and those involved in counting votes appeared to cope with this innovation without serious trouble, although the level of invalid ballots was a little higher than the average over recent years.

After more than 70 years of proportional representation, an essentially two-party structure has been retained in Tasmania. Although there have been attempts to establish the National (formerly Country) party in Tasmania, as in most of the other states, these have not succeeded. There have been some difficulties in maintaining the Westminster-style of government on occasions, but it is important to remember that the House has only 35 members, so that no party is likely to have a large majority with any electoral system except one capable of considerable distortion in party representation.

When the quota-preferential system was introduced for the federal Senate, the number of people eligible to vote was approaching 5 million, with nearly 2 million in the state of New South Wales. Some procedures different from those in the Hare-Clark system were incorporated, presumably with the idea of simplifying the scrutiny with the larger numbers of voters.[9] One unfortunate feature of the previous majority-preferential system was retained when the change to proportional representation was made. The marking of preferences for all candidates was made a condition in order to achieve validity of votes, although there was strong opposition during the debates in 1948. One consequence is that the incidence of incomplete ballots has been high. In the election of 1974, following the dissolution of both houses, ten senators were elected from each state. In New South Wales, there were 73 candidates, and 12.31% of the votes were rejected as incomplete. This level was unusually high, but levels between 9% and 10% have been usual. For comparison, the proportions of incomplete ballots in simultaneous House of Representatives elections have been about 2.5%.

In the staggered Senate elections, with five vacancies in each state, the major parties have usually endorsed only three candidates, the largest number each would hope to see elected. They also issue how-to-vote recommendations. These practices are undoubtedly designed to limit the choice available to voters so that control of the parliamentary representation of the parties remains with those who control endorsement. Most party supporters have followed party "tickets." In Tasmania, many major party supporters, used to freedom of choice within parties in their state elections, exercise the same freedom in Senate elections. In recent years, substantial numbers of voters in all states have supported Senate candidates outside the major parties, and nonmajor-party candidates have been elected in every recent election. Agreement between party vote share and seat share has been good.[10] Elections for the Legislative Council of New South Wales were held in 1978 and 1981 using a method very similar to that used for federal Senate elections. In each election, 15 vacancies were filled, the quota for election thus being 6.25%. In both cases, more than 90% of the voters saw the election of their first-preference candidates, and the numbers of seats won by the parties agreed with their voting support. In 1978, with 46 candidates, all the seats were won by the Labour party and by the Liberal-National Country party coalition, which together received 91.19% of the first preferences. In 1981, there was stronger support for nonmajor-party candidates; and the result, with 48 candidates, was Labour 8 seats, Liberal-NCP coalition 5, Australian Democrats 1, and Call to Australia 1.

The party-list system of proportional representation that was introduced for elections of the South Australian Legislative Council in 1973 was used for only two elections, in 1975 and 1979. It was replaced in 1981 by a quota-preferential system practically identical with that used for the New South Wales Legislative Council. This system has so far been used for only one election, in November 1982, when the result was 5 Liberal, 5 Labour, and 1 Australian Democrat.

Political Consequences

Electoral systems based on single-member districts with majority-preferential voting apply to the lower houses in all states except Tasmania and to the federal House of Representatives. Even in Tasmania, where the quota-preferential Hare-Clark system applies to elections of the House of Assembly, elections of the House of Representatives and the State Legislative Council take place with single-member-district systems; and the parties there are branches of the Australia-wide parties, so that they are influenced considerably by the thinking of party officials whose backgrounds are in activities concerned with single-member-district systems.

There is much talk among politicians about the desirability of cooperation in the national interest, but the single-member-district systems undoubtedly encourage a confrontation style of politics. While a Westminster-inspired system carries an implication that the opposition has a duty to oppose, confrontation between Labour and the conservative parties is continuous, with disagreement on practically all publicly discussed issues. In election campaigns, the emphasis is on differences in policies. Since there is only one seat to be won in each district and only one candidate from each party, the parties have found it profitable to concentrate on parties and party leaders rather than on local candidates or issues. Most campaigning in recent years has been done through the media, especially television.

The practice of single endorsement by each party has a significant effect on the quality of candidates and elected members. A person considering serving in a Parliament, recognizing that there is very little chance of election without the backing of a major party, must build up a reputation within a party that will lead eventually to endorsement for a winnable seat, usually after exposure on one or two occasions in districts safe for an opposing party. It is likely that many talented people who might consider serving as representatives never seek endorsement, being unwilling to accept the accompanying limitations on freedom of thought and action.

Although one of the classic arguments for single-member-district systems has been that they encourage two-party political systems, there has been a more complex party structure in Australia for many years. The federal Parliament since about 1920 has had a three-party structure, the main party in the non-Labour coalition having to depend on the rural-based National party for its ability to govern. With its support concentrated in a relatively small number of districts, the National party has been able to win a disproportionate number of seats and to exert a major influence on coalition policies. Other smaller parties, as discussed earlier, have been able to influence the policies of the major parties although they have not won seats.

The feasibility of quota-preferential systems has been well established by the continuous use of the Hare-Clark system in Tasmania for over 70 years. Perhaps the most significant feature of Tasmanian House of Assembly elections is that voters regularly make use of the freedom of choice provided by the system. In the only recent attempt by a party to regiment its supporters, the Labour party recommended an order of preference in a by-election in the district of Denison in February 1980. Over 99% of Labour supporters did not follow the party's how-to-vote instructions.

The maintenance of a two-party structure in Tasmania is almost certainly associated with the freedom of choice available to voters. In other applications of quota-preferential methods in Australia, the parties have chosen to limit endorsements and to urge their supporters to follow party directions for preference marking. This has generally led to substantial support for candidates outside the major parties. In particular, elections of the federal Senate have generally involved the election of nonmajor-party candidates, and five Australian Democrat senators and one independent were elected in March 1983.

There have also been some recent instances of party supporters rejecting party directions. In the 1980 Senate election, about 46,000 Labor voters in Victoria gave their first preferences to a sitting woman senator who was placed third on the party's ticket. In Queensland, the wife of the National party state premier was given first place on the party's ticket before two sitting senators. More than 56,000 party voters gave their first preferences to the second and third candidates.

Without exception, quota-preferential systems in Australia have given substantially higher proportions of voters the representation they wanted than have the single-member-district systems. They have also consistently given parties seats in numbers in agreement with their voting support. In spite of efforts by parties to limit the choice offered to voters, quota-preferential systems have not led to splintering of the parties; and in Tasmania, where the choice available to voters has been widest, a two-party structure has continued, while three or more parties have developed in other parts of Australia.

If good government is government consistent with the will of the people, quota-preferential systems have certainly performed better than single-member-district systems, even when these have incorporated preferential voting. In spite of fears expressed by some that proportional representation would lead to fragmentation of the party system, this has not happened; and in the case of the best technical embodiment of the quota-preferential method, the Tasmanian Hare-Clark system, the party structure is less fragmented than where single-member-district systems apply. On the other hand, the effective participation of voters under quota-preferential systems in the selection of candidates as well as in the determination of party seat numbers has influenced the behavior of politicians and the nature of the parties. Perhaps the most significant political consequences of the use of quota-preferential systems will eventually be seen to have less to do with changes in the numbers of seats won than with improvements in the quality and public standing of elected representatives.

Notes

1. The Commonwealth of Australia came into existence in 1901 through the federation of the six states. These had developed over the preceding century from settlements at various points around the coast and in Tasmania, the island state south of the mainland. At present, the federal Parliament consists of a Senate of 76 members and a House of Representatives of 148 members, 145 of them from the states in numbers approximately proportional to the numbers of voters in each state, 2 from the Australian Capital Territory, and 1 from the Northern Territory. The Parliaments of the states are all bicameral except that of Queensland, where the upper house was abolished in 1922. There is also a Legislative Assembly in the Northern Territory, and an elected House of Assembly in the Australian Capital Territory has limited powers under the Commonwealth Department of Territories. In all states, there is a system of local government with elected councils, the precise arrangements varying from state to state. Australia is one of the few countries where voting is nominally compulsory. Failure to record a vote is an offense under the laws relating to all parliamentary elections in Australia. Since voting is by secret ballot, there is no real compulsion to vote, as an unmarked ballot paper can be placed in a ballot box.

2. The term *quota-preferential* is used in this paper to refer to electoral methods involving preferential voting *and* election by quota. Such methods are commonly referred to as "single-transferable-vote methods," but I have avoided the use of this term because of possible confusion with the preferential method used in single-member-district elections in Australia, which is a single-transferable-vote method leading to a majority decision. This latter method is also commonly known as the alternative vote.

3. Very few people voting in present-day Australian elections, other than people who have migrated from other countries, have had any experience with plurality voting in public elections.

4. The main changes were the replacement of a simple quota by a Droop quota and the introduction of a superior procedure for the transfer of surplus votes of elected candidates. In each district, the quota for election was the whole number just above one seventh of the formal votes. Surplus votes of elected candidates were transferred to the continuing candidates shown as next preference by the procedure recommended by Gregory (Priesse, 1913, p. 44). With this procedure, the ballot papers of the elected candidate are credited to the candidates shown as next preferences, each paper having a transfer value calculated by dividing the surplus by the number of papers.

5. In 1917, the Electoral Act was amended to provide that a casual vacancy should be filled by reexamination of the papers forming the quota of the vacating member to find which of the continuing candidates was the next choice of those whose votes formed the quota. Besides ensuring that the balance of representation would not be disturbed when casual vacancies were filled, this provision has had the effect of encouraging the parties to endorse more candidates than they have expected to see

elected so as to be sure that they would not lose seats when casual vacancies were filled.

6. It became apparent after several elections that the choice of an even number of seats in each electoral district led to some problems. To win 3 of the 6 seats in a district, a party required 42.87% of the votes, and for 4 seats, 57.16%. Thus, it was possible for a party to win more than half the votes in a district and to fail to win more than half the seats. In 1955 and again in 1956, each of the major parties won 15 seats. Following these two results, a select committee on electoral reform was set up to consider possible changes in the system. It noted that "since the system was first used in 1909, the only real complaints made about it have been voiced when electorates have returned an even number of members from each of the two main parties." The committee stated its belief that "a majority of electors within an electorate should be guaranteed the right of returning a majority of elected members" and recommended "the election of seven instead of six members from each of the five existing Commonwealth-State electorates" (Tasmania House of Assembly Select Committee on Electoral Reform, 1957, p. 2). The recommendation was adopted, and the 7-member-district system has applied in all elections of the House since.

7. In 1969, a new party, the Centre party, associated with the Federal Country party, was formed. Its most prominent member was K. Lyons, a former Liberal. He was elected to the last seat in the district of Denison after substantial numbers of later preferences of people who had given their first preferences to Liberals were transferred to him. Lyons supported the Liberals, who held 17 seats, and was made deputy premier in a Liberal government. In 1972, after a severe disagreement between Lyons and the Liberal party, the House was dissolved and an election was held. Lyons was not a candidate.

8. Ballots that are incomplete (and thus invalid) are known as informal ballots.

9. The main difference is the use of a procedure involving random sampling of ballot papers from those showing next preferences for candidates rather than crediting all such papers to the respective candidates at the calculated transfer values, as in Tasmania.

10. There have been cases of difference in political balance between the Senate and the House of Representatives, due largely to the arrangement for overlapping terms in the Senate. There is also a provision in the Constitution whereby casual vacancies are filled by the Parliaments of the states where the vacancies occur. Before 1977, the choice was left to the state Parliaments; and, although there was a convention that a replacement should be from the same party as the vacating senator, this was not always observed. There have been examples of "hostile" Senates. The crisis of 1975 resulted from the failure of the Senate to pass budget bills within a specified time. In this case, the coalition controlled the Senate after two state Parliaments had departed from the convention in filling casual vacancies. In 1977, the Constitution was amended by referendum to provide that a state Parliament, in filling a casual vacancy, is obliged to choose a person of the same party as that of the vacating senator unless no such person is available.

CHAPTER 8

The Rise, Decline, and Resurrection of Proportional Representation in Local Governments in the United States

Leon Weaver

Experiences with proportional representation (PR) systems in the United States must be assessed from a relatively small number of cases. An examination of these experiences permits generalizations to be made concerning the adoption, survival, and political effects of such systems.

Extent of Use

Use of proportional representation systems in the United States has been limited to local government and to the single-transferable-vote variety (PR/STV), although party-list (PR/PL) systems have been proposed in several local governments, and the system of election of both houses of the Puerto Rico legislature can be considered essentially a PR/PL system (Puerto Rico Constitution, Art. III, Sec. 7; *Cintron-Garcia v. Romero-Barcelo,* 671 F. 2d 1, 1982).[1] The principal reason for the contrast between PR/STV adoptions and the PR/PL nonadoptions probably lies in the channeling of most of the resources of PR supporters into advocacy of PR/STV and their preference for the nonpartisan ballot, which would rule out PR/PL.

PR systems have constituted a very small sample—a fraction of 1% — when compared with the total number of electoral systems in this country, most of which are single-member-district (SMD) systems (all national, virtually all state, and many local legislative seats); at-large (AL) systems, which are found mostly at the local level; or combined SMD/AL systems, also at the local level.

PR systems have been used in approximately two dozen cities (for city councils and school boards). These cases might conceivably be counted as five dozen if one wished to count the school committees in Massachusetts PR cities and in the New York City community school boards as separate cases. (Childs, 1952, chap. XXVI; 1956, pp. 65–68; Bromage, 1962, p. 16; Hermens, 1941, chap. XIV; Shank and Conant, 1975, pp. 66–67).

Figure 8.1 and Tables 8.1 and 8.2 summarize the experiences with PR systems in municipal governments in the United States during the middle half (1915–1970) of this century. The picture is one of a heyday of 22 adoptions in the 20s, 30s, and 40s canceled out by abandonments, with continued use in Cambridge as the conspicuous exception. The year 1971 marks the resurrection of PR (comparatively speaking), when New York City, mandated by state statute, began electing 32 community school boards by PR/STV.

Contrary to the impression one might gain from some standard works (such as Bromage, 1962, p. 16), acquaintanceship with political life in present PR systems in Cambridge and New York City leaves no doubt that in these comparatively few situations (miniscule in comparison with the frequency of other election systems used in this country), PR is still alive and well. Also, there do not appear to be any substantial initiatives to eliminate it in those instances, although in New York PR may be attacked indirectly through an attack on the basic concept of decentralization of some decision-making powers to community school boards. These statements may be surprising to some, since most of the literature on PR in the United States was written prior to 1970 and ended with the abandonments, and of course could not reflect the New York school district elections.

Adoptions

In order to understand the abandonments of PR, it is necessary to understand why it was adopted. The adoptions for use in city council elections and for school committees in Massachusetts without exception came about as a part of municipal reform movements in the cities concerned.[2] The adoption for New York City community school

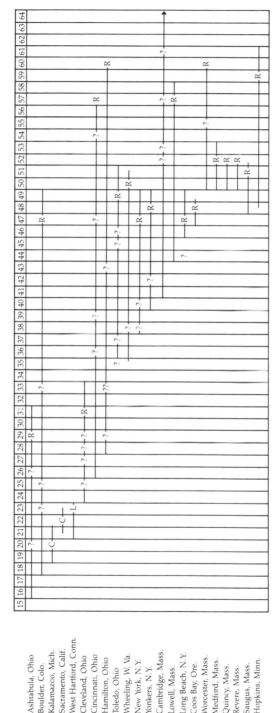

FIG. 8.1. The stormy experience of PR in 22 American cities, 1915–1964. There were 49 attempts to repeal, of which 21 succeeded, leaving Cambridge the sole survivor. PR was used about 180 times, including 37 times for school boards in the Massachusetts cities. Lines represent years PR was in effect; ? = repeal referendum failed; C = declared unconstitutional by Court; L = banned by legislature; R = repealed by referendum. (From Childs, 1965, p. 67.)

141

boards, a generation later (in 1969), was somewhat analogous in that it was an expression of concern for making representation systems more accessible to groups which had been excluded or underrepresented in previous systems—to an extent that some analysts saw in this an important cause of the tearings of the social fabric during the turbulent 60s and 70s.[3]

With the conspicuous exception of New York City, the use of PR in council elections was a feature of council-manager charters; thus, with the exceptions of New York City and Ashtabula, Ohio (where PR was added by referendum amendment to a council-manager charter adopted a few years earlier), "adoption of PR" was really "adoption of a council-manager charter *containing PR*" (unlike most council-manager charters)[4] and containing distinctive concomitants characteristic of the reform model, such as elections separate from state and national elections, a nonpartisan ballot,[5] nomination by petition, a small council, and a mayor elected by the council rather than directly by the voters and whose duties were essentially limited to ceremonial functions and to presiding over the council. It should also be noted that these adoptions came about by local referenda; what were established by local referenda were vulnerable to disestablishment in the same manner.

These concomitant features have been a source of confusion in the debates concerning the effects of PR and the reasons for the abandonments. For example, one of the important reasons for the abandonments was the opposition of party organizations and their leaders. Their enmity to the PR electoral system was caused in part by their loss of influence over nominations due to the nomination-by-petition concomitant, as well as by their aversion to PR counting methods. Other examples of difficulties in sorting out the effects of the various concomitants are discussed in the following sections.

Abandonments

Appreciation of the circumstances under which council-manager charters containing PR were adopted or (in Ashtabula and New York City) PR was added as part of a municipal reform movement helps to illuminate the principal common features discernible in the abandonments, which may be summarized as follows.

1. PR was vulnerable to local repeal referenda, particularly after repeated attacks by anti-PR forces, in ways that systems mandated by state statute are not.

2. PR incurred the enmity of leaders of the majority and sometimes

the minority party, since the charters or PR amendments were enacted by reform forces appealing "over the heads" of party leaders directly to the electorate. Loss of influence over nominations by party leaders (as a result of the nomination-by-petition feature) was an exacerbating factor.

3. In some instances anti-PR campaigns were viewed by PR supporters and opponents alike as a struggle for tactical terrain that would facilitate an attack on the manager feature. However, in all except three cities (Cleveland, Ashtabula, and Quincy), attacks on manager government did not succeed, and in the latter two cases succeeded only several years after the abandonment of PR. Manager government usually gained more of a constituency than PR. Cleveland was the exception.[6]

4. There was a decline in the resources and zeal of reform forces;[7] while they may not have been "morning glories" as characterized by George Washington Plunkett, in many PR cities pro-PR forces did not recruit new enthusiasts to replace the ones who led the initial charge after they retired, died, or moved away; Cambridge, of course, is the conspicuous exception; Cincinnati is a partial exception in that, although they could not save PR after five attacks, the Charter Committee organization and tradition of reform government remains strong.

5. In some cities PR-repeal campaigns represented a venting of voters' wrath generated by actions of reform council members; the ire was focused not only against such incumbents but also against the PR election system perceived to be producing them. Labor elements in Toledo and Hamilton would be examples of anti-PR forces mobilized in such a fashion.[8]

6. The successful and well-publicized PR-repeal campaign in New York, with its spurious linkage to the "Communist issue" (Zeller and Bone, 1948), probably was influential in a few other repealer campaigns after World War II, although explicit mention of that issue was rare.

It is also important to realize what factors did *not* enter into the abandonments in any meaningful way. When one scans the records of the abandonments, one is struck with how little attention was given in those campaigns to the *pros*[9] and *cons*[10] of proportional systems (as compared to the alternatives) which preoccupy political scientists. In assessing the rhetoric of such campaigns, it is useful to distinguish between arguments based on ostensible reasons—such as the alleged complications of PR for the voter and/or counting officials—and the real reason: whether the various political actors perceived themselves to be advantaged or disadvantaged by PR. Proponents tended to be-

lieve correctly that they were advantaged because their more programmatic politics and more disciplined approach (e.g., platform statements and slates) gained them a following more likely to vote all or
most of their numbered preferences. Opponents, who tended to be
machine candidates or independents with lower-class personal fol-
lowings, did not benefit as much from transfer votes (Weaver, 1982).[11]
The most economical and cogent explanation of the success of PR-
repeal forces is that political actors who perceived themselves (usually
correctly, occasionally incorrectly) to be disadvantaged were able to
mobilize more voters than were those who perceived correctly that
they were advantaged. Cambridge was the exception in that reform
forces successfully staved off five attempts at repeal (Weaver, 1982, p.
2). A critical element in such contests was the existence and effectiveness of an ongoing pro-PR political organization, in effect a municipal
party, such as the Cincinnati Charter Committee and the Cambridge
Civic Association (Shaw, 1966; Weaver, 1982, p. 2).

Nor should the decline in the use of PR, in the opinion of this
writer, be attributed to its unfortunate consequences for the body
politic such as election of extremists, "factionalism," and indecision,
as perceived by critics such as Professor Hermens,[12] although flawed
application of the STV method may have been a minor contributing
factor in some cases – for example, Boulder (Winter, 1982). Nor should
the decline be attributed to the perceived unsuitability of the method
to the personality of voters or to the politics in this country.[13] Rather,
the rise and substantial decline of PR in municipal government in this
country is best explained by the particular circumstances that provided the political context for the adoptions and abandonments – in
short those "local factors" or "local issues" cited by political pundits as
explanatory of many political phenomena. The local factors, however,
exhibited some common features which help explain why adoptions
frequently passed by wide margins only to be followed usually by
abandonments by usually emphatic majorities and usually with
higher turnout rates, although this generalization has several exceptions and must be subjected to qualifications.[14] (See Table 8.1 and 8.2.)

The history of PR abandonments in municipal governments is in
stark contrast with the high survival rate of semiproportional (SPR)
systems, such as cumulative voting (CV) and limited voting (LV) systems[15] in this country (Weaver, 1984). The reasons are not hard to
divine: (1) SPR adoptions were made in partisan systems and represented bargains between the parties; thus the party people are allies
of, and investors in, the system rather than enemies as in the case of
PR. (2) Most of the adoptions were by state statute or constitution and

thus were beyond the reach of repealer referenda at the local level, although many exceptions exist in LV provisions in Connecticut home-rule charters. (3) The greater simplicity of the voters' task and of counting methods deprived critics of some of the arguments present in PR repealer campaigns. These considerations suggest conditions conducive to the survival of PR systems, although slating and party-like organizations may, if they are strong and persistent enough, off-set opposition by party organizations.

Political Effects of PR

If, as just ventured, the rise, decline, and resurrection of PR systems in their admittedly limited numbers was related but little if at all to its theoretical merits and demerits, can it be said that the adoptions and abandonments resulted from the real or perceived political effects of PR? The answer to this question is as follows: (1) *Yes*, up to a point which is quickly reached with the generalization that whether PR was voted up or down was determined largely by whether those who perceived themselves advantaged by it were able to muster more votes than those who perceived themselves to be disadvantaged. (2) Beyond that point, *no* in the sense that the effects of the PR feature of the systems involved have not been well enough documented to permit a careful sifting of the evidence and a synthesis of sometimes conflicting findings of investigators looking at only one community or one part of a political system, such as the city manager (his role, his tenure, etc.). The more that one looks at the complicated mosaic of local experi-ences with PR in this country the more one is driven to an attitude of skepticism concerning the existing or potential validation or invalida-tion of much that has been written concerning the political effects of PR. Resolution of such doubts by acceptable research methods must await a more systematic and deeper probe of experiences with PR than is possible within the present resources of this writer. In the meantime we must supplement the meager research findings by intui-tion and speculative thinking.

Some of the assertions in the PR literature must be true, of course, but how do you prove them? This problem exists largely because of the *ceteris paribus* problem: the difficulty or impossibility of isolating the effects of PR from the effects of other concomitant features of the reform model. (New York, of course, is an important exception with regard to all of these features.) Effects which have been attributed by some writers to PR seem to be more reasonably attributable to other features of the system. A few examples will have to suffice:

TABLE 8.1. Analysis of PR Adoptions and Abandonment Votes

City and State	"For PR"[a]	"Against PR"	Majority %	Participation % [g,h]	Election [g,h]
		ADOPTIONS			
Ohio					
Ashtabula[b]					
Cincinnati	92,510	41,105	67	29	Gen.
Cleveland	77,888	58,204	57	17	Gen.
Hamilton	5,555	5,377	51	21	Spec.
Toledo	33,263	28,125	54	21	Gen.
Mass.					
Cambridge[c]					
Lowell	16,477	14,135	54	30	Gen.
Medford	15,830	4,467	78	31	Gen.
Quincy	17,187	7,745	69	30	Spec.
Revere	13,931	2,059	87	43	Spec.
Saugus	3,252	816	80	24	Spec.
Worcester	42,179	22,154	66	32	Spec.
New York					
Long Beach	1,575	1,378	53	33	Gen.
New York City					
— Council	923,186	555,217	62	20	Gen.
— School Boards[d]					
Yonkers	24,072	21,160	53	32	Gen.
Sacramento, Calif.[e]					
Boulder, Colo.	691	131	84	7	Spec.
West Hartford, Conn.[f]					
Kalamazoo, Mich.[e]					
Hopkins, Minn.	1,148	555	67	22	Spec.
Coos Bay, Oreg.	976	873	53	35	Gen.
Wheeling, W. Va.	8,789	7,339	54	26	Spec.
		REPEALS			
Ohio					
Ashtabula[b]					
Cincinnati	54,004	65,593	55	24	Spec.
Cleveland	51,831	61,448	54	13	Gen.
Hamilton	12,872	15,790	55	40	Spec.
Toledo	30,378	56,760	65	29	Spec.

TABLE 8.1. (*Continued*)

City and State	"For PR"[a]	"Against PR"	Majority %	Participation % [g,h]	Election[g,h]
Mass.					
Cambridge[c]					
Lowell	12,881	21,214	62	37	Gen.
Medford	11,728	16,706	59	43	Gen.
Quincy	10,310	29,921	74	48	Gen.
Revere	2,821	11,014	80	38	Spec.
Saugus	548	1,299	70	11	Spec.
Worcester	30,386	46,873	61	38	Gen.
New York					
Long Beach	1,783	2,884	62	30	Spec.
New York City					
−Council	586,170	935,222	61	19	Spec.
−School Boards[d]					
Yonkers	26,800	31,133	54	38	Gen.
Sacramento, Calif.[e]					
Boulder, Colo.	1,370	3,159	70	23	Spec.
West Hartford, Conn.[f]					
Kalamazoo, Mich.[e]					
Hopkins, Minn.	455	1,016	69	13	Spec.
Coos Bay, Oreg.	250	700	74	15	Spec.
Wheeling, W. Va.	6,579	13,456	67	34	Gen.

See note 19 for sources.

[a]In most cases the vote was on new charters containing the usual features of the council-manager plan. Exceptions, where the PR adoption vote was on a separate PR proposal, were Ashtabula and the New York City Council.

[b]Not available.

[c]Excluded from this analysis because there was no abandonment of PR.

[d]Excluded from this analysis because they were mandated by state statute and still continue.

[e]Excluded from this analysis because PR was abolished by court decision.

[f]Excluded from this analysis because PR was abolished by the legislature.

[g]Percent of population.

[h]Elections held the second week of November of even-numbered years are classified as "General," and all others as "Special."

TABLE 8.2. Analysis of Participation Rates in PR Cities Classified by Types of Elections Used in PR Adoptions and Repealers

Adoption and Repealer at General Election			Adoption and Repealer at Special Elections			Adoption at General, Repealer at Special Election			Adoption at Special, Repealer at General Election		
	A	R		A	R		A	R		A	R
[a]Cleveland	17	13	Hamilton	21	40	[a]Cincinnati	29	24	Medford	31	43
Lowell	30	37	[a]Revere	43	38	Toledo	21	29	Quincy	30	48
Yonkers	32	38	[a]Saugus	24	11	[a]Long Beach	33	30	Worcester	32	38
			Boulder	7	23	[b]New York City	20	19	Wheeling	26	34
			[a]Hopkins	22	13	[a]Coos Bay	35	15			

Note. Derived from data in Table 8.1. A = Adoptions; R = Repealer. Figures are percentage of population voting. PR adoptions were adoptions of council-manager charters with PR provisions except in the case of Ashtabula (for which election figures are not available) and New York City, where PR was adopted as a separate amendment.

[a]Cities in which participation rates at repealer elections were lower than at adoptions.

[b]Statistical difference treated as insignificant.

1. Lower participation rates in PR elections than in previous elections have sometimes (e.g., Dobrusin, 1955) been attributed to the PR feature; it seems more reasonable to attribute declines in turnout to an absence of a head-to-head mayoral contest.

2. Splits, delays in decision making, and shifting alliances in PR-elected councils have sometimes been inferred to be the result of the PR electoral system. A special case of this proposition exists in the contention that PR was conducive to long delays in the election of a mayor (in Ashtabula, Cincinnati, and Cambridge, for example) as a result of factional polarization within the council.[16] These phenomena seem to be more readily explained by the method of electing the mayor (by the council) than by the method of electing the council. The problem yields readily to the direct popular election of the mayor. Another special case exists in the dismissals of managers attributed to shifting alliances within the council perceived to be the effect of PR. If for the sake of argument the greater attrition of managers in PR systems is granted, there is a dearth of evidence that changing managers changed policy in any significant way, and there is reason to believe that in a PR system (or in any system which minimizes departures from proportionality in the seats-votes relationship) policy swings will be more gradual than in winner-take-all systems. In both of the special cases, and probably in other cases of perceived ill effects of PR, a fallacy exists in focusing on the STV method of election rather than on its result, which is representativeness. In a community with definite cleavages a representative council will presumably have a more difficult time of finding a consensus[17] than would a council which overrepresents one element or a few elements of the community. Thus, any electoral system (including SMD and SPR ones) which tend to maximize the representative character of a body rather than its decisiveness will be subject to the same criticism, a relationship which Price (1941) recognizes, but which some other critics of PR do not. The implied obverse is: the more proportional the representation system is, the less vulnerable it is to reversals of policy.

3. "Better" candidates recruited and elected in PR systems have been one of the effects perceived by its proponents. While PR has probably tended to give more representation to "good government" candidates in cities in which good government appealed only to a minority than would have been the case otherwise, probably still more such candidates could have been elected in winner-take-all situations where good-government ideology commands a majority. Thus, singling out PR as *the* decisive element fails to give sufficient recognition to other factors, such as support in the electorate and the exist-

ence or absence of a strong political organization supporting the good-government slate. The ability of the Cincinnati Charter Committee to make alliances with one of the major parties and to preserve its influence in an at-large system adopted after the repeal of PR would be a case in point.

Some generalizations may be supportable on the basis of consensus of knowledgeable observers and perhaps, in some cases, more objective data. Examples of likely hypothesized relationships possibly amenable to such validation are as follows:

1. PR-elected councils were more diverse in their composition than were their predecessor and successor councils from the standpoint of greater representation of minority parties, significant ethnic groups, and perhaps other elements of the community.

2. PR affects campaigning styles in at least two important ways. (a) Competition for transfer votes provides an incentive for candidates to mute personal attacks on other candidates (including those on opposing slates) lest they alienate those candidates' first-choice supporters; such competition may, however, tend to cause frictions among candidates on the same slate, thus undermining group discipline. (b) Despite the nonpartisan ballot, PR tends to promote or induce the use of parties or partylike groups, as East (1965) suggests, because programmatic politics and disciplined voting by party or slate supporters is advantageous to the extent that such supporters vote all or several of their available choices rather than just one or a few as is the tendency of the supporters of candidates who run as independents relying on a personal following or machine candidates who must find much of their support among lower-class voters. While this relationship also exists in systems other than PR systems, it probably tends to be more pronounced in the latter system with its more numerous available choices for the voter. Whether these relationships impart a class bias to PR, rewarding the more sophisticated and affluent voters with more influence (as a result of exercising more choices) than the poor and uneducated is an interesting question. It may be that there are more significant lines of cleavage; for example, the most disadvantaged group may be newcomers to the city, regardless of status, who have not been reached with voter-education materials concerning how to vote under PR.

Conclusion

Although the battle cries have often been phrased in normative political-science terms, the local controversies over PR in the United

States have been dominated more by considerations of who gets or keeps power than by abstract considerations of what is the best polity.[18]

Notes

1. The principal features are as follows: In the event a party elects more than two thirds of either house (from a combined single-member-district and at-large system), the underrepresented parties shall have their delegations increased until their proportion in the legislative body approximates their proportion of the vote for governor. From this point on, PR will be used as shorthand for the PR/STV systems under analysis unless circumstances call for the more specific terminology of PR/STV.

2. In some of the smaller cities the adoptions were fairly sedate affairs, but in the larger cities, such as Cleveland, Cincinnati, and New York City, the adoption campaigns took on the characteristics of a *jihad* of reform politics with its rhetoric of antibossism and anticorruption which at times took on overtones of an antiparty and antipolitician nature.

3. In "cities where the local government is more sensitive to the citizens' feelings, riots are less probable. These are cities having a large number of city councilmen and thus smaller districts, in which residents feel closer to their elected officials" (Schanberg, 1965, quoting Stanley Lieberson, Department of Sociology, University of Wisconsin. Also, see Zimmerman, 1971; Hamilton, 1969; Campbell, et al., 1970).

4. In the early part of the century, only a little over 1% of cities used the council-manager form of government.

5. New York and Cleveland were exceptions. Where the ballot was nonpartisan, these cities (as in the case of non-PR cities) exhibited wide variations in the amount and kind of party involvement as is well documented in the literature on nonpartisan elections (e.g., Adrian, 1959; and Weaver, 1971).

6. There was a tendency by some early reformers to proffer PR to counter arguments of opponents of the manager plan who insisted it was "undemocratic" (*National Municipal Review,* 1915, p. 59; 1917, p. 177). Cleveland was also exceptional in that the PR abandonment was voted at the same election which saw the abandonment of the manager plan; its demise has been attributed largely to its having become embroiled in patronage-oriented politics (Bromage, 1964, p. 23; Shaw, 1966).

7. In some cities, such as the small Massachusetts cities in which the last adoptions occurred (after World War II), PR's roots apparently were very shallow to begin with; apparently the PR option of the manager plan proffered by the National Municipal League's Model Charter was adopted somewhat uncritically and quietly shelved a few years later with little or no effort to mount a campaign in defense of PR.

8. Not necessarily typical of labor groups in other cities, such as Cincinnati, where labor elements were among the staunchest supporters of PR.

9. Such as the close relationship that exists between votes and seats.

10. Such as the alleged tendency to elect extremists; "factionalism"; and *immobilisme.* New York City might be considered a partial exception because of the Communist issue (Zeller and Bone, 1948), but to this writer the issue falls more under the category of ostensible reasons than real reasons. The Communist issue entered into

a few other abandonment campaigns but not significantly (Hopkins, Minn., and Cambridge would be examples), and in most not at all.

11. Why some leaders of minority parties which stood to gain from PR were against it or neutral is a puzzle, the solution to which must await further analysis and possibly filling gaps in the existing record. The most likely explaination is that in one-party-dominance situations the leadership of the minority party may find more benefits in cooperation or collusion with the majority party while underrepresented than in vigorous competition when proportionally represented.

12. This statement is made despite the following considerations: The Communist issue was prominent, and perhaps decisive, in the New York City repealer campaign (Zeller and Bone, 1948), and the influence of the New York City example was felt in subsequent repealer campaigns; for instance, in Cincinnati, Cambridge, and other Massachusetts cities. The arguments of Professor Hermens (1941) and his occasional personal participation (at the invitation of proponents of repeal) in some cities became a part of the debate. However, the judgment of this writer is simply that such effects were outweighed by "local factors" as discussed in the text. Also, the Communist issue could hardly have influenced the abandonments before 1945.

13. As seems implicit, for example, in Bromage (1962).

14. The exceptions were Cleveland, Revere, Saugus, Hopkins, Cincinnati, Long Beach, and Coos Bay. A more detailed analysis of Tables 8.1 and 8.2 leads to the following qualifications and exceptions: (1) Note that participation rates are calculated as a percentage of *population* and should be considered only a rough approximation, since registration data were not available for most of the cities. (2) In cities where the "adoption of PR" (adoption of a council-manager charter containing PR provisions) was at a special election and the repeal referendum was on a general election ballot, it is to be expected that the participation rate would be higher in the balloting on the repeal proposal since it was on a general election ballot, and all four cases conform to this expectation (Table 8.2, column 4). (3) Where the opposite set of circumstances existed (adoption at a general, repealer at a special election, Table 8.2, column 3), as would be expected, participation rates were usually lower in the repeal referendum (in a special election). Toledo was the exception. (4) In cities where the general *versus* special election parameter was a constant (Table 8.2, columns 1 and 2), participation rates were lower in repealer referenda as often as they were higher. The lower ones are probably explainable in terms of pro-PR forces providing no campaign or an ineffectual one, as Shaw (1966) has pointed out with regard to Cleveland. (5) The substantially higher participation rate in repeal referenda in Toledo and Hamilton, Ohio, was probably due at least in part to the opposition of labor organizations that had been alienated by actions of reform members of the council. (6) Boulder perhaps should have been eliminated from the analysis because the participation rate in the adoption referendum was so abnormally low. (7) Although the differences in the figures for New York are considered insignificant from a statistical point of view, the fact that participation in the special election repealer campaign was almost as high as in the general-election adoption (of a separate PR amendment) attests to the relatively high voter interest and effective campaigning of both PR proponents and opponents. (8) Some future researcher should investigate the possibility that in some cities, especially Cleveland and Cincinnati, substantial population increases (or decreases in the cases of Lowell and Worcester) and migrations in and out may have changed the demographic mix to the disadvantage of PR supporters.

15. Limited voting systems allow the voter to vote for only fewer candidates than there

are seats to be filled. In cumulative voting systems the voter is given as many votes as there are seats to be filled, and he may give them all to one candidate or otherwise distribute them between candidates as he sees fit.

16. See Straetz (1958, chap. V) for a discussion of such occurrences in Cincinnati. Similar deadlocks occurred in Ashtabula and Cambridge. There appears to be no generally available study of the workings of council election of mayors in non-PR cities; that these situations also produced deadlocks or were perceived as having such potential is probably one of the reasons for the decline of council elections of mayors in council-manager cities in favor of direct election which rose from 40% in 1945 to 57% in 1982.

17. Heisel's (1982) study of PR councils in Cincinnati and Heilig's (1983) study of the election of councillors by districts suggest that voting on substantive policy issues is unaffected by the method of election. This is probably due to the nature of local government issues. However, voting behaviors on mayors and managers may be responsive to different considerations than voting on substantive policy issues.

18. In the research literature the arguments seem to swirl around a central issue posed by the fact that the concept of representative government combines two ideas between which there seems to be some tension: *representing* and *governing*. Although there is usually a tendency to assume that "too much" representativeness militates against decisive governing, there must be situations where indecision results from overrepresentation of one or more elements of a community in which there is a clear majority opinion, but if so, such cases have not gained commensurate attention from political scientists.

19. *Sources for Table 8.1.* Abbreviations: NMR (National Municipal Review). PRR (Proportional Representation Review).

Ashtabula: PRR, 1915, No. 33: 19; No. 34: 43. 1921, No. 57: 15. NMR, 1914: 482. 1916: 56. 1920: 623. The manager plan was converted to the mayor-council pattern in 1948, 19 years after the repeal of PR, although the directly elected "mayor" is titled "Manager."

Cincinnati: NMR, 1925: 69; 1926: 465. Straetz (1958, p. xi).

Cleveland: "Why Cleveland Abandoned the Manager Plan," National Municipal League Archives; University of Cincinnati Library, Box 2, File 1953: 15. PRR No. 61, 1922; No. 69, 1924.

Hamilton: PRR, 1927, No. 81:3. NMR, 1960: 623,642.

Toledo: NMR, 1934; 703; 1950: 566. The Background of City Government and Politics in Toledo. Department of Political Science, University of Toledo, 1950, esp. p. 50.

Lowell: NMR, 1942; 642; 1957: 350.

Medford: NMR, 1947: 631, 646; 1952: 578.

Quincy: NMR, 1947: 631, 646; 1952: 578.

Revere: NMR, 1947: 631, 646; 1955: 592.

Saugus: NMR, 1947: 409; 1951: 540.

Worcester: NMR, 1947: 631, 646; 1960: 623.

New York City: Zeller and Bone, (1948, pp. 1127, 1137).

Long Beach: NMR, 1943; 1947: 649.

Yonkers: NMR, 1938: 616; 1948: 609.

Boulder: Lien (1925: 248); NMR, 1947: 650.

Hopkins: NMR, 1948: 52; 1959: 370.

Coos Bay: NMR, 1944: 629; 1949: 53.

Wheeling: NMR, 1935: 276; 1951: 46.

The Limited Vote and the Single Nontransferable Vote: Lessons from the Japanese and Spanish Examples

Arend Lijphart, Rafael Lopez Pintor, and Yasunori Sone

In the choice of an electoral system, the main alternatives are the plurality method and proportional representation (PR). One must not forget, however, that there are several intermediate systems that combine some of the features of both plurality and PR. These may appropriately be referred to as "semiproportional systems" (Lakeman, 1970, pp. 80–89). The limited vote – including, as a special category of the limited vote, the single-nontransferable vote or SNTV – is both the most important kind of semiproportional system and the most straightforward and logical compromise between the plurality and PR principles.

The limited vote uses multimember districts in which each voter has fewer votes than there are seats at stake in the district; when each voter has only one vote, the limited vote may be called the single-nontransferable vote. The winners are those candidates who have collected the largest numbers of votes. Hence the limited vote appears to be very similar to plurality. It also has some of the principal advantages claimed for plurality, especially the fact that the voters vote for individual candidates, instead of groups of candidates organized as party lists, and its great simplicity for both voters and vote counters: The voters simply give their one or more votes to the candidate(s) they like best, and each candidate's votes are added up to determine the election result. For these reasons, the limited vote is in fact frequently called a plurality method (Johnston, 1979a, p. 54; Katz, 1980, pp. 9, 31; Mackie and Rose, 1982, p. 406; O'Leary, 1979, p. 49). We prefer a stricter definition of plurality systems which specifies that the voters have as many votes as the number of seats available in the district. Moreover, in national elections the plurality method is usually applied in single-member instead of multimember districts. The most important difference is that the limited vote does, whereas plurality does not, facilitate minority representation. In this respect, the limited vote resembles PR. It is therefore more accurate to call the limited vote, including SNTV, a semiproportional system rather than a plurality system.

In this chapter, we shall examine the operation of the limited vote and SNTV in the two countries—Japan and Spain—that use these systems for elections at the national level. We shall analyze the extent to which they allow the representation of minority parties. And we shall compare them with both the plurality method and PR: Are the limited vote and SNTV really semiproportional in the sense that they are halfway in between plurality and PR?

The Japanese and Spanish Examples

Although the limited vote and SNTV appear to be promising combinations of plurality and PR, they are rarely used in practice. The electoral system that has been used for the election of the Japanese House of Representatives since 1900 is the most important and the best-known example of SNTV, although it has been neglected in comparative studies of electoral systems; for instance, Lakeman (1970, pp. 84–85) and Mackenzie (1958, pp. 57–58) give it scant attention, and Duverger (1963) and Rae (1971) do not mention it at all. Mackenzie's (1958, p. 58) assertion that "there has been so little study of these elections that it would be unwise to draw conclusions from them" is by and large still valid today. The Japanese upper house, the House of Councillors, was also elected by SNTV until 1983 when a partial shift to PR took place. Japan is the only country in which SNTV is currently used at the national level (Stockwin, 1983).

Examples of the limited vote, in which the voter has two or more votes, mentioned by Bogdanor (1981, pp. 101–104), Lakeman (1970, pp. 80–83), Mackenzie (1958, pp. 58–59), and Carstairs (1980, p. 12), are some of the constituencies in British general elections in the period between 1867 and 1885: 12 three-member districts in which each voter had two votes, and the four-member district of the City of London, in which each voter could cast three votes. Lakeman (1970, pp. 83–84) also calls attention to the limited vote elections of the city council of Gibraltar until 1969: Each elector had four votes, and seven councillors had to be elected. The only contemporary national-level example of the limited vote—other than SNTV in Japan—is the electoral system used for the election of the Spanish upper house, the Senate, since 1977. The politically much more important lower house in Spain, the Congress of Deputies, is chosen by PR (Georgel, 1981, pp. 316–328).

We shall analyze two recent elections: the Japanese House of Representatives election that took place in 1980 and the election of the Spanish Senate in 1982. Before we turn to this analysis, a few minor exceptions must be stated with regard to both electoral systems: Neither is an *exclusively* limited vote system. In Japan, each voter has one vote and most of the districts are three-member, four-member, and five-member districts. However, there is one single-member district: the Amami Islands. A single-member district with one vote for each voter necessarily entails a plurality system instead of SNTV. We shall exclude this one district from our analysis and concentrate on the election of an "artificial" 510-member House of Representatives instead of the real 511-member House.

In Spain, the basic rule is that each province is a four-member district for the election of the Senate, and that each voter has three votes. There are different arrangements, however, for the island provinces and for the two enclaves of Ceuta and Melilla: 3 three-member districts, 2 two-member districts, and 7 one-member districts. In the three-member districts, each voter has two votes, and these districts are therefore clearly also limited vote districts. But the two-member and one-member districts are plurality districts, because each voter has two votes and one vote, respectively. We shall ignore these plurality districts and restrict our analysis to the 47 four-member and 3 three-member districts. We shall also ignore the additional 31 senators who are indirectly elected by the regional legislatures. For our purposes, therefore, the Senate will be a 197-member body instead of the real 239-member chamber. We should emphasize, however, that our vote totals for both Japan and Spain are close to the national vote totals, because the excluded districts are much smaller in population than any of the other districts.

Minority Representation

How conducive are the limited vote and SNTV to minority representation? One way to measure this is to determine how high a threshold a minority party has to surmount in order to win a seat in a district. Two thresholds must be distinguished: the threshold of representation and the threshold of exclusion (Rae, et al., 1971; Lijphart and Gibberd, 1977). The threshold of exclusion is the percentage of the vote that will guarantee the winning of a seat even under the most unfavorable circumstances. For example, in a three-member SNTV district, the least favorable situation for a minority party is to be faced with one large majority party with three candidates, each receiving exactly equal shares of the majority supporters' votes. However, if the minority has only one candidate who receives slightly more than 25% of the votes, the minority candidate is assured of election; the three majority candidates have to share the remaining votes, totaling slightly less than 75%, and hence they cannot have more than 25% each. The threshold of exclusion in this case is therefore 25%.

A simple example of the threshold of exclusion in a limited vote system other than SNTV is the following: Assume a limited vote district with three seats and two votes for each of the district's 1,000 voters. Here again, the most unfavorable situation for a small party is to be confronted by one large party that has nominated three candidates who are equally supported by the majority party's voters. If the majority numbers 600 voters out of the total of 1,000 in the district, they can cast 1,200 votes for the three candidates—400 votes for each candidate, if the votes are distributed evenly. If the minority prudently nominates only two candidates, they will also receive 400 votes each. Consequently, if the minority is slightly larger than 40%, it is sure to win a seat; if it is slightly smaller, the majority may win all three seats. Thus the threshold of exclusion is 40%.

The general formula for the threshold of exclusion is:

$$\frac{v}{v+m} \times 100\%$$

in which m is the number of seats to which the district is entitled (the district magnitude) and v is the number of votes each voter can cast (Newland, 1982, p. 33). In the Japanese SNTV system, the threshold of exclusion is 25% for the 3-member districts, 20% for the 4-member districts, and 16.7% for the 5-member districts. In Spain, the 4-member districts (in which $m=4$ and $v=3$) have a threshold of exclusion of 42.9%, and the three-member districts ($m=3$, $v=2$) have a threshold of exclusion of 40%. The formula shows that the threshold of exclusion decreases—and hence that the chances for small parties improve—as the number of seats increases and as the number of votes of each voter decreases. As far as the latter variable is concerned, the optimal limited vote for small parties is a system in which the number of votes of each voter is as small as possible; that is, one. In other words, the optimal limited vote system from the point of view of minority representation is SNTV. This is, of course, also the reason why this category of the limited vote is given a special name.

In SNTV systems, the chances for small parties must be judged to be approximately as good as under the single-transferable vote (STV), which is a form of PR. In the Irish STV system; for instance, the number of votes that entitles a candidate to be declared elected is known as the Droop quota: the total number of valid votes, divided by the number of seats plus one (and rounded up to the next integer). A quick glance at our formula for the threshold of exclusion reveals that this threshold for SNTV is virtually identical with the Droop quota in STV.

Furthermore, it is quite possible for a minority party to win a seat with a number of votes that is well below the threshold of exclusion (the minimum vote necessary to win a seat under the *least* favorable circumstances). We can also ask: Which proportion of the vote may be sufficient for winning a seat in the *most* favorable situation; this lower threshold is the threshold of representation. The limited vote, including SNTV, has the unusual property that its threshold of representation is almost zero. If, for instance, all but two of the voters in a three-member SNTV district concentrate their votes on one candidate, two other candidates can be elected with one vote each. And in our earlier example of a three-member limited vote district with two votes for each of 1,000 voters, two candidates could be elected with 999 votes each, and two minority candidates could get one vote each—the latter two would have to draw lots to determine the winner.

Handicaps for Large Parties

This discussion of the threshold of representation calls attention to the fact that the limited vote and SNTV entail special problems for the larger parties; that is, those parties that can reasonably expect to win more seats than the number of votes available to each voter. The small parties can follow a simple strategy: They should nominate as many candidates as each voter has votes—one candidate under SNTV, two when $v=2$ under the limited vote, and so on—and encourage their supporters to vote for these candidates.

The larger parties have to solve two serious problems. First, they have to decide how many candidates they can safely nominate. If their estimate is wrong, they can suffer a severe loss. Let us once more use the example of a limited vote three-member district with 1,000 voters casting two votes each. If the majority party believes that it will be supported by more than 60% of the voters, it may be tempted to nominate three candidates in the hope of winning all three seats. It may be too optimistic, however, and, instead of more than 600 voters, only 597 voters may give their two votes to the party's three candidates—yielding 398 votes for each candidate if the votes are equally distributed. The minority party's two candidates will get 403 votes from the 403 minority voters. Two candidates of a minority of about 40% would be elected, and only one candidate of the majority of about 60%.

The second handicap for a large party nominating more than the completely "safe" number of candidates, unlike for its smaller competitors, is that it has to try to instruct its supporters very carefully to distribute their votes as equally as possible among its candidates. This may require a substantial organizational effort. The basic problem is that all of the votes received by a candidate above the number necessary for victory are wasted votes; it would be preferable for the party if these votes had been cast for another of the party's candidates. Another way to characterize this problem is to call it the problem of nontransferability of votes. In a system of transferable votes, like STV, any vote surplus will be transferred to other candidates, usually to candidates of the same party. In this respect, SNTV differs sharply from STV—and it is a difference that mainly disadvantages the larger parties.

The problems of finding the best strategy of nomination and vote distribution are illustrated in Table 9.1. It shows the results in three districts in the 1980 House of Representatives election in Japan. In the first example, the Liberal Democrats made the mistake of undernomination; that is, nominating fewer candidates than they might have been able to elect. If they had nominated three candidates, and if the 147,120 Liberal Democratic voters had spread their votes equally among these three, each candidate would have won 49,040 votes. All three would have been elected, and the Communist candidate would have been defeated. The second example shows an optimal nomina-

TABLE 9.1. Examples of Undernomination, Overnomination, and Unequal Vote Distribution in the Japanese House of Representatives Election, 1980

A. Undernomination: Tokyo, 8th district, 3 seats		
Takashi Fukaya (Lib. Dem.)	76,254	elected
Kunio Hatoyama (Lib. Dem.)	70,866	elected
Mitsuhiro Kaneko (Comm.)	46,208	elected
Yoshimi Nakagawa (Komeito)	45,029	
Yuji Sato (Soc.)	16,476	
Total votes	254,833	
B. Unequal vote distribution: Niigata, 4th district, 3 seats		
Katsuhiko Shirakawa (Lib. Dem.)	67,549	elected
Osamu Takatori (Lib. Dem.)	65,434	elected
Kihei Kijima (Soc.)	57,261	elected
Toru Tsukuda (Lib. Dem.)	53,886	
Tomosaburo Sudo (Comm.)	7,089	
Total votes	251,219	
C. Overnomination: Oita, 1st district, 4 seats		
Isamu Murakami (Lib. Dem.)	104,522	elected
Chubun Hatano (Lib. Dem.)	86,255	elected
Eijiro Hata (Lib. Dem.)	72,093	elected
Keinosuke Kinoshita (Dem. Soc.)	70,206	elected
Tomiichi Murayama (Soc.)	69,466	
Kimitake Hongo (Soc.)	65,081	
Koichi Hamada (Comm.)	11,450	
Total votes	479,073	

Source. Adapted from *Asahi Nenkan 1981* (Tokyo: Asahi Shinbunsha, 1981), pp. 236-239.

tion strategy on the part of the Liberal Democrats but an insufficiently even allocation of the votes among the three Liberal Democratic candidates. Too many votes were collected by candidates Shirakawa and Takatori and too few by candidate Tsukuda. A completely equal distribution of Liberal Democratic votes would have yielded about 62,290 votes for each candidate, victory for all three and the defeat of the Socialist candidate.

The final example of Table 9.1 illustrates the problem of overnomination. The Socialists nominated two candidates, supported in nearly equal proportions by the Socialist voters. Both candidates fell just short of the minimum number of votes required for election. If the Socialists had put up only a single candidate, this one candidate

TABLE 9.2. Seats Lost and Gained by Undernomination, Overnomination, and Unequal Vote Distribution in the Japanese House of Representatives Election, 1980

	Seats Gained By				
	Soc.	Comm.	Kom.	Dem. Soc.	Total
Seats lost by:					
Liberal Democrats					
Undernomination	9	4	4	0	17
Unequal vote distribution	7	3	2	1	13
Socialists					
Overnomination		1	0	1	2
Total	16	8	6	2	32

Source. Based on *Asahi Nenkan 1981*, pp. 236-239.

would almost certainly have been elected, and the candidate of the Democratic Socialist party would not have won a seat.

Table 9.1 merely contains illustrations. The more important question is: How do the problems of overnomination, undernomination, and unequal vote distribution affect the different parties? The seats lost by some of the parties and won by other parties as a result of these problems are shown in Table 9.2. Of the 510 seats, a total of 32 (6.3%) were affected. Two conclusions may be drawn from the table. One is that almost all of the seats that were lost—30 of the 32 seats—were lost by the largest party, the Liberal Democrats, and gained by the smaller parties. Secondly, the seats lost by the Liberal Democrats were lost because of undernomination and unequal vote distribution in approximately equal proportions; they lost no seats by overnomination. The only seats lost by overnomination were seats that the Socialists, the second largest party, might have been able to win.

As explained earlier, the risks of overnomination in limited vote and SNTV systems are so severe that large parties naturally tend to be too conservative, instead of not conservative enough, in their nomination strategies. Since the smaller parties also tend to be prudent, the overall pattern in Japan is one of relatively few candidates competing for the seats at stake. Of the 129 SNTV districts in the 1980 election, only 26 (20.2%) were contested by at least twice as many candidates as there were seats in the district. The limited choice that this entails for the voters may be considered a disadvantage of SNTV.

The limited vote system for the Senate in Spain encourages even

TABLE 9.3. Examples of Undernomination and Prudent Nomination in the Spanish Senate Election, 1982

A. Undernomination: Cádiz, 4 seats	
Francisco Arias Solís (Soc.)	293,807 ⎤
Esteban Caamaño Bernal (Soc.)	288,009 ⎥
Jose Manuel Durate Cendán (Soc.)	285,847 ⎥ elected
Migual Arias Cañete (A.P.)	93,860 ⎦
Manuel M. Garcia de Veas Vaquero (A.P.)	89,174
Jose Maria Pemán Domecq (A.P.)	88,629
Miguel Campos Varela (Comm.)	23,276
22 other candidates with fewer votes	214,832
Total votes	1,377,434
B. Prudent nomination: Guadalajara, 4 seats	
Francisco-Javier Solano Rodriguez (Soc.)	33,899 ⎤
Rafael de Mora Granados Marull (Soc.)	33,639 ⎥
Alfonso Trillo Hernando (Soc.)	33,207 ⎥ elected
Antonio Zahonero Celada (A.P.)	31,894 ⎦
Jose-Manuel Paredes Grosso (A.P.)	31,560
Jose-Isidoro Ruiz Ruiz (A.P.)	31,461
Feliciano Román Ruiz (U.C.D.)	12,629
21 other candidates with fewer votes	52,057
Total votes	260,346

Source. Adapted from data supplied by the Ministry of the Interior, Madrid.

greater conservatism. The typical pattern is for the parties to nominate exactly as many candidates as each voter has votes: three candidates in most of the districts, which are four-member districts, and two candidates in the few three-member districts. For a small party, there is obviously no advantage in nominating more than three or two candidates, respectively; it is also wise not to have fewer candidates than exactly this number in order not to induce its supporters to give some of their votes to the candidates of other parties. For the largest party in a district, there is little to gain and potentially much to lose by overnomination. It can safely count on winning three of the seats in a four-member district; if it tries to win more, it may end up with only one seat. This is illustrated in Table 9.3. In the province of Cádiz, the three Socialist candidates won more than three times as many votes as their closest competitors; in all probability, the presence of four Social-ists on the ballot would have resulted in a total Socialist victory. But in Guadalajara, the nomination of four Socialist candidates and an even distribution of the votes among them would have led to the election of three Popular Alliance candidates and only one Socialist.

How many districts could have been swept by the largest party if it had pursued a more aggressive nomination strategy and if it had successfully instructed its voters to spread their votes evenly among its candidates? Under these—obviously very demanding—conditions, 31 out of the 50 districts could have elected candidates of only one party. The actual most prevalent result in the 47 four-member districts was the election of three members of the largest party and one of the next largest: This occurred in 43 of the 47 districts. In three of the remaining four-member districts, the two largest parties were closely matched and won two seats each; and in one district, the division was two to one, with one successful independent candidate. In all three of the three-member districts, two candidates of the largest and one of the next largest party were elected.

Unless a large party is overwhelmingly strong in a district, a conservative nomination strategy is clearly dictated by partisan self-interest. It should also be emphasized, however, that this tendency is reinforced by a genuine respect for fair play and for the principle of minority representation. Because the basic idea underlying the limited vote system in Spain is to permit the election of one minority representative from each province, a large party that would try to defeat this purpose would make a very selfish impression.

SNTV in Japan: Comparisons with PR and Plurality

Considering the advantages that the limited vote, and SNTV in particular, offer to small parties and the handicaps that they present for the larger parties, it seems surprising that the Japanese House elections and the Spanish Senate elections do not yield very proportional results. In order to measure the proportionality of the Japanese 1980 and the Spanish 1982 election, we shall use the index proposed by Rose (1984): the sum of the differences between each party's percentage of votes and its percentage of the seats, divided by 2 and subtracted from 100. Another way to define this index is as the total percentage by which the overrepresented parties are overrepresented—which is the same, of course, as the total percentage by which the underrepresented parties are underrepresented—subtracted from 100. As table 9.4 shows, the index of proportionality for the 1980 election in Japan is 90.7%. When we compare this index with the indexes computed by Rose (1984), we see that it is similar to the indexes of the less proportional PR systems but also to the indexes of the more proportional non-PR systems. In this respect, it indeed behaves like a semiproportional system. The index of proportionality for

TABLE 9.4. Votes, Actual Seats Received, and Three Hypothetical Seat Allocations in the Japanese House of Representatives Election, Excluding the Amami Islands, 1980, in Percent

		Seats	Hypothetical Seat Allocations		
	Votes	SNTV	Plur.	STV	LR
Liberal Democrats	47.8	55.5	95.9	55.5	49.0
Socialists	19.3	21.0	0.8	21.0	22.5
Communists	9.8	5.7	1.0	5.3	7.3
Komeito	9.0	6.5	0.0	6.7	9.0
Democratic Socialists	6.6	6.3	0.8	5.9	6.1
Others	7.4	5.1	1.6	5.7	6.1
Total	100	100	100	100	100
Index of Proportionality		90.7	52.0	90.7	95.6

Source. Based on data in *Asahi Nenkan, 1981,* pp. 236-239.

the 1982 Senate election in Spain is a much lower 79.3%, placing this limited vote system among the least proportional of the non-PR systems (see Table 9.6).

It is also worth noting that both elections yielded what Rae (1971, pp. 74–77) calls "manufactured majorities": parties that receive less than a majority of the votes but to which the electoral system awards a majority of the seats. The Japanese Liberal Democrats won 55.5% of the seats (not counting the seat they won in the Amami Islands district) with 47.8% of the votes. In Spain, the Socialists won 65.0% of the 197 seats in the limited vote districts with 47.2% of the votes. As Rae notes, manufactured majorities occur much more frequently under plurality than under PR. In this respect, therefore, the Japanese and Spanish systems resemble plurality.

How can the relative disproportionality of the two systems be explained? One factor concerns the inherent properties of the limited vote and SNTV formulas. The other factor is the small magnitude of the districts—an average of slightly less than four seats per district both in Japan and in Spain—and the malapportionment of these districts. Especially with regard to Japan, many observers have noted that the Liberal Democrats are greatly helped by the fact that they are strong in the rural districts which tend to have more representatives than they would be entitled to on the basis of an equal-population standard. McNelly (1982, p. 13; see also Stockwin, 1983, p. 219) states,

"In Japan, the electoral system is flawed . . . by the malapportionment that results from the failure to redistrict as the population has shifted to the cities."

Table 9.4 compares the 1980 SNTV results in Japan with the hypothetical results of the application of plurality and two forms of PR in the same districts. Only parties with more than 5% of the popular vote are listed separately. For plurality, we assume that the party whose candidates receive the most votes in a district would have won all of the district's seats. The Liberal Democrats would have been the overwhelming beneficiary of this rule, winning 95.9% of the seats. The corresponding index of proportionality is an extremely low 52.0%. This result is in accordance with the well-known tendency of plurality systems to become increasingly disproportional if, instead of single-member districts, multimember districts of increasing magnitude are used—an average magnitude of about 4 in the hypothetical Japanese case (Blondel, 1969, p. 192). The SNTV results are obviously much more proportional than those of multimember district plurality.

We can compare SNTV with STV by assuming that the votes cast in the 1980 election are perfectly transferable among the candidates of the same party and by assuming that no transfers to other parties take place. Under these assumptions, the election outcomes in several districts change; for instance, the Socialists capture the Democratic Socialist seat in the Oita first district (see Table 9.1). But the overall result remains almost exactly the same, and the STV index of proportionality is identical with the SNTV index. Moreover, under STV the Liberal Democrats retain their manufactured majority. One reason is that STV is not the most proportional of the PR formulas and that it tends to discriminate somewhat against small parties (Lijphart, chap. 10, in this volume). The most evenhanded PR formula is that of the largest remainders. And indeed, when this formula is applied to the 1980 election, the index of proportionality goes up and the Liberal Democrats lose their manufactured majority.

How can we assess the effects of malapportionment? The method that we chose is to calculate the exact number of seats to which each district would be entitled according to the standard of perfectly equal representation, and to assign the appropriate weight to each of the seats in the district. The first calculation is based on the number of valid votes in each district (instead of the total district population or the number of eligible voters) in order to control not only for malapportionment but also for unequal voter turnout rates. For instance, on the basis of the valid votes cast in the Miyagi first district, it should

TABLE 9.5. Votes and Three Hypothetical Seat Allocations in Perfectly Apportioned Districts in the Japanese House of Representatives Election, Excluding the Amami Islands, 1980, in Percent

		Hypothetical Perfectly Apportioned Seat Allocations		
	Votes	SNTV	STV	LR
Liberal Democrats	47.8	53.5	52.8	47.1
Socialists	19.3	20.5	20.8	21.9
Communists	9.8	6.2	6.0	7.9
Komeito	9.0	7.4	7.8	9.9
Democratic Socialists	6.6	6.6	6.2	6.4
Others	7.4	5.8	6.4	6.7
Total	100	100	100	100
Index of Proportionality		93.2	93.5	96.4

Source. Based on data in *Asahi Nenkan 1981,* pp. 236-239.

have 6.5 seats instead of 5 seats. Each of the 5 seats can therefore be given a weight of 1.3 in order to obtain perfectly equal apportionment. The weights range from .606 to 1.911.

Table 9.5 recalculates the results of the 1980 election by giving each winning candidate a weighted seat instead of one seat. It is clear that malapportionment plays a role, but it should not be exaggerated. The SNTV index of proportionality for the weighted results is higher than that for the real election, but only by 2.5%. Even in perfectly apportioned districts, SNTV—and STV, too—give the Liberal Democrats a manufactured majority. Only the largest remainders formula can undo this advantage. The persistent overrepresentation of the largest party under SNTV and STV is mainly due to Japan's low-magnitude districts. Unless the PR formula is completely evenhanded, like largest remainders, PR and semi-PR systems require districts with relatively many seats in order to attain a high degree of proportionality (Rae, 1971, pp. 114–125).

The Limited Vote in Spain: Comparisons with PR and Plurality

Tables 9.6 and 9.7 summarize the differences between the Spanish limited vote results on the one hand, and the PR and plurality results on the other hand, according to an analysis similar to the one just applied to Japan. Only the three parties that gathered more than 5% of the popular vote and the two main ethnic parties are listed sepa-

TABLE 9.6. Adjusted Votes, Actual Seats Received, and Four Hypothetical Seat Allocations in the Spanish Senate Election, Excluding the Nine Plurality Districts, 1982, in Percent

| | Adj. Votes | Seats LV | Hyp. Seat Allocations | | | |
			Max. LV	Plur.	STV	LR
Socialists	47.2	65.0	79.7	81.7	54.8	47.7
Popular Alliance	25.6	26.9	13.7	10.7	31.0	29.9
Union of the Democratic Center	7.0	0.5	0.5	0.0	6.6	12.7
Catalan Nationalists	4.2	3.6	2.5	3.0	2.5	2.5
Basque Nationalists	2.0	3.6	3.0	4.1	2.5	1.5
Others	14.0	0.5	0.5	0.5	2.5	5.6
Total	100	100	100	100	100	100
Index of Proportionality		79.3	66.4	63.4	86.4	89.4

Source. Based on data supplied by the Ministry of the Interior, Madrid.

rately. The votes are adjusted votes in the sense that the votes in the few three-member districts, in which each voter could cast two votes, were increased by 50% in order to make them equivalent to the votes cast in the four-member districts. The vote percentages shown in Tables 9.6 and 9.7 correspond closely to the votes cast in the PR election of the lower house that was held simultaneously.

TABLE 9.7. Adjusted Votes and Three Hypothetical Seat Allocations in Perfectly Apportioned Districts in the Spanish Senate Election, Excluding the Nine Plurality Districts, 1982, in Percent

| | Adj. Votes | Hypothetical Perfectly Apportioned Seat Allocations | | |
		LV	STV	LR
Socialists	47.2	67.7	56.4	49.4
Popular Alliance	25.6	23.0	31.2	28.1
Union of the Democratic Center	7.0	0.2	3.3	7.9
Catalan Nationalists	4.2	4.9	4.4	4.4
Basque Nationalists	2.0	4.1	2.8	1.5
Others	14.0	0.1	1.9	8.7
Total	100	100	100	100
Index of Proportionality		76.7	84.2	94.2

Source. Based on data supplied by the Ministry of the Interior, Madrid.

The index of proportionality for the limited vote is 79.3% — a relatively low index but one that is closer to the index for the hypothetical STV result than for the hypothetical plurality outcome. The main reason, as discussed earlier, is that the largest party in each district did not "abuse" the limited vote by trying to capture all of the seats. The hypothetical results of a successful "abusive" strategy are shown in the third column of Table 9.6: They hardly differ from the plurality results. As in the Japanese case, the Socialist manufactured majority is maintained under STV rules but is eliminated by largest remainders.

The Spanish Senate districts are even more malapportioned than the Japanese House districts, but malapportionment may be considered more legitimate in the Spanish case. The Senate is the upper house in which the basic principle is that the provinces should be equally represented (with additional seats for the regional communities) — similar to the equal representation of the states or cantons in the United States, Australian, and Swiss federal chambers. Nevertheless, we can get a more accurate conception of the operation of the limited vote if we control for the effects of "malapportionment." This entails the assignment of weights to the seats, ranging from .142 to 6.161 — much greater differences than found in Japan. Using the perfectly apportioned districts, we find that the limited vote results become less instead of more proportional. The reason is that in Spain the largest party, the Socialist party, is stronger in the larger provinces with major urban centers — unlike the more rurally based Liberal Democrats in Japan. Table 9.7 also shows that even in perfectly apportioned districts the limited vote and STV fail to eliminate the Socialists' manufactured majority; only the largest remainders method is able to achieve this.

Conclusions

The Japanese and Spanish examples show that the limited vote and SNTV combine several of the important features of plurality and PR. Their allocation of seats tends to be more proportional than the plurality method but less proportional than PR. Within the limited vote, there is a wide variety of options that affect the proportionality of the election outcome. The least proportional results are likely when the number of votes of each voter is large and when the district magnitude exceeds this number by one, exemplified by the electoral system for the Senate in Spain. The most proportional results are likely when the district magnitude is high and each voter has only one vote. The Japanese SNTV system exemplifies the one-vote-per-voter criterion, but its districts are relatively small. At best, SNTV can achieve approximately the same level of proportionality as STV but not a perfect or near-perfect proportionality. This conclusion must be further qualified by stating that the similarity of SNTV and STV is based on the aggregate nationwide result and that, if one is in favor of SNTV, one has to tolerate disproportionalities at the district level as shown in Table 9.1. On the other hand, the limited vote, and especially SNTV, have the attractive simplicity of the plurality rule: Voters have an extremely easy task, and the votes can be counted just as easily. For better or for worse, the limited vote and SNTV are indeed semiproportional and semiplurality systems.

CHAPTER 10

Degrees of Proportionality of Proportional Representation Formulas

Arend Lijphart

I t is a well-established proposition in the literature on electoral systems that proportional representation (PR) is generally quite successful in achieving its principal goal—a reasonably proportional
translation of votes into seats—especially in comparison with plurality
and majority formulas. One of Rae's (1971, p. 96) "differential propositions" is that "proportional representation formulae tend to allocate
seats more proportionally than do majority and plurality formulae." It
is also known that different PR formulas are not equally proportional,
but students of PR disagree about which of the formulas are more and
which are less proportional.

The purpose of this analysis is to establish a rank order of the
principal PR formulas according to their degree of proportionality. I
shall use Blondel's (1969, pp. 186–191) ranking of the single-transferable vote, Sainte-Laguë, d'Hondt, and largest remainder systems—the
most important attempt to rank order PR formulas undertaken so
far—as my preliminary hypothesis. In addition to the four formulas
analyzed by Blondel, I shall also try to include the two Imperiali
formulas in my ranking.

The degree of proportionality may be defined in terms of two elements. One is the degree to which the seat percentages of the different parties correspond to their vote percentages. The second is the

degree to which large and small parties are treated equally. It is the second element that provides a clear criterion for judging the proportionality of PR formulas, because deviations from proportionality are not random: They tend to systematically favor the larger and to discriminate against the smaller parties.

Blondel's Ranking

Blondel (1969, p. 191) ranks four PR formulas in the following decreasing order of proportionality:

1. Single transferable vote (STV)
2. Sainte-Laguë
3. D'Hondt
4. Largest remainders

STV is therefore the most, and the largest remainder method the least, proportional formula, according to Blondel. Other, more limited, attempts to determine the proportionality of PR systems tend to (1) ignore the STV method, (2) agree with Blondel's judgment that the d'Hondt formula is less proportional than the Sainte-Laguë formula, and (3) disagree with Blondel's placement of the largest remainder formula at the bottom of the list.

Loosemore and Hanby (1971) consider three of Blondel's four formulas, and they arrive at the following rank order:

1. Largest remainders
2. Sainte-Laguë
3. D'Hondt

Their relative placement of Sainte-Laguë and d'Hondt is in agreement with Blondel's, but they conclude that the largest remainder formula is the most proportional of the three. Rae (1971, p. 105) also finds that the largest remainder method is more proportional than the other two lumped together. Balinski and Young (1980) confirm the Loosemore-Hanby finding that the Sainte-Laguë formula, equivalent to the Webster method of apportionment of the U.S. House of Representatives, yields more proportional results than the d'Hondt formula, which is the equivalent of the Jefferson method of apportionment.

Most of the literature confines itself to a pairwise comparison of the d'Hondt and largest remainder formulas. The consensus is that d'Hondt disproportionally favors the larger parties and that the largest remainder formula is more proportional and more favorable to the smaller parties (Van den Bergh, 1955, pp. 24–26; Mackenzie, 1958, pp. 78–80; Lakeman, 1974, pp. 93–97; Berrington, 1975, pp. 366–368; Nohlen, 1978, pp. 77–80; Bon, 1978, pp. 96–100). This consensus deviates from Blondel's ranking. In the next section, I shall show that the consensus is right and that Blondel is wrong.

Comparing d'Hondt and Largest Remainders

A pairwise comparison of the d'Hondt and largest remainder formulas is a good starting point for our exercise because it also supplies us with the key we need for the ranking of the other PR methods. How can we explain the different results of these two basic PR formulas?

The initial difficulty is that the d'Hondt and largest remainder formulas appear to use completely different methods for allocating seats on the basis of the parties' votes. Table 10.1 gives a concrete illustration. The largest remainder formula first calculates the electoral quota or quotient (often called the Hare quota): the total number of valid votes cast (v) divided by the total number of seats in the district (s). The parties' votes are divided by this quota, and each party receives a seat for every whole number in the result. The remaining seats are then awarded to the largest of the unused "remainders" or remaining votes. The d'Hondt formula does not require the calculation of an electoral quota. As Table 10.1 shows, each party's votes are divided by the series of divisors 1, 2, 3, and so forth, and the seats are given successively to the highest of the resulting values, usually referred to as "averages."

It is possible, however, to interpret the d'Hondt highest average formula in such a way that it becomes comparable to the largest remainder formula. The purpose of the d'Hondt formula may be said to be the improvement of the largest remainder formula by finding an electoral quota, lower than the Hare quota, which allows us to allocate all of the seats exactly according to the largest remainder rule but without having to take any remaining votes into account (Van den Bergh, 1955, pp. 68–72). This lower d'Hondt quota is equal to the last of the "averages" to which a seat is awarded. In the example of Table 10.1, the d'Hondt quota is 14 votes. When the parties' votes are divided by this quota, party A is entitled to 2 seats, B to 2, C to 1, and D and E to none; all of the seats have been allocated and the remaining votes can be ignored.

TABLE 10.1. Hypothetical Example of the Operation of the Largest Remainder, D'Hondt, and Pure Sainte-Laguë Formulas in a District with 100 Votes, 5 Seats, and 5 Parties

| | | Largest Remainders[a] | | | |
Parties	Votes	Initial Allocation of Seats	Remaining Votes	Allocation of Remaining Seats	Final Seat Allocation
A	36	1	16	1	2
B	30	1	10	0	1
C	14	0	14	1	1
D	12	0	12	1	1
E	8	0	8	0	0

| | | D'Hondt[b] | | |
Parties	$v/1$	$v/2$	$v/3$	Total
A	36 (1)	18 (3)	12	2
B	30 (2)	15 (4)	10	2
C	14 (5)	7		1
D	12			0
E	8			0

| | | Pure Sainte-Laguë[b] | | |
Parties	$v/1$	$v/3$	$v/5$	Total
A	36 (1)	12 (4)	7.2	2
B	30 (2)	10		1
C	14 (3)	4.67		1
D	12 (5)	4		1
E	8			0

[a]The electoral quota is 100/5 = 20.
[b]The numbers in parentheses indicate the sequential order of the allocation of seats.

The reason for the disproportionality of d'Hondt now becomes clear. The remaining votes that it disregards are a relatively small portion of the votes of the larger parties but a very large portion of the small parties' votes — and, of course, the entire vote total of a party that does not receive any seats. As a result, the seat shares of the larger parties will tend to be systematically higher than their vote shares, and the smaller parties will tend to receive seat shares that are systematically below their vote shares. In contrast, the largest remainder method treats large and small parties equally: The initial allocation of seats is exactly proportional, and small and large parties compete for the remaining seats on an equal basis.

Sainte-Laguë

Like d'Hondt, the Sainte-Laguë formula is a highest average method but, in Sainte-Laguë's original proposal, the divisors are the odd integers 1, 3, 5, and so forth, instead of the d'Hondt divisors 1, 2, 3, and so forth (for an English translation of his article, written in 1910, see Lijphart and Gibberd, 1977, pp. 241–242). Table 10.1 illustrates this method of translating votes into seats. The Sainte-Laguë formula can also be interpreted as a variant of the largest remainder method in that it tries to find a quota that it considers more suitable than the Hare quota. Unlike d'Hondt, however, it aims to be completely proportional and even-handed as between large and small parties. The Sainte-Laguë quota equals twice the last of the "averages" to which a seat is given. In Table 10.1, for example, it is 24. For each quota of votes the parties receive 1 seat, and all remaining votes of half a quota or more are also honored. Party A with 36 votes receives 1 seat for its first 24 votes and a second seat for its remainder of 12 votes, which is exactly half of the Sainte-Laguë quota. Party C's remaining votes are 14, more than half of the quota and hence good for a remaining seat.

The crucial difference between d'Hondt and Sainte-Laguë is that the latter does honor some of the remainders. If all remainders were honored with a seat, a strong bias in favor of the small parties would result—just as the d'Hondt rule of ignoring all remainders entails a bias against the small parties. By setting a boundary of half a quota above which remainders do, and below which they do not, qualify for a seat, Sainte-Laguë treats all parties in an even-handed manner. In this respect, it resembles the largest remainder formula, and both have to be regarded as equally proportional. In most cases, they also yield exactly the same results (as in Table 10.1), but this is not necessarily always the case.

In practice, the Sainte-Laguë formula is not used in its original and pure form. The Scandinavian countries use a modified formula in which the first divisor is raised to 1.4 in order to make it more difficult for small parties to win a first seat. The divisor series 1.4, 3, 5, and so forth, can be made comparable to the d'Hondt and pure Sainte-Laguë divisors by dividing each of these divisors by 1.4. The modified Sainte-Laguë divisor series can therefore also be stated as 1, 2.14, 3.57, 5.00, 6.43, and so forth. It is clear that the distance between these divisors is greater than in the d'Hondt series but smaller than in the pure Sainte-Laguë series. The modified Sainte-Laguë formula is therefore less proportional than the pure form—and hence also less proportional than largest remainders—but more proportional than d'Hondt.

It should be noted that, as Rosensweig (1981; see also Grofman, 1975, p. 316) has pointed out, this conclusion also applies to the chance that a small party has to win its first seat. The 1.4 divisor makes modified Sainte-Laguë less proportional than pure Sainte-Laguë, but it would have to be raised to 1.5 to be equivalent to d'Hondt as far as the winning of the first seat is concerned. Hence Rae (1971, p. 34) is mistaken when he argues that modified Sainte-Laguë entails a "higher cost of the initial seat" than d'Hondt, and Taylor and Johnston (1979, p. 67) erroneously state that modified Sainte-Laguë is "relatively more severe on small parties" than d'Hondt. Elder (1975, p. 187) commits the same error.

The relative proportionality of the three PR formulas considered so far can be summarized as follows, with the proviso that here and henceforth Sainte-Laguë signifies the modified formula as used in Scandinavia:

1. Largest remainders
2. Sainte-Laguë
3. D'Hondt

The Single-Transferable Vote

The difficulty of comparing STV with these three formulas is that in STV systems the voters cast their votes for individual candidates instead of for party lists. There are two ways to solve this problem. One is to assume that all voters will vote for the candidates of only one party, so that intraparty, but no interparty, transfers will take place. Under such conditions, the STV rules become virtually equivalent to those of the largest remainder formula. The second solution is to look at the votes in the final round of counting, which is the basis on which the seats are allocated. Applying the largest remainder rule to this final count will yield the same results in all but very exceptional circumstances.

There is one important difference between the largest remainder formula and STV: The former uses the Hare quota while the latter normally uses the Droop quota, defined as the total number of votes divided by the total number of seats plus one—$v/(s + 1)$—and then usually rounded up to the next higher integer. The consequence of using the Droop instead of the Hare quota as well as its relationship with the d'Hondt formula is stated succinctly in one of the oldest treatises on PR by Humphreys. After discussing the largest remainder method, Humphreys writes:

> The rule subsequently devised aimed at reducing the importance of remainders in the allotment of seats. The total of each list was divided by the number of seats plus one. This method yielded a smaller quota than the original rule and enabled more seats to be allotted at the first distribution. The final improvement, however, took the form of devising a rule which should so allot the seats to different parties that after the first distribution there should be no seats remaining unallotted. This is the great merit of the Belgian or d'Hondt rule (Humphreys, 1911, p. 188).

Humphreys's comment makes clear that the Droop quota is lower than the Hare quota but higher than the d'Hondt quota. The Droop quota and STV based on it are therefore less proportional than the largest remainder method with the Hare quota, since it honors fewer remainders, but more proportional than d'Hondt, since it usually does honor some remainders. In order to rank it among the three previously ranked formulas, we also have to compare it with Sainte-Laguë. Unfortunately, no unambiguous relative placement is possible here; it depends on the numbers of parties, the number of seats, and the sizes of the small parties. If there are small parties that would be barred from representation by the 1.4-divisor, the Droop quota is more favorable; it should be remembered that the 1.4-divisor makes Sainte-Laguë almost like d'Hondt as far as the first seats are concerned. Once the small parties have gained their first seats, however, Sainte-Laguë becomes more favorable to them, because it is, from this point on, completely proportional.

With this reservation, we can now rank the four methods as follows:

1. Largest remainders
2. Single-transferable vote   ⎤
3. Sainte-Laguë   ⎦ overlapping
4. D'Hondt

The Imperiali Formulas

Two other formulas—variously referred to as the "Imperiali" and "Imperial" formulas—have been discussed in the literature on electoral systems. One is the Imperiali largest remainder formula (Rae, 1971, pp. 34–36; Grofman, 1975, p. 309; Wertman, 1977, pp. 45–47; Brew, 1981, p. 420), and the other is the Imperiali highest average formula (Van den Bergh, 1955, p. 25; Nohlen, 1978, p. 78; Laakso, 1979, p. 162).

The distinctive feature of the Imperiali largest remainder method is that it uses a quota that is lower than the Hare and Droop quotas. It equals the total number of votes divided by the total number of seats plus 2: $v/(s + 2)$. As it is used in Italy, its other special characteristic is that the remaining votes and seats are not handled at the district level but gathered into a national pool. For our purposes, it is important to recognize that the Imperiali quota is lower, and hence less proportional, than the Droop quota but usually higher and more proportional than the d'Hondt quota. It is incorrect to state, as Rae (1971, p. 34) does, that Imperiali is a variant of the largest remainder formula "intended to lower the price of the initial seats, helping weak parties." Similarly, Wertman (1977, p. 45) is mistaken when he argues that the $(s + 2)$ denominator "lowers the quota and thus increases the small parties' chances to gain seats in the Chamber of Deputies." As Carstairs (1980, p. 159) points out, the quota used in the 1948 and 1953 Italian elections was even lower than the Imperiali quota: $v/(s + 3)$ instead of $v/(s + 2)$. The change to the higher quota was "made in response to the demands of the smaller parties": The denominator "used for calculating the quota of votes necessary for election was reduced from seats *plus three* to seats *plus two*. This meant that there would be more remaining seats to be allocated."

A more difficult question is what the relative ranking of Imperiali and Sainte-Laguë is. The answer is analogous to the relationship that we found between the Droop quota and Sainte-Laguë. With regard to the first seats, Sainte-Laguë behaves very much like d'Hondt and is therefore less proportional than Imperiali, although the Imperiali quota is usually close to the d'Hondt quota. After the first seats have been obtained, Imperiali obviously becomes much less proportional than Sainte-Laguë. In the overall ranking, the former should therefore be placed below the latter, but with the proviso that there is some overlap.

The second Imperiali formula is completely different from the first, in spite of the similarity of the name. It is a form of highest averages that looks deceptively similar to d'Hondt since it uses the divisors 2, 3, 4, 5, and so forth; the crucial exception is that the first divisor of 1 is omitted. In order to make these divisors comparable to the d'Hondt divisors, they have to be divided by 2. The Imperiali divisors then become 1, 1.5, 2, 2.5, 3, 3.5, and so forth. It is immediately clear that, because the distance between the divisors is much smaller than in d'Hondt, the Imperiali highest average formula is considerably less proportional than d'Hondt. In the example of Table 10.1, Imperiali would give party *A* 3 seats, instead of the 2 awarded under the d'Hondt rule, and it would take away party *C*'s 1 seat.[1,2]

Our final ranking, including the two Imperiali formulas, is as follows:

1. Largest remainders
2. Single-transferable vote ⎤ overlapping
3. Sainte-Laguë ⎦ ⎤
4. Imperiali largest remainders ⎦ overlapping
5. D'Hondt
6. Imperiali highest averages

Notes

1. A formula that is also sometimes compared with the other PR formulas is the so-called "Danish method" (Laakso, 1979, p. 162). It is a highest average formula that uses the divisors 1, 4, 7, 10, and so forth. The distance between the divisors is greater than in the pure Sainte-Laguë method, and the Danish method would therefore be even more favorable to small parties. I have not included it in my ranking for two reasons. (1) It would have to be ranked above the largest remainder formula because it favors the small parties more. However, this characteristic derives not from the basic proportionality of the formula, as in the case of the largest remainder and pure Sainte-Laguë formulas, but from the fact that the Danish method is *disproportionally* favorable for small parties. (2) In Denmark, this method is not used for the translation of votes into seats: It "has nothing to do with the allocation of supplementary seats among parties. It is solely related to the geographic distribution *within* parties over regions and constituencies" (Johansen, 1979, p. 47).

2. There are two crucial qualifications that must be added to the above ranking of PR formulas according to proportionality.

   First, the proportionality of PR systems is not only a function of the kind of formula that is used. A more important factor is the magnitude of the electoral district. As James Hogan has forcefully pointed out, "the decisive point in PR is the size of the constituencies: the larger the constituency, that is, the greater the number of members which it elects, the more closely will the result approximate to proportionality. On the other hand, the smaller the constituency, that is, the fewer the number of members which it returns, the more radical will be the departure from proportionality" (Hogan, 1945, p. 13).

   Second, although I find that the largest remainder formula is the most proportional of the six, my conclusion should not be read as meaning that it is therefore also the "best" method. One may be in favor of PR without wanting to maximize proportionality. A special disadvantage of largest remainders is that it may give rise to the Alabama paradox: the phenomenon that a party would lose a seat if the total number of seats available in the district would be increased (Brams, 1976, pp. 137–166). This problem does not occur in any of the highest average systems, since these allocate seats sequentially. If one should want to maximize proportionality while avoiding the Alabama paradox, the pure Sainte-Laguë formula is preferable to largest remainders. However, both methods suffer from a more serious weakness: They may encourage party splits. In the example of largest remainders in Table 10.1, party *B* could win an additional seat, at the expense of party *D*, if it would present two separate lists, each of which would get 15 votes. Pure Sainte-Laguë would have the same effect. This tendency declines as PR formulas become less proportional, and it disappears entirely under the d'Hondt rule—certainly a very powerful argument in favor of this not maximally proportional formula (cf. Balinski and Young, 1983).

PART **III**

Evaluating the Impact of Electoral Laws: Plurality Systems

CHAPTER 11

The Geography of Representation: A Review of Recent Findings

Peter J. Taylor, Graham Gudgin, and R. J. Johnston

Because political representation in most countries is organized on a territorial basis, it has attracted the attention of geographers as a research topic. Sauer (1918), for instance, suggested that congressional districts should be designed around geographic regions; and Bunge (1966), reflecting a new theoretical geography, recommended hexagons as the solution to the districting problem. As part of the tendency toward quantification in geography there were contributions from geographers on measuring compactness (Schwartzberg, 1966) and in designing region-building algorithms to produce constituencies (Cope, 1971). These technical contributions have been of minimal relevance to our understanding of political representation, however. More recently, emphasis has moved from pattern to process in an attempt to identify the mechanisms that operate to produce alternative representations. It is this latter research which is reviewed here.

The starting point of this research has been to study elections as consisting of the interaction between two spatial distributions: the pattern of votes and the network of constituency boundaries. This then leads on to the districting problem of single-member district plurality elections that states that different locations of boundaries will likely produce different election results in terms of seats won by a party even when the distribution of the party's vote remains constant

(Taylor, 1973). It is this phenomenon that makes gerrymandering a possibility, of course. Much recent work on the geography of representation has set out to explore this problem. In what follows we will present a list of "findings" emanating from this work. Some are already familiar to students of politics (although they may appear here in more precise form), while others seem to be new and in some cases quite surprising. It is from among the latter that political geography can claim to have made a distinctive contribution to debates on political representation.

The Distribution of Party Voters

If a party's vote proportion over a set of districts is arrayed as a frequency distribution of districts by vote proportions, then the *shape* of the frequency distribution will directly affect the number of seats won by the party. Many of the succeeding findings refine this general statement in terms of, first, what mechanisms produce the shape and, second, what aspects of the shape produce different effects. This basic distribution is referred to as the "constituency proportion distribution" (CPD) (Gudgin and Taylor, 1974; 1979, pp. 13–20).

The CPD can be modeled as the outcome of a Markov probability process which generates a normal distribution. This is particularly interesting because of numerous empirical observations that CPDs are sometimes normal in shape (Gudgin and Taylor, 1979, pp. 20–36). A normal CPD implies a seat-vote relationship very close to a power law of the form.

$$S = V^k/(V^k + (1-V)^k)$$

where S and V are a party's seat and vote proportions, respectively. When $k=3$, we have the well-known cubic law of seat proportions or "cube law." For a plurality single-member district system this occurs when the standard deviation of the normal distribution is 0.137 or 0.133 (depending on the approximation used for matching the power law to the normal distribution). Between 1945 and 1970 the standard deviation for the major parties in British general elections ranged from 0.135 to 0.149, which explains why the cube law seemed to "work" in Britain (Gudgin and Taylor, 1979, pp. 26–30).

The Markov model can be interpreted as a model of the voting process as the outcome of the interaction of four spatial components. The size of the constitutency will directly determine the degree of mixing of party voters. If we assume that voters are segregated by

TABLE 11.1. A Selection of Alternative Combinations of Spatial Components for Producing the "Cube Law"

Size of Constituency (Voters)	Size of Areal Clusters	No. of Clusters per Constituency	Homogeneity of Clusters[a]	Spatial Autocorrelation of Clusters[b]	Std. Dev. of CPD
60,000	500	120	0.7	0.983	0.137
15,000	6,000	2.3	0.7	0.543	0.137
250,000	12,000	20.83	0.7	0.908	0.137
60,000	500	120	0.6	0.996	0.137
60,000	6,000	10	0.9	0.543	0.137

[a]Proportion of voters for cluster's majority party.
[b]Probability of neighboring clusters supporting same party.

party of support into areal "clusters" of voters representing one or other party, then the larger the constituency the more clusters and hence more chance of including a range of different clusters. This relation will obviously also depend upon the size of the areal clusters. The larger the clusters, the less per constituency and hence the less potential for mixing. The key relationship is the number of clusters per constituency.

The clusters may also vary in terms of voter homogeneity. This will depend upon the nature of the party system and its relationship to the processes of residential segregation operating (e.g., by class, ethnic group, or religion). Under some situations the clusters may not be very solid, say 60% support for the cluster party, whereas in other cases 80 or 90% solidarity may be achieved for a party in a cluster of voters. Obviously the effect of mixing clusters will depend upon this cluster homogeneity. The pattern of the cluster will also be important. If like clusters are found close to one another (which we will term *spatial autocorrelation*) to produce large patches of clusters, then this will lessen the possibilities of the mixing of clusters within districts.

Alternative combinations of these four spatial components will generate different CPDs. Table 11.1 shows 6 alternative ways in which a CPD with a standard deviation of 0.137, the cube law, may be produced.

Which particular combination of spatial components will produce a cube law or any other power law can only be derived empirically. In such a study of four Newcastle upon Tyne constituencies for the February 1974 election the following parameters applied:

Number of Clusters per Constituency   =   45
Proportion of Votes for Cluster Party   =   0.7

Spatial Autocorrelation of Clusters   =   0.94
Derived Standard Deviation of CPD   =   0.118

These results imply a power law of about 3.3 rather than the cube law (Gudgin and Taylor, 1979, pp. 39–54).

Malapportionment will affect the results for a party only insofar that its support is overrepresented in either large or small constituencies. A party's *effective* vote in an election is its average vote proportion per constituency, *not* its direct proportion of the overall vote. The difference between these two values is a measure of the malapportionment effect on a particular party. Rowley (1970) has shown the existence of malapportionment effects in recent British elections (Taylor and Gudgin, 1976a; 1979, pp. 55–59).

When the swing between two parties over a pair of elections is not uniform, this will change the shape of the resulting CPD. A uniform swing implies a distribution of constituency swings with a standard deviation of zero. Empirical investigation shows actual deviations to range from 0.014 to 0.037 in Britain (1945–1974), 0.051 to 0.056 in the United States (1952–1960), 0.020 to 0.029 in New Zealand (1957–1975), to a very high value of 0.123 for Canada (1972–1974). The precise distortion of a CPD depends on the size of these standard deviations and their relationship to the distribution of party votes (Gudgin and Taylor, 1979, pp. 59–61). When the relationship between swing and party votes is random, its effect on a normal CPD is to increase the standard deviation. For instance, a normal distribution's standard deviation of 0.137 is changed to 0.146 by a nonuniform random swing with a standard deviation of 0.05. This, in effect, converts a cube law to a power law of 2.74 (Gudgin and Taylor, 1979, pp. 61–63).

In order to prevent an increase in CPD standard deviations, a slight negative association between swing and party vote is required. In Britain with its swing standard deviations of the order of 0.02, the CPD can be maintained with swing-vote correlations of the order of −0.014, whereas the United States when its swing standard deviation was of the order of 0.05, required a correlation of −0.035. A positive swing-vote relation will, on the other hand, accentuate the increasing standard deviation of the CPD. How far this process may account for part of the general increase in CPD standard deviations has not been researched (Gudgin and Taylor, 1979, pp. 63–64).

Empirical CPDs are, of course, never exactly normal. Two deviations from normality can be identified. A skewed CPD means that the two major parties are treated unequally by the seats-votes relationship. A positively skewed CPD will result when a party has an overconcentration of supporters in a few constituencies. In this situation these excess votes are wasted and the party is at a disadvantage due to the spatial distribution of its support. This is typically the fate of left-wing parties whose support is concentrated in industrial zones. The degree of kurtosis of the CPD directly relates to the "peakedness" of the distribution and hence may affect the number of seats changing hands for a given swing independent of the CPD standard deviation. Platykurtic ("flat") CPDs will tend to produce stability across elections. The classic case of this is the current bimodel CPD for U.S. congressional elections (Gudgin and Taylor, 1974; Ibid., 1979, pp. 65–73; Morrissey and Johnston, 1984).

This approach to studying seats-votes relations through the CPD can be used to provide a decomposition of the electoral bias (the difference between seat and vote proportions). For a party that wins an election we may state that its electoral bias equals the malapportionment effect, plus turnout effect, plus minor party effect, plus the interaction of these effects, plus a cube law winner's bias, plus additional normal segregation, plus a nonnormality effect. For the British Conservative party in 1979 these terms were, respectively,

$$0.0162 = -0.0113 + 0.0021 + 0.0080 - 0.0061 + 0.0650 - 0.0191 - 0.0224$$

(Taylor and Gudgin, 1976a; Johnston 1976a, b; Gudgin and Taylor, 1981). For three-party elections an electoral triangle can be employed to show the distribution of vote proportions for each party. The "shape" of these two-dimension distributions within the triangle determines the seat-vote relation (Gudgin and Taylor, 1979, pp. 93–96). For the third (minor) party the larger the standard deviation of its vote proportions the lower the overall vote threshold required for representation. With a standard deviation of 0.137, seats are picked up with about 10% of the vote; for 0.05 about 25% of the vote is required; and for a zero standard deviation no seats are won until 33.3% of the vote is won by the party (Gudgin and Taylor, 1979, pp. 103–105).

For the third (minor) party the larger the standard deviation of its vote proportions the more rapid its growth in seats once it passes its vote threshold. With a zero standard deviation it becomes the largest party immediately after it passes an average of 33.3% of the overall vote, whereas with a standard deviation of 0.137 it only reaches that status with 38% of the overall vote (Gudgin and Taylor, 1979, pp. 102–103). It is better for the minor party to attract votes in equal amounts from the two major parties. For instance, the effect of attracting 80% of its new votes from one major party lessens the effectiveness of the third party's seat winning potential by the equivalent of about 3% of the vote. This means that it will win approximately the same number of seats with 37% of the vote and equal attraction from both major parties as with 40% of the vote and 80% of its votes gained from one major party (Gudgin and Taylor, 1979, pp. 99–102).

In empirical studies of election triangles for Britain it is the Conservative party that consistently suffers most with a Liberal revival. For example, when the overall vote is split evenly at 33.3% to each of the three parties (Liberals attracting new votes equally from Labour and Conservative), seat proportions are predicted as follows: Labour 0.44, Conservatives 0.28, and Liberals 0.28 (Gudgin and Taylor, 1979, pp. 109–116).

The Distribution of Constituency Boundaries

The districting problem reflects the fact that there are many different combinations of base units that may make up an electoral district. With no constraints except equal numbers of base units per district, the number of combinations of n base-units to produce m districts is given by

$$n!/(m(n/m)!m!)$$

With 20 base-units to be divided into 4 districts of 5 units each, this comes to 24,310 solutions! The addition of a continguity constriant on the solutions will reduce this number. For Newcastle upon Tyne 20 wards combine into 334 solutions of contiguous patterns of 4 constituencies, for example. The reduction is dramatic, but many "feasible" solutions remain (Taylor and Gudgin, 1975; 1976b; Gudgin and Taylor, 1979, pp. 140–143; Johnston and Rossiter, 1981b).

In problems involving generation of just two districts, an interesting finding emerges. All solutions may be arranged along a scale that measures the degree of polarization between the two districts. High polarization means districts are very different in their levels of party support. It so happens that the aggregation effect tends to produce more low-polarization solutions than high-polarization solutions. Hence nonpartisan districting agencies (boundary commissions and neutral computer districting) will usually choose a low-polarization solution simply because these are the most common. However, partisan gerrymanderers for the overall majority party will also choose low-polarization solutions because these will provide majority party victories in both districts. The converse is that bipartisan districting agencies (such as state electoral commissions or bipartisan computer districtors) will tend to produce highly polarized solutions like partisan gerrymanderers for the minority party (in order to win one district). Clearly, not the procedural intention but the political effect is what is important: Nonpartisan districting is equivalent to partisan gerrymandering for the majority party; bipartisan districting is equivalent to partisan gerrymandering for the minority party (Taylor and Gudgin, 1976b; Gudgin and Taylor, 1979, pp. 146–154).

Extension of this finding to more than two district problems is difficult, as the relationship between polarization and party fortunes becomes much more complicated. Nevertheless, a very frequent electoral result can be found from among the different solutions, and just such a solution was found to be chosen by boundary commissioners for Newcastle upon Tyne and by partisan gerrymanderers for the state of Iowa (Taylor and Gudgin, 1976b; Gudgin and Taylor, 1979, pp. 154–160; O'Loughlin and Taylor, 1982; Johnston and Rossiter, 1982). Application of this methodology of finding all feasible solutions to British cities has, in addition, shown that the boundary commissioners are very partial to compact solutions even though they are not obliged to enact a compactness or shape rule. In twelve separate problems the boundary commissions chose the most compact solution on five occasions and the second or third on another three occasions. In each problem there were several hundred feasible solutions (Johnston and Rossiter, 1981a, b).

Alternative Voting Systems

In voting systems that use a majority rather than a plurality criterion for election by district (alternative vote in Australia, and double ballot in France), the election triangle can be employed to define "winning regions" for each party. These can be defined on the basis of second preferences or second votes. In this way it can be shown that the Australian Labour party has a far smaller winning region than has the Liberal party, hence accounting for its dearth of electoral success (Taylor and Gudgin, 1977; Gudgin and Taylor, 1979, pp. 165–176).

With the single-transferable vote system the spatial organization of the election affects the results through the choice of the number of seats per constituency. The ideal situation is to have an even number of seats in constituencies where your party is relatively weak so that you share the spoils and, conversely, to have an odd number where your party is strong and can win a majority of seats. These abuses are well-known in Ireland (Paddison, 1976; Gudgin and Taylor, 1979, pp. 176–188; Mair, this volume).

The additional member system as used in the German Federal Republic is a mixture of single-member districts and a proportional representation list system (Kaase, 1985, forthcoming; Irvine, 1984). Biases can still occur because seats won in the constituency section are kept as "bonus seats" even if they produce a nonproportional result overall. The likelihood of this occurring can be modeled using the CPD. For instance, under the Hansard Society's (1976) proposals for British parliamentary reform the Labour party would have 3% bonus seats if it won 40% of the vote under cube law assumptions (Gudgin and Taylor, 1979, pp. 188–195).

From Representation to Power

Most arguments for electoral reform have been aimed at achieving some form of equity in the context of Mill's famous dictum, "one man, one vote; one vote, one value." In the United States, for example, the "reapportionment revolution" of the 1960s equalized voting power in terms of one man, one vote. In Great Britain for many decades, and especially again since about 1974, substantial arguments have been presented for the adoption of a proportional representation electoral system which would ensure equity according to the one-vote, one-value demand. Under the single-member constituency, plurality voting system electoral bias has been considerable (O'Loughlin, 1980; Rae, 1971); a majority in Parliament has been "manufactured" at each election, since no party has achieved a majority of the votes, and small parties—especially those lacking a clear regional or sectional base—have achieved much smaller proportions of seats than of votes.

The claims of electoral reformers regarding the greater "fairness" of a proportional representation electoral system have been analyzed. The results of these analyses make it very clear that "proportional representation" cannot be equated with "proportional power." With the use of game theoretic approaches to the study of bargaining power in coalitions (Laver, 1981), it has been shown that "fair representation" (Balinski and Young, 1982a, 1983) is rarely, if indeed ever, translated into a fair distribution of bargaining power. Studies of various E.E.C. institutions (notably the Council of Ministers and the European Assembly) have shown the impossibility of allocating votes to the member countries which are both fair in terms of the ratio of votes to population (the one-man, one-vote requirement) and fair in terms of the ratio of bargaining power to voters (the one-vote, one-value requirement). Because of the configuration of votes, some countries have (relative to their size) much more bargaining power—that is, the ability to influence the policy of a viable coalition having a majority of the votes—than do others. Recent analyses have shown that in some circumstances it is possible to establish a majority level—at 55% of the votes cast in Parliament, say—at which bargaining power is relatively equal. Establishment of this level in a partisan-dominated Parliament could be undertaken only after each election, however (Johnston 1977a, 1983a, 1983b; Johnston and Hunt, 1977; Taylor and Johnston, 1978, 1979).

The distribution of bargaining power among parties can be extremely volatile, with only relatively small shifts in the allocation of seats. This was illustrated by simulations of a potential Welsh Parliament, with four parties. Changes in the allocation of only a few seats among the parties (presumably resulting from shifts in the distribution of votes, and hence "fair" in the context of proportional representation) created major shifts in their relative bargaining power (Johnston, 1979b, 1982a).

Many blocs of votes are themselves "coalitions" involving separate views on particular matters. Each country's delegation to the European Assembly comprises members of separate party groups, for example. Certain votes may be taken on party rather than on national lines, so that each country's power within the European Assembly is a combination of, first, its power in the individual party groups and, secondly, the power of those party groups in the Assembly as a whole. Such "dual-level" bargaining further distorts the relationship between representation and power (Johnston, 1977b).

In a single-member constituency system such as Britain's, the achievement of "one man, one vote" via equality of electorates can considerably distort the relative power of groups within the constituencies, notably those on which the major electoral cleavages are based. There may, for example, be two parties competing for votes in a system, across three social groups. One group may traditionally support party *A*, whereas another traditionally supports party *B*. The third group, with 15% of the votes overall, may have no stable allegiance. Depending on the geography of the system—where the third group lives and where the constituency boundaries are—the third group may be extremely influential (its votes control the result in a majority of the constituencies), or it may have very little bargaining power (Johnston, 1977c, 1979a). Thus "positive gerrymandering," such as that undertaken to ensure representation for black electors in the

United States (Morrill, 1981; O'Loughlin, 1982a), need not necessarily be the most sensible allocation of voting power to those groups; it all depends on the total social configuration of the constituencies (Johnston, 1982a).

In many national Parliaments, the parties are ranged on a left-right continuum, and coalition formation is constrained by relative positions on this continuum. Not only does this virtually ensure a "centrist" coalition so that parties on the extremes of the continuum have much less bargaining power than representation, it also means that parties (and groups within parties or even groups of parties) can wield considerable power over such coalitions if they are prepared to depart from the traditional continuum; nationalist parties, national groups within parties, and nationalist groups from several parties can benefit from such action (Holler, 1982; Johnston, 1977c, 1982a; Laver, 1981; Laver and Underhill, 1982).

Conclusions

Election results are determined not just by the quantity of votes returned to each party but also by the spatial distribution of those votes and the location of constituency boundaries around them. The interaction of these factors produces the distribution of seats within a Parliament, and that distribution in turn determines the distribution of power among parties, groups of voters, and places. Elections and their outcomes involve interactions among people, *places*, and votes: these paragraphs briefly review investigations by political geographers of those interactions during the last decade.

CHAPTER 12

Social Choice and Pluralitylike Electoral Systems

Peter C. Fishburn

The purpose of this chapter is to consider the analysis of alternative electoral systems for large-scale elections, especially those in which more than two viable candidates compete for a single office. Our discussion is motivated by two axioms of political behavior. (1) Different election procedures can affect not only the conduct and outcomes of elections, but might also influence basic political structures. (2) Politically powerful individuals are often wary of proposed electoral changes and will strongly oppose proposed changes that they perceive to be inimical to their interests. I call attention to two implications of these axioms.

First, in a society whose powerful individuals or political parties are more or less satisfied with present electoral procedures, it is extremely difficult to institute significant changes in these procedures. This conclusion is borne out by historical evidence. For example, the electoral college method of choosing a president of the United States has remained intact for many decades despite periodic attempts to change the presidential election system. Another example is provided by two three-candidate senatorial elections in New York. In 1970, James Buckley defeated Charles Goodell and Richard Ottinger by a plurality of 39% to 24 and 37%, respectively, despite the likelihood that either Goodell or Ottinger would have beaten Buckley in a direct majority contest between the two (Stratmann, 1974; Brams and Fishburn, 1978, 1983). Although many observers were dissatisfied with the plurality voting method used in that election, the system was not changed. Then, in 1980, Alphonse D'Amato defeated Elizabeth Holtzman and Jacob Javits by a plurality of 45% to 44 and 11%, respectively, though the polls indicated that Holtzman would have easily beaten D'Amato if Javits had not been a candidate.

The second implication of axioms (1) and (2) is that if a proposed change is to have a significant chance of being adopted, it must be examined from a number of perspectives and shown to be superior to the status quo system for most, if not all, of these perspectives. Otherwise, powers who are comfortable with the present system and, rightly or wrongly, fear the effects of the proposed change, will often be able to sway the tide their way.

Elsewhere (Fishburn, 1983) I have identified twelve dimensions of election procedures that deserve close examination in any serious attempt to supplant one electoral system by another. I will review several of these briefly so as to give an idea of what is entailed by the task of comparing different systems.[1] The next section of this paper then notes several pluralitylike electoral systems that either enjoy widespread use or could be serious contenders to present systems. In particular, I focus on plurality, plurality-with-runoff, and approval voting, although other methods will be mentioned. I then discuss selected dimensions among the twelve on which these pluralitylike systems have been compared. The highlighted dimensions involve candidate and voter strategies, evaluative factors of aggregation procedures, and effects on institutions.

Ballots, or vote-expression mechanisms, can affect elections. Obvious examples are open versus secret ballots and voting machines versus paper ballots. Less obvious factors are the order in which candidates are listed on ballots and, for sequential-elimination procedures, the order in which candidates are voted on. The *ballot response profile* identifies how ballots are recorded for tallying. More complex election procedures often require more detailed response profiles for the purpose of computing the winner. The *ballot aggregator* defines the specific counting procedure that is used to determine the winner from the ballot response profile. For practical reasons, aggregators must not allow ties unless they also have tie-breaking provisions.

Casual reflection shows that the various aspects of election procedures can intertwine in numerous ways. In particular, the ballot aggregator can directly affect candidate and voter strategies, ballot form and responsible profile, and costs and may well interact with the other dimensions. The ensuing discussion is organized around different balloting and aggregation methods.

Plurality and Related Systems

A plurality system is one in which each eligible voter either abstains from voting, or votes for one candidate. The candidate with the most votes wins. Since ties are extremely rare in large-scale elections conducted by plurality and closely related systems, they will be ignored here.

The only system besides plurality that is used extensively in the United States is the two-ballot plurality-with-runoff system (also known as the double-ballot system). The first ballot is like the plurality ballot. If one candidate gets at least 40% (or perhaps 50%) of the votes on the first ballot, then the candidate with the most votes wins, and there is no runoff. Otherwise, there is a simple-majority runoff ballot between the two candidates who receive the most votes on the first ballot. This system appears most often in primary elections where three or more candidates compete for a place on the ballot in the general election.

Plurality and plurality-with-runoff are sometimes referred to as nonranked systems since neither asks voters to rank-order candidates on the first (or only) ballot. By contrast, preferential voting systems (including the method of single-transferable votes, which is used for some major elections in Australia, Ireland, and South Africa) requires voters to order the candidates from most preferred to least preferred. Its ballot response profile shows how many voters have each best-to-worst order of candidates. In some situations, preferential voting is used to elect two or more candidates to seats in a legislature on the basis of the ballot response profile by means of a sequence of vote transfers as described, for example, in Fishburn and Brams (1983) and Hare (1861). If only one candidate is to be elected and if there are only two or three viable candidates among the nominees, then majority-preferential voting is virtually tantamount to plurality-with-runoff. The obvious differences are that preferential voting requires voters to order the candidates and never needs a second ballot. Excepting these differences, later remarks about plurality-with-runoff also apply to preferential voting for a single office when there are three or fewer strong contenders.

I shall focus henceforth on nonranked systems, in part because they are so widely used and in part because they are simple for voters to understand. Moreover, they are the most elementary systems from the standpoint of ballots, response profiles, and aggregators. Non-ranked systems that use a single ballot, like the plurality system, entail similar costs, while plurality-with-runoff and other multiple-ballot systems may cost substantially more.

Two other single-ballot nonranked systems are the double-plurality and approval voting systems. Double plurality requires each nonabstaining voter to vote for two candidates, which would usually be his first and second choices. The candidate with the most votes wins. In a field of many candidates, double plurality seeks to gather more information about voters' preferences than does plurality, although it makes no distinction between first and second choices. It also seeks to correct the wasted-vote problem of plurality that arises when a voter's first choice is an unpopular candidate who has no chance of winning.

Approval voting (Brams and Fishburn, 1978, 1983) allows each voter to vote for any number of candidates. The voter does not rank the candidates he votes for, and each of these candidates receives a full vote from the voter. The candidate with the most votes wins. If it is true that voters vote for the candidates they approve of, then approval voting elects the candidate who is approved of by the most voters. Like double plurality, approval voting avoids the wasted-vote problem of the plurality system. In particular, a voter can always vote for his favorite without penalty: If his favorite is unpopular, he can vote for one or more others who have better chances.

There are other single-ballot nonranked systems, but the three just sketched will suffice for our present discussion. There are also numerous multiple-ballot nonranked systems besides plurality-with-runoff, including double plurality and approval voting with runoffs. However, since none of these has been shown to have significant advantages in large-scale elections over plurality-with-runoff or the single-ballot systems, I shall not consider them further.

Thus, ensuing remarks focus on the three single-ballot systems and on plurality-with-runoff. Aspects of some of the twelve dimensions identified in Fishburn (1983) for these systems have already been touched on. Others will be considered in the next section.

Dimensional Analysis and Comparisons

In this section we shall concentrate on the dimensions involving strategy, evaluative aspects, and effects on institutions.

Candidate Strategy

Granberg and Brent (1980) discuss how candidates use polling data to determine where people stand on issues, and how they try to manage voters' impressions. Allocation of campaign funds for optimal effect is considered by Brams and Davis (1974), Shane (1977), and Young (1978), among others. Beginning with Downs (1957), an extensive literature has emerged on candidates' chances of being elected as a function of their issue positions and the distribution of voters over the issues.

Much of this work has concentrated on plurality elections between two candidates. When different election systems and three or more contenders are considered, variations in candidate strategy arise. Under plurality voting, the main objective of a viable candidate is simply to get enough votes to win. In addition to persuading the uncommitted, it may be important to appeal to voters whose favorites have slim chances since a sizable fraction of one's votes might come from such voters.

Similar comments apply to double plurality and approval voting. Moreover, because of the multiple-vote feature, a strong candidate may attempt to convince supporters of other strong candidates to vote for him. There is some concern that this may encourage candidates to adopt diffuse or ambivalent issue positions, leaving voters with no substantive bases for choice, but this seems unlikely since it is doubtful that bland candidates would gather enough support to surpass candidates with more definitive positions. We presently lack both theoretical models and election experience to assess the effects of multiple-vote systems on candidate strategies. However, experience pertaining to the initial ballots in plurality-with-runoff elections may provide clues for this.

Plurality-with-runoff adds a new—and significant—wrinkle because of its emphasis on making the runoff. Four interrelated aims operate here: to win outright on the first ballot, to prevent someone else from winning outright, to come in at least second on the initial ballot, and to ensure that one's opponent in the runoff can be beaten in that round. Depending on circumstances, one or more of these may take precedence. For example, if a candidate believes that nobody will win outright and that he is sure to make the runoff, he may try to divert some of his strength to another candidate who he feels he can defeat in the runoff. Clearly, plurality-with-runoff offers strategic possibilities not available for the single-ballot systems, not all of which are geared toward ensuring the election of the "best" candidate.

Voter Strategy

Research on voter strategy, as exemplified by Farquharson (1969),

TABLE 12.1. The Effect of Double Plurality and Approval Voting on the Wasted-Vote Problem

	Actual Vote	Estimates	
		Double Plurality	Approval Voting
Reagan	51	71	59
Carter	41	58	49
Anderson	7	71	50

Source. Brams and Fishburn, 1982.

Gibbard (1973), Pattanaik (1978), and Satterthwaite (1975), shows that virtually all voting systems involving three or more candidates have scenarios in which some voters may find it advantageous to vote contrary to their true preferences. Even if a voter does not engage in "strategic misrepresentation," he may be faced with several voting choices. We consider both possibilities for our four systems. For convenience, the common behavior of registering disinterest or disgust by abstaining will not be discussed. It should be noted, however, that different systems can encourage substantially different rates of voter participation. For example, voter participation might increase in some elections if they were conducted by approval voting rather than by plurality owing to the greater opportunity to show one's preferences on the approval-voting ballot.

Under plurality, a voter whose favorite has a fair chance of winning has a clear choice. However, if that favorite is an underdog, he will often vote strategically for another candidate he approves of who has a better chance. As we know from numerous elections, the latter effect can be substantial. For example, the popular-vote percentages in the 1980 presidential election were 51 for Ronald Reagan, 41 for Jimmy Carter, and 7 for John Anderson. Using available data from several sources, Brams and Fishburn (1982) estimated that if the same voters had voted their true preferences, then the percentages would have been about 40 for Reagan, 35 for Carter, and 24 for Anderson. Thus more than 70% of those who favored Anderson voted for either Reagan or Carter. The underdog status of Anderson nearly turned the election into a two-candidate race between Reagan and Carter.

Because double plurality and approval voting alleviate the wasted-vote problem and are much less likely than plurality to encourage strategic misrepresentation, they would have presented a rather different picture for the 1980 election (see Table 12.1). The dramatic effect here is, of course, the better showing of Anderson for the multiple-vote systems.

Double plurality has the obvious defect of forcing a voter to vote for a candidate he may dislike in order to vote for his favorite. Approval voting has an advantage in this regard since the voter is not forced to vote for a specific number of candidates. Instead, it offers an array of choices that reflect how strongly the voter feels about the various candidates. Different assumptions have led several people (Weber, 1979; Merrill, 1979; Fishburn and Brams, 1981) to the same conclusion that optimal voting strategies would have voters vote for about half of the candidates they are knowledgeable about if their preferences are spread out; but if they strongly favor only one or two candidates, then they will vote for only one or two. In addition, it is highly unlikely (Brams and Fishburn, 1978, 1983) that voters will misrepresent their preferences under approval voting in the sense of not voting for a candidate who is preferred to a candidate they vote for.

As with candidate strategies, plurality-with-runoff opens up new strategic possibilities for voters on the initial ballot. The wasted-vote problem seems less severe than for plurality, but we now face the possibility that some voters, perhaps organized for the purpose, will vote for a nonpreferred candidate that their favorite can defeat in the runoff.

Evaluative Aspects

I shall comment on only a few of the many evaluative aspects of aggregation, and on comparisons between collective decisions and social choices, that have been discussed in the literature.

Perhaps the most important of these is the propensity of a voting system to elect a candidate who best represents the desires and preferences of the voting public. While it may be true that this is of minor concern in the large number of elections that have a clear favorite who would be elected by any of our four systems, it can be crucial in close contests.

A most-representative or socially most-preferred candidate can be defined in several ways. One of these, used by Weber (1979), is based on a notion of a random society and maximization of the sum of voters' utilities or values. His analysis shows that approval voting is significantly better than plurality in electing candidates whose utility sums over the voters approach the maximum that is possible. I suspect that this is true also of approval voting versus double plurality. Weber's analysis was not designed to include runoff systems.

A decidedly different measure of representativeness is the extent to which a system elects the consensus majority candidate—who would

TABLE 12.2. Random Distribution of Voters' Preference and Consensus Majority Candidate

	Three Candidates %	Four Candidates %
Plurality	76 to 81	66 to 69
Double Plurality	72 to 74	72 to 76
Approval Voting	75 to 79	64 to 70
Plurality-with-Runoff	96 to 98	89 to 92

Source. Fishburn and Gehrlein (1982).

defeat every other candidate in face-to-face majority votes, given that such a candidate exists. Practical as well as theoretical analyses (Gehrlein, 1983) indicate that there will be consensus majority candidates in most elections of the kind considered here. Studies by Fishburn and Gehrlein (1982) give percentages, in ranges, of elections with a consensus majority candidate in which this candidate is elected when it is assumed that voters' preferences are randomly distributed, voters do not misrepresent their preferences, and nobody abstains (see Table 12.2). Under the noted assumptions, the runoff system is much better than the single-ballot systems at electing consensus majority candidates.

The picture changes considerably when abstentions are accounted for. In this case Gehrlein and Fishburn (1979) define consensus majority on the basis of the preferences of the entire electorate, including abstainers. They estimate the percentages of cases in which the consensus majority candidate is elected when there are three viable candidates (see Table 12.3). Hence, if the initial ballot for the plurality-with-runoff system has low voter participation, it may be no better than a single-ballot system at electing consensus majority candidates.

A second evaluative aspect that differentiates among our systems is the criterion which says that a winner should remain a winner when one or more voters change their votes in his favor. This monotonicity condition (Fishburn, 1982) clearly holds for the single-ballot systems, but it can fail for plurality-with-runoff. To illustrate this with an example, suppose 27 voters are divided into six groups with the following best-to-worst preference orders on candidates a, b, and c:

Order:	abc	cab	bca	bac	cba	acb
Number of Voters:	6	6	6	4	2	3

With no misrepresentation, a, b, and c receive 9, 10, and 8 votes,

TABLE 12.3. Abstentions and Consensus Majority Candidate

		Percent Turnout, Single-Ballot, or Runoff Ballot	
		50	80
Single-Ballot Systems		60	69
Runoff System:	20	60	68
percent turnout	50	66	75
for first ballot	80	70	80

Source. Gehrlein and Fishburn (1979).

respectively, on the initial ballot; so that a and b go into the runoff, where a defeats b by 15 to 12. Now suppose that 3 of the 4 *bac* voters change to *abc* and that the two *cba* voters change to *cab*. All of these changes favor a, the original winner. The new profile of preferences is

Order:	abc	cab	bca	bac	cba	acb
Number of Voters:	9	8	6	1	0	3

Now a, b, and c receive 12, 7, and 8 votes, respectively, on the initial ballot; so that a and c go into the runoff, where c defeats a by 14 to 13. Hence candidate a loses after the changes in his favor.

A third evaluative aspect concerns the degree to which each voter carries equal weight or is treated equitably by the voting system. In one sense, plurality, double plurality, and plurality-with-runoff treat voters equally since each voter casts the same number of votes in these systems. It may also appear that, under approval voting, voters are not treated equitably when they vote for different numbers of candidates. In fact, Fishburn and Brams (1981) show that this is true only when there are four or more candidates, where a slight advantage is gained by voters who vote for about half of the candidates. With only three candidates, a voter's ability to influence the collective decision is the same whether he votes for one or two candidates. Moreover, as shown by Weber (1979) and Fishburn and Brams (1981), approval voting is actually better than plurality in the sense that, on the average, it yields a greater utility to the individual voter.

Effects on Institutions

Because plurality and plurality-with-runoff have been widely used for many years in the United States, their institutional effects in this country should be well-known. Perhaps the most important effect is the tendency of these systems to perpetuate two major political parties. This is due in large measure to the wasted-vote phenomenon. The actual results of elections like the 1980 presidential election maintain the impression of two widely supported parties even when this is illusory.

Since approval voting has not been used in general elections, judgments about its institutional effects are conjectural. It appears, however, that because approval voting does not compel supporters of third-party candidates to vote only for others when they want their votes to count, third parties may find it easier to get candidates into office when approval voting is used in general elections. Although this could be to the good of society, it may be a threat to vested interests and to present institutional arrangements, so approval voting may not find ready acceptance for use in general elections. On the other hand, approval voting could strengthen the two-party system by forcing the major parties to be more responsive to the electorate's wishes if they are to remain in power. But, as already stated, this is conjectural.

The use of approval voting in party primaries with their often numerous contenders poses no immediate threat to the parties themselves, although it could be opposed by intraparty factions that fear a loss of influence. However, since it offers a simple and attractive way of assessing relative strengths of candidates within parties, it could find a measure of use in primary elections within the not-too-distant future.

Acknowledgments. I would like to express my indebtedness and thanks to Steven Brams and William Gehrlein for their collaboration on much of the research reported in this chapter.

Notes

1. As might be expected, there is a vast literature on these topics. One access to this literature is Fishburn (1983) and works cited there. Historically interesting material will be found in Black (1958), Hare (1861), and Hoag and Hallett (1926). Discussions that emphasize political, economic, sociological, and psychological aspects of collective decision making are given by Downs (1957), Lipset (1960), Campbell et al., (1960), Riker (1962), Buchanan and Tullock (1962), Olson (1965), Key (1966), Rae (1967), and Granberg and Brent (1980). Technical treatments of social choice theory include Arrow (1951), Farquharson (1969), Sen (1970), Fishburn (1973), Kelly (1978) and Pattanaik (1978). A recent and extensive analysis of the simple types of electoral systems discussed in the rest of this paper is provided by Brams and Fishburn (1983).

CHAPTER 13

The Effect of At-Large Versus District Elections on Racial Representation in U.S. Municipalities

Richard L. Engstrom and Michael D. McDonald

Whether the members of a city council should be selected through at-large, citywide elections or through geographically designated (usually single-member) districts within a city has been a major election law issue in the United States for many years. Election at large has been one of the central planks in the platform of the American municipal "reform" movement. The first model city charter issued by the National Municipal League in 1899 recommended that this electoral system be adopted in place of the single-member district or ward system used at that time; this recommendation has been retained in all subsequent editions of the model charter. At-large elections, these reformers argued, would attract a "better class" of council members and improve the quality of councilmanic decisions. Successful candidates within this system would have to appeal to more than a particular neighborhood or ethnic group, and therefore were more likely to be people of education and accomplishment (or expressed differently, wealth and social standing). These "better-qualified" councilmanic representatives were in turn expected to make decisions on the basis of what they perceived to be good for the entire city, not just one geographic or social segment of it. This combination of council members with better judgment and a citywide decisional referent, these reformers maintained, would improve dramatically the quality of municipal government (see, e.g., Judd, 1979, pp. 87–100).

The municipal reformers were remarkably successful in that their recommended electoral system was widely adopted (often in combination with a nonpartisan ballot). A survey conducted in the early 1970s of cities with populations exceeding 10,000 discovered that in over three fourths of these cities (78.2%) at least some members of the city council were elected at large; in 63.3%, the *entire* council was elected at large (Svara, 1977, p. 168). A more recent survey of the largest central cities within each standard metropolitan statistical area (SMSA) has disclosed that in 83.6% of the cities, some of the members of the council are elected at large, and in 47.0% *all* of the members are elected at large.[1] The municipal reform campaign was so successful, in fact, that for many commentators at-large elections, in combination with the nonpartisan ballot and city manager plan, became virtually synonymous with the idea of "good government" itself.

This association with good government has not been accepted by everyone, however. In recent years what might be called "a new wave of reformers" (Grofman, 1982a, p. 124) has been active, attempting to undo much of what the earlier reformers had accomplished. This second generation of reformers, unlike the first, is predominately black, and its activity has been concentrated largely within the American South.

The "new reformers" argue that cities should elect council members from districts within the city because this electoral system is much "fairer" than are at-large elections—a city council elected in this fashion is likely to be more "representative" of the municipal population. Specifically, black opponents of at-large elections complain that citywide elections are discriminatory toward the racial minorities residing within America's cities. Given the racially polarized voting patterns often found in American cities, the black minority has enormous difficulty electing the candidates of its choice, especially black candidates. The white majority, it is argued, effectively controls access to all of the at-large seats on the council, an especially serious matter when the entire council is elected in that manner. White council members electorally accountable to a white majority, they complain, are not likely to be very responsive to the needs of the black minority. If the city is divided into districts, however, the black minority can often take advantage of being residentially concentrated and control the selection of one or more council members, who will be more directly accountable to, and presumably responsive toward, the black electorate.

This new wave of reform has been especially pronounced in the American South, a region in which the municipal reformers had been especially successful (see, e.g., Wolfinger and Field, 1966; Dye and MacManus, 1976). The 1972 survey just noted disclosed that over eight in ten (81.7%) of the cities with a population above 10,000 and located within the southern and border states elected at least some of the council members at large; almost three fourths (74.6%) elected all members of the council at large (Svara, 1977, p. 171). The more recent survey of central cities likewise found that 89.3% of the cities in the South (defined as the 11 states of the Confederacy) elected at least some council members at large, while 59.2% elected all of them at large. The South was the region of the country with the highest proportion of cities utilizing at-large councilmanic elections in the later survey.[2]

The South is also the region in which blacks have been the most severely underrepresented on city councils. The percentage of a city's council members who are black is usually less than the percentage of a city's population which is black. Numerous studies have documented the fact that this is especially true of cities in the South (see, e.g., Jones, 1976; Karnig, 1976; Taebel, 1978; Karnig and Welch, 1980, chap. 4; Engstrom and McDonald, 1982; and Heilig and Mundt, 1983). Much of this underrepresentation, the new reformers maintain, is attributable to the extensive use of at-large elections within the region. Indeed, at-large elections have been at the center of the *vote dilution* controversy in the South.

Since passage of the Voting Rights Act in 1965, the barriers to black people registering to vote and actually casting ballots have been largely removed throughout the American South, and as a consequence black registration and electoral participation have increased significantly (see, e.g., Engstrom, forthcoming). Despite these gains, however, the issue of racially discriminatory electoral laws continues to be an important legal and political issue within that region. The nature of that issue has changed, however; as the black electorate has grown, the previous preoccupation with denial of the vote has shifted to a more contemporary concern, dilution of the vote. Blacks have become acutely aware of the fact that when voting patterns are polarized along racial lines, the actual impact of the votes they cast may well be dependent upon the way in which electoral competition is structured. Placing electoral decisions in the hands of a white citywide majority is commonly cited as one of the major techniques for reducing the potential impact of the black vote. Blacks in the South, therefore, have launched an aggressive campaign against the continued use of at-large elections, seeking through referendum and/or litigation the substitution of single-member districts.[3]

A survey conducted by Peggy Heilig and Robert Mundt in 1980–1981 of cities with populations exceeding 10,000 and in which at least 15% of the population was black in 1970 has documented the southern focus to this latest "reform" activity. Their survey disclosed that 93% of the cities in which attempts were made to switch from at-large to single-member districts during the 1970s were located in the South. Such efforts, which were almost invariably initiated by black groups, occurred in 55% of the southern cities which in 1970 used at-large elections to select council members (Heilig and Mundt, 1983, p. 394; see also Claunch and Hallman, 1978). Efforts to switch to districts were especially likely to have occurred, not surprisingly, in the southern cities in which blacks were the most severely underrepresented on the council (Mundt and Heilig, 1982, pp. 1042–1043). These more recent "reform" efforts have not been without success, as 33% of the southern cities employing at-large elections in 1970 were found to have switched to geographic districting by 1980.[4]

This new reform movement, as just noted, is premised upon two important propositions: (1) that the black minority will be better able to convert its voting strength into the selection of black representatives if elections are conducted within districts rather than at large, and (2) that councilmanic decisions (and municipal policies generally) will become more responsive to the needs and interests of the black community as the percentage of black council members increases. Considerable empirical research has addressed the first proposition, and efforts to verify the second have been reported recently. The following section reviews and evaluates the evidence for these propositions.

Election Systems and Descriptive Representation

Numerous studies have addressed the issue of whether blacks are more likely to be elected to city councils if districts rather than at-large elections are used. The central concept in virtually all of these studies has been what Hanna Pitkin has called "descriptive representation," the correspondence between the black percentage of a city's population and the percentage of seats on that city's council to which black people have been elected (Pitkin, 1967, pp. 60–91). The focus of inquiry has been to account for why blacks are more or less proportionately represented across city councils.

Despite the tremendous variation of sampling criteria employed in these studies (e.g., cities with different size populations and having various proportions of black residents) and the variety of analytic designs applied, there is an overwhelming consensus among the researchers that when blacks are a citywide minority, their presence on the city council is likely to be less proportionate when elections are held at large rather than through districts (see, e.g., the review of these studies by Grofman, 1982b). Black candidates, these studies suggest, are simply much less likely to be elected if forced to compete citywide. Indeed, few generalizations in political science appear to be as well verified as the proposition that at-large elections tend to be discriminatory toward black Americans.

There is not, however, unanimity among researchers on this issue. A dissenting view has been put forward which maintains that the electoral framework through which city council members are selected is actually little more than a relatively unimportant intervening variable — a structural dimension which happens to intervene between more explanatory socioeconomic factors and the level of black representation. The degree to which blacks are elected is far better accounted for, according to this view, by the socioeconomic characteristics of a city's population than by the city's electoral structure. We will focus on those studies which we believe offer the most persuasive evidence of the discriminatory impact of the at-large format, studies utilizing both cross-sectional and longitudinal data, and also on those studies which have formed the basis for the dissenting viewpoint.

Described by Grofman as "the best of the cross-sectional studies" (Grofman, 1982b, p. 7), Engstrom and McDonald (1981) treat the electoral format as a specifying variable which affects the rate at which blacks are able to convert their voting strength into the election of black council members. The major independent variable, the variable expected to have the greatest effect on the black percentage of council members, is the percentage of the population which is black (in only a few cities is the race of registered voters recorded). The study attempts, by regressing the black council percentage onto the black population percentage, to assess how the relationship between these two variables will differ, depending on the electoral structure being employed. The results of this analysis, based on a 1976 survey of the largest central city within each SMSA ($N = 239$), are displayed in Figure 13.1.[5]

In cities in which all of the members of the council are elected from districts, the relationship between the black population and the black membership on the council is virtually proportional. Although excep-

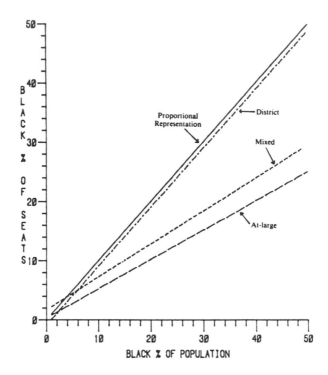

FIG. 13.1. Relationship between black percentage of population and black
percentage of city council in different electoral formats. (From Engstrom and McDonald, 1981, p. 348.)

tions can always be cited, as a general matter blacks can be expected to
be almost proportionally represented if districts are the exclusive medium through which council members are selected. If at-large elections are used, however, blacks can be expected to be underrepresented. The correspondence between the population percentages and
council percentages drops dramatically if some councilmanic seats are
filled through citywide contests (the mixed category), and even further if all of the council members are elected in that manner. The
electoral format, according to this analysis, has a major impact on how
black electoral strength translates into black elected officials.

It is further estimated in this study that this differential impact will
be present even when the black percentage of the population in a city
is quite small. In Figure 13.2, 90% confidence bands have been added
to the regression lines for cities employing either districts or at-large
elections exclusively (i.e., we can be 90% confident that the actual

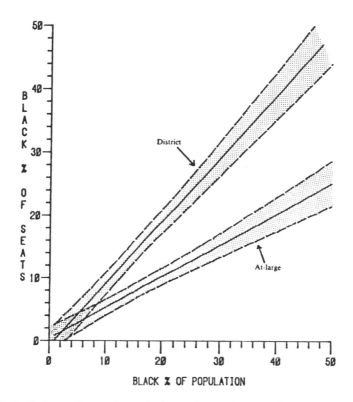

FIG. 13.2. Estimated seats/population relationships with 90% confidence bands in districted and at-large electoral formats. (From Engstrom and McDonald, 1981, p. 349.)

seats/population relationship lies within the band). Because these bands separate completely at a point below 10% black population, the authors argue that the 10% figure can be (conservatively) considered to be a threshold or critical point — whenever blacks constitute 10% or more of the population, at-large elections are likely to have an adverse impact on how proportionately they are represented. The differential impact of election structures was not affected in this study when statistical controls were applied for a variety of socioeconomic factors which other researchers have suggested might relate to the election of blacks (such as the educational, occupational, and income characteristics of the cities' populations).

Another cross-sectional study which complements the Engstrom-McDonald analysis very well is that by Albert Karnig and Susan Welch (1982). This study, based on a 1978 survey of all cities with

TABLE 13.1. Representational Indices for Mixed Cities by Electoral Format

	Representa-tional Ratio	Representa-tional Deficit	Percent of Cities Without Any Black Council Member
A. Districts + At-large (N=50)			
District seats	.952	−2.4	14.0
At-large seats	.499	−11.6	72.0
B. Districts + At-large with Residency Requirement (N=6)			
District seats	1.047	+1.4	12.0
At-large seats	.478	−12.0	50.0

Source. Karnig and Welch (1982, p. 105).

populations greater than 25,000 in 1970 and in which black people constituted at least 10% of the population (N=264), focuses special attention on the representational situation in cities employing mixed electoral arrangements. This approach was adopted because in those cities, differences in how proportionately blacks have been elected to the at-large seats and how proportionately they have been elected to the seats allocated to districts can be attributed directly to the different electoral contexts. Other variables which may be expected to have an impact on the election of black council members are "naturally controlled" in this approach.

> When comparing two election forms within the same city, socioeconomic, demographic, political context, and other variables are controlled, since aggregate indicators of income, education, percent blacks, region, partisanship, form of government, and so on, are precisely the same for both the at-large and the district parts of the election in the same municipality (Karnig and Welch, 1982, pp. 103–104).

In this analysis, the dependent variables are two measures of the deviation from proportional racial representation in each city. One measure, the representational ratio, is simply the quotient obtained when the black population percentage is divided into the percentage of council members who are black. This ratio is, of course, zero when no blacks serve on the council and 1.0 if the two percentage figures are equal. If the percentage of black council members is higher than the population percentage, then the ratio will exceed 1.0. The other measure, the representational deficit, is the result obtained when the population percentage is subtracted from the council percentage. With this

TABLE 13.2. **Representational Indices for Single Format Cities by Electoral Format**

	Representa- tional Ratio	Representa- tional Deficit	Percent of Cities Without Any Black Council Member
District Elections	.922	−1.3	10.0
At-large Elections	.616	−9.6	44.0
At-large Elections with Residency Requirements	.443	− 14.0	45.0

Source. Karnig and Welch (1982, p. 107).

measure, a score of zero reflects perfect proportionality, and scores above or below zero register the relative degree of over- or underrepresentation respectively.[6] Different electoral arrangements are then treated as independent variables affecting the scores for various cities on these measures.

Reported in Table 13.1 are the average scores within the districted and at-large components across cities in which both of these electoral mechanisms were used to select council members. In 50 of the cities, a combination of districts and "pure" at-large elections (i.e., candidates residing in any area of the city may compete for any at-large seat) were used. In 6 others, a residency requirement was attached to the at-large component (i.e., only candidates residing in specified areas of the city were permitted to compete for certain at-large seats). It is disclosed in Table 13.1 that blacks come very close to winning a proportional number of district-based seats in these cities, while winning a disproportionally low number of the at-large seats (including those in which council members are required to live in dispersed areas throughout the city). One reason why the representational indexes reflect such a greater deviation from proportional representation within the at-large components is apparent in the third column of the table; blacks are often excluded completely from election to the at-large seats, while winning at least one of the districted seats in almost every city.

Although the evidence from the cities with mixed electoral systems is quite impressive, Karnig and Welch find additional evidence for the differential impact thesis in their analysis of those cities using only one electoral format as well. Reported in Table 13.2 are the representational indexes for those cities in which only district elections are used to select council members, those in which only "pure" at-large elections are used, and those using only at-large elections with specific residency requirements. Once again, blacks are close to being proportionally represented when districts are employed but are considerably "underrepresented," and often excluded completely, when elections are held at large. These differences between electoral systems remained when statistical controls for a number of demographic and other variables were applied.

Most of the evidence which has been marshaled in support of the argument that at-large elections have a racially discriminatory impact has been cross-sectional in nature (see also Kramer, 1971; Jones, 1976; Karnig, 1976; Taebel, 1978; Robinson and Dye, 1978; Latimer, 1979; and Engstrom and McDonald, 1982). As noted, however, the recent movement to force the abandonment of at-large elections in favor of districted arrangements has not been without success. Heilig and Mundt (1983; p. 394), for example, discovered that among the southern cities in their sample which were electing council members at large in 1970, one third had switched to either a mixed or districted system by 1980. This has created an opportunity to approach the differential impact question using longitudinal rather than cross-sectional data, that is, examining the level of black representation within a city both *before* and *after* the adoption of a different electoral arrangement.

Two studies have brought longitudinal data to bear on this question. The first to be reported was that by Chandler Davidson and George Korbel (1981). They report scores for both the representational ratio and the representational deficit for blacks and Mexican-Americans (combined) for all 21 municipalities in Texas which switched from elections at large to either a mixed or districted arrangement between 1970 and 1979. The differences between the before and after scores in these cities were dramatic—the average ratio was .28 prior to the systemic alteration and .86 after, while the average deficit was –18.7 before the change and only –3.3 after. While this is impressive evidence of the impact of these structural revisions, the absence of any "control" group of cities in this analysis (cities in which electoral arrangements were not altered) does leave open the possibility that these increases in minority representation are a result of some other factor or factors. Without a control group,

> [I]t is difficult to be sure that increased equity in minority representation is occurring *because* of change of election system—especially in a period where some minority groups (in particular, Blacks in the South) have been making extensive electoral gains based on increased voter registration and

TABLE 13.3. Representation Ratios for Southern Cities, 1970s and 1980

	Representation Ratio		
	1970s	1980	Difference
At-large ($N=122$)	.31	.37	+ .06
Mixed ($N=10$)	.44	.57	+ .13
Districts ($N=13$)	.45	.74	+ .29
Changed from At-large to Mixed ($N=19$)	.16	.70	+ .54
Changed from At-large to Districts ($N=25$)	.15	.87	+ .72

Source. Heilig and Mundt (1983, p. 396).

the easing of traditional barriers such as intimidation (Grofman 1982b, pp. 5–6).

This problem is at least partially overcome in the second analysis employing longitudinal data. Heilig and Mundt (1983) have examined the representation ratios over time for blacks in 209 southern cities (i.e., cities located in the former Confederacy) in which there are more than 10,000 residents, at least 15% of which are black. Heilig and Mundt employ a "natural" experimental design (see, e.g., Shively, 1980, pp. 92–93)—differences in representational ratios over time are compared across groups of cities, some of which have altered their electoral arrangements and some of which have not. In their analysis, those cities which used only at-large, mixed, or districted systems during the period 1970–1980 serve as "control" groups, while those in which a systemic change from an at-large to a mixed or districted arrangement occurred sometime during the 1970s serve as "treatment" groups. The average representation ratio for these groups in 1980 is compared to the average ratio throughout the 1970s for the control groups, and the average ratio in the 1970s prior to the systemic adjustments for the treatment groups.

The results of the Heilig and Mundt analysis, which are presented in Table 13.3, strongly support the differential impact thesis. Changes in the representational ratios were much greater in the treatment groups than in the control groups. The average ratio in 1980 for the 25 cities switching to districts exclusively was .72 higher than the average ratio for those cities prior to the adoption of districts. For the 19 cities adopting a mixed plan, the average ratio increased .54. Among the control groups, the average ratio increased substantially within only one group, that in which districts had been employed over the entire period. This increase (.29), however, was still well below that for either of the groups of cities in which there had been a change. In the other two groups the ratio changed only minimally, + .06 for cities employing only at-large elections over the entire period and + .13 for those using a mixed arrangement.

Although this analysis does employ "control" groups against which before and after scores can be compared, it does not solve completely the inferential problem just noted. Alternative explanations for the increased minority representation in the treatment groups, beside that of the alteration in the electoral systems, are still possible because cities, although "matched" by region (i.e., all are located in the South), have not been placed into the treatment and control groups randomly (a situation which is characteristic of the "natural experiment"). This leaves open the possibility that another factor or factors may be responsible for both the change in the electoral system and the increase in the number of blacks elected to the councils. One such factor, for example, might be a high degree of political mobilization or organization within the black community. As Grofman has noted,

> [C]ities which change from at-large to ward elections are *ipso facto* more likely to be characterized by a minority political organization of some strength which will be likely to generate greater minority representation under *any* electoral system . . . (Grofman, 1982b, p. 6).

The fact that the representation ratios for the treatment groups in this analysis during the period in which at-large elections were employed were substantially below those for the at-large control group during the 1970s (.15 and .16 vs. .31) and that the ratios for 1980 were substantially above those for the respective control groups in 1980 (.57 vs. .70 for those with mixed systems, and .74 vs. .87 for those with districts only) suggests that another factor or factors may also be at work. While alternative explanations for these "experimental" results therefore cannot be precluded, the Heilig and Mundt analysis does provide impressive empirical support for the differential impact thesis.

The longitudinal and cross-sectional analyses just described provide, we believe, a solid basis from which to generalize about the racial consequences of alternative electoral structures. As just noted, however, there has not been unanimity among researchers on this matter. Dissenting voices have been raised which argue that different electoral frameworks have only minimal, if any, impact on the election of blacks to municipal councils.

The most extensive analysis in which electoral structures have been reported to be relatively unimportant was conducted by MacManus (1978). Utilizing data gathered in 1975 on 243 central cities of SMSAs, MacManus discovered that differences in the local electoral structures across those cities had virtually no impact on how proportionately blacks were represented within them. Various demographic character-istics of these cities, however, such as population size and growth, median family income, median school years completed, and the pro-portion of workers employed in white-collar occupations, were related to the representation levels. This leads MacManus to suggest that these environmental factors were the more important determinants of the rate at which blacks were elected, while the councilmanic election system was "only an intervening variable" (MacManus, 1978, p. 159) which itself had very little effect on whether or not blacks were elected.

The analysis conducted by MacManus, however, does not provide an adequate basis for abandoning the differential impact notion. The basic problem with the study concerns the use of the representational deficit (the percentage of council members who are black *minus* the black percentage of the city's population) as the measure of descrip-tive representation without also requiring that the cities included in the study contain at least some minimal number or percentage of black residents (a threshold commonly set at 10% or 15%). In cities in which there are proportionately very few black residents, no more than a minimal level of underrepresentation can be recorded on this measure, even if the municipal council is composed exclusively of white members. One can hardly expect any electoral system to have a racially discriminatory impact in these virtually all-white cities.

Sixty of the cities in the MacManus analysis in which no black was serving on the council also had black population proportions of *less than 5%*. In over half of these cities, councilmanic elections were con-ducted *at large*.[7] It should not be surprising, then, to discover that the electoral system variable has little impact on the scores recorded by the deficit measure—blacks can hardly be seriously disadvantaged by the use of at-large elections in places such as Fargo, North Dakota; Provo, Utah; Dubuque, Iowa; and Sioux Falls, South Dakota! Nor should it be surprising, given the absence of any minimal black popu-lation threshold, that MacManus ultimately concluded that blacks are most likely to be equitably represented in "small [central] cities, char-acterized by growth, greater wealth, and more highly educated populations . . . regardless of the plan of electing council members" (Mac-Manus, 1978, p. 160). These are precisely the types of cities most likely to have minimal percentages of blacks in their populations and therefore cities in which blacks cannot be seriously underrepresented, by definition (given the deficit measure). There is a strong negative relationship between the percentage of blacks in the populations of cities and the representation scores recorded on the deficit measure, and when statistical controls are imposed for these black population percentages, the relationships between the environmental variables Mac-Manus focused upon and black representation levels virtually disappear (see Engstrom and McDonald, 1981, pp. 350–351). The Mac-Manus analysis, therefore, does not provide a very solid foundation upon which to challenge the differential impact thesis.

A second study which also questions the differential impact notion is a much more limited analysis by Cole (1974). Examining the 16 cities in New Jersey with a population of 25,000 or more, at least 15% of which were black, Cole discovered that it was not possible to distinguish, on the basis of their electoral systems, between those cities in which blacks were close to being proportionally represented (in 1972, based on the deficit measure) and those in which they were not. Cole (1974, pp. 23–28) concluded, therefore, that the differential impact thesis had been exaggerated and, like MacManus, suggested that the socioeconomic characteristics of a city's residents were much more important determinants of black electoral success. Blacks were more likely to be equitably represented, he reported, in those cities in which the municipal population had the highest levels of formal education, largest proportions of residents employed in relatively prestigious occupations, and the highest median annual incomes.

Although the analysis performed by Cole does not suffer from the methodological problems present in the analysis by MacManus, the data base is clearly too limited to provide a basis for generalization (see, e.g., Karnig, 1976, p. 224). Given that other, more extensive cross-sectional studies have controlled for these and similar environmental variables without equivalent results (e.g., Engstrom and McDonald, 1981; Karnig and Welch, 1982; Robinson and Dye, 1978; and Latimer, 1979), it hardly seems appropriate to abandon the differential impact thesis on the basis of Cole's limited analysis.

There is substantial evidence for the first proposition upon which the campaign against at-large elections is premised—that the black minority will be better able to convert its voting strength into the selection of black representatives if councilmanic elections are held within districts rather than citywide. This appears to be especially true for cities within the South, the region in which this campaign is most intense. Southern cities tend to have the most racially segregated residential patterns, and therefore the blacks in these cities are likely to benefit the most from the adoption of geographic districting (see, e.g., Van Valey et al., 1977; Vedlitz and Johnson, 1982; and O'Loughlin and Taylor, 1982).

The impact of this campaign on the racial composition of municipal councils in that region has already been impressive. The data reported by Heilig and Mundt (1983, p. 396) demonstrate that the dramatic increase over the past decade in the number of black people serving on city councils in the South can be attributed almost entirely to the adoption of district elections. The regional differences (South vs. non-South) in how proportionately blacks are represented were, by 1980, only slight in those cities employing districted or mixed electoral arrangements, yet still substantial in those employing only at-large elections. Heilig and Mundt have concluded, therefore, that the continued adoption of district elections "is the key to increasing black representation in the South" (Heilig and Mundt, 1983, p. 396). Indeed, it has been estimated that if the distribution of electoral systems across southern cities were the same as that across cities outside the South, not only would the relative underrepresentation of southern black people disappear, but blacks within that region will be likely to be more proportionately represented on city councils than black people outside the South (Engstrom and McDonald, 1982).

Black Representation and Responsiveness

While electing black people to city councils is a major goal of the new reform movement, that in itself is of course "only half the battle [and] perhaps the lesser half at that" (Karnig and Welch, 1980, p. 150). Black demands to employ district-based elections are premised on the expectation that the election of black council members will result in a difference in the way in which a municipal government responds to the needs and interests of its minority citizens. As expressed by Eisinger,

> A central assumption in the practice of ethnic [or racial] politics is that a particular group will be in a more powerful position to have its demands met if it has a coethnic in a position of authority than if it must supplicate an officialdom controlled by other groups (Eisinger, 1982, p. 388; see also Bullock, 1975, p. 727; and Keech, 1968, pp. 57–58).

The presence of blacks on city councils, therefore, is expected to result in more than "symbolic representation"; it is expected to translate into "substantive representation" as well (see, e.g., Preston, 1978).

The second proposition upon which this more recent reform movement is based, however—that councilmanic decisions (and municipal policies generally) will become more responsive to the needs and interests of the black community as the percentage of council members who are black increases—has not been documented anywhere near as impressively as the initial proposition linking different electoral systems to black electoral success. While there is impressionistic evidence suggesting that black elected officials do make the expected difference (see esp. Cole, 1976, pp. 221–223), only a few efforts at systematic empirical verification of this second proposition have as yet been attempted. Although these initial attempts at verification have been limited (and must be considered far from conclusive), they do suggest that it would be wise, at least at this time, to heed Marguerite Barnett's warning against any naive acceptance of "the *careless equation* of black political presence with black political power" (Barnett, 1982, p. 28; emphasis added; see also Walton, 1972, pp. 196–202).

Measuring the influence of black elected officials in the policy-making process, especially across a large number of municipalities, is admittedly an investigative task "fraught with methodological and conceptual difficulties" (Karnig and Welch, 1980, p. 115). One of the initial, and most serious, conceptual problems researchers working in this area must confront is the specification of the types of impact that black council members can be expected to have on municipal policies and programs. Mack Jones has provided a useful approach to this problem by identifying three conceptually distinct areas in which the impact of black elected officials may be evaluated. According to Jones,

[T]he political power of black officeholders may be assessed in terms of: (1) their success in *reordering the priorities* of their boards and commissions and persuading them to seek novel solutions to outstanding problems, particularly those especially salient in black communities; (2) garnering for the black community a *more equitable distribution of existing benefits and services* provided by government; (3) *thwarting the passage of measures inimical* to the welfare of their constituents (1978, pp. 98–99, emphasis added).

The efforts to verify the increased responsiveness thesis have to date examined the first and second of Jones's dimensions; the third has yet to be the subject of systematic, comparative inquiry.

Undoubtedly the most dramatic form of increased responsiveness is the reordering of public priorities. This was the focus of the first broadly based comparative study to attempt to link different levels of black councilmanic representation to changes in municipal policies. Albert Karnig and Susan Welch (1980) attempted to determine whether the changes in the amount of money spent for different categories of municipal functions (both per capita and as a proportion of the total budget) could be attributable to the level of black representation on municipal councils. They had hypothesized that as the black percentage on a council increased, there would be *greater increases* in spending on social welfare functions (health, housing, welfare, and education) and *smaller increases* in spending for protective services (fire and police), physical facilities (streets, sanitation, sewage, and hospitals), and amenities (parks and libraries). When they related the percentage of council members who were black (the average percentage for 1970 and 1972) in 139 cities (each greater than 50,000 in population) to the changes in the municipal expenditures in these categories between 1968 and 1969 and 1974 and 1975, however, they discovered that the level of black representation had minimal, if any, impact on any of the policy areas, including the social services category (Karnig and Welch, 1980, pp. 124–141).[8]

Karnig's and Welch's results surely will not bring comfort to those who assume (or hope) that a linkage exists between the presence of blacks on municipal councils and the policies and programs of municipalities. But these results must be considered, at best, as only suggestive. It would be premature to dismiss the increased responsiveness thesis on the basis of this analysis alone. While the findings certainly are not supportive of that thesis, neither are they, by themselves, a sufficient basis for rejecting it.

Karnig and Welch have relied upon changes in the amount of money spent in various functional areas as an indicator of changes in "responsiveness." The relationship between these budgetary categories and the actual needs and/or demands of minority residents, however, is far from clear, and, as Karnig and Welch (1980, p. 117) acknowledge, may vary from municipality to municipality. Eisinger has argued that "assigning special racial interests to broad functional expenditure categories is an exercise fraught with ambiguity," one which requires the researcher to make "questionable assumptions" (Eisinger, 1982, p. 382)—such as assuming that blacks will place a relatively low priority on spending for protective services, despite the fact that they are disproportionately the victims of both crimes and fires. Even if such racial assignments could be made, the problem of assuming a constant set of minority needs or demands across cities remains.

Schumaker and Getter have commented in this regard that "[T]here is no single, a priori distribution of policy which can be considered responsive" (Schumaker and Getter, 1977, p. 249; see also Getter and Schumaker, 1978). Ideally, a study assessing changes in responsiveness should have an independent measure or measures of minority needs and/or demands so that responsiveness could be inferred from a relationship between variables, rather than defined through the researcher's own selection of a dependent variable or variables.

Another problem with the use of aggregate expenditure levels as a medium for assessing the impact of black council members is that the level at which budgetary categories are funded is something over which council members may have minimal control, especially in the short run. As expressed by Thomas Dye and James Renick, "Much of a city's budget is composed of 'uncontrollables'—items over which neither black nor white . . . council members have much authority" (Dye and Renick, 1981, p. 475). To expect dramatic changes in the levels at which existing programs and services are funded is to impose, therefore, a very stringent test on the increased responsiveness thesis. A more important problem with the use of aggregate expenditure figures, however, is that the level at which programs and services are funded may not be a good indicator of who is actually benefiting from the expenditures. Money spent in functional areas assumed to be important to blacks may or may not be spent in a fashion directly benefiting the black community. This relates, of course, to the second dimension of possible impact identified by Jones—"garnering for the black community a more equitable distribution of existing benefits and services" (Jones, 1978, p. 98). This, in fact, may be the area in which black council members can be expected to have the greatest influence. As Karnig and Welch suggest:

> It is quite possible, owing to financial straits as well as the difficulty of changing policy in other than an incremental fashion, that the emphasis of black officials may be on shifting program benefits from white to black neighborhoods. For example, the stress may be on more police protection in black neighborhoods, more spending on black schools, improved paving and repair of streets in black areas, and so forth (Karnig and Welch, 1980, p. 153).

This type of change in policy, as Karnig and Welch recognize, "may occur without changing the distribution of expenditures in the overall policy categories" (Karnig and Welch, 1980, p. 153).

Support for the expectation that black councilmanic representation will result in blacks being treated more equitably has been found in a study of municipal employment patterns. Unlike broad categories of expenditures, "the distribution of public-sector jobs is clearly divisible by race" (Eisinger, 1982, p. 382) and can be used, therefore, to measure differences in how equitably blacks are treated, both across communities and over time within specific municipalities. Dye and Renick have suggested that this is one area in which black council members are most likely to have an impact.

> If there are any policy consequences at all which stem from increased minority representation, certainly increased minority employment in government ought to be one of those consequences. Even if minority council members cannot solve all of the problems confronting the nation's cities, they can still act to obtain more and better city jobs for their minority constituents. (1981, p. 476)

When Dye and Renick compared the race of full-time municipal employees across various occupational categories for 42 cities in 1977 (all with populations of 25,000 or more, at least 10% of which were black) with the percentage of councilmanic seats filled by blacks in 1976, they discovered a very pronounced relationship. The greater the percentage of black council members in a city, the higher the percentage of blacks employed in administrative, professional, and protective (police, fire, corrections, etc.) positions, regardless of the relative size and the educational and income characteristics of the black population within a city. For each of these employment categories, the level of black representation was the variable most strongly related to the level of black employment, prompting Dye and Renick to conclude that "black representation on city councils is a *crucial link* in improving black employment opportunities" (1981, p. 485, emphasis added).

Eisinger (1982) has analyzed data very similar to that relied on by Dye and Renick, however, and reached a conclusion inconsistent with theirs. Examining employment data for 43 cities with populations exceeding 50,000 and which were also at least 10% black (only 14 of which were included in the Dye and Renick study), Eisinger discovered that the degree to which blacks were represented on a city council in 1977 had virtually no impact on the percentage of blacks in administrative or professional positions in 1978. (The presence of a black mayor, however, was related to black employment in these categories.) Eisinger's indicator of black representation, however, was the ratio measure frequently utilized in studies of "descriptive representation"; that is, the percentage of council members who were black divided by the percentage of the population which was black, and the results of the analysis therefore cannot be considered a test of the increased responsiveness thesis. The causal variable specified by that thesis is *not* how proportionately black people are represented but the proportion of the council which is black. When the issue is the policy impact of black representatives, the latter is clearly the more appropriate variable. In this regard, we are in agreement with Karnig and Welch, who state:

> An equitable proportion on the city council is probably less important to meeting policy objectives than is the absolute representation that blacks possess on the council. That is, we would expect blacks to have greater influence where they hold 60% of the council seats, even if that is only 80% of the equitable rate, than where they hold one quarter of the seats and this reflects an equity ratio 1.5 times their share of the population (Karnig and Welch, 1980, p. 116; see also Meier and England, 1982, p. 13).

Much more research obviously needs to be completed before the increased responsiveness thesis, the second proposition upon which the new reform movement is based, can be considered empirically sound. The degree of congruence between a greater variety of measures of "policy" and indicators of the needs and/or demands of black residents needs to be investigated. In addition, some important analytic issues concerning the assumed linkage between black representation and policy outputs need to be resolved. One such issue is the degree to which increased responsiveness may be a function of the race of the representative, or the race of the represented. Earlier research has reported that municipal policies are more responsive to the interests and needs of blacks in those cities in which council members are elected by district, rather than at large (see, e.g., Liebert, 1974, pp. 781–782; Karnig, 1975, pp. 99–100; Lyons, 1978, pp. 126–129; and Schumaker and Getter, 1977, pp. 265, 273–275; 1983, p. 25). The race of councilmanic representatives was not included in these analyses. Because districted systems presumably create situations in which black voters have more electoral influence, these studies suggest that the important variable may be the ability of blacks to hold representatives electorally accountable, regardless of the race of those representatives. In other words, responsiveness may result from a fear of electoral retribution by black voters, a fear that is presumably shared by black and white officeholders alike (and is felt more immediately by a greater percentage of council members in districted cities). The efforts to assess responsiveness to date have included either the electoral system variable or the black representation variable, but never both. Each needs to be included in future research designs so that the relative impact of each can be better clarified. Another related issue concerns a more complete elaboration of the manner in which the presence of blacks on a city council affects responsiveness. Is the percentage of blacks on a council best understood as an intervening variable in a causal sequence (as suggested by Dye and Renick, 1981, p. 485) and therefore viewed as having a direct affect on the adoption of policies that are congruent with the needs or demands of blacks, or is it best understood as a specifying variable which establishes conditions under which the relationship between black needs or demands and policies will vary? In statistical terms, should it be viewed as having an additive or a multiplicative impact? These, and undoubtedly other issues, will have to be addressed in future research efforts before we have an adequate empirical basis upon which to accept the increased responsiveness thesis.

Conclusions

At-large councilmanic elections have been a central plank in the platform of municipal reformers for many years. These elections, it was assumed, would result in the selection of "responsible" council members from the middle and upper classes, who would make decisions on the basis of a citywide, "public-regarding" viewpoint (see Banfield and Wilson, 1963, pp. 87–96, and Lineberry and Fowler, 1967). Many American municipalities have adopted and are today using this "reformed" electoral structure as the means for selecting council members. This electoral system has drawn an adverse reaction from America's black minority, however, which has argued that at-large elections are often racially discriminatory. District-based electoral systems, they maintain, would provide black people with a much more equitable opportunity to elect fellow blacks to city councils, a situation which in turn is expected to result in municipal governments being more responsive to minority needs and interests. This has stimulated another "reform movement," focused largely on municipalities within the southern portion of the United States, which seeks to substitute single-member districts for the at-large arrangement.

The empirical evidence for the two propositions upon which this new black reform movement is based has been reviewed in the preceding pages. The first proposition, that blacks will be represented more proportionately on councils if district-based rather than at-large elections are employed, has been impressively documented. Indeed, this proposition is among the best verified empirical generalizations in political science. The second proposition, however, that governmental responsiveness will increase as the level of black representation increases, does not rest upon nearly as solid an empirical foundation as the first. Systematic efforts to verify this second proposition have begun only recently and have reached inconsistent conclusions. It would seem prudent, therefore, to exercise considerable caution before generalizing about the policy consequences associated with different levels of black councilmanic representation. It is not possible, as yet, to state with any confidence whether these inconsistent findings are related to the type of policy dimensions analyzed (priorities or equitability of distributions), the measurement of black strength on the council (black proportionality or black percentage), and/or the failure to account for other factors that might make a difference (such as variation in black needs or demands or the likelihood of greater electoral accountability generally in districted as opposed to at-large systems).

Even if the impact that black elected officials have on municipal policies and programs should prove to be of less magnitude than many black reformers would like, this should not suggest that the current electoral reform movement is therefore unimportant. District-based election systems do generally facilitate the election of blacks to city councils, and the presence of blacks on councils may serve other important functions beside that of altering policies. The presence of blacks on a council may very well result in increased constituency service for black citizens (see, e.g., Jewell, 1982, pp. 145–146). And feelings of political competence and affect among blacks may increase as a result of blacks being in decision-making positions. As expressed by Michael Preston:

> [S]ymbolic representation is not only desirable but necessary for black Americans. Because of past historical conditions, blacks need role models in government; they need representatives that they believe will represent their interests; they need to know that good leadership (or bad) is not dominated by one race or group. Most important, blacks must become more self-reliant. Self-reliance is a basic ingredient of political influence. To be self-reliant is to believe in oneself, and to seek out others who can be influenced to act in one's behalf (Preston, 1978, p. 198; see also Karnig and Welch, 1980, p. 109).

Regardless of the type of impact that black council members may (or may not) ultimately have, the better electoral prospects for black candidates in districted as opposed to at-large systems will continue to compel the racial minority to view districted systems as the more fair alternative, in the sense that "the fairness of the electoral method depends on whether substantial numbers of voters who wish to elect one of their own members . . . can, in fact, do so" (Lijphart, 1982, p. 144). On this dimension, the black reformers are unquestionably correct.

Notes

1. This data was collected through a telephone survey of city clerks' offices during the spring of 1982. The authors wish to thank Albert Ringelstein for assisting with this survey.
2. The South was second to the West in the proportion of cities utilizing at-large elections in the earlier study of cities with populations exceeding 10,000. For the regional percentages in the earlier survey, as well as the definition of the West employed in both, see Svara (1977, p. 171).
3. The litigation has been premised on the Fourteenth and Fifteenth amendments to the United States Constitution and on section 2 of the Voting Rights Act. For an excellent discussion of the history of this litigation, and commentary on the standards applied, see O'Rourke (1982).
4. Efforts to switch to at-large elections in those southern states covered by section 5 of the Voting Rights Act, which requires federal "preclearance" of any changes in laws affecting elections, are generally prevented by the Department of Justice, or the United States District Court for the District of Columbia, on the grounds that they may have a racially discriminatory effect (see Motomura, 1983, pp. 210–214).
5. Four central cities in which blacks constituted a *majority* of the population were excluded from this analysis.
6. The correlation between these two measures is exceptionally high when they are applied to cities having populations which are at least 10% black but is reduced dramatically if a lower black population threshold is applied (see Engstrom and McDonald, 1981, p. 346).
7. These figures are based on the data collected in 1976 by Robinson, not the data collected by MacManus. For analyses of the data collected by Robinson, see Robinson and Dye (1798) and Engstrom and McDonald (1981, 1982).
8. Karnig and Welch (1980, p. 120) attempted to minimize the impact that the differences in the functional responsibilities of cities might have on these results by examining changes over time within each city's budget and by eliminating from the analysis of each category of expenditures any cities that did not have expenditures in that category in either of the two observed fiscal years. On the importance of taking these differences into account, see Liebert (1974).

CHAPTER 14

The Nonpartisan Ballot in the United States

Carol A. *Cassel*

In a majority of U.S. municipal elections (probably about two thirds), candidates run for office on tickets without party labels.[1] Such nonpartisan elections are a product of the municipal reform movement of the early twentieth century which attempted to limit the power of corrupt party machines, insulate local elections from the influence of state and national party politics, facilitate more efficient and businesslike administration of local government, and encourage recruitment of superior candidates for local office who might be reluctant to associate themselves with party organizations (Lee, 1960; Weaver, 1971). Nonpartisan elections provide an interesting contrast with elections where party labels are present.

Behaviorally oriented political scientists of the mid-twentieth century questioned the validity of the reformers' theory. A revisionist theory developed based on observations of nonpartisan elections in practice and a theoretical recognition of the functions of political parties in political systems. The classic statement of such reassessment was made by Adrian (1952), who hypothesized that nonpartisan elections tend to be issueless in nature, that incumbents are advantaged and less accountable to the public in nonpartisan systems, that nonpartisan bodies lack collective responsibility, and that channels for recruitment to higher office are restricted by nonpartisanship.

It is the purpose of this essay to review the generation of empirical studies since 1952 which examined the political effects of the nonpartisan ballot. Although several scholars conducted major studies of nonpartisan elections which tended to support the revisionist theory (Hawley, 1973; Lee, 1960), scholars generally have turned only recently from studies of one or several communities to comprehensive comparative analyses. These comparative analyses have challenged some, but not all, of the findings of the earlier empirical work.

Description of Use of the Nonpartisan Ballot

Before examining the effects of nonpartisan elections on political factors such as voting behavior, types of candidates advantaged, and municipal public policy, it is useful to provide the reader with background information on the use of the nonpartisan ballot in the United States. The nonpartisan ballot is a Progressive municipal reform of the early twentieth century and is related strongly to demographic region, apparently for historical reasons. Cities in the Northeast, formed early in U.S. history, are most likely to have partisan elections (68.5%); whereas cities formed later in the West were most likely to be influenced by the Progressive movement of the early twentieth century and adopt nonpartisan elections (92.9%). It has been asserted that nonpartisan elections occur more frequently in smaller and more middle-class cities, but there is no evidence of significant relationships between ballot form and city size or income (Cassel, 1985).

A majority of all forms of government (mayor-council, council-manager, etc.) have nonpartisan elections, although the nonpartisan ballot is associated most closely with the reform model council-manager form of government. Likewise, the nonpartisan ballot is used in a majority of all council constituency types, but it occurs most frequently with the reform model at-large election constituency. When the proportions of cities which fall into various combinations of the municipal government structures are assessed, the structure of U.S. city governments clearly is characterized more by diversity than by the reformed or unreformed model (Cassel, 1985).

Voting Participation

There are both theoretical and empirical reasons to believe that the nonpartisan ballot inhibits voter turnout in municipal elections. The literature on participation produced during the last two decades established a clear theoretical link between strength of partisanship and voter turnout at the national level. Since the nonpartisan ballot is intended to make every voter an independent, it is logical to hypothesize that turnout is lower in nonpartisan elections.

Empirical studies found that voter turnout is lower in nonpartisan than in partisan elections (Alford and Lee, 1968; Hamilton, 1971; Hansen, 1975; Karnig and Walter, 1977; Lee, 1963). In 1975, median turnout in all U.S. cities with populations of 25,000 and above was 36% in partisan elections and 27% in nonpartisan elections (Karnig and Walter, 1977). Yet other features of municipal reform structure, such as holding elections independent of state and national elections and council-manager government, are associated with the nonpartisan ballot and also tend to depress voter turnout.

In cities holding elections independent of state and national races, median turnout in elections for mayor is 39% in partisan elections and 30% in nonpartisan contests (Karnig and Walter, 1977). This 9-percentage point differential may not be entirely attributable to the nonpartisan ballot, since the mayor's role in reformed nonpartisan/council-manager cities is less important than in less reformed nonpartisan/mayor-council cities. When there is no mayoral contest but election for council only, median turnout in partisan cities is 25% and in nonpartisan cities 21% (Karnig and Walter, 1977).

The evidence seems clear that nonpartisanship depresses municipal turnout at least a few percentage points when city elections are held independently. This conservative estimate represents 15% to 20% of the municipal voting electorate. Such a reduction of public participation supports the revisionists' preference for a partisan ballot. Yet a more effective means to encourage municipal participation is to schedule municipal elections concurrently with state and national elections: When elections are held concurrently, not only is municipal turnout substantially higher, but there is virtually no difference in the level of turnout in nonpartisan and partisan cities (Karnig and Walter, 1977).

Republican Turnout Advantage?

Early empirical studies of a limited number of cities suggested that lower voter turnout in nonpartisan elections is advantageous to Republicans (Salisbury and Black, 1963; Williams and Adrian, 1959). A more comprehensive study questioned this early claim. Hawley (1973) compared the success of Republican mayoral candidates with the success of Republican presidential and congressional candidates in

California and found that lower turnout alone does not work to the advantage of Republicans.

The Voter's Choice

Most of the empirical literature on voting behavior which proliferated in the last three decades examined presidential and congressional elections. This literature is based primarily on national surveys of voters which are conducted at the University of Michigan and made available to the political science community. Since such data for the municipal level are not available, studies of voting behavior in city elections are relatively rare, and our knowledge of voting behavior in nonpartisan elections remains limited.

Candidate Voting

Adrian was the first to suggest that scholars address apparent unanticipated consequences of the nonpartisan ballot, proposing that party labels suggest policy positions to voters, and that without such labels the voter comes "as a last resort in his confusion, to choose 'name' candidates" (Adrian, 1952, p. 773). Empirical studies did find that such candidate characteristics as personality, celebrity status, name resemblance to a well-known politician, ethnicity, and even ballot order influence the voter's choice in nonpartisan elections (Greenstein, 1970; Lee, 1960; Pomper, 1966; Kamin, 1958; Lorinkas, Hawkins and Edwards, 1969; Arrington, 1978; Bain and Hecock, 1957). It does not necessarily follow that nonpartisan and partisan elections differ in this respect; such candidate characteristics also are known to influence voting in partisan contests.

However, there is evidence from several systematic studies that voting for candidates on the basis of ethnic name identification or ballot order is greater in nonpartisan than in partisan elections. A comparison of voting in Newark's nonpartisan city election with voting in the partisan state assembly contests found that ethnicity is strongly related to voting in the nonpartisan situation but is not related to voting in the partisan election (Pomper, 1966). Several experimental studies found that voters are influenced by ethnic name identification and ballot order when selecting candidates from a nonpartisan ballot, but neither name nor ballot order affects candidate choice when party labels are present (Kamin, 1958; Lorinkas, Hawkins, and Edwards, 1969). Additional studies found that ballot order is influential in nonpartisan elections (Bain and Hecock, 1957), and that ethnic voting declines when elections are partisan (Arrington, 1978).

Unlike studies at the presidential level, studies of local elections have not explored candidate voting on the basis of candidate characteristics such as competence, integrity, and experience. Instead, only voting on the basis of trivial candidate characteristics such as name is discussed in the literature on nonpartisan elections, leaving the impression that the nonpartisan ballot only has confused voters by removing party labels. It is impossible to determine from studies presently available whether or not the nonpartisan ballot encourages city electorates to judge candidates on the basis of individual merit, as the reformers intended.

Issue Voting

Reform literature is somewhat ambiguous about the role of issues in nonpartisan elections. It is argued that the removal of party names from the ballot will insure that voting in local elections is based upon local issues. Somewhat at variance with this position is the argument that local government is largely a matter of good business management or "housekeeping," suggesting that meaningful issues or political cleavages do not exist at the local level of government. Adrian provided a typical statement of the revisionist argument that nonpartisanship encourages the avoidance of issues of policy in campaigns. "Fence straddling is much more tempting than under the conventional election system, since in the latter the presence of a party label suggests some sort of 'position' to the electorate" (Adrian, 1952, p. 773).

In their four-city study, Williams and Adrian (1959) found that in nonpartisan local elections, the more issues are stressed in campaigns, the more voting patterns conform to voting patterns in partisan elections. Thus cleavages of opinion on local issues may be associated with partisanship, and removal of party labels from local ballots may not affect the pattern of issue voting which would have occurred in a partisan election.

Lee (1960) characterized nonpartisan city elections in the San Francisco Bay Area as personality oriented and generally issueless, but stressed the local nature of these elections rather than the nonpartisan ballot as the cause of issueless politics. This assessment was based on results of a survey of 192 cities, in which city officials reported that three fourths of the election campaigns were personality-oriented. In the remaining one fourth of the local election campaigns, issues were believed to be a deciding factor.

Lee noted that "verification of the general feeling that personality factors predominate in influencing city elections must await the use at the local level of survey research techniques employed in *The Voter Decides*" (Lee, 1960, p. 131), a reference to public opinion polling of voters. This feeling remains to be verified regarding local nonpartisan elections. For example, in the most comprehensive study of nonpartisan elections since Lee (1960), Hawley (1973) did not discuss issue or candidate voting. And even today, studies which make systematic comparisons of issue voting in nonpartisan and partisan elections have not been conducted. The effect of the nonpartisan ballot on issue voting in municipal elections remains a matter of speculation.

Party Voting

Although the term *nonpartisanship* describes a situation where party designations do not appear on the ballot, political parties are known to operate in many nonpartisan systems. Adrian's (1959) classic four-category typology for nonpartisan cities categorizes cities by their varying degree of party activity. At one extreme, in some nonpartisan elections (e.g., Chicago), only those candidates who are supported by the dominant party organization ordinarily have a chance to win. At the other extreme, political parties are not important in nonpartisan elections, and candidates run on an individual basis. According to Adrian (1959), nonpartisan cities where party organizations have little or no role in campaigns and where voters consider party affiliation to be irrelevant are by far the most prevalent type of nonpartisan elections in the United States.

A number of attempts have been made to assess partisan patterns of candidate support in nonpartisan elections. Most studies (Williams and Adrian, 1959; Salisbury and Black, 1963; Jennings and Zeigler, 1966) found that votes in nonpartisan elections are related to partisan variables—even in cities with no overt party activity. A different conclusion was reached in a study (Arrington, 1978) which found that the nonpartisan ballot produced predominantly racially motivated municipal voting in a southern municipality; however, even this study found some evidence of party-related voting in nonpartisan elections.

A variant of the nonpartisan election, where no party labels appear on the ballot, is the partisan election where only local party designations are permitted. Approximately 5% of U.S. cities permit local, but not national, party affiliation of candidates on election ballots.[2] A study of one such local election system (Freeman, 1958) reported that partisan patterns of candidate support in the local party system and national party system are related.

Although advocates of the nonpartisan ballot asserted that "there is no Democratic or Republican way to pave a street," and although this argument for insulation of local elections also motivated some cities to adopt local party election systems, most studies found that municipal voters behave as though their interests at different levels of government are related. Even in nonpartisan systems, partisan interests are one determinant of voting behavior.

Voting for Incumbents

It is commonly asserted that nonpartisanship increases the electoral advantage of incumbents, because the voter often resorts to selecting a familiar name on the ballot in the absence of party labels (Adrian, 1952; Gilbert and Clague, 1962; Greenstein, 1970). It is also believed that the tendency of voters to select incumbents in nonpartisan elections inhibits the ability of voters to remove unsatisfactory elected officials. This effect of the nonpartisan ballot on incumbency is considered to be an undesirable unanticipated consequence of the municipal reform movement.

Adrian (1952) observed that the nonpartisan ballot in Minnesota and Nebraska state legislative elections increased the electoral advantage for incumbents. In fact, most nonpartisan incumbents in Minnesota were able to maintain their legislative seats during the early 1930s, despite drastic changes in partisan elected officials. Similarly, Welch (1978) observed an 84% success rate among incumbents running for reelection to the nonpartisan state legislature in Nebraska, compared with a 46% success rate among incumbents in Michigan and Wisconsin. Yet Rosenthal (1981) reported a 29-state average incumbent reelection rate of approximately 90% in state legislatures, challenging the conclusion that nonpartisan incumbents are more secure than partisan incumbents in state legislatures.

Contrary to conventional wisdom, both Lee (1963) and Karnig and Walter (1977) found that at the municipal level, incumbent candidates for mayor fare better in partisan elections. Their conclusions are convincing, since both studies are based on surveys of all U.S. cities with populations of 25,000 and above. In 1975, the incumbent success rate for mayors was 75% in partisan cities and 61% in nonpartisan cities "probably as a consequence of the stabilizing influence party identification has on structuring electoral choices" (Karnig and Walter, 1977, p. 68). Also, since voters have more information about mayoral than legislative candidates, the name recognition advantage attached to incumbency in less visible contests may not be as significant in mayoral elections.

Incumbent council members also appear to be helped in their re-election efforts by the partisan ballot, although the advantage is modest. It appears that the incumbent electoral advantage increased in partisan cities in recent years, creating the relative advantage for partisan incumbents. In 1975, 82% of partisan and 76% of nonpartisan incumbent council members who sought reelection were successful (Karnig and Walter, 1977); whereas in 1962, 76% of partisan and 75% of nonpartisan incumbent council members who sought reelection were successful (Lee, 1963).

An exception to this generalization may be that the nonpartisan ballot favors incumbents more than the partisan ballot when voters are dissatisfied with city government and attempt to "throw the rascals out." Karnig and Walter (1981) reported that voters are more likely to defeat a majority of city council members in the same election in partisan than in nonpartisan contests. In the one election in eight in which city voters remove a majority of the council members from office, the partisan ballot provides a convenient collective label for the voters to identify the "ins" and "outs."

It seems that, as Adrian (1952) noted, the hypothesis that nonpartisan elections foster greater voting for incumbents than do partisan elections applies only when comparisons are made between nonpartisan situations and competitive two-party elections. But instead of being competitive, many municipal elections are dominated by one party. In such elections, incumbents have the advantage of both a majority party base and name recognition. In the real world of noncompetitive municipal elections, it is actually the partisan incumbent whose office is more secure.

Types of Candidates Recruited and Elected

Nonpartisan ballots may encourage certain types of candidates and discourage others from competing in municipal elections. Municipal reformers who supported the nonpartisan ballot argued that "better" candidates would choose to run in nonpartisan contests, and that nonpartisan elections would eliminate political party "hacks" and open municipal government to civic-minded individuals unwilling to become involved and identified with political party organizations.

Since reformers wanted municipal government to be managed on a businesslike basis, "better" candidates presumably would be those from the business and professional communities. Also, good candidates from the minority party would stand a better chance to obtain office under the nonpartisan system.

Revisionist interpretations of the municipal reform movement argue that the nonpartisan ballot biases elections in favor of candidates who have access to nonparty resources necessary to wage a successful election campaign. Thus the revisionist interpretation views nonpartisan contests negatively: Wealthy candidates and those with support of the business community would seem more likely to be elected and less likely to be concerned with the well-being of the community as a whole than candidates with more diverse social backgrounds. Because affluent candidates tend to be Republican, it is commonly assumed that nonpartisan elections have a Republican candidate bias. Additionally, nonpartisan elections are viewed negatively because it is believed they do not provide a channel for recruitment to higher partisan office.

Social Background

Lee found the nonpartisan system "pretty bad" (Lee, 1960, p. 171) in terms of the representativeness of local elective officials. Affluent, white Protestant males were clearly advantaged in California municipal elections. Lee remarked that evidence was not then available to discern whether or not successful candidates in cities using the partisan election system would be any different.

Despite the revisionist theorists' claim that the nonpartisan election system biases candidate selection and inhibits recruitment to higher partisan office, only a few studies have compared social and political backgrounds of elected officials in nonpartisan and partisan systems (except studies which examined the impact of election systems on blacks and females, discussed in the following section). One study (Rogers and Arman, 1971) found that officials elected in nonpartisan systems in Ohio have higher-status occupations, higher income, and are older than officials elected in partisan systems. A second study (Feld and Lutz, 1972) suggested that partisan elections provide a stepping stone to higher office, whereas nonpartisan contests generally do not: Nonpartisan city councils may attract "an older, more established man seeking a prestigious diversion"; partisan contests may attract "a young breed of politician" (Feld and Lutz, 1972, p. 927).

These studies suggested several propositions tested by Cassel (1985) with a survey of all U.S. cities of population 2,500 and above. First, it was suggested that partisan elections have a greater tendency to facilitate recruitment to higher political office than do nonpartisan elections, which result in nonpartisan city councils whose members are older and fewer of whom are attorneys than for partisan city councils. Instead, Cassel (1985) found the average age of city council members is virtually identical in nonpartisan and partisan cities (average age is 47 in nonpartisan cities and 47.3 in partisan cities), and there is virtually no difference in the proportion of attorneys on nonpartisan and partisan city councils. Thus, there is no evidence based on age or attorney occupation that career ambitions vary in nonpartisan and partisan cities or that the nonpartisan movement has inhibited political recruitment in the United States.

Second, studies suggested that nonpartisan council members tend to be of higher socioeconomic status than partisan council members, resulting in nonpartisan city councils which contain a higher proportion of persons with high-status occupations and high levels of education. The second proposition was supported, in part. There are occupational, although not educational, differences between nonpartisan and partisan city councils. Within each category of council constituency (at-large, district, or combination), the proportion of council members with high occupational status is higher in nonpartisan cities. At the extremes, reformed cities with both nonpartisan and at-large elections have a majority of occupational elites on city councils (53.8%); and unreformed cities with both partisan and district elections have a clear minority of occupational elites on city councils (37.7%) (Cassel, 1985).

Reformed election systems (nonpartisan, at-large) result in relatively more elitist city councils in terms of council members' occupational status. Whether or not the nonpartisan ballot results in election of better candidates, as the reformers had hoped, is a value judgment which cannot be confirmed or denied. The data do indicate that reform institutions exaggerate the differences in socioeconomic status between cities' populations and their legislative bodies.

Republican Candidate Bias?

A number of studies attempted to assess the potential partisan candidate bias of nonpartisan elections. The conventional wisdom, which is part of the revisionist critique of nonpartisan elections, is that nonpartisan elections benefit Republican candidates because wealth and access to wealth, which Republicans are more likely to have, are more important in nonpartisan contests; and Democrats are hurt more than Republicans by the lack of party organization. The latter is presumably true because the working-class Democratic electorate is harder to mobilize and is less politically informed than its middle-class Republican counterpart.

Early empirical studies supported the notion that nonpartisanship benefits Republican candidates, although tentatively. For example, Williams and Adrian's (1959) study of four cities and Salisbury and Black's (1963) study of Des Moines supported the Republican benefit thesis. Lee examined six California cities from 1931 to 1955 and reported that "the evidence of this study is persuasive that, in terms of membership, the minority (Republican) party has the lion's share of local political office in California" (Lee, 1960, pp. 180–181). Yet Lee (1960) also reported that the minority Republican party dominated California's partisan state government.

Other studies did not find evidence of a Republican bias. Hagansick concluded that in Milwaukee, "the nonpartisan ballot has not substantially increased formal Republican representation on local governing bodies" (Hagansick, 1964, p. 119); Orleans (1968) found the same is true in a large undisclosed western city; and Wildavsky (1964) reported that the shift from partisan to nonpartisan elections in Oberlin, Ohio, resulted in an advantage for Democratic (minority party) council candidates.

The Republican benefit thesis was tested most systematically by Hawley (1973), who compared the vote for council members elected in 88 nonpartisan municipalities in the California Bay Area with the vote for state and federal officials in those same municipalities from 1957 to 1966. Hawley's data supported the general conclusion that nonpartisanship benefits Republicans although the bias is substantial only in large cities whose population exceeds 60,000. "In these cities the average Republican bias is 35.1%; that is, Democrats would have won more than a third more of the races for councilman and mayor in these cities than they did between 1957 and 1966 had elections been partisan rather than nonpartisan" (Hawley, 1973, p. 82). Additionally, Hawley found that the Republican bias is greater in lower SES cities.

Since none of the cities in the Bay Area used district elections, the Republican bias appears attributable solely to the nonpartisan ballot. Although the Republican bias potentially is a serious problem in large, low-SES cities, Hawley hypothesized that it might be mitigated by factors such as district election, party activity, or a heavily Democratic electorate.

Election of Blacks and Females

Studies consistently reported that nonpartisan elections favor candidates of higher socioeconomic status than do partisan elections, but it is not certain that nonpartisan elections inhibit the election of blacks. On the basis of social status alone, black candidates would seem to fare better in partisan systems. But successful black candidacy in partisan systems depends on black access to party resources and support.

It is possible that political parties provide black candidates access to party nominations and support, especially through the practice of balancing tickets to include nominees from a city's minority and ethnic populations. On the other hand, ticket balancing may not be widespread in partisan systems, and black candidates may find it difficult to penetrate local party organizations. If this were the case, black candidates might find it easier to run for office and be elected in nonpartisan systems, despite their socioeconomic disadvantage.

Robinson and Dye (1978) and Karnig and Welch (1980) assessed the effect of the nonpartisan ballot on black election to city councils and concluded that nonpartisan elections contribute to underrepresentation of blacks, although Karnig and Welch did not find the positive association between partisan elections and black candidate success to be statistically significant.

Karnig and Welch (1980) also examined the electoral success of black mayoral candidates and found they are more likely to be elected in nonpartisan than in partisan systems. In the 1970s, 8% of partisan cities and 21% of nonpartisan cities elected a black mayor. Karnig and Welch speculated that a possible reason why partisan elections inhibit the election of black mayors may be that party leaders tend to slate black candidates for less important city offices. In summary, it appears that the nonpartisan system of election inhibits the election of black council members but promotes the election of black mayors. On balance, since the office of mayor is more important, the nonpartisan system seems beneficial to blacks.

Several studies (Karnig and Walter, 1976; Welch and Karnig, 1979) examined the relationship between ballot form and the election of females to municipal office. These studies reported that the relationship between nonpartisanship and female office holding is extremely weak. Ballot form appears to have the same general effect on female as on black electoral success, only weaker.

Policy Effect

Researchers have investigated the effect of reformed local governmental structures on municipal policy. These studies commonly assess the relationship between (1) socioeconomic factors; (2) reform structures (ballot form, council-mayor relationship, and council constituency); and (3) per capita municipal taxation and expenditures. Because adoption of the nonpartisan ballot and other reforms attempts to take "politics" out of local government and to administer municipalities in an efficient, businesslike manner, it seems logical to hypothesize that the nonpartisan ballot contributes to lower levels of municipal taxing and spending. This also seems likely because nonpartisan elections contribute to the election of persons with high-status occupations and to the election of Republicans who generally prefer more limited government than do Democrats.

In the first comparative local policy study of its kind, Lineberry and Fowler (1967) found that reformed cities tax and spend less than their unreformed counterparts and are less responsive to social cleavages. Although Lineberry and Fowler concluded that the effects of reform institutions (nonpartisanship, at-large elections, and council-manager government) are additive, their data indicate that taxation and expenditure levels are virtually no different in nonpartisan and partisan cities.

Findings of subsequent studies are mixed. In a reanalysis of Lineberry and Fowler's study, Liebert (1974) contended that the conclusion that reformed cities tax and spend less is not supported when a control is introduced for functional inclusiveness of cities. "Unfortunately, spending on most major municipal expenditure items is determined less by community policy commitments than by whether city hall, a county, a special district or a state is responsible for these items" (Liebert, 1974, p. 765). Lyons (1977) reported that although there is no evidence that the effects of reforms are additive, nonpartisan cities spend less.

Hansen's (1975) study of citizen-leader agreement on the salience of local problems also supported the thesis that nonpartisan governments are less responsive to the local community, although policy attitudes, rather than actual policy outcomes, were measured. However, Morgan and Pelissero report that "changes in city government structure have almost no impact on changes in taxing and spending levels" (Morgan and Pelissero, 1980, p. 1005), in an analysis of taxation and expenditures in cities which changed their form of government.

Karnig (1975) reported findings which are congruent with Lineberry and Fowler's conclusions in a similarly designed comparative analysis using different independent and dependent variables. Karnig examined the relationship between civil rights group mobilization and the development of local private-regarding programs which benefit particular groups within a community. According to Karnig, "the association between private-regarding group mobilization and private-regarding public policy is lower in nonpartisan, at-large and council-manager cities" (Karnig, 1975, p. 103).

In summary, studies have not resolved the dispute over whether or not governmental structure affects municipal policy. Taxation and expenditure levels have been the focus of most studies because budgetary figures represent policy outcomes of political systems and because these data are readily available. Yet, as the Karnig study suggests, cities may vary in resource allocation in ways not revealed in analyses of aggregate budgetary data, even when expenditures for police, sanitation, and other categories of local government budget items are measured separately.

Conclusions

Municipal reformers of the early twentieth century and political scientists of the mid-twentieth century developed conflicting theories about the effects of nonpartisan elections on municipal politics. Reformers viewed nonpartisan elections as a means to recruit superior candidates for municipal office and to insulate municipalities from irrelevant state and national partisan issues. Reformers also were motivated by their desire to reduce the potential for domination of politics by corrupt party machines, but merit personnel systems and other reforms have made this rationale for nonpartisan elections far less relevant for the 1980s. Revisionist theorists questioned the desirability of nonpartisan elections, their principal argument being that removal of party labels from municipal ballots reduced the responsibility of the rulers to the ruled by promoting issueless elections and favoring election of incumbents and other "name" candidates.

In this essay, three decades of empirical research have been reviewed. Neither the reformist nor the revisionist theory of nonpartisan municipal elections is generally supported by empirical studies. The differences between partisan and nonpartisan systems appear to be less than both the proponents and critics of nonpartisanship argue.

However, there are some discernible and measurable differences. It does appear that Republicans, members of the business community, and professionals are elected more frequently in nonpartisan than in partisan systems. Yet as just suggested, the differences do not seem to translate into notable policy differences. Perhaps the Republican policy preference for lower taxes and spending at the state and federal level is not applicable to local government, or at least not to the same extent. Republicans may actually prefer local responsibility for certain kinds of governmental services and may have no reason to tax and spend less than their Democratic counterparts where spending outcomes visibly enhance a local community in ways beneficial to many businesses. And even if Democrats elected to partisan office prefer to increase municipal services to their constitutents, they may find that policy options are extremely narrow; not only is political support for increased taxation difficult to obtain, but experience has shown that higher tax rates tend to drive a city's businesses and residents elsewhere.

Partisan elections do appear to provide better access to local office to persons who are not community elites. The somewhat less representative nature of nonpartisan legislative bodies appears to be the major revisionist critique of nonpartisan elections supported by empirical evidence, although there also is evidence that voting on the basis of a candidate's name (ethnicity) is more prevalent in nonpartisan than in partisan contests. Empirical studies fail to confirm other important revisionist criticisms, such as notions that nonpartisan elections are issueless in nature and that nonpartisan elections insulate incumbents. Empirical studies also fail to confirm the reform argument that nonpartisan elections insulate local elections from partisan concerns or that the nonpartisan system of elections results in more efficient administration of municipalities. There remain significant gaps in our knowledge of the effects of the nonpartisan ballot on voting behavior and of the policy effects of nonpartisan elections.

The insignificant differences between partisan and nonpartisan systems can be better understood if consideration is given to relevant elements in the broader pattern of the political system as it has developed in the United States. One of these elements is the nature and extent of party competition or lack thereof. Adrian (1952) qualified his revisionist propositions about nonpartisan elections by stating that such propositions were made presuming comparison with a competitive two-party system. In reality, competitive two-party situations tend to be the exception rather than the rule in U.S. municipalities.

Thus empirical studies typically compare nonpartisan elections with elections where one party dominates.

In noncompetitive partisan systems, if elections are contested at all, they must be contested in primaries of the dominant party where there are no labels and only names to guide voters, just as in nonpartisan elections. Such contests are sometimes between the more conservative and more liberal elements of the community. Studies by Williams and Adrian (1959), and Salisbury and Black (1963) suggest that such factions develop in nonpartisan communities as well. Partisan elections also may resemble the nonpartisan model when one party dominates and factions develop around personal characteristics of candidates rather than issues or ideology. Perhaps these similarities in the dynamics of both types of contests help explain why turnout, policy, and other differences in the two systems appear to be so small. Additionally, the contemporary weakness of party structures in the United States would seem to blunt the differences between nonpartisan and partisan models.

Acknowledgments. This chapter is based on a paper delivered at the XII World Congress of the International Political Science Association, Rio de Janeiro, August 9–14, 1982. The author is especially indebted to Leon Weaver for support and assistance in numerous ways.

Notes

1. Approximately 63% of municipal elections are nonpartisan. The 63% figure is a weighted estimate from the International City Management Association (ICMA) 1981 survey of the universe of U.S. cities, *Form of Government*. The ICMA surveyed 6,761 cities; 4,659 of which responded (69%). Regional response rate varied substantially, ranging from 63% in the Northeast to 81% in the West. See Sanders 1982, pp. 178–179. Because of the strong association between ballot form (nonpartisan/partisan) and region, the survey is weighted by regional response rate to estimate the proportion of nonpartisan cities in the United States. The same figure (63%) is obtained when weighting by the form of government item. (Response rate is highest among council-manager cities.) Because these varying response rates bias this survey and previous surveys, the incidence of municipal reform structures (nonpartisan elections, council-manager form of government, and at-large elections) may be exaggerated slightly in reported studies. For example, when the 1981 survey is not weighted for response bias, it appears that 70% of U.S. cities have nonpartisan elections.
2. Estimated from the ICMA 1981 survey.

CHAPTER 15

Ballot Format in Plurality Partisan Elections

Howard A. Scarrow

Ever since the 1880s, when the American states first began to print an official ballot paper, there has been significant variation in its format. Such variation has stemmed from (1) America's federal structure; (2) the large number of format possibilities which a long ballot presents; (3) the competing demands of professional politicians and political reformers, both of whom have always believed that ballot format makes an important difference on election outcomes; and (4) Americans' willingness to employ innovative mechanical devices, in this case the voting machine, and more recently the punch card and the optical scanner. Other democracies have lacked this tradition of federalism, bossism, reformism, and mechanical innovation. It has been among American political scientists, accordingly, that the study of ballot format has received most attention.

Single Versus Multiple Choice

A frequently studied question has been the respective impact of the single-choice and the multiple-choice ballot format, the former usually referred to as the "Indiana" or "party-column ballot," and the latter as the "Massachusetts" or "office-block ballot." With the first type a voter can, with a single mark (or lever or card punch) cast a vote for all of a party's candidates appearing on the ballot. The multiple-choice ballot, in contrast, requires the voter to expend separate effort (mark, lever, and punch) for each candidate he wishes to support; if 20 offices are to be filled, 20 acts are required. The impact of these different formats has been discussed in terms of (1) straight-ticket versus split-ticket voting, usually in the context of "coattails" or in the context of the insulation of state from national politics; and (2) roll-off, or voter fatigue; that is, the failure of voters to cast a vote for candidates whose names appear at the lower end of the ballot. Roll-off not only is a measure of nonstraight-ticket voting but also has been considered important in its own right, in the context of voter participation.

All of the studies have concluded that ballot format does have an impact on the two variables mentioned. With the multiple-choice ballot there is more ticket splitting and more roll-off than there is with the single-choice ballot. The hunches of the professional politicians and political reformers have thus been confirmed. Exactly how much difference ballot format makes on election outcomes or voting behavior is, however, less certain. One reason is that the various studies have employed different methodologies, and hence their findings cannot be directly compared. Another problem is that the studies based on aggregate data have been subject to the usual ecological-fallacy warning.

Only the Campbell and Miller (1957) study allows firm conclusions regarding individual voter behavior. Using survey responses from the 1956 election, the authors found a difference of 11 percentage points between the proportion of Eisenhower voters who voted the straight Republican ticket in the single-choice states (59%) and the proportion of such voters who did so in the multiple-choice states (48%). A difference almost as large (9 points) characterized the Stevenson voters in the two groups of states. Cummings (1966, pp. 172–183), using aggregate data, found that during the period 1932–1964 the discrepancy between a party's proportion of a district's congressional (House) vote and its proportion of the district's presidential vote was much larger in districts located in multiple-choice states than in districts located in single-choice states. For example, 24% of the former type district displayed discrepancies of over 10 points; in contrast, discrepancies of that size occurred in only 9% of the single-choice districts. Rusk (1970) also found larger discrepancies in the multiple-choice states. Examining elections at the turn of the century (1890–1908) for all statewide offices, he found the mean discrepancy between a party's highest office percentage and its lowest office percentage to be 4.8

points in the multiple-choice states but only 2.8 points in the single-choice states. Walker (1966) looked at percent roll-off (i.e., decline) from the total vote cast (all parties) for president (or governor) and that cast for the office of congressman; he found that during the period 1950–1962 the roll-off in the multiple-choice states averaged between 3% and 4%, whereas in the single-choice states it averaged only between 2% and 3%. Before-and-after analysis of individual states which switched to the multiple-choice format revealed a similar pattern. Dubois (1979), looking at judicial offices in 9 states for the period 1948–1974, found roll-off usually higher in the multiple-choice states (average 8%) than in the single-choice states (5%).

One of the most important findings of several studies is that the impact of ballot format on voter behavior varies with characteristics of the individual voter. Campbell and Miller (1957) found that a multiple-choice format encouraged split-ticket voting much more among voters who were only weakly motivated by partisan loyalty and by knowledge of candidates and issues than it did among strongly motivated voters. Using census data, Walker (1966) found that the multiple-choice ballot produced roll-off much more in counties populated by persons of low education than it did in counties of high educational levels. The analysis by Zauderer (1971) of city wards in Ohio produced a similar finding.

Granted that ballot format has produced differences in voting behavior—at least among voters of specified characteristics—what political consequences have stemmed from these differences? Have elections been won or lost as a result of ballot format? This is a question which studies have usually not addressed. An exception is Weber's (1980) analysis of 79 gubernatorial elections during the 1970s. Unified party control of the governorship and lower house of the state legislature resulted from 67% of the single-choice elections but from only 50% of the multiple-choice elections.

One of the problems encountered by all of the foregoing studies is that the labeling of states as single choice or multiple choice does not produce two homogeneous groupings. The amount of effort required of the voter varies considerably within each classification. New York's voting machines (compulsory since 1938), while styled "office block" and lacking a master party lever, in fact make straight-party voting very easy since all of a party's candidates are located on a single horizontal row or, as in New York City, in a single vertical column; one sweep of the hand along the row or column will produce a straight-party vote. Walker (1966) noted that the office-block paper ballot in Montana was printed in a way which actually *discouraged* roll-off. Connecticut illustrates that a single-choice format, too, can be distinctive. Until 1965 in that state not only *could* a voter pull the straight-party lever, but he was forced to do so in order to activate the machine. Only after pulling that lever could the voter, if he wished to do so, undo some of the choices and support candidates of another party. Mayhew (1971, p. 268) believes that this distinctive format accounted for some of the wild swings in district election outcomes.

Finally, it should be noted that none of the authors mentioned identify ballot format as the only factor affecting the degree of party voting and/or roll-off. Burnham (1965) specifically treats these phenomena more as the product of the electorate's orientations toward the political system than of ballot format. Rusk (1970) takes the opposite view.

Ballot Position

The other subject which has received scholarly attention has been the effect of the ordering of candidates' names on the ballot. Although roll-off studies focus on one aspect of candidate ordering, namely, voter participation, ballot-position studies investigate what advantage accrues to the candidate whose name appears first, second, and so forth on the ballot. Depending on the ballot format, analysis may be in terms of (1) a candidate's position in a vertical or horizontal list of names, especially where the voter is asked to vote for more than one name; or (2) a candidate's position in a first row (or column), as opposed to subsequent rows (or columns). Again, the hunches of the professional politicians have suggested the research agenda. As far back as 1916, for example, a candidate presented to a New York court evidence purporting to show that when an office-block ballot presented a list of many partisan candidates, arranged by lot, to fill 4 to 6 judicial vacancies, top placement was worth 20,000 votes (Bain and Hecock, 1957, p. 24). Reflecting such practitioner insight, state election laws have invariably stipulated the method for determining ballot position—for instance, alphabetical, lot, rotation, and party strength.

Understandably, most of the ballot position studies have focused on nonpartisan primary elections, where the voter is deprived of the normal party cue and hence where the effect of ballot position is likely to be most pronounced. The most ambitious study, carefully designed in terms of statistical significance, is that of Bain and Hecock (1957). Examining a number of primary and nonpartisan elections in Michigan, the authors found that in a vertical list the top name was always favored, that the names immediately following were also usually favored, and that where there was a long list the bottom name was favored over some of those above. Mueller's (1970) analysis of a non-partisan election in Los Angeles, based on regression analysis, confirmed the importance of candidate ordering. With 133 candidates on the list, alphabetically arranged, a top-to-bottom order effect was found to follow a logarithmic pattern, except that, as in the Michigan study, the bottom name seemed more favored than some of those above. A British study of within-party variation in at-large local council elections (within-party being equivalent to nonpartisan) also found a clear ordering effect: the higher a candidate's name (in lists of three, four, and five), the more votes he polled (Upton and Brook, 1975). All of the studies have found that the effect of ballot position diminishes when the voter is presented with other cues, such as name recognition.

Because of the wide use of voting machines, the findings of Bain and Hecock relating to machine ordering are of particular interest. They found a definite advantage for the candidate whose name appeared on the top row, within his opponent immediately below on the second row. The authors' report (Bain and Hecock, 1957, pp. 14–22) of two election outcomes in other states provided even stronger evidence, since these elections were general elections with partisan labels. In Colorado 30 candidates, listed alphabetically, occupied two rows of 15 each on the machine; with one exception, the vote of each top-row candidate exceeded the vote of the second-row candidates. In Ohio, under a rotation scheme, a congressional candidate's name appeared sometimes on the top row, sometimes on the second row, and sometimes on the third row; each candidate was found to be greatly disadvantaged when his name appeared third.

The question of ballot placement lends itself nicely to experimental study. Taebel (1975) administered two versions of the same ballot choices to a group of respondents and found not only that being listed first (in groups of two, three, or four) was to a candidate's advantage, but also that the advantage increased for offices listed at the end of the ballot (nine offices were to be filled). Bagley (1966), in a more complex experiment, reported contrary findings: In a list of two candidates the second one is favored, in a list of three candidates the middle candidate is favored, and in a list of four candidates the third is favored.

Conclusions

Political scientists today seem less interested in the study of ballot format than were those of a previous generation. As can be seen, much of our knowledge is based on studies completed in the 1950s.

Obviously lacking are more studies of the effect on voting behavior of the various mechanical devices. For example, what are the relative impacts of the Shoup (vertical column) and Automatic Voting Machine (horizontal row) formats? And is it true, as some plaintiffs have charged in state courts, that in the horizontal format voters mistakenly believe that in a multimember district contest they are prevented from voting for a candidate in row *B* (or *A*) if they have already pulled the lever for a candidate positioned immediately above (below), thus diminishing the vote of a candidate perceived as being paired against a popular incumbent? The most fundamental question, however, is still that of what difference, if any, ballot format makes in determining which candidate, and especially which party, wins an election.[1]

Notes

1. Key, in the fourth edition of his classic text (1958, p. 694) notes Taft's observation that some 200,000 of his 1950 senatorial vote total could be attributed to the fact that Ohio had recently switched to the office-block format. Impressive as that figure may sound, Taft's margin of victory was over twice that size; American politics had been affected not in the least.

CHAPTER 16

Cross-Endorsement and Cross-Filing in Plurality Partisan Elections

Howard A. Scarrow

Cross-endorsement refers to the practice of a candidate for office running as the nominee of more than one political party. In cross-filing a candidate simultaneously seeks the nomination of more than one party. Both practices appear peculiar to U.S. politics, although a phenomenon roughly similar to cross-endorsement occurs in other democracies when two parties form an electoral alliance in support of a single candidate. Recent examples of the latter practice have been the alliance between Socialists and Communists in France and between Liberals and Social Democrats in Britain. What has distinguished the American practice of cross-endorsement has been that the respective parties have officially, under state law, nominated the same candidate for an office, and that the names of the respective nominating parties have, accordingly, been printed on the ballot.

In the early part of the century and even before, there were more instances of cross-endorsements in the United States than there are today. The Congressional Quarterly's *Guide to U.S. Elections* (1975), for example, shows that during the period 1890–1920 there were 56 gubernatorial elections, spread across 19 states, in which at least one of the candidates was the nominee of more than one party. In contrast, for the next 30-year period the *Guide* lists only 12 such instances, confined to only six states. The decline in cross-endorsed candidacies stemmed from modifications in the states' election laws. As of 1910 there were 19 states whose laws effectively banned cross-endorsements. By 1960 the list of states with such laws had expanded to include all but three states—New York, Connecticut, and Vermont. Major additions to the list were made in 1935 and 1959 when Pennsylvania and California, respectively, enacted cross-endorsement bans.

What were, and what are, the consequences stemming from the cross-endorsement practice? The question can be answered most profitably by looking at the two most noteworthy examples of the practice, California and New York.

Cross-Filing in California

The term *cross-filing* originated with a 1913 amendment to the California election law. The state's direct primary law, enacted in 1909, had mandated a primary system which was "closed" not only in the sense that primary voters had to be able to demonstrate their past support for the party but also in the sense that primary candidates, too, were required to demonstrate past party support. The 1913 amendment eliminated this latter requirement; from now on a candidate could file petitions to enter his own party's primary, and/or he could cross-file in another party's primary.

The 1913 amendment attracted little attention at the time of its enactment (Findley, 1959, p. 703). For one thing, the amendment simply restored the legal situation as it existed prior to 1909, when multiple party nominations (by conventions) were not uncommon. More important, the 1913 amendment was enacted by a Progressive-dominated legislature in the spirit of nonpartisanship. The assumption was that its major effect would be to allow a party to seek and nominate a candidate who was worthy, regardless of his partisanship.

It soon became apparent, however, that the 1913 amendment provided a useful device for partisan candidates to increase their chances of electoral success. A Republican or a Democratic candidate could run both in his own party's primary and also, at the same time, "raid" the primary of the other major party and, if successful in both contests, be assured of victory in the general election. This ploy became very popular; by the mid-1950s over three quarters of all candidates for statewide, state legislative, and national legislative office were attempting to win election this way. Altogether, according to one study (Pitchell, 1959, p. 462), some 47% of all candidates for these offices during the period 1914–1956 resorted to the cross-filing tactic, and half of the elections during this period—some 1,350 contests—were in effect won at the primary election. One conspicuous example was Earl Warren's Republican and Democratic gubernatorial candidacy in 1946.

Making successful raids possible was the fact that the primary election ballot did not indicate the party affiliation of the respective candidates. It was thus possible for a candidate to "masquerade" before the voters, not stressing his party ties (McHenry, 1950). The importance of the information gap became apparent after the election law was changed, in 1952, to require the printing of party labels on the primary ballot. The number of cross-filings, as well as the success rate, immediately plummeted (Baker and Teitelbaum, 1959, p. 288). With such a decline, the stage was set for the total repeal of the cross-filing system, which finally occurred in 1959.

Two conspicuous consequences of the cross-filing system were identified by its critics. The first was the advantage given to incumbents. With no party labels to guide the primary voter, name recognition became especially important. A full 80% of all successful cross-filers during the 1914–1956 period were incumbents (Pitchell, 1959, p. 471). The second consequence of the cross-filing system was that it completely undermined party responsibility. A primary contest among unlabeled candidates, it was argued, was no substitute for a general election contest between two major party candidates, each identified with a party record, a party platform, and with fellow party candidates. "The most important step toward establishment of party responsibility in California," concluded McHenry (1950, p. 232) was "abolition of cross-filing."

A third consequence of California's cross-filing system was the boost it gave to minor parties. The reason the Progressive faction of California's Republican party decided to form a separate party organization in December 1913, was that the amendment to the election law enacted earlier that year resolved the doubts of those within the Progressive movement who questioned the wisdom of such a move (Findley, 1959, p. 704). With the change in the law the Progressives could form a new party and yet continue to challenge regular Republicans in Republican primaries. The following year the candidates of the new Progressive party succeeded in capturing Republican nominations for five of the statewide offices, and in 1916 the party's U.S. senatorial candidate (Hiram Johnson) was similarly successful. As the popularity of the Progressive movement declined, the raiding tactic became of diminished value; indeed, the tactic was turned on the Progressive party itself. Nevertheless, the Progressive Party showed that the disadvantage suffered by a "third" party under the single-member-district, plurality election system can be partially overcome by tampering with the nomination system—just as the French and British parties mentioned earlier do so today.

The Progressives were not the first minor party to make this discovery. Long before 1913 minor parties in various American states had exploited such opportunities. The tactic they usually used, however, was simply that of nominating as their own candidate the nominee of one of the major parties. Of the 56 joint gubernatorial nominations during the period 1890–1950, mentioned earlier, all but two were major-minor party combinations, and most of these seem to have been the product of this latter variety of the cross-endorsement practice.

Cross-Endorsement in New York

It was in New York that this variety of cross-endorsement found its most conspicuous expression (Scarrow, 1983). One reason was New York's ballot format. At the beginning of the century New York, like California and most other states, used the party-column ballot. Accordingly, when two or more political parties nominated the same candidate, the name would appear in two more columns of the ballot. The candidate's total vote would be calculated by adding together the votes received at each ballot position. This format carried three great advantages for a minor party which nominated as its own candidate the nominee of one of the major parties. First, the minor party's organizational autonomy was visibly emphasized on the ballot. Second, the size of the vote polled in the minor party's ballot column could be used to demonstrate the importance of the party's endorsement. Finally, the arrangement allowed the option to an independent-minded voter who wanted to support the candidate nominated by a major party but did not want to support the candidate's party. For these reasons, then, multiple ballot placement, much more so than multiple nomination alone, provided a means by which a minor party could play a significant role in an election, despite the disadvantages imposed on it by the winner-take-all election system.

Early in the century these advantages became especially apparent in New York City. There the only way the powerful Tammany Democratic organization could be defeated was for various reform groups to join Republicans in a so-called fusion movement, each group forming a petition-initiated party which would list in its ballot column the common slate of anti-Tammany candidates. The all-time record for multiple candidacies occurred in the mayorality election of 1909, when the fusion movement sponsored four ballot columns and the Tammany forces countered with eight columns of their own.

The importance of multiple ballot placement to New York's cross-endorsement practice became apparent after 1913, the year New York state switched from the party column ballot to the office-block ballot, a change California made two years earlier. Under the new format the name of a jointly nominated candidate would appear on the ballot only once, with the names of the respective nominating parties printed beside it. In the first New York City mayorality election held under the new format the anti-Tammany coalition was reduced to only two petition-initiated parties, down from five in the previous election. In the following three elections fusion coalitions disappeared entirely from the ballot. Mayorality elections became straight fights between Democratic and Republican candidates. Clearly the new ballot format was inhospitable to minor party activity. Not until 1933 was the fusion idea revived by La Guardia, who ran that year as the candidate of the Republican Party and also of a petition-initiated Fusion party.

By this time, however, another change had occurred in the ballot format—the introduction of the voting machine. As presented on the voting machine, the office-block ballot was virtually indistinguishable from the party-column paper ballot of old. Although there was no machine lever for straight-party voting, all of a party's candidates for the various offices were listed in a separate vertical column (or, outside the city, in a horizontal row), thus reintroducing the three advantages for a minor party of separate ballot placement—autonomy, the recording of size of support, and the option for the independent-minded voter. Only because of the voting machine was La Guardia able to revive the fusion idea in 1933 (the second election in which machines were used). The same tactic has been used in every mayorality election since then.

The impact of the voting machine on minor party growth in New York State was most profound in statewide, congressional, and state legislative elections, the arena in which the officially recognized political parties compete. After the introduction of the office-block ballot in 1913, New York State had become, for all practical purposes, a two-party system.[1] Then in 1936 came the American Labor party (ALP), formed by labor leaders who believed that there were many New Yorkers who would not vote for President Roosevelt's reelection as the candidate of the Democratic party but who would vote for him on another party's ballot line. (Some 275,000 voters chose this option.) Then in the 1940s came the Liberal party, a breakaway faction of the ALP which continued to thrive after the ALP lost its official status. The Liberals perfected the "blackmail" potential of the cross-endorsement system, agreeing to support a major party's candidate (usually the Democrat's) only if the nominee were sufficiently "liberal" or, in later years, only if sufficient patronage was promised. Seeing how successful the Liberals were in playing the blackmail game, conservative Republicans formed a Conservative party in the 1960s, and in the late 1970s antiabortion forces formed a Right to Life party. The latter party carried the cross-endorsement game to a new level, demanding a signed antiabortion pledge of any candidate it endorsed.

Thus evolved today's five-party system in New York. As can be seen, under the New York election law the single-member-district, plurality system of election actually favors multiparty growth. With the stakes defined as all or nothing, a major party is willing to pay a considerable price, in terms of policy promises or patronage, for the relatively few votes which a minor party's endorsement is worth. It should be noted that California did not adopt the voting machine but stayed with the paper, office-block ballot. This difference no doubt helps to explain the different role played by minor parties in the two states. The Pennsylvania experience is also instructive. Until that state banned dual nominations in 1935, most of the combinations were between a major party and a minor one, as in New York; also like New York's voting machine format, the Pennsylvania ballot allowed separate party placement.

There is, however, one additional provision of New York's election law which must be mentioned as providing the foundation for New York's thriving multiparty system. In 1947 a Republican legislature, reacting to several ALP raids on Republican congressional primaries, enacted an antiraiding law. Similar to the California law of 1909, the Wilson-Pakula law, as it is known, provided that in order for a candidate to enter a party's primary his voter registration must show that he is enrolled in that party. Had the amendment stopped there, the practice of cross-endorsement might have come to an end. The law contained one escape clause, however: A party's executive committee could authorize the entry into its primary of a nonmember. Hailed at the time as a law which would preserve the two-party system, the law turned out to lead to precisely the opposite result. As the major parties came to appreciate the value of having the additional line on the ballot, they were forced to bargain with the minor parties; the raiding option was closed to them. Accordingly, since the 1950s each preelection season has featured negotiating sessions between major and minor party leaders, culminating in cross-endorsement agreements (critics call them deals) relating to most or all of the offices at stake. Under the agreement, in return for appropriate policy or patronage concessions the minor party leaders agree to authorize entry into their primary of one, and only one, candidate from the major party and to fight anyone from within their own ranks who tries to win the nomination.

Critics have identified four undesirable consequences which have stemmed from New York's system of cross-endorsement. First, the system has allowed minor parties to exert influence which is far in excess of their electoral strength. Minor party influence can be seen reflected in the candidates nominated by the major parties, as well as in the policy positions adopted by candidates and elected officials. A second consequence has been minority election outcomes. On those occasions when minor parties enter their own separate candidates, the chances are high that the winner in the election will receive less than a majority of the vote (New York's junior senator received 45%). A third consequence of the cross-endorsement system is that it sometimes produces Republican-Democratic candidates, as in California prior to 1959. When this happens (e.g., Mayor Koch's candidacy in 1981), voters are deprived of a meaningful general election. Finally, the preelection cross-endorsement "deals" among the party leaders, in which patronage considerations play a conspicuous part, have generated more than the usual amount of cynicism with "politics."

Conclusions

The experience of California and New York leaves little doubt that election laws may have profound consequences for the working of a political system. The impact of the cross-endorsement practice became especially noticeable in these states as they came to be among the few in the nation which had not outlawed the practice. At the same time, the California and New York experience demonstrates that laws which are enacted in order to achieve a specified goal (e.g., nonpartisan elections in California, and a "reformed" ballot in New York) may turn out to have unforeseen consequences, and even consequences which are precisely the opposite from those intended.

Notes

1. Because in New York official party status is determined by the number of votes polled by a party's candidate for governor, the office-block ballot format provided for multiple voting squares for gubernatorial candidates nominated by more than one party. Unfortunately for the minor parties, voters tended to place their X in the square nearest the candidate's name, which was the major party square, and hence only parties which were able to poll sufficient votes for their own separate candidates (e.g., Prohibition) managed to survive the change in ballot format, (Scarrow, 1983).

PART **IV**

Redistricting

CHAPTER 17

Whatever Happened to the Reapportionment Revolution in the United States?

Gordon E. Baker

The period 1982–1984 marks the twentieth anniversary of the reapportionment revolution – those landmark U.S. Supreme Court decisions that transformed American political institutions in a manner unparalleled in the nation's history. The intervening years have witnessed the reshaping of legislative constituencies on the basis of one person, one vote at virtually all levels from the federal House of Representatives down to the smallest school district.

A distance of two decades provides an ideal opportunity to survey the most salient results of the new conditions. We might ponder such questions as: How do the institutional patterns of representation compare "before" and "after"? In particular, what were the aims and expectations of those reformers and commentators who triggered the reapportionment revolution? To what extent have these aims been achieved? And, if the analogy to revolution is appropriate, have there been, as in nearly all revolutions, unintended – even counterproductive – consequences?

In approaching this problem, we should initially note the main characteristics that prompted judicial entry into what had been widely recognized as a "political thicket."

The 1960 census revealed widespread and extreme disparities in the populations of state legislative districts. After completion of postcensus reapportionments, statistics showed that in only six states were both houses of the legislature apportioned so that at least 40% of the state's population was required to elect a majority in each. Only 20 states had even one house so apportioned. Finally, in 13 states, one third or less of the population could elect a solid majority of both legislative houses (National Municipal League, 1961, p. i).

On the eve of *Baker v. Carr* (1962), an influential statistical survey of state legislative representation revealed that, on a national basis, counties with a population under 25,000 held a representative strength well over double that of counties with over 100,000 (David and Eisenberg, 1961). Population disparities among state legislative constituencies ranged as high as 987–1 and as low as 2.2–1.

While population discrepancies among congressional districts were understandably less severe than in state legislatures, the extremes were still substantial. Even after the reapportionment and redistrictings of 1961–1962, districts, nationally, varied in population from 177,431 (upstate Michigan) to 951,527 (Dallas, Texas), or a ratio of 5.4–1. The 20 most populous districts in the nation (nearly all of them metropolitan) had a total of 13,941,475 people, compared with only 4,550,061 in the 20 least inhabited districts (all rural or small-town). Small wonder that an earlier recommendation of a committee of the American Political Science Association that congressional districts should fall from a maximum deviation of plus 15% to minus 15%, or a total range of 30%, seemed utopian indeed (*American Political Science Review*, 1951, pp. 153–157).

Such were the general contours of legislative representation prior to judicial intervention. After *Baker v. Carr*, holding that apportionment controversies are justiciable, lower courts readily accepted the floodtide of litigation, and new district patterns had emerged even before the 1964 decisions establishing the doctrine of representative equality for both houses of state legislatures and for the national House of Representatives. As early as the 1964 elections, half of the 50 states had made significant changes in apportionment patterns in at least one legislative house. And, by the 1966 elections, most legislative houses and congressional districts substantially approximated a population standard. Moreover, this institutional revolution was accomplished with remarkable speed. Within a few short years the political maps of the nation reflected new—in some cases, dramatically new—patterns, even though opposition at times reached a fever pitch in the chambers of Congress and state capitols (Baker, 1966, pp. 39–40, 82).

Agenda for Reform

As indicated, the standard of one person, one vote had been achieved in a remarkably short time after judicial intervention. But we might well ask: What were the aims of those pressing for per capita equalization of legislative districts? What kinds of institutional or political metamorphoses were envisaged, and why?

In probing such questions, it is first necessary to briefly sketch the nature of the problem as viewed by analysts and commentators (ranging from academic scholars to civic and social interest groups) before judicial involvement changed expectations. The census of 1950 focused particular attention on vast population mobility during and after the Second World War and the concomitant failure of American representative institutions to reflect increasingly urban and suburban trends. This situation, long in the making, was approaching a near-critical stage. The adaptability and resiliency of governmental institutions appeared to be tested by unprecedented challenges. Moreover, during the period from World War II until *Baker v. Carr,* remedies for growing malapportionment seemed largely unavailing. The precedent of *Colegrove v. Green* in 1946 (despite its scant four-to-three plurality) was widely regarded as a clear signal that courts were not a likely source of reform.

Under the circumstances, those analyzing malapportionment had little occasion to adjust their sights beyond the immediate condition of the growing disparities between areas of voters and representation. Calling attention to the problem and its seeming consequences was the immediate task – perhaps in a sense presaging Justice Frankfurter's later invocation of an "appeal for relief . . . to an informed, civically militant electorate" – though few could share Frankfurter's apparent hope that "an aroused public conscience" necessarily "sears the conscience of the people's representatives" (dissenting in *Baker v. Carr*). Critics of the *status quo* regarded the problem as basically one of political legitimacy posed by the gap between theory and practice. The generally accepted norm of democratic self-government through representative equality contrasted with the reality of oligarchies not responsible to a majority of the electorate.

This general concern with the problem of democratic theory and practice was often accompanied by a focus on rural versus urban political power (Baker, 1955). With the balance of population shifting over the years to the cities, political tension and conflict grew between urban spokesmen and state legislatures still dominated by rural and small-town areas. By the middle of the twentieth century, elected city leaders, led by the United States Conference of Mayors, singled out unequal representation as the major source of troubles for municipalities. In their view, most urban residents were victims of taxation without adequate representation.

The impact of malapportionment on state social and economic policies posed yet another concern. Long-standing rural overrepresentation in many capitols meant that organized agricultural interests were usually in a favorable position to influence state legislation, with a corresponding disadvantage to certain urban and suburban interests. Inaction could be as important as actual legislation, so that malapportionment of even one house might be decisive (Baker, 1955, pp. 23–25). Because many variables affect legislative decision-making, the impact of representative patterns was not easily measurable, and one intensive study of a single rural-dominated state (Florida) found that the influences, while clear, were often "subtle and deeply imbedded in the structure of government" (Havard and Beth, 1962, p. 77).

Another consequence of disproportionate rural legislative strength that drew the attention of scholars was the impact on the party system. For years it was said that the New York legislature was "Republican by constitutional law," indicating the results of apportionment formulas in the state constitution that limited the number of seats allotted to largely Democratic New York City. Similar conditions could be found in other states as well, with an increased likelihood of divided party government. In several northern states, Democrats could capture the governorship with a statewide majority that found one or both legislative houses out of reach because of districting patterns more favorable to the opposing party with greater rural strength (Baker, 1955, pp. 19–23; Key, 1956, pp. 64–67).

These were the more central problems identified by critics of malapportionment, but there was little optimism before the 1960s that significant change could be expected soon. Implicit in much of the analysis was the expectation that attainment of equal representation would ultimately bring about different consequences from those just identified.

Judicial intervention in 1962 transformed the earlier discontent into a more specific agenda for reform. Five months after *Baker v. Carr*, Charles S. Rhyne, successful counsel for appellants, confidently asserted the following prognosis:

> Reapportioned state governments will become more effective parts of our governmental machinery.

The oft-repeated words "states' rights" will now assume real meaning as states begin again to exercise their governmental powers.

Unshackling of long-dormant state powers will enable urban problems to be dealt with at state capitols with lessened reliance upon Washington.

Cities after decades of denials and frustrations will have the votes to secure essential home rule powers to meet local needs. It is certain that archaic state legislative machinery will now be modernized.

Genuine state constitutional reform is now possible.

The extensive nation-wide dialogue on the fundamentals of our system of government provides an opportunity to restudy and reallocate public powers and functions to those levels of government best able to perform them under twentieth-century conditions (*National Civic Review*, 1962).

Most scholarly assessments were more cautious, though inclined to anticipate some significant changes. Following the 1964 decisions, Professor of Law Robert B. McKay, pondering the consequences of reapportionment, suggested: "At the very least it should be expected that state legislators will show greater concern for the critical urban and suburban problems of education, housing, and transportation, to mention only the most acute. Since the more populous areas have always contributed a proportionately larger share of the state revenues, while receiving a significantly smaller share in return, some readjustment may be anticipated" (McKay, 1965, p. 268).

One political scientist offered this carefully balanced analysis of the evolving reapportionment revolution:

. . . reapportionment will probably increase the frequency with which governor and legislature are of the same party, but this effect may be attenuated by other factors; urban, but especially suburban, people will be more heavily represented in state legislatures, but in what directions and to what degree this will alter the nature of the policy output of legislatures remains to be seen; the effect of reapportionment on the two major parties will vary by state and will depend greatly on the political pattern that suburban people develop, though in the populous states of the north and east the immediate effect will be to benefit the Democratic party (Fesler, 1967, p. 566).

But perhaps the loftiest and hence the most elusive goal of representative equality was asserted by Chief Justice Earl Warren when he declared that "the achieving of fair and effective representation for all citizens is concededly the basic aim of legislative apportionment" (*Reynolds v. Sims*, pp. 565–566).

Reapportionment's Accomplishments

The most obvious transformations caused by the one-man, one-vote decisions were structural. Within a remarkably short span of a few years, virtually all state legislative and congressional districts represented, in Chief Justice Warren's words, "people, not trees or acres" (*Reynolds v. Sims*, p. 567). The shift in political power was substantial, as older rural and small-town areas yielded representative strength to urban and suburban localities. Moreover, an unprecedented influx of new legislators signaled a major turnover of representatives. One report noted that the proportions of new lawmakers amounted to 80% in Maryland, over 50% in Connecticut, and nearly 50% in California (McKay, 1968, p. 230).

One consequence of increased urban representation, especially in the South, was the election of more black legislators, with the national total rising from 94 in 1964 to 238 in 1973. (Black members of Congress rose from 5 to 16 in approximately the same time period) (Smith, 1975).[1] While some of this growth in minority representation resulted from the Voting Rights Act of 1965, the fact that the greatest numerical increase of black lawmakers occurred outside the South suggests that reapportionment was also a factor. In his study of eight states of the South (including the border state of Kentucky) Malcolm E. Jewell concluded: "The drastic changes that are occurring in the apportionment of Southern legislatures are important because they will accelerate changes already under way in the South—notably the growing political power of Negroes and of Republicans. The result of these related trends seems certain to be an increase in competition, as fewer legislative contests are controlled by political cliques and more of them become wide-open races in which a variety of interests play a part" (Jewell, 1967, p. 137).

A significant impact on political party fortunes was widely anticipated, but with uncertainty as to its nature and extent. During the summer of 1964 the national chairmen of the Democratic and Republican National committees welcomed the reapportionment decisions handed down in June (Baker, 1966, pp. 12–13). Spokesmen for both parties could understandably foresee prospective advantages from the changes in representation then under way. While the effects would vary greatly from state to state, Democrats could generally look for gains in major cities, while Republicans could reap benefits from newly recognized suburban strength.

But Republicans were victims of unfortunate timing in 1964. The late Robert G. Dixon, Jr., made the point with his customary insight: "By

TABLE 17.1. Years of Party Control in Selected States, 1947–1965

State	Senate		House			Governorship	
	D	R	D	R	Tie	D	R
Illinois	0	18	4	14		8	10
New Jersey	0	18	6	12		10	8
Michigan	0	18	0	16	2	14	4
Connecticut	12	6	2	16		12	6
New York	0	18	0	18		4	14
Ohio	4	14	4	14		12	6

coincidence, in the fall of the same year, the Goldwater debacle in the presidential election had the side effect of ousting 500 Republican state legislators from office at the very time when legislative reapportionment, and potential future control of the legislature for years to come, was by judicial order in top position on most state legislative calendars" (Dixon, 1968, pp. 3–4). Evidence of Democratic Party gains from reapportionment emerged from an extensive analysis of 38 nonsouthern legislative chambers between 1952 and 1968. Democratic increase was greatest in states that initially were most malapportioned and which had disproportionate Democratic electoral strength in urban areas (Erikson, 1971).

Another consequence of the reapportionment revolution appears to be the reduced likelihood of divided party control between the legislature and governor. The figures in Table 17.1 reveal the prereapportionment disparities in selected states over a period of 18 years. With legislative districts distorted for partisan or rural advantage, Democrats could often elect a governor but not one or both legislative chambers. While many other factors—including weak local party organization, less well-known candidates, and "wasted" votes through heavy concentration of party strength in one or a few areas—can contribute to a discrepancy between a party's electoral and legislative strength, malapportionment was also a key factor. Table 17.2 suggests a significant reduction in divided party control in the 18 years following the major restructuring of constituencies in the mid-1960s. The one curious anomoly is the enormous increase in Democratic control of the Michigan legislature while that party was consistently losing the governor's office that it had previously held for all but four years of the earlier period. (In 1982, the Democrats regained the governorship.)

The problem of divided party control of state legislative and executive branches had long interested many political scientists, especially

TABLE 17.2. Years of Party Control in Selected States, 1965–1983

State	Senate D	R	Tie	House D	R	Tie	Governorship D	R
Illinois	8	10		8	10		8	10
New Jersey	12	6		14	4		12	6
Michigan	12	2	4	16	2		0	18
Connecticut	16	2		14	4		14	4
New York	2	16		12	6		8	10
Ohio	6	10	2	10	8		4	14

Sources. Data drawn from Council of State Governments, *Book of the States* (Lexington, Ky.) for the years covered. The idea for the tables and earlier data on four of the states is based on a similar table in Jewell, 1962, 1969, chap. 2. The figures in both Tables 1 and 2 are for the legislative sessions ending in 1965 and 1983, respectively, and hence do not reflect results of the elections of 1964 or 1982.

those concerned about attaining a heightened degree of party responsibility (Key, 1956, chap. 3). This view asserted that there should be some proximate correspondence between the actions of policymakers and the interests of the voters who elected them. The whole rationale of the two-party system is that it should offer the electorate alternative choices of candidates and programs. In this way, the parties give meaning and purpose to public sentiment, while serving to strengthen the element of responsibility among governing officials. Ideally, parties should contest for public support in such a way that votes can be translated into some sort of public policy. In a democracy there should be a reasonably direct relationship between predominant public opinion and the power to govern. Yet one ironic counterproductive feature of this reduction in divided party control is the fact that it removes what may be the only check on partisan gerrymandering, a venerable distortion of representation that has reached new levels of effectiveness, as spelled out in the next section.

The impact of vastly new apportionment patterns on social and economic policies of the states is the most difficult consequence to analyze and measure because of the many variables that produce public policy. The early returns appeared encouraging to some proponents of reapportionment. While conceding that legislative remodeling was too new to permit definitive evaluation of its impact, McKay added, "However, there were observable trends in the form of increased aid for schools, greater home rule, increased consumer protection, stronger civil rights legislation, curbs on air and water pollution, and reform of criminal justice" (McKay, 1968, pp. 230–231).

On the other hand, some political scientists had attempted to measure the earlier impact of malapportionment prior to judicial entry into the political thicket. Employing a variety of statistical methods comparing state districting patterns with policy outcomes, these studies found little correlation between malapportionment and public policies unfavorable to urban areas or "liberal" causes. The implication, seized on by critics of the Warren Court's one-person-one-vote decisions, was that the reapportionment revolution had been waged to no avail because it would not produce the results widely anticipated. While these "skeptics" generally stated their conclusions with a high degree of certitude, one of them, Dye, had the prudence to attach this caveat: "Quantification necessitates a simplification of what may be a very complex question. The consequences of reapportionment may be so subtle and diverse that they defy quantitative measurement. Perhaps the consequences in each state will vary so much that interstate comparisons are inappropriate" (Dye, 1965, p. 600).

In 1971, Bicker subjected these impact studies to a searching and penetrating analysis, concluding that they were flawed by a variety of methodological problems and did not constitute tests of either the arguments by "reformers" or of the potential impact of the Court's reapportionment decisions. Bicker (1971) declared a mistrial. Moreover, subsequent studies began to find some effects of changing representative patterns, suggesting that institutional transformations may require time to trigger results.[2]

Taking account of previous research (including Bicker's caveats), O'Rourke (1980) devised a conceptual framework for an in-depth comparative analysis of six states. Using a four-level theoretical framework, O'Rourke reasoned:

> In order for reapportionment to bring about measurable policy change, a series of developments rather than the single event of redistricting must transpire. First, reapportionment must lead to abnormally high turnover or, at the very least, enough district modification to alter legislative representation in a detectable fashion. To the degree that policy reflects group demands, redistricting must produce sufficient modification of group representation in the legislature (for example, the distribution of urban-rural or partisan interests) to make policy change likely or possible. If these first two conditions are met, measurable policy change would still require surmounting a variety of institutional barriers. Within the legislature, for example, stability in committee chairmanships and party leadership positions might mitigate major policy innovation despite substantially altered membership. In addition, legislative decision making must function within the context of previous decisions or laws and budgetary restraints

which can limit policy innovation. It should be readily apparent that fourth-level effects, being several steps removed from the immediate impact of reapportionment, are likely to result only if reapportionment has produced sweeping changes in patterns of representation. (O'Rourke, 1980, p. 5).

His investigations confirmed O'Rourke's initial expectations. First- and second-level effects were most immediate and discernible, while institutional patterns, established rules and customs, revenue limitations, and past policy commitments tended to render third- and fourth-level effects more diffuse. Changes were least noticeable in Oregon and South Dakota, which had been well or fairly well apportioned prior to 1962. Impact appeared greater in states where changes in district patterns were most sweeping, replacing artificial nonmetropolitan legislative majorities. But effects were also mitigated in states with strong two-party competition. Reapportionment helped to increase the number of black legislators in Tennessee, Kansas, and New Jersey and stimulated two-party competition for legislative control in Tennessee and Kansas. As for fourth-level (policy) effects, O'Rourke concludes, "The evidence presented suggests that reapportionment has affected selected policies in all sample states, but that the overall influence of reapportionment on policy has been rather limited and immeasureable" (O'Rourke, 1980, p. 51).[3] Among fourth-level effects were the more favorable distribution of state expenditures to central cities in most sample states and generally more "liberal" policies and possibly a more favorable climate for labor interests in all six states.

Now . . . the Bad News

In spite of the fact that the reapportionment revolution achieved some of the earlier aims of reformers, from the perspective of two decades it has won only a partial victory, one that appears to have raised questions as serious and vexing as those resolved. While any major institutional revamping carries with it inevitable negative side effects, the reapportionment experience was exaccerbated by the almost pell-mell pace of events. The sweep and speed of the Supreme Court's 1964 decisions as interpreted by lower courts increasingly left less and less room for imaginative accommodation of the one-person, one-vote rule to the myriad of other democratic values involved, including initiative and referendum. A legal scholar sympathetic to the basic goal of representative equality posited by the Court cautioned:

Even if it is assumed that the rights vindicated in the *Reapportionment Cases* are "individual and personal," there are also at stake "important political rights of the people." The State "as a polity" is involved when fundamental questions concerning the nature of representative government are decided. It is strange that the Court should conclude that the consent of the governed can be given no weight in the process of decision." (Auerbach, 1964, pp. 84–85)

Some had hoped that judicial intervention into apportionment might serve a more subtle, yet promising, function. This was the potential reexamination of the whole concept of representative government in a complex modern society. "It should open the way at last," in the words of Professor Dixon, "to a fresh dialogue—long overdue—about the character and function of representation in a Twentieth Century mass democracy" (Dixon, 1964). Professor Dixon perceptively pointed out that the Supreme Court's emphasis on representative equality as an individual right obscures the crucial fact that the personal civil right of the voter is necessarily intertwined with group activity in the process of representation. These relationships needed a new exploration which was not undertaken while the debate on representation was necessarily conditioned by the struggle over population equality.

Unfortunately, such an exploration—or fresh dialogue—did not take place except sporadically as problems arose. Indeed, any genuine and sober reappraisal of representation would likely have required a more selective entry by the Court into the political thicket, on a case-by-case basis. Instead, disposing of appeals from 15 states employing a wide diversity of representative patterns on two decision days in June of 1964 tended to suggest a more uniform approach than the high tribunal professed to intend. Still, basing the doctrine of one vote, one value on the equal protection clause of the Fourteenth Amendment led almost inevitably to an increasing preoccupation with population equality and little else. This in spite of persuasive suggestions by some legal scholars that using either the due process clause of the Fourteenth Amendment, or the guaranty (Republican Form of Government) clause would have allowed the essence of representative equality but with more adaptability to differing circumstances. (Auerbach, 1964, pp. 84–87; Dixon, 1968, p. 135).

In spite of such considerations, the Supreme Court in its 1964 decisions did take pains to indicate the degree of discretion still left to state legislatures in devising districts of substantially equal populations. In doing so, Chief Justice Warren's opinion made specific reference to multimember districts. For example, the Court said: "One body could be composed of single-member districts, while the other could have at least some multimember districts"; and again, "Single-member districts may be the rule in one state, while another state might desire to achieve some flexibility by creating multimember or floterial districts" (*Reynolds v. Sims*, pp. 577, 579).

The election of legislative delegations at large poses two distinct kinds of problems. One involves the differences in influence between voters situated in districts of varying populations which elect proportionate numbers of legislators. The usual "commonsense" assumption is that legislative strength should be proportionate: that a county five times as populous as an average single-member district should be assigned five times the number of seats in order to equalize representation. This is true *if* single-member district lines are drawn in the more populous county, but if the five legislators are elected at large, a different situation obtains. John F. Banzhaf (1966) has demonstrated that a vote in the larger, multimember districts has considerably more effective influence on elections and legislative outcomes than does a vote in a single-member or smaller multimember district, assuming proportionate populations. Using a standard mathematical technique (related to the use of game theory in measuring power distributions in legislative bodies and other groups), Banzhaf showed that voter influence was in proportion to the square root of the population of the district. Moreover, the ratios of effective representation are substantial—far more so than the variations in district populations that have concerned the judiciary.[4]

The second problem of multimember districts is the impact of winner-take-all elections on minority groupings in a particular district. This issue would still exist if, for example, Banzhaf's objections were corrected by a system entirely composed of multimember districts of approximately equal population, each electing an identical number of legislators. Of course, the inferior status of political minorities, while accentuated in at-large elections, is not exclusively confined to them. A district electing but one legislator obviously cannot expect him to represent all minority viewpoints. But single-member districts are more likely to do so *in toto*, because the creation of a large number of constituencies is more likely to accommodate significant minority groupings (such as blacks, Hispanics, Mexican-Americans, suburban Republicans, or city Democrats, depending on the state and area involved). Such minorities frequently have sufficient geographic concentration in metropolitan areas to comprise their own districts.

Both problems posed by multimember, at-large elections are extensively found in all sections of the United States. Court-ordered reapportionments typically resulted in adding legislative representation to urban centers. These augmented delegations have, in turn, frequently been elected at large and usually have produced windfalls for political majorities in these areas. The result, though not always the intent, is a species of gerrymander. Courts have groped cautiously around this part of the political thicket, invalidating some multimember districting that appeared tainted by discriminatory racial intent. But while not holding multimember districts unconstitutional, the Supreme Court demonstrated a preference for single-member districts by insisting that they be used by lower federal courts in court-drawn plans unless there were "insurmountable difficulties" (*Connor v. Johnson*, pp. 690, 692).

Judicial involvement in the details of redistricting had been particularly expanded because of the Voting Rights Act of 1965 (extended in 1970, 1975, and 1982). Based on the enforcement provisions of the Fifteenth Amendment, these acts affected several states, mostly in the South, plus scattered counties elsewhere. State or local governments brought under the coverage of the act (due to low voter registration or participation) were required to obtain federal approval of any new voting laws, standards, practices, or procedures, before implementing them. Within a few years, legislative apportionment suits were routinely brought under the act, even though this was not its original aim. New targets included not only the impact of district lines on minority areas, but especially the use of multimember districts that elect an entire delegation at large. When the Voting Rights Act of 1982 was being considered, the debate over intent versus effects was a central one. A compromise resolved the issue by providing that minority groups had no right to proportional representation, but that lack of representation was one of a "totality of circumstances" that courts could consider in determining if an electoral law produced a discriminatory effect (Congressional Quarterly Weekly Report, 1982, p. 1504). Clearly, the courts will continue to be involved in making such delicate interpretations, not to mention trying to resolve the continuing conflicts among ethnic/racial group interests that surfaced in *United Jewish Organizations v. Carey.*

The most troublesome question not only remained unsettled but loomed ever large in significance. The gerrymander—the intentional manipulation of districts for partisan or factional advantage—comprised the heart of the political thicket that the judiciary skirted most gingerly. Moreover, by 1969[5] the Supreme Court had paradoxically encouraged the potential for widespread gerrymandering by developing a single-minded quest for mathematical equality. Even though the Court in 1973[6] articulated a somewhat less stringent population standard for state legislatures, the common misconception remained that a redistricting plan is to be judged by how closely it approximates numerical equality.

Extensive gerrymandering can obviously undermine the basic aim of "fair and effective representation for all citizens." It can effectively dilute, indeed, even render impotent, the voting power of certain individuals and magnify the effective power of others—depending on their geographic locations. The party in power in the year of redistricting is able to condition the fate of the opposition by diminishing its legislative voice. Finally, the reflection of future changes in public sentiment can be cushioned and even forestalled.

We might ask whether gerrymandering is worth the worry or the struggle required to minimize it. After all, we have been accustomed to that practice for most of our history as a nation, and the polity has survived. Moreover, experience has shown that the best-laid plans of political cartographers are often only partially successful and, at times, thwarted altogether. An answer to this logical query entails, first, an understanding of the kinds of restraints that have conditioned boundary manipulation in the past; and, second, some appreciation of why there is now reason to conclude that such constraints are less likely to be operative in the future.

Prior to the reapportionment revolution of the 1960s, state constitutional provisions typically prohibited the breaking of county lines in forming districts. Consequently, gerrymanders were more common in urban than rural areas, and in a number of state legislatures urban delegations were elected at large. In others, a city or urban county was allotted only a single seat in one or both houses. This was, of course, a form of gerrymander written into the constitution, but one that obviated periodic line-drawing. Then, too, a large number of states simply failed periodically to redistrict. This resulted in status-quo gerrymanders, but disturbing them required extraordinary efforts. For example, district lines for Congress were typically redrawn only in states—usually a minority—that lost or gained seats. Finally, population mobility, especially after World War II, frustrated boundary manipulation in many areas in ways previously unanticipated.

Events during the 1960s completely changed these considerations. Reapportionments following the 1970 census were the first in American history to witness revisions of legislative and congressional boundaries in *all* states. Prior constitutional restrictions regarding county or other boundary lines had already been undermined by the need to construct districts of almost precisely equal population. In 1970, the coordinator to Senate majority Republicans in New York State candidly observed to the *New York Times*: "The Supreme Court is just making gerrymandering easier than it used to be" (Baker, 1971, p. 137).

As a result, reapportionments after the censuses of 1970 and 1980 were characterized by even more elaborate gerrymanders in many states (see insert). The use of computers brought a new degree of sophistication to boundary manipulation. The results were likely to be far more durable than the comparatively crude guesswork that formerly characterized even the more professional efforts at drawing constituencies for partisan advantage. These conclusions, while difficult to prove empirically, stem both from the logic of a situation mandating far more frequent and extensive redistricting activity, with population equality the sole standard, and from the observations of knowledgeable observers.[7] In state after state, grotesquely shaped districts completely ignoring local subdivision lines or communities of interest are justified by politicians and approved by judges with the solemn chant, "one person, one vote."

Some attachment to community representation has long been entrenched in our thinking and practice and, together with a standard of approximate population equality, can help approach the goal of "fair" representation. Even though the justification of gross malapportionments prior to *Baker v. Carr* invoked — often quite artificially — representation of communities that were hardly delineated by ancient subunit boundaries, the complete abandonment of such lines in the quest for precise population equality poses a potential hardly envisaged by either the reformers or the Supreme Court between 1962 and 1964. The aim of representative equality did not rule out some retention of traditional ground rules, including local boundaries whenever possible, in forming districts. The view was best expressed by Chief Justice Warren in *Reynolds v. Sims*: "A state may legitimately desire to maintain the integrity of various political subdivisions, insofar as possible, and provide for compact districts of contiguous territory in designing a legislative apportionment scheme. Valid considerations may underlie such aims. Indiscriminate districting, without any regard for political subdivisions or natural or historical boundary lines, may be little more than an open invitation to partisan gerrymandering. . . ." (pp. 578–579).

What Is To Be Done?

This retrospective critique of the U.S. reapportionment revolution over the past two decades reveals a kaleidoscopic pattern, reflecting diverse and changing accomplishments and failures. It is time for a candid reappraisal, especially by those who have been involved from the start. The sober fact is that some of the reformers, depending on conditions in the states where they live, may find the brave new world no better than the one it replaced. Equipopulous districts, drawn by incumbents for perpetual political longevity, may offer no more prospect of translating electoral shifts into representational changes than did the old "rotten boroughs" that were the proper target of the reformers. In the blunt words of the late Robert G. Dixon, Jr., "A mathematically equal vote which is politically worthless because of gerrymandering or winner-take-all districting is as deceiving as 'emperor's clothes'" (Dixon, 1968, p. 22).

Perhaps one problem is the lofty ideal set forth by Chief Justice Warren in 1964. In an absolute sense, "fair and effective representation for all citizens" is not possible. Even assuming the most dispassionate and "neutral" drafting of districts, it is difficult to find a magic formula granting every voter a competitive choice, with the resulting statewide pattern representing a close approximation to the public at large. We want a number of *desiderata* that are not always (perhaps ever) entirely compatible — effective voter choice, proportionality, representation of communities, and effective majority decision-making. Which is to say

Opposite page. Competition for the decennial Elbridge Gerry Memorial Award for Creative Cartography was especially keen in the wake of the 1980 census. Yet California managed to retain the prize it had captured a decade earlier (Baker, 1972, pp. 280–282). One clear advantage was the opportunity to enact a second redistricting, since Republicans had mounted a successful referendum challenge to the 1981 districts. After calling the Democratic-controlled legislature into a hurried special session, Governor Edmund G. (appropriately nicknamed "Gerry") Brown approved the new districts shortly before his Republican successor took office. The 1981 winner, the 6th Congressional district, attracted widespread publicity in the national press and weekly news magazines. It was replaced in 1982 by more conventional boundaries. But the new Congressional districts for the Los Angeles area offer a number of strong possibilities, with the 32nd and 42nd districts being narrowly edged out by the 27th, which "goes to sea at Redondo Beach, sails around the Palos Verdes Peninsula, and lands at San Pedro to pick up the harbor populations" (*California Journal*, 1983: S.S.4). Copyright 1981, 1983, The California Center. (Shading supplied by author.)

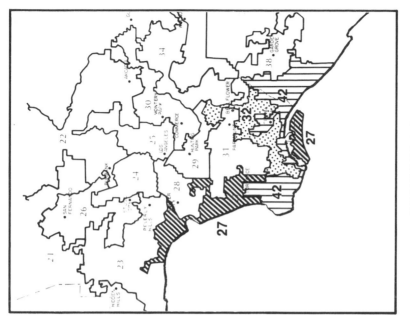

CONGRESSIONAL DISTRICTS
Los Angeles Area 1982

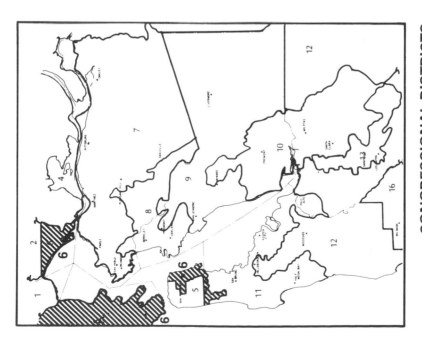

CONGRESSIONAL DISTRICTS
Bay Area 1981

that we cannot expect the best of all worlds and must settle for some kind of trade-off (Niemi and Deegan, 1978). But at least a higher degree of fair and effective representation should be a continuing goal. This requires our ability to learn from mistakes, to experiment, to revise.

What is needed in the future is that long-overdue "dialogue" about the fundamentals of representation rather than continued reliance on sterile and mechanistic rituals — a return, in other words, to the spirit that animated the 1964 decisions. What are the prospects of fine-tuning or reforming the negative consequences of the reapportionment revolution?

As for multimember districts, more will predictably be replaced by single-member districts, especially in areas covered by the Voting Rights Act. But it does not seem likely that the Supreme Court will declare at-large, winner-take-all arrangements unconstitutional per se. Not only were they specifically approved in *Reynolds v. Sims*, but they also persist in a majority of local elections of city, county, and school boards. Courts are more impressed by evidence of actual electoral effects on minority representation than by abstract, mathematical proof that multimember districting is inherently discriminatory.

Finding ways to check partisan gerrymandering that has proliferated in the wake of the one-person, one-vote rulings is probably the most pressing challenge. The fact that the redistricting function in most states is vested in the legislatures poses an obvious conflict of interest. While not referring specifically to reapportionment, James Madison put the matter succinctly in these words: "No man is allowed to be a judge in his own cause, because his interest would certainly bias his judgment, and, not improbably, corrupt his integrity. With equal, nay with greater reason, a body of men are unfit to be both judges and parties at the same time. . . ." (*The Federalist*, No. 10).

Transferring the function of redrawing constituencies to noninvolved parties is a move considered basic by many. In November 1977, one reform organization (Common Cause, 1977, p. 11) reported a total of 17 states with redistricting commissions, though eight of these were either advisory or backup agencies in the event of legislative failure. Common Cause and others, such as the National Municipal League, have advocated further adoption of independent, nonpartisan, or bipartisan commissions.[8] While neutrality and objectivity in so political an undertaking are illusions, a key consideration should be a decisive role for nonlegislators. Even though guardian angels are in scarce supply, it seems reasonable to believe that citizens of diverse political affiliations can approach the problem differently from those with a direct stake in the outcome.

One final item deserves serious consideration—the need for Congress to fulfill its responsibilities under Article I, Section 4 of the Constitution to make or alter the manner of holding elections for representatives. From 1842 through 1911, decennial statutes apportioning representatives among the states included specific standards, beginning with single-member districts (to replace statewide "general ticket" elections in smaller states), later to include requirements of contiguity, compactness, and approximate equality of district populations. No redistribution among the states took place after the 1920 census, due to resistance from rural legislators fearing the consequences of America's rapid urbanization. To preclude a recurrence of that lapse, Congress in 1929 enacted an "automatic" reapportionment statute establishing formulas to be implemented by presidential decree after each census in the absence of new legislation by Congress. But all previous districting standards were omitted, perhaps because they had not been enforced. The only type of enforcement that was then conceivable was refusal by the House to seat members elected from improperly drawn districts—a severe sanction.

It could now be convincingly argued that the Supreme Court's interpretation of Article I announced in 1969—that a state "must make a good-faith effort to achieve precise mathematical equality" among congressional districts—was made in the absence of congressional guidelines on a subject matter in which Congress has primary responsibility. Such legislative action could help save the Supreme Court from itself. Over the past decade a clear majority of the highest tribunal have objected to the goal of precise population equality, with some justices even warning that so single-minded an approach would enhance gerrymandering. But adherence to *stare decisis* kept the Court in 1973 and 1983 faithful to its 1969 rationale in which only a minority of the nine justices subsequently believed.[9]

Insistence on precise equality of district population *within* states is especially curious in light of the fact that distribution of 435 seats *among* the 50 states (with at least one to each state) inevitably entails greater divergences between the states in population/representation ratios. What sense does it make to insist that all 22 districts in Illinois must be mathematically equal with each other, while all of them are 7.3% more populous than all six districts in Colorado and 4.4% less populous than all nine districts in Missouri?

The time has arrived for Congress to reenact standards for districts, in addition to the small one added in 1967 that reinstituted the requirement of single-member districts (*United States Code*, Title 2, Sec. 2c). Formulation of other standards should include consideration of such issues as contiguity, compactness, communities of interest, and attention to local subdivision boundaries whenever possible. A reasonable population variance should be specified by extending the lessons of the decennial apportionment among the states. For example, if states were required to draw congressional districts so that all fell within one standard deviation of the mean of the average number of persons per district in each of the 50 states, it would yield a reasonable result—for instance, a range of about 6.4% plus or minus after the 1970 census. Such a measure would eliminate from consideration the more extreme state deviations and emphasize that a national standard would apply *within* as well as *among* the states. Legislation could also specifically indicate that federal courts continued to have jurisdiction over districting challenges. But under this proposal, the judiciary would have specific legislative standards to apply rather than its own vague "natural law" conceptions of what Article I really means.

To sum up, it is clear that there is still much work to be done to approximate the goal of fair and effective representation for all citizens, as expressed by Chief Justice Warren in 1964. Some possible items on the agenda have been suggested, and others will emerge; for the pursuit of fairness, like the pursuit of happiness, is endless. The reapportionment experience of the past two decades amply illustrates a point made by Thomas Jefferson 160 years ago. "The generation which commences a revolution can rarely compleat it."[10]

Notes

1. The seeming incongruity between the data presented in the article and its title is explained by the author's measuring success by proportional representation.
2. See references in O'Rourke, 1980, pp. 139–145; also see Saffell, 1982.
3. The author's findings might have been more conclusive as to impact had at least one highly malapportioned southern state (prior to *Baker v. Carr*) been included in his sample.
4. Banzhaf (1966), applying the mathematical technique to legislative houses in five states employing mixed single and multimember systems, computed effective representation variances ranging from 200% to 374%. Also see Grofman, 1982a.
5. *Kirkpatrick v. Preisler*, p. 526; *Wells v. Rockefeller*, p. 542.
6. *Mahan v. Howell*, p. 315; *Gaffney v. Cummings*, p. 735.
7. *Congressional Quarterly Weekly Report* (1981, p. 2155) concluded, "Those curves and squiggles are part of the new gerrymandering, a refinement of the traditional art of drawing districts for political purposes. It is in large part a creation of the Supreme Court."
8. For the Common Cause Model Proposal, see Common Cause, 1977, pp. 26–35.
9. *Kirkpatrick v. Preisler*, p. 526, and *White v. Weiser*, p. 783, respectively.
10. To John Adams (September 4, 1823), in Cappon, 1971, p. 596.

CHAPTER 18

Constituency Redistribution in Britain: Recent Issues

R. J. *Johnston*

Single-member constituency electoral systems are more likely to produce a mismatch between the proportion of the votes and the proportion of the seats won by a party than are any other widely used systems (Rae, 1971). This mismatch, widely known as electoral distortion or bias—although the latter term is sometimes used with a different meaning (see, e.g., Niemi and Deegan, 1978)—comes about for a variety of reasons, most of which are related to one or both of the following general factors: (1) variations in the size, that is, number of electors, of constituencies; and (2) the relative concentration of supporters of particular parties in certain constituencies only. Both of these factors can be induced through political manipulation of constituency boundaries—producing malapportionment in the first case and gerrymandering in the latter—although they can equally well be the product of "neutral" decision-making, whereby the boundary-drawers have no intention to produce a mismatch (Gudgin and Taylor, 1979; Johnston, 1979a).

The nature of these mismatches is widely recognized and has led to preventative action. Thus with regard to deliberate malapportionment and gerrymandering there have been moves to ensure equality in constituency sizes and to take decision-making regarding boundary delimitation out of the hands of politicians. Such neutral redistricting ensures a "fair" procedure. It does not necessarily ensure a fair result, however. The neutral counterpart of malapportionment can be avoided by ensuring that constituency electorates do not vary substantially. But the neutral counterpart of gerrymandering cannot readily be countered, because there is no objective standard against which any redistricting can be compared. However, it is unlikely that a neutral procedure will perpetrate a major gerrymander. But if it does not, and malapportionment is thus prevented, this does not remove the potential for electoral bias resulting from operation of the neutral procedure. It is for this reason that some groups in society, notably those who suffer most from the electoral bias, promote electoral reform policies and the adoption of different electoral systems.

Both redistricting by neutral bodies and electoral reform are political issues, because of the likely electoral impacts of various courses of action. Both have been the focus of considerable political debate in Britain in recent years. Some issues with regard to electoral reform have been discussed elsewhere (Johnston, 1984). The concern of the present essay is redistricting. The following sections deal, in turn, with the context of redistribution in Britain, with the most recent redistribution exercise, with a legal (political) challenge to that exercise, and with the political consequences of the recent exercise.

Redistricting in Britain: The Context

As in the United States and elsewhere, the need for regular redistricting in Britain was realized as necessary to counter the consequences of malapportionment. Population redistribution—from country to town and city, from region to region, and from city to suburb—has created substantial discrepancies in the size of the various constituencies returning members to the House of Commons, and agitation for reform has led to parliamentary action. In the nineteenth century, this was associated with the various reform acts, which also altered the franchise (Seymour, 1915; Butler, 1963; Taylor and Johnston, 1979). Although these removed many of the most glaring abuses, it was not until the 1940s that a series of regular redistributions, undertaken by neutral commissions (one for each of England, Northern Ireland, Scotland, and Wales), was introduced.

The first of these "modern" redistributions took place in 1946, following a recommendation that all constituencies should be within 25% of the average electorate. The boundary commissions asked to be released from this requirement, because it was impossible to achieve the specified equality; the constituencies that they created in 1947 ranged in number of electors from under 40,000 to over 80,000.

This apparent inability of the commissions to avoid the neutral equivalent of malapportionment influenced the wording of the Act of Parliament passed in 1949 – the House of Commons (Redistribution of Seats) Act, 1949 – with regard to electoral equality. No objective standard was identified, and the act refers only to the electorate of each constituency being "as near the electoral quota as is practicable." (Electoral quota is the total electorate of the country divided by the number of constituencies there prior to the redistribution.)

Although the avoidance of malapportionment and the inequalities of representation that it creates, irrespective of any electoral bias, was a major *raison d'être* of the 1949 act, achieving equality of representation was not the prime goal. Traditionally, the House of Commons had been composed of representatives from the shires (now the counties) and from the boroughs (thereby providing representatives of the rural- and urban-landed interests, respectively). Although by 1949 Britain had a universal franchise, these territorial units remained the infrastructure within which representation was to be organized. Three rules lay down an operating procedure for the commissions.

Rule 4 (as amended by the Local Government Act, 1972) states that in England and Wales

> no county or any part thereof shall be included in a constituency which includes the whole or part of any other county or part of a metropolitan borough; . . . (and) no metropolitan borough or any part thereof shall be included in a constituency which includes the whole or part of any other metropolitan borough.

There are currently 45 counties in England, and 32 metropolitan (i.e., London) boroughs. Rule 5 states that

> The electorate of any constituency shall be as near the electoral quota as is practicable having regard to the foregoing . . . and a Boundary Commission may depart from the strict application of the last foregoing rule if it appears to them that a departure is desirable to avoid an excessive disparity between the electorate of any constituency and the electoral quota, or between the electorate thereof and that of neighbouring constituencies in the part of the United Kingdom with which they are concerned.

Finally, Rule 6 allows a commission to

> depart from the strict application of the last two foregoing rules if special geographical considerations, including in particular the size, shape, and

accessibility of a constituency, appear to them to render a departure desirable.

These rules have been interpreted by the commissions as requiring them (a) to determine the national electoral quota, (b) to use this to allocate constituencies to the counties and boroughs, (c) to consider constituencies crossing county and/or borough boundaries only to avoid "excessive disparities," and (d) to use their discretion with regard to strict application of Rules 4 and 5 where there are "special considerations." Such an interpretation gives primacy to the representation of the major units of local government; equality of representation of electors is secondary.

This interpretation was bolstered by an amendment to the rules incorporated in the House of Commons (Redistribution of Seats) Act 1958. Introduction of this act resulted from concern among MPs and the political parties with both the frequency of redistributions, at least once every 4–7 years, and the lack of continuity of representation and local party organization that this implied. Thus the time between redistributions was extended to 10–15 years, and a further rule was introduced stating that the commissions need not

> aim at giving full effect in all circumstances to the rules set out in . . . the principal Act, but they shall take account, so far as they reasonably can, of the inconveniences attendant on alterations of constituencies other than alterations made for the purposes of rule 4 of these rules, and of any local ties which would be broken by such alterations.

This clearly indicates the primary importance of "representation of places" (i.e., counties and boroughs) relative to "representation of people;" the crucial issue is the relative weight of the two, and the interpretation of the phrase "as near the electoral quota as practicable" in Rule 5 (On the work of the commissions, see Butler, 1955, 1963; Craig, 1959; Taylor and Gudgin, 1975).

The Commissions in Operation

The commissions operate in the following way. A joint decision is made regarding the need for a redistribution within the statutory period, and a base date is chosen for calculating the electoral quota. Each commission then allocates constituencies to the counties and boroughs and produces proposals for the boundaries of those constituencies. These are published seriatim, as they are ready. Comments on the published proposals are invited; and if sufficient critical representations are received, a public inquiry is held, presided over by an assistant commissioner, in the county/borough. The report on this inquiry is considered by the commission, which then publishes its final proposals. All of the final proposals are then submitted to the Home Secretary in a single report. The Home Secretary transmits them to Parliament and lays down an Order in Council scheduling their acceptance.

The commissions reported on their initial review in 1949, on the first periodic review in 1955, and on the second in 1969. A further review was due between 1979 and 1984. Because of the major reorganization of local government in the mid-1970s plus rapid population redistribution, a third periodic review was commenced in 1976, using electoral data for that year. (For Scotland, 1978 data were used; for Wales, 1981 data; and for Northern Ireland, 1979 data.) The procedure was completed in late 1982, and the report laid before Parliament in February 1983.

Challenging the Commissions

In 1982, two legal actions were initiated by interested parties (both associated with the Labour party, then the major opposition party in the House of Commons) against the Third Periodical Review of the Boundary Commission for England. Both sought greater equality in "representation of the people" than was apparently produced in the review. One, brought by the leader (Michael Foot), chief whip, secretary, and national agent of the Parliamentary Labour party (though acting as individuals), challenged the entire review, claiming that it was inconsistent with the "equality of representation of people" requirement in Rule 5. The other, brought by three elected councils (all with Labour party majorities) in the county of Tyne and Wear, challenged the decision to allocate only 13 constituencies to the county, claiming that it should have received 14. (According to the electoral quota, it was entitled to 13.48. The county of Lancashire was entitled to 15.47 and was allocated 16; Buckinghamshire was entitled to 5.47, and was allocated 6.) Both cases were lost.

The basic aim of the first (general) case was to prove that the commission had not followed the rules closely enough because of the disparity in electorates. The goal was to get the courts to establish a standard of no more than a certain percent variation around the electoral quota, except in special circumstances. The case was argued with regard to both intracounty and interborough discrepancies.

Examples of variations within a county included some taken from Lancashire. There, one of the proposed constituencies (Blackburn) had a 1976 electorate of 76,628 (16.54% above the national quota of 65,753), whereas another (Morecambe and Lunesdale) had an electorate of 52,154 (20.68% below). It was shown how small changes in boundaries could rectify this anomaly.

Much of the general case focused on the 32 London boroughs. Rule 5 was not operated at all with regard to crossing boundaries, leading to a maximum discrepancy among the 84 constituencies of 37,908 (from 84,401 to 46,493; 58% of the national quota). Furthermore, there were major discrepancies between neighboring constituencies (as, for example, between Barnet, Finchley, with 57,995 and Haringey, Wood Green, with 84,401).

That the commission chose not to cross London borough boundaries to produce equality of electorates represented it "misdirecting" itself, according to the plaintiffs. (Interestingly, the commission responded that in 1977, and again in 1979, it consulted with the major political parties, which unanimously agreed that borough boundaries should not be crossed. The plaintiffs countered that this was before they became aware of the excessive disparities that would be produced.)

The final main argument in the general case was that the commission had been inconsistent in its treatment of district boundaries in the definition of constituencies. (The districts are subsidiary units with counties: prior to the Local Government Act, 1972, the rules required the commissions to respect district boundaries.) Thus the proposals for Greater Manchester and Tyne and Wear counties involved cross-district boundary constituencies (as did the final proposals for West Yorkshire); whereas in South Yorkshire, where the potential disparities were as large, no proposals for crossing district boundaries were presented. Moreover, it was argued, holding separate inquiries in each of the four districts precluded questioning of this policy.

The unanimous judgments in the Divisional Court (December 21, 1982; see *The Times*, January 5, 1983) and the Court of Appeal (January 25, 1983; *The Times*, January 26, 1983) covered a large number of issues, including the standing of the plaintiffs, the timing of the case, and the function of the courts in reviewing the reports of commissions established to advise Parliament. On the merits of the case, two major conclusions stand out:

1. That the courts were not prepared to lay down an absolute standard as the definition of excessive discrepancy, and that indeed they

were very unsure as to whether such a standard could be defined (even one as broad as 20%). This is because of the large number of criteria laid out in the rules and the relative insignificance of the discrepancy rule; the commission must weigh all the relevant criteria and should not be shackled by an absolute standard on one criterion.

2. That the evidence presented relating to the electoral discrepancies proposed and the lack of any proposals to cross county/borough boundaries could not properly lead to the inference that the commission had "misdirected" itself. There was no evidence that the commission had "closed its mind" to certain courses of action, and no evidence that it had failed to consider all the criteria laid down by the rules. It was not for the commission to prove that it had considered many options (although evidence suggested that it had), nor was it necessary for it to seek to identify the "best" set of constituencies. It had to take account of all the relevant considerations and, after consultation, to advise Parliament on a reasonable set of new constituencies. There was no evidence that it had failed to do this. Thus, as stated by Lord Donaldson (Master of the Rolls), in the judgment of the Court of Appeals,

> Though the relevant disparities are substantial in some of the instances ruled on, they are in no case so large as to point per se to the conclusion that the Commission wholly failed to have regard to the provisions of Rule 5 relating to electoral equality

and

> the framework of the Rules of 1949 itself make it plain that as a matter of general policy Rule 5 was to be regarded as subordinate to Rule 4 and not vice versa.

On this interpretation, then, "representation of places" (the major units of local government) takes priority over equal "representation of people."

In the Tyne and Wear case, the plaintiffs claimed that the commission misdirected itself by allocating only 13 constituencies and that by proposing one constituency that crossed a major physical feature forming a district boundary (the lower Tyne separating Newcastle and Gateshead) it failed to pay due attention to local ties, as required in the 1958 act. (The courts, not surprisingly, noted that this contradicted one of the issues in the general case.) In the end, the case focused on whether the assistant commissioner who conducted the local inquiry misdirected himself because he accepted the commission's original proposal for 13 constituencies and excluded consideration of the alternative of allocating 14; as a consequence, it was claimed, he misrepresented the views expressed at the inquiry in his written report.

The Divisional Court dismissed the claim. They found that the local inquiry had been properly conducted, that the assistant commissioner properly reported it to the commission, and that the commission had in no sense misdirected itself by recommending 13 constituencies in its initial proposals.

Evaluation: A "Reapportionment Revolution" That Wasn't

The two cases discussed here represent the first full attempt to involve the British courts in an oversight of the work of the boundary commissions and to obtain a clearly defined standard of electoral equality, which is undefined in the relevant act. The general case was a lengthy one and produced a long, and in parts highly critical, judgment in the Divisional Court. Although the court decided that because of the issues of standing and delay the plaintiffs had no case, nevertheless it did hear the case on its merits. It did not rule that cases could not properly be brought, but it made clear that there would need to be much clearer evidence of the commission misdirecting itself than the circumstantial evidence of some substantial electoral disparities and that it would require much larger disparities than those adduced before it would conclude that the commission had misinterpreted the rules. Nevertheless, in Justice Webster's words, the court would not equate excessive disparity with "any arbitrary limit"; it required clear evidence that "the commission had failed to perform a procedural duty or even that . . . it had misdirected itself as to the law," and it had been presented with no such evidence.

Full evaluation of this decision requires a much more detailed examination than can be provided here. Two conclusions can be drawn at this stage, however. The first relates to the nature of parliamentary democracy under the (unwritten) British Constitution and its interpretation in the House of Commons (Redistribution of Seats) Act. This is that, despite the universal franchise and the implicit concept of "one man, one vote; one vote, one value," equality of representation for *people* is secondary to that of representation for *places*. And yet those places are relatively new creations (the counties were reconstituted in 1972, and the London boroughs were created in 1963) and can be radically revised by decision of Parliament. There is substantial evidence that there are few local ties relating to these units of local administration (Rose, 1982b) and therefore no clearly identifiable communities for which separate representation might be sensible. The incorporation of relatively vague, subjective criteria in the rules, the likelihood that they may be inconsistently interpreted (Johnston, 1982b, 1983c), the lack of any absolute standards, and the absence of any need for the commission to justify its proposals leave the nature of representative democracy in Britain in some doubt.

The second conclusion is a comparative one. In the United States, two vague statements in the Constitution have been interpreted (Article I for the House of Representatives, the Fourteenth Amendment for state legislatures) as requiring equality of electorates among constituencies, including some very strict interpretations of the degree of deviation allowed (Johnston, 1979a), interpretations that have been put into effect (Grofman, 1982c). In England (the only country covered in the cases) an apparently firmer ground for requiring electoral equality (Rule 5) has not been substantiated, and very broad tolerances have been allowed. This illustrates the futility of seeking generalizations in many aspects of the social sciences, exemplifies the role of judges and bureaucrats as interpreters of vague texts (Johnston, 1983c), and indicates the great variety of interpretations that can be placed on the concept of representative democracy.

Political Consequences

The redistricting procedure is of great importance to the political parties in Great Britain, because of its likely impact on their parliamentary representation. It was for this reason that the "minimal change" rule was introduced in the 1958 act and the period between redistributions was extended to 10–15 years. (Initially, in the 1940s it had been intended to have a redistribution before each general election; the United Kingdom House of Commons does not have a fixed term, however, only a maximum term.)

Of the two major parties that have fought all of the general elections between 1945 and the present (Conservative and Labour) it is widely accepted that a redistribution disadvantages Labour. This is not to say that it creates an electoral bias in favor of Conservative, however. Rather, it indicates that over the period between redistributions a relatively small bias (less than 5% of all seats in the House of Commons) develops in Labour's favor. This is brought about by what might be called creeping malapportionment." (Orr, 1969, in a slightly different context calls it a "silent gerrymander.") A major aspect of population redistribution in recent decades has been substantial decline in the inner cities countered by growth in the suburban belts and small towns of, especially, southern England. The inner city contains many Labour strongholds; the suburbs and beyond are the heartland of Conservative support. Thus, as the constituencies age, Labour's inner city seats become smaller, and it benefits in exactly the same way as it would if it were able to operate a malapportionment strategy (Johnston, 1976a).

Each redistribution removes this advantage from Labour, therefore; and the predictions are that, as at the previous redistribution proposed in 1969 but not instituted until after the 1970 general election (Johnston, 1979a), the present review will lead to a net loss of 20–30 seats for Labour. (There is a small, anti-Labour gerrymander effect which results from its having more "safe" seats: Johnston, 1976a.)

An example of these predictions for Greater London (i.e., the 32 London boroughs) is taken from *The Economist* (March 11–15, 1983):

Type of Seat	Before Redistribution	After Redistribution
Safe Conservative	29	30
Marginal Conservative	13	9
Marginal Labour	12	12
Safe Labour	38	33

(The predictions take no account of the possible impact of the Liberal/SDP Alliance. They are based on estimates, since voting data below the constituency scale are not available.) Labour is clearly the net loser, because of the removal of the "creeping gerrymander"; London was a major focus of much of the general case.

The possibility of a gerrymander-equivalent on a national basis is very unlikely in the British context, at least for the Conservative and Labour parties. (The third party in British politics, Liberal, has suffered the equivalent of a "cracked gerrymander"–Johnston, 1979a– throughout the period since 1945, however, winning many fewer seats than its percentage of the vote suggests it is "entitled" to: The nature of this "cracked gerrymander" is analyzed by Gudgin and Taylor, 1979.) Nevertheless, there is the potential of achieving a gerrymander at the local level, because of the way in which the set of constituencies for each county/borough is constructed. This is why the parties are very active at the public local inquiries held in each county/borough on the commission's proposals. The extent of gerrymandering, then, depends on the degree to which it is accidentally introduced by the commission (research has shown that in almost every county/borough there is electoral bias, with the party getting the largest percentage of the vote getting an even larger percentage of the seats: Johnston, 1982b; Johnston and Rossiter, 1982) and on the success of the parties in convincing the commission to introduce one. (Partisan issues are never directly discussed at the inquiries!)

One further potential for gerrymandering involves the structure of local government areas within which the boundary commissions work. The network of counties/boroughs is not constitutionally fixed. It can be, and is, changed by the central government and, as has been demonstrated (Johnston, 1979a, 1982b), the nature of such changes in recent decades indicated the importance of electoral considerations.

Within the counties/boroughs, the commissions use the local government electoral units, the wards, as the "building blocks" for the creation of constituencies. Definition of wards, with electorates that are "as equal as practicable," is undertaken at least once every ten years. It is done by local government boundary commissions, which do not produce their own proposals but act on those brought before them by interested bodies, including the elected councils of the local authorities and the political parties. This is a clear invitation to attempt a gerrymander of local electoral arrangements (which can then influence the creation of parliamentary constituencies). There is little doubt that the parties accept this invitation and that the commissions often "rubber-stamp" their work: indeed, some local parties seek to gerrymander the boundaries of polling districts, which are the building blocks for wards.

The political consequences of electoral redistributions are quite substantial in Britain, therefore. At the national level, the removal of "creeping malapportionment" removes advantages gained by the Labour party as a result of inner city population decline, whereas at the local level manipulation of ward and constituency boundaries can have a marked influence on the partisan composition of constituencies. Thus the political parties are closely concerned with the latter proceedings, the only level at which they can influence the outcome directly.

At the national level, parties can seek to influence the redistribution procedure via the rules which are set by Parliament for the boundary commissions—hence the 1958 act. The court cases in 1982–1983 were the first major attempt to involve the judiciary, in a very similar way to the American "reapportionment revolution," by asking the courts to translate the general wording of the rules into objective, quantified standards. The cases failed, however, because of the nature of the judicial review procedure in Britain and the clear unwillingness of the judges to identify objective standards and to "interfere" with what has always been a parliamentary procedure. The loser in the short term has been the Labour party, because it was unable to prevent the removal of the creeping malapportionment effect. (It has been suggested that this was the main rationale for the case—certainly for appealing as far as the House of Lords—in that the party wanted the next general election to be fought in the old constituencies.)

Conclusions

The redistribution of parliamentary constituencies in Britain is a very subjective procedure, undertaken by neutral bodies operating within a relatively vague set of rules and with attempted partisan influence. The neutral bodies, the boundary commissions, report to and advise Parliament. Their reports indicate why they have offered the advice, but the results of recent litigation indicate that they do not have to make a full defense to interested parties as long as they did not "misdirect" themselves by ignoring or misinterpreting the rules, and that they do not have to produce the "best" set of advice. The consequence politically is somewhat unpredictable locally, although nationally it almost certainly removes any major electoral bias toward Labour developed since the preceding redistribution.

The case brought in 1982–1983 sought unsuccessfully to make the reapportionment procedure more certain, with clearer guidelines and objective standards. But, as has happened with many issues brought before the U.S. Supreme Court, judicial involvement may bring an issue to prominence on the political agenda. Members of all parties have expressed their concern about the present procedure—about its length and about the lack of computer usage. Almost certainly, this review will have been the last conducted in that way.

Acknowledgments. I am extremely grateful to Gerry Bermingham for involving me in the general case discussed here and for providing me with much of the detailed information on which this essay is based.

CHAPTER 19

Districting Choices under the Single-Transferable Vote

Peter Mair

This chapter deals primarily with the impact of constituency size on electoral outcomes under the single-transferable vote (STV) system of proportional representation. The data which are used concern elections in the Republic of Ireland, which has used STV for its parliamentary elections since the foundation of the state. The second section of the chapter will briefly outline how STV works, the third section will discuss the merits of STV, and the final section will concern the drawbacks of the system, in this case concentrating mainly on its accessibility to partisan manipulation by means of modifying the size of constituencies.

The Irish Constitution specifies that Dàil (i.e., legislative) elections be held using STV in multimember constituencies. On two occasions in the postwar period (in 1959 and 1968) the then governing party, Fianna Fail, sponsored referenda which sought to remove this constitutional requirement and to change the electoral system to the simple British and U.S. type of first-past-the-post in single-member districts. In both cases the proposal was rejected by the voters—by 51.8 versus 48.2% in 1959, and by a massive 60.8 versus 39.2% in 1968.

From one perspective it may have seemed odd that Fianna Fail would wish to abolish a voting system which had served the party so well over the previous decades. Since first taking office in 1932, Fianna

Fail by 1959 has won seven of the nine subsequent elections and has since gone on to win five of the eight elections since 1959, including that of 1969, which followed just one year after its referendum defeat. But at the time of the first referendum, Fianna Fail was feeling somewhat insecure. Coalition governments had been in office—and Fianna Fail in opposition—from 1948 to 1951 and from 1954 to 1957; Fianna Fail's own government from 1951 to 1954 commanded only 47% of Dàil seats, while the participants in the first coalition government accounted for only 46%, and those in the second coalition government for little over 47% (this excludes one minor party, Clann na Poblachta, which supported the coalition but remained outside the Cabinet). Moreover, at least on the face of it, the Fianna Fail leader Eamon de Valera was opposed to the type of postelection bargaining for a coalition agreement which he saw as an inevitable consequence of the multiplicity of small parties (O'Leary, 1979, p. 50).

Since the defeat of these two proposals the question of changing the electoral system has been dormant in Ireland, at least until recently, when the lack of an overall majority for either Fianna Fail or the Fine Gael-Labour coalition following the 1981 and February 1982 elections put the issue back on the political agenda in terms of a very clear dichotomy between the value of a proportional or "fair" result on the one hand versus an "effective" result on the other. Given the distribution of electoral support in contemporary Ireland, a proportional outcome may leave neither of the main contenders, Fianna Fail or Fine Gael-Labour, with an overall Dàil majority. If such an overall majority is desirable, therefore, it perhaps can be achieved only at the cost of failing to provide a distribution of Dàil seats which adequately reflects that of popular votes.

But more of that later. Suffice it for now to say that though STV may be subject to challenge in contemporary Ireland, it is, on the contrary, often seen in a very favorable light by proponents of electoral reform in Britain, where it is viewed as an ideal form of proportionally representing the increasingly heterogeneous spectrum of British political opinion while at the same time maintaining some degree of the individual MP accountability which is associated with the present first-past-the-post system based on single-member constituencies.

How The System Works

STV in Ireland is based on multimember constituencies in which voters rank-order the candidates on a 1, 2, 3 . . . n basis. Candidates are elected if they receive a *quota* (Q)—known as the Droop quota—of the total valid poll (*TVP*) in the constituency, this quota being calculated according to the number of seats (*S*) in the constituency. The exact calculation is as follows:

$$Q = \frac{TVP}{S+1} + 1$$

which, in a hypothetical 4-seat constituency with a valid poll of 50,000 is:

$$\frac{50,000}{4+1} + 1 = 10,001$$

As is immediately evident, no more than 4 candidates can receive this quota, in that 5 quotas, or 50,005 votes, amount to 5 votes more than the total valid poll. If no candidate receives a quota on the basis of the count of first preferences, the lowest polling candidate is eliminated and all of his votes transferred to other candidates according to his second preferences. Alternatively, if one or more candidates receive sufficient first preferences to equal or surpass the quota, and if not all of the seats are distributed at the end of the first preference count, any of their surpluses over and above the quota are distributed to the other candidates in proportion to the second preferences of *all* the ballot papers of the elected candidates. Thus, if candidate X has a surplus of 2,000 first preferences over and above an 8,000 quota (i.e., 10,000 votes in all), then these 2,000 votes are distributed in proportion to the second preferences on all 10,000 of X's ballot papers. This process of electing/eliminating candidates and distributing their surpluses/total votes according to the next ranking preference continues until all the seats have been filled. As is often the case, a number of ballot papers do not show some or all possible preferences; and, at various stages, these are deemed *nontransferable*. Since this reduces the number of votes in circulation, the last seat (*s*) in a constituency is regularly awarded to a candidate who, though not reaching the quota, has an unbeatable lead or is the only one remaining in the contest.[1] Table 19.1 gives an example of an actual count in the constituency of Cork North-West in the February 1982 General Election and nicely illustrates this last point.

Having briefly looked at how the system works, the remainder of this paper will be devoted to discussing some of the merits and drawbacks associated with STV as it has operated in the Irish Republic.

TABLE 19.1. Election in Cork North-West, February 18, 1982

Electorate: 40,156 *Total Valid Poll:* 33,494 *Seats:* 3 *Quota:* 8,374

Candidates	First Count[a]	Second Count[b]		Third Count[c]		Fourth Count[d]	
Creed, Donal (FG)	7305	+ 733	8038	+ 77	8115	+ 22	8137
Crowley, Frank (FG)	7240	+1102	8342	+ 412	8754	–	8754
Donegan, M. (FF)	3726	+ 227	3953	–3953	–	–	–
Meaney, Tom (FF)	7025	+ 408	7433	+2604	10,037	–1663	8374
Moynihan, Donal (FF)	5137	+ 219	5356	+ 739	6095	+1636	7731
Smith, Michael (Lab)	3061	–3061	–	–	–	–	–
Nontransferable	–	+ 372	372	+ 121	493	+ 5	498
Total	33,494		33,494		33,494		33,494

Source. Irish Times, February 22, 1982.
[a]Smith eliminated.
[b]Donegan eliminated.
[c]Meaney and Crowley elected; distribution of Meaney's surplus shown.
[d]Creed elected without reaching quota.

Particular attention will be paid to the potentiality for electoral engineering created by the system, primarily through the impact of constituency size on the degree of proportionality achieved in the distribution of seats.

Merits

Candidate Accountability

Based as it is on the preference ordering among individual *candidates*, STV has the major advantage of combining on the one hand the individual accountability associated with first-past-the-post electoral systems based on single-member constituencies with, on the other, the proportional representation of *parties*. Indeed, in the Irish case, the multimember constituencies can often be regarded as simply sets of single-member constituencies, as individual TDs (TD = Teachta Dala = MP) carve out personal bailiwicks within the larger constituency which represent specific subconstituencies from which their particular support derives (Sacks, 1970). A good example of such a division of territory is afforded by the Sligo-Leitrim constituency in 1977, where Fianna Fail was attempting to win two seats in a very marginal 3-seat constituency. The constituency was dominated by one major urban center, Sligo town, and was otherwise a predominantly rural area. One of the two Fianna Fail candidates (Ray McSharry) based his support in Sligo town, while the other (James Gallagher) was based in the southern end of the county, a mainly farming area with small market towns such as Ballymote, Coloony, and Tubbercurry (Gallagher's home town). In this particular case, the bailiwicking was easily effected: MacSharry had the town and coastal strip, or what he referred to as the area "from Bundoran to Ballina, between the mountains and the sea," while Gallagher had the remaining and admittedly smaller part of the constituency. In the former area the Fianna Fail posters urged supporters to "vote No. 1 McSharry and No. 2 Gallagher," and in the latter "vote No. 1 Gallagher and No. 2 McSharry." A border was clearly delineated by both candidates, and so the contest was organized. In the event, Fianna Fail did win two of the three seats with an overall vote of 48% (almost 31% for McSharry and just over 17% for Gallagher), and with over 72% of McSharry's surplus passing to Gallagher in the second count.

But not all intraparty bailiwicking can be effected so easily (indeed, there were even a lot of strains in the Gallagher-McSharry arrangement), nor prove so successful. More often than not Fianna Fail, and to a lesser extent, Fine Gael, will nominate more candidates than they can really hope to win seats. In 1977 in Sligo-Leitrim two candidates were nominated in the hope of winning two seats; but in neighboring Roscommon-Leitrim (3 seats) three candidates were nominated for a contest in which Fianna Fail could at most win two seats while, further north, the party nominated four candidates in Donegal (5 seats), again in the knowledge that only two of the seats were actually winnable. Such overnomination is the norm in Fianna Fail, and with as many arguments in favor of such a strategy as there are against it (e.g., Cohan et al., 1975; Katz, 1981; Lijphart and Irwin, 1979), it is obviously impossible to decide its value one way or the other. What is undeniable, however, is that such a strategy promotes an intense level of intraparty competition in which, for example, Fianna Fail candidates will vie against one another rather than against the other parties over, say, which of the three nominated will take the only two winnable Fianna Fail seats in a four-seat constituency.

In general, such intraparty conflict finds expression in the assertion by rival candidates of their individual merits as constituency or sub-constituency representatives. As members of the same party and as supporters of a common party program, the individual candidates are unable to compete on grounds of policy or ideology. Rather, they compete in terms of individual effectiveness or competence in a manner which does much to *depoliticize* electoral competition.[2] As such, candidates often rely primarily for their success (and voters for their choice) on an ability simply to service constituencies or particular bailiwicks. The result is a Dàil characterized by very good local representatives and very careless legislators, though whether this is a merit or a drawback is open to question. The ultimate point, however, is that STV in Ireland does encourage a high degree of concern with constituency service and individual candidate accountability.

Proportional Outcomes

As just noted, STV ideally combines such individual candidate accountability with the proportional distribution of parliamentary seats. Having already looked at the first of these two facets, let us now look briefly at the system's record as far as proportional outcomes are concerned. On the face of it, and as can be seen from Table 19.2, STV in Ireland has effected a reasonable correspondence between the electoral balance of the parties and their relative strengths in the Dàil: Indexes for electoral and legislative fractionalization correspond very closely, with the difference ranging from a high of .06 (1969) to a low of just .01 (1951 and 1965), while the mean difference is just .03.

A closer look at the performance of the individual parties shows a less rosy picture, however. As can be seen from Table 19.3, which shows the index of proportionality (O'Leary, 1979, chap. 9) for Irish political parties in the postwar period, Fianna Fail and Fine Gael have generally received a disproportionately large share of Dàil seats vis-à-vis their electoral performance. Fianna Fail has been consistently overrepresented throughout the postwar period, while Fine Gael has been underrepresented on only two occasions, in 1965 and 1977. Conversely, Labour, the smallest of the three main parties, has been overrepresented only three times—in 1948, 1954, and November 1982—while its average Dàil representation is well below its average electoral strength. Indeed, of the minor parties and independents (the latter treated as a group), only Clann na Talmhan has generally benefited from any STV bonus, a factor which largely can be accounted for by the geographically concentrated nature of its support base in the 1940s and 1950s.

In sum, then, STV can be said to provide a "reasonably" proportional outcome, albeit with a tendency to overrepresent the larger parties and/or those with a geographically concentrated electorate.

Stable Governments

Among the many merits associated with the STV variety of proportional representation is the Irish experience of (relatively) stable gov-

TABLE 19.2. Irish Elections, 1948–1982: Electoral and Legislative Fractionalization

	1948	1951	1954	1957	1961	1965	1969	1973	1977	1981	1982 (Feb)	1982 (Nov)	Mean
Electoral Fractionalization	.75	.69	.69	.68	.69	.63	.65	.63	.63	.65	.63	.63	.66
Legislative Fractionalization	.72	.68	.67	.63	.64	.62	.59	.61	.58	.62	.61	.60	.63
Difference	.03	.01	.02	.05	.05	.01	.06	.02	.05	.03	.02	.03	.03

Note. Figures show the value of Rae (1971, pp. 53–58) index. Independent TDS have been grouped together as a single unit in calculating the value of the index.

Source. 1948–1981: Official figures published by the Stationery Office, Dublin; 1982: *Irish Times*, February 22, 1982 and November 27, 1982.

TABLE 19.3. Irish Elections 1948–1982: Indices of Proportionality[a]

Party	Mean vote 1948–1982 %	1948	1951	1954	1957	1961	1965	1969	1973	1977	1981	1982 (Feb)	1982 (Nov)	Mean
Fianna Fail	46.0	110	101	103	111	112	105	113	103	113	103	103	101	107
Fine Gael	31.9	107	107	107	103	103	96	103	108	96	108	102	108	104
Labour[b]	11.8	115	96	102	82	91	95	74	97	94	92	99	102	95
Clann na Talmhan	3.1	91	141	110	83	93								104
Clann na Poblachta	4.2	52	34	55	41	58	88	22						55
Sinn Fein/H. Block	3.0				51	c					48	c		50
Sinn Fein Workers Party	2.0								c	c	35	78	37	50
Others/ Independents	5.3	96	100	60	92	103	67	36	48	48	71	80	42	68

[a]The Index of Proportionality was devised by Cornelius O'Leary, and is calculated on a base of 100 by dividing the percentage of seats by the percentage of votes. Full proportionality is therefore 100, while 100+ signifies disproportionately high representation and 100– disproportionately low representation (O'Leary, 1979, chap. 9).
[b]Includes National Labour.
[c]Indicates that the party stood for election but failed to win any seats.
Source. O'Leary (1979); official figures published by the Stationery Office, Dublin, and Irish Times, February 22, 1982 and November 27, 1982.

ernment. Though the validity of the argument that PR can lead to fragmented party systems, fragile coalitions, and ineffective government has been strongly challenged (e.g., Sartori, 1968a), conventional Anglo-American wisdom, based as it is on long experience of the decisiveness of simple pluralities, remains inclined to associate PR with governmental instability. In such circumstances, the Irish case, and hence STV in general, is seen to provide a rather happy counterexample: On only two occasions since the war has an Irish government been led to resign as the direct result of a defeat in the Dàil. The defeats were those which precipitated the most recent elections in Ireland, in February and November 1982, and were caused by the rejection of the Fine Gael-Labour coalition budget in the first case and the passage of a vote of no confidence in Fianna Fail in the second.[3] Moreover, and again this is a source of comfort to British electoral reformers, 7 of Ireland's 12 postwar governments have been single-party governments (see Table 19.4) which, excluding the most recent, have had an average duration of 3 years and 10 months.

Even the coalition governments have reasonable lifetimes in Ireland, at least until recently: Excluding the short eight-month coalition government which came to office in 1981, the three previous coalitions had an average duration of three years and six months. Yet despite this record of stability, it can be seen from Table 19.4 that as many as 5 of these 12 governments failed to command a majority of Dàil seats, while another, that of Fianna Fail in 1965, held exactly 50%. But notwithstanding the insecurity which led Fianna Fail to propose the abolition of STV in 1959 and 1968, minority governments have been rarely problematic in Ireland. In general, the party or parties in government have had a plurality of seats, and the balance of Dàil power has usually been held by independent TDs who were normally reluctant to precipitate another general election and who therefore tended to support whatever party or parties were in a position to form a government. More recently, however, in 1981 and from February to November 1982, the balance of power was held by minor left-wing parties, such as the Workers party, or left-wing independents, who offered their support only in return for specific policies and who, in the absence of such policies, were willing to vote with the opposition— hence the defeat of the coalition budget in January 1982 and of Fianna Fail in November 1982. If, as could be argued, Irish STV offered proportional representation with stable and effective government, then in retrospect it can be suggested that a condition of this was the presence of independent TDs who were willing to simply serve their constituencies and not to take a stand on general government policies. As the

TABLE 19.4. Government Formation, 1948–1982

Period	Type of Government	Percentage of Dáil Seats	Parties Involved in Government	Duration Years	Months
1948–51	Minority Coalition	46.3	Fine Gael, Labour, National Labour, Clann na Talmhan, Clann na Poblachta, one Independent	3	4
1951–54	Minority Single Party	46.9	Fianna Fail	3	0
1954–57	Majority Coalition	50.3	Fine Gael, Labour, Clann na Talmhan, with a pledge of support from Clann na Poblachta	2	10
1957–61	Majority Single Party	53.1	Fianna Fail	4	7
1961–65	Minority Single Party	48.6	Fianna Fail	3	6
1965–69	Minority (?) Single Party	50.0	Fianna Fail	4	3
1969–73	Majority Single Party	52.1	Fianna Fail	3	8
1973–77	Majority Coalition	50.7	Fine Gael, Labour	4	3
1977–81	Majority Single Party	56.8	Fianna Fail	4	0
1981–82	Minority Coalition	48.2	Fine Gael, Labour	0	8
1982–82 (Feb) (Dec)	Minority Single Party	48.8	Fianna Fail	0	8
1982– (Dec)	Majority Coalition	52.1	Fine Gael, Labour	n.a.	
Average Duration, 1948–1982 (Dec):				3	2

style and caliber of independent TDs have changed, so too may Ireland's capacity to produce the sort of durable governments normally associated by commentators with plurality voting systems.

Drawbacks: Redistricting and Gerrymandering

If we exclude the fact that STV in Ireland has encouraged intense intraparty rivalry, with the result that it tends to create simply good constituency representatives rather than effective legislators; and if we also exclude the inevitable depoliticization of electoral contests associated with such intraparty rivalry, since these facets may be arguably termed merits rather than drawbacks; then the only real drawback to STV in the Irish experience has been its openness to the abuse of partisan political engineering. This was at least the case until 1979, when an independent electoral commission was established to draw up new Dàil constituencies, a task which up to then had been the prerogative of the government of the day.

There are three basic ways in which constituencies can or have been revised in Ireland in order to maximize partisan advantage. The first of these, what might be called *the relocation gerrymander,* is also the most straightforward and consists of redrawing the border between two constituencies so as to maximize one's own chances and to minimize those of one's opponents. When the Fine Gael-Labour coalition government revised the constituency map in 1974, for instance, they transferred a sizable section of the South Tipperary constituency into the North Tipperary constituency. The section involved contained a relatively high proportion of the Labour votes which had elected Sean Tracey as a Labor TD for South Tipperary in 1973. Since Tracey had then been appointed Ceann Comihairle (i.e., speaker), he would be deemed reelected automatically at the subsequent election. These Labour votes were thus no longer so vital in South Tipperary and hence were transferred in an effort to strengthen Labour's marginal seat in the North Tipperary constituency. The results of the next election (held in 1977) showed a drop in Labour's South Tipperary vote from 20.6% to 16.2% and an increase in its North Tipperary vote from 19.1% to 22.6%. The lower vote in the former constituency was largely irrelevant, since Tracy was automatically reelected, while Labour's seat in North Tipperary was substantially reenforced.

This form of gerrymander is particularly effective in Ireland, given the parties' well-attested knowledge of voting patterns at even the most microterritorial level. But since this gerrymander is also feasible

under almost all types of electoral systems and not peculiar to STV, it
need not further concern us here.

The second type of gerrymander, the *rotten-borough gerrymander*, is
also reasonably simple. This involves the unequal distribution of the
electorate between constituencies, such that, for example, a territorial
pocket with 100,000 voters who support one's opponent will be allocated, say, two seats, while a similar-size area dominated by one's own
supporters will be allocated four seats. Again, this need not concern
us here. Apart from its simplicity and its potential applicability to
many different types of electoral systems, such a strategy is virtually
impossible in Ireland, where the constitution stipulates that the ratio
of deputies to the population should be uniform across the whole
country (Art. 16.2.3) and that this ratio should not exceed 1 deputy per
20,000 inhabitants or be less than 1 per 30,000 inhabitants (16.2.2).
Indeed, a 1961 constituency revision which failed to follow these parameters had to be withdrawn following a challenge to its constitu-
tionality before the High Court. In general, Irish governments have
tended to stick fairly closely to the lower limit of 1 deputy per 20,000
inhabitants, a practice which led to the number of Dàil seats being
increased from 144 in 1973 to 166 in 1981 in response to the sudden
population growth of the 1970s.

While these constitutional restrictions therefore effectively prevent a
rotten-borough strategy, they do have one singular advantage for partisan political engineers in that they necessitate regular revisions of
the constituency map and therefore allow politicians many opportunities to experiment with the *district-size gerrymander*. This, the third
basic type of gerrymander, takes the total number of seats as a given
and involves deciding on the number of constituencies into which to
divide these seats. Thus, for example, if 60 seats are to be distributed,
those who determine their allocation between constituencies will have
to decide whether it be 6 with 10 seats, 12 with 5, 15 with 4, or 20 with
3, and so on; or, indeed, whether there should be a combination of
different-size constituencies such as, 6 with 5 seats, 6 with 4 seats,
and 2 with 3 seats. The possibilities are endless, but clearly some
distributions will be more favorable to some parties than to others. It
is here that STV shows its greatest potential for partisan political
engineering, and it is here that we find the greatest (potential) drawback in this particular electoral system.

The District-Size Gerrymander

As was just shown, the quota necessary to be elected in an STV contest is determined by dividing the total valid poll by one more than the total number of seats and then adding one to the result. It is clear from this that *as the number of seats increases, then the quota decreases as a percentage of the total valid poll.* In a 3-seat constituency, the divisor is 4 (3 + 1), and the quota is therefore approximately 25% of TVP. In a 9-seat constituency, the divisor is 10 (9 + 1), and therefore the quota is just 10% of TVP. Thus, for a minor party with a fairly even geographic spread of support, the larger the constituency (in terms of seats), the greater is the opportunity to win seats.

In Ireland, since 1947, no constituency has been allocated more than 5 seats, nor less than 3. *Ceteris paribus*, this means that, in order to be successful, a party—or individual candidate—needs between some 17% (5 seats) and 25% (3 seats). In order to gain Dàil representation, therefore, smaller parties such as Labour or the Workers party and, in the earlier period, Clann na Talmhan or Clann na Poblachta, need to rely on having either strong individual candidates—whose local personal following far exceeds the average level of support won by the party on a national basis—or geographically concentrated support, such as that enjoyed by Clann na Talmhan in the 1940s and 1950s or Labour in the Dublin area in 1969. Neither pattern is particularly favorable in the long run, however. Geographical concentration can facilitate organizational persistence, but only in very favorable circumstances can a regionally based party "nationalize" its electoral appeal. Strong personal candidates, on the other hand, may be useful in the short run, but their eventual deaths or retirements can lead to the disappearance of the party's basis of support.

But this is incidental. The major point is that, *ceteris paribus*, the potentiality for providing proportional outcomes with STV increases as the size of the constituency—in terms of seats—is expanded, a point already established quite clearly by Rae (1971, p. 115). The *ceteris paribus* clause is also important, since in practice increased proportionality is associated with large constituencies *only* given certain voting distributions (Gallagher, 1975). Indeed, in the Irish experience, while the average vote-seat deviation per party between 1927 and 1973 shows a secular decline as one moves from 3- to 4- to 5-seat constituencies, the deviation is nevertheless at its highest levels in the 7-, 8-, and 9-seat constituencies which formed a small part of the prewar constituency maps (Gallagher, 1975, Table 7). Moreover, recent evidence now suggests that the rule does not now apply even at the 3-, 4-, and 5-seat level. As can be seen in Table 19.5, which shows the average vote-seat deviation by constituency type in 1977, 1981, and the two elections of 1982, the average deviation was lowest in the 3-seat constituencies

TABLE 19.5. Average Vote-Seat Deviation by Constituency Size, 1977–1982

Year	Number of Seats in Constituency		
	3	4	5
1977	2.7	3.2	2.4
1981	0.9	3.0	1.5
1982 (Feb)	0.8	1.2	1.1
1982 (Nov)	0.8	2.9	1.5
Mean	1.3	2.6	1.6

Note. Calculation based on formula of Rae (1971, pp. 84–86).

(1.3) and highest in the 4-seat constituencies (2.6), and only in 1977 did the 3-seat constituencies show a value greater than unity.

In brief, therefore, while in theory proportionality should increase as constituencies become larger, in practice the proportionality of STV is dependent upon the actual distribution of electoral preferences. Larger districts will clearly suit smaller parties, but what is often not recognized, though what has been clearly shown by Gallagher (1975) and others, is that the converse is not necessarily true. In other words, smaller districts will not necessarily favor larger parties. Rather, depending on its *precise* vote, a large party may prefer a 4-seat to a 3-seat constituency or a 5-seat to a 4-seat constituency.

A simple example will suffice here: If party X wins 51% of first preferences in area Y, then, *ceteris paribus*, it will win 2 seats if Y is a 3-seat constituency, 2 seats also if Y is a 4-seat constituency, and 3 seats if Y is a 5-seat constituency. In other words, a 51% vote will win it 67% of seats in one case, 50% in another case, and 60% in the third case.[4] Thus if party X is in control of the constituency allocation, and if it is sure it can win 51% of the votes in area Y, then it will divide area Y into 3-seat constituencies (the smallest constituency permitted by the Irish Constitution). Conversely, if it expects its vote to drop to around 40% to 45% in area Y, it will divide Y into 4-seat constituencies, on the grounds that it can expect to win 50% of the seats with 40% to 45% of the vote. Finally, if party X *thinks* it can win 51%, and divides area Y into 3-seat constituencies, and then finds it *actually* wins only 40%–45% of the vote, then party X is in trouble; it has effectively allowed the opposition the advantage which it itself had hoped to gain. In these circumstances, if party X finds itself unable to accurately predict its vote, it is better advised to opt for 5-seat constituencies. If it then wins 51% of the vote, it still maintains a 3:2 majority of seats which, though not as advantageous as a 2:1 majority, is a majority nevertheless. If its vote falls to 40% to 45%, then it still manages 2 out of every 5 seats, which is a lot better than 1 out of every 3 if the constituencies each had 3 seats. Of course, it could again opt for the safe, 4-seat alternative; but, if its vote does indeed rise to 51%, it will not have gained a commensurate majority of seats.

Prior to 1979, the allocation of constituencies was in the (partisan) hands of the government of the day; and, normally, no major mistakes were made. In 1974, however, when the new coalition government got its first ever opportunity to revise the constituency map, it effectively decided to go for broke. Dublin city in 1969 and 1973 had been allocated 27 seats, which were divided between six 4-seaters and one 3-seater. In both elections Fianna Fail had won 2 seats in each of the 4-seaters, and Fine and Labour (contesting independently of one another in 1969) also won 2. In both cases also, Fine Gael and Labour took two of the seats in the 3-seat constituency, with Fianna Fail taking the third. Overall, the coalition parties won 50% of the Dublin vote in 1969 and 54% in 1973, while Fianna Fail won 39% and 42%, respectively. Given the predominance of 4-seat constituencies, however, this massive electoral majority resulted in only 14 seats for the coalition parties as against 13 for Fianna Fail.

Since the coalition enjoyed such an electoral dominance in Dublin in 1969 and 1973, it was then not surprising to find that their 1974 revision allocated the city's 27 seats among nine 3-seat constituencies. The logic of the new arrangement, as has already been stated elsewhere (Mair and Laver, 1975), was based on the assumption that their Dublin vote would hold up and that they could therefore win two seats in each of the 3-seat constituencies. In 1969 and 1973 they had won 14 of the 27 (52%) seats with a vote just over 50%; with a similar vote at the subsequent election, it was reckoned that they could increase this figure to 18 out of 27 (67%), and so do much to secure their return to office.

In the event, the gamble failed miserably. Fianna Fail won almost 44.5% of the Dublin city vote in 1977, as against just 45.1% for the coalition. Coupled to this, the contenders' relative strengths varied substantially from one Dublin constituency to another, with Fianna Fail spreading between a maximum of 51.6% (Finglas) and a low of 31.1% (South Central), while the party also maintained a higher rate of intracandidate vote transfer than that achieved by the coalition parties (Mair and Maguire, 1978). The result was that the coalition ended up with just 12 of the city's 27 seats (44%), as against the hoped for 18, while Fianna Fail alone won 14 (52%).

In this particular case, then, what was seen as a very obvious gerrymander[5] backfired very badly on its designers. Moreover, the sheer partisanness of this particular gerrymander led to the creation of the first independent electoral commission, which was placed in charge of devising the new 1981 constituencies.

In keeping with what had been the postwar practice of government-devised constituency maps, the new independent commission was specifically enjoined to use only 3-, 4-, and 5-seat constituencies. Though this stipulation effectively maintained the high threshold of a minimum of 17% of votes for minor parties and independents, the results of the 1981 and 1982 elections were reasonably proportional by comparison with those of earlier years (see Table 19.3). Paradoxically, however, precisely because the proportionality of the outcomes in1981 and February 1982 left neither of the alternative governments with an overall majority and instead gave the balance of power to the new left-wing parties and independents, the results of the commission's work precipitated quite a volume of protest against the electoral system itself.[6] But what is really at issue here is not the validity of STV as such; rather, in 1981 and February 1982 Ireland experienced the unanticipated consequences of what was intended to be a fair distribution of constituencies and which turned out instead to have the effect of muffling the impact of the electoral swing between government and opposition (Mair, 1982).

For a variety of reasons, such as the social composition of the different electorates, varying patterns of party indentification, differing levels of concern with issues as cues for voting as against more traditional loyalties (Mair, 1981), the eastern—more urban and more prosperous—part of the country tends to be much more electorally volatile than the western—poorer and more rural—area. Since 1948, for instance, the average swing between Fianna Fail on the one hand, and Fine Gael, Labour, and various other minor parties on the other, has been 5.0% in Dublin and 4.2% in the East and Midlands, as against only 2.3% and 2.2% in the West and Border peripheries, respectively. And while the brief 8-month span separating both the elections of 1981 and February 1982, as well as the two 1982 elections, acted to dampen average swings in the country as a whole; the swings which occurred in 1981, the first election to be held in the new commission's constituencies, replicated almost precisely the average patterns of postwar volatility. In other words, in 1981 the Dublin and East and Midlands areas swung most sharply against the Fianna Fail government, while the change registered in the West and Border was quite minimal (Mair, 1982).

The second important interregional difference which is relevant here is that Fianna Fail has tended to win a larger proportion of the vote in the more rural and peripheral areas than in the center. The contrast is particularly marked between the western region on the one hand, where Fianna Fail has averaged 53.6% of the vote between 1969 and 1982, and the Dublin region, where its 1969–1982 average vote has been just 41.5%.

If we then tie together these two characteristics – a more volatile and on average lower vote in Dublin as against a higher and more stable vote in the West – we can begin to see how the new electoral commission's particular allocation of 3-, 4-, and 5-seat constituencies dampened the effects of a substantial shift of votes in 1981. More specifically, with an average Dublin vote for Fianna Fail of 42%, with an actual range of about 39% to 46%, and recalling that candidates can be elected without actually reaching a full quota, a preponderance of 3-seat constituencies in the city could be expected to particularly favor the party in its "up" periods, and particularly penalize it in its "down" periods. In other words, 3-seat constituencies are those which would most exaggerate a shift in electoral preferences in this very volatile region. Conversely, and recalling an earlier point, 4-seat constituencies are those which would be most likely to fail to register such a swing in electoral preferences, since Fianna Fail would hope to win 2 out of every 4 seats whether in its up periods or in its down periods. At the same time, given the party's very high average vote in the West and given also the comparatively low level of volatility, Fianna Fail would clearly benefit from 3-seat constituencies in the West, since it could expect to win 2 seats in every 3 in both its down and its up periods. In short, given the distribution of electoral preferences and given the interregional differences in volatility, changes in electoral majorities are more likely to be reflected in Dàil majorities if 3-seat constituencies are concentrated in the marginal Dublin area rather than in the more electorally consistent West.

The new independent electoral commission did precisely the opposite: Whereas 18 of the West's 31 seats were distributed as 3-seat constituencies in 1981, the greater Dublin area was allocated five 5-seat, five 4-seat, and only one 3-seat constituency. The (arguably) unanticipated consequences in 1981 were as follows: In the 3-seat constituency, a coalition electoral majority gave it a 2:1 majority; in all of the 5-seat constituencies, the coalition also had an electoral majority/plurality and ended up with 14 of the 25 seats, as against 10 for Fianna Fail and 1 going to an Independent; in the 4-seat constituencies, however, the coalition's electoral majority/plurality in 3 of the 5 gave it just an even division of the seats with Fianna Fail. One type of constituency, therefore, turned a coalition electoral majority/plurality into a 2:1 seat majority; another type turned it into a 3:2 seat majority; while the third type left it simply with an even split of the seats. Had all of these constituencies been allocated as 3-seaters, on the other hand, the outcome would have been very different. Given that Fianna Fail had a majority/plurality in 2 of the 4-seat constituencies and yet also only won 2 seats in each of these, a division of greater Dublin into just 3-seat constituencies would have benefited that party in certain areas. But given also that the coalition parties were dominant in most of greater Dublin, a 3-seat division could have been expected to give them some 30 of the 48 seats. As it was, the coalition won 23 seats, as against 21 for Fianna Fail and 4 for the minor parties of Independents.

The point may be perhaps more clearly stated if these results are contrasted with those of the greater Dublin area in 1977, when 39 of the then 43 seats were allocated as 3-seat constituencies.[7] In the earlier election, Fianna Fail won 23 (53%) of the 43 seats as against 19 (44%) for the coalition; yet the party's vote was just 47% as against 45% for the coalition. In 1981, by contrast, with only one 3-seat constituency, the coalition's 48% vote won it just 48% of the seats, whereas Fianna Fail won 44% with a vote of slightly more than 41%. In this case, then, a 7% plurality for the coalition gave it a 4% plurality of seats, whereas a 2% plurality for Fianna Fail had given that party a 9% plurality of seats in 1977.

To be sure, the outcome in Dublin in 1981 was significantly more proportional than that of 1977; but, and perhaps more to the point, precisely because it was more proportional the outcome did not reflect the substantial swing in electoral preferences.

This, then, is the essential problem: With what end in mind does one design a constituency map for a STV election? If the purpose is partisan, then there should be no problem. Intelligent guesswork about the size and distribution of one's party's vote will determine the number and allocation of 3-, 4-, 5-seat constituencies. The only difficulty, then, becomes that of the guesswork; since, like the coalition design for the 1977 Irish election, unanticipated election results can doubly defeat the strategist's original purpose.

But if the purpose is nonpartisan, such as one must assume is the case for Ireland's new independent electoral commission, then there really may emerge a conflict of interests between effecting a proportional outcome on the one hand or a disproportional but decisive outcome on the other. The first, probably involving a heavy reliance on 5-seat constituencies, may effect a closer correspondence between votes and seats than has normally been achieved in Ireland (though note the figures in Table 19.5); given the general distribution of party support, however, such a distribution may also leave neither of the two main alternative governments with an overall majority. The second, which would almost certainly involve a heavy reliance on 3-seat constituencies in the more volatile and marginal area of greater Dublin, is likely to give large parties a substantial bonus in terms of seats but can only do so at the cost of squeezing out the smaller parties and independents. The establishment of an independent electoral commission may have cured the ills of Irish Gerrymandering for once and for all, but despite the more clear-cut outcome of the November 1982 election, it has also raised once more the thorny question of proportionality versus decisiveness.

Acknowledgments. An earlier version of this paper was presented to the 1982 meeting of the American Political Science Association. The author would like to acknowledge financial support given under the Nuffield Foundation Small Grants Scheme.

Notes

1. For a detailed account of the counting process see Chubb (1978); see also Casey (1977), and Hand (1979).
2. This may now be changing, in that divisions within Fianna Fail over the party leadership have been occasionally reflected in more generalized faction fights at local level. On the developing factional disputes in the party, see Garvin (1981).
3. On two other occasions, both also involving coalition governments in 1951 and 1957, government resignations were precipitated either through fear of a Dàil defeat or because of internal dissent within the coalition ranks, see Chubb (1974, p. 56).
4. In practice, though for the sake of argument it is assumed otherwise here, a party often needs less than 51%, since it can gain lower preference transfers from other parties and candidates or retain its own transfers while those of its opponents become nontransferable; see Cohan et al. (1975); Mair and Laver (1975).
5. In fact it was known in Ireland as a Tullymander, after James Tully, the Labour TD and Minister in charge of devising the new constituencies.
6. See, for example, the *Irish Times,* 22 February, 1982.
7. There may be some confusion here: whereas earlier reference was made to the Dublin *city* area, this present discussion concerns greater Dublin; that is, the city and the county.

References List/Author Index

Numbers in parentheses following each reference indicate the page or pages on which the work is cited. Below is an alphabetical listing of coauthors cited in references, followed by the name of the senior author under whose name a complete entry will be found. Many of these coauthors' names will also be found listed as senior authors for other works.

At the end of the References section there is a separate listing of court cases, each followed by the page number(s) in parentheses where the case was cited.

Adrian, C. See Williams, O.
Apter, D. E. See Eckstein, H.
Arman, H. D. See Rogers, C.
Ashworth, H.P.C. See Ashworth, T. R.
Bardi, L. See Katz, R. S.
Beth, L. See Havard, W.
Black, G. See Salisbury, R. H.
Bone, H. A. See Zeller, B.
Boyes, W. J. See Amacher, R. D.
Brams, S. J. See Fishburn, P. C.
Brent, E. See Granberg, D.
Brook, D. See Upton, G.J.G.
Butler, D. See Bogdanor, V.
Cazzola, F. See Spreafico, A.
Clague, C. See Gilbert, C. E.
Conant, R. W. See Shank, A.
Davis, M. D. See Brams, S. J.
Deegan, J. See Niemi, R.
Dye, T. R. See Robinson, T. P.
Edwards, S. D. See Lorinkas, R. A.
Eisenberg, R. See David, P.
England, R. E. See Meier, K. J.
Field, J. O. See Wolfinger, R.
Fiorina, M. P. See Ferejohn, J. A.
Fishburn, P. C. See Brams, S. J.
Fishburn, P. C. See Gehrlein, W. V.
Fowler, E. P. See Lineberry, R. L.
Gehrlein, W. V. See Fishburn, P. C.
Getter, R. W. See Schumaker, P. D.
Gibberd, R. W. See Lijphart, A.
Good, I. J. See Mayer, L.
Gudgin, G. See Taylor, P. J.
Hallett, G. H. See Hoag, C. G.
Hallman, L. C. See Claunch, R. G.
Hanby, V. J. See Loosemore, J.
Hawkins, B. W. See Lorinkas, R. A.
Hecock, D. S. See Bain, H. M.
Heilig, P. See Mundt, R. J.
Hunt, A. J. See Johnston, R. J.
Irwin, G. A. See Lijphart, A.
Johnson, C. A. See Vedlitz, A.

Johnston, R. J. See Morrissey, M. J.
Johnston, R. J. See Taylor, P. J.
Karnig, A. K. See Welch, S.
Keech, W. R. See Chappell, H. W., Jr.
Korbel, G. See Davidson, C.
Laver, M. See Mair, P.
Lee, E. See Alford, R.
Lutz, D. S. See Feld, R.
Mackie, T. T. See Craig, F.W.S.
MacManus, S. A. See Dye, T. R.
Maguire, M. See Mair, P.
Maley, M. See Maley, B.
McDonald, M. D. See Engstrom, R. L.
McKinlay, R. D. See Cohan, A. S.
Michel, P. See Ginsburgh, V.
Miller, W. E. See Campbell, A.
Mughan, A. See Cohan, A. S.
Mundt, R. J. See Heilig, P.
Ordeshook, P. C. See Riker, W. H.
Pelissero, J. P. See Morgan, D.
Penniman, H. R. See Butler, D.
Ranney, A. See Butler, D.
Renick, J. See Dye, T. R.
Rose, R. See Mackie, T. T.
Rossiter, D. J. See Johnston, R. J.
Sartori, G. See Sani, G.
Sanders, E. See Bensel, R. R.
Schumaker, P. D. See Getter, R. W.
Simon, C. P. See Keech, W. R.
Smock, A. C. See Smock, D. R.
Taylor, A.M. See O'Loughlin, J. O.
Taylor, P. J. See Gudgin, G.
Teitelbaum, B. See Baker, G. E.
Tullock, G. See Buchanan, J. M.
Wagner, R. E. See Buchanan, J.M.
Walter, B. O. See Karnig, A. K.
Welch, S. See Karnig, A. K.
Wilson, J. Q. See Banfield, E. C.
Young, H. P. See Balinski, M. L.
Zeigler, H. See Jennings, M. K.

References

Adrian, C. (1952). Some general characteristics of nonpartisan elections. *American Political Science Review* 46: 766–776. (226, 229, 230, 231, 232, 233, 240)

Adrian, C. (1959). A typology for nonpartisan elections. *Western Political Quarterly* 12: 449–458. (151)

Aldrich, J. H. (1976). Some problems in testing two rational models of participation. *American Journal of Political Science* 20: 713–733. (39)

Alford, R., and E. Lee (1968). Voting turnout in American cities. *American Political Science Review* 62: 796–813. (228)

Allum, P. A. (1964). Il voto di preferenza e l'elettorato Napoletano. *Nord e Sud* 11: 58–78. (87)

Amacher, R. D., and W. J. Boyes (1978). Cycles in senatorial voting behavior: Implications for the optimal frequency of elections. *Public Choice* 33 (3): 5–13. (105)

American Political Science Review (1951). The reapportionment of Congress. XLV: 153–157. (258)

Arrington, T. S. (1978). Partisan campaigns, ballots and voting patterns: The case of Charlotte. *Urban Affairs Quarterly* 14: 253–261. (229, 230, 231)

Arrow, K. J. (1951, 1963). *Social Choice and Individual Values*. New York: Wiley. (95, 104, 202)

Ashworth, T. R., and H.P.C. Ashworth (1900). *Proportional Representation Applied to Party Government: A New Electoral System*. London: George Roberts. (23)

Auerbach, C. A. (1964). The reapportionment cases: One person, one vote – One vote, one value. In P. Kurland (ed.), *Supreme Court Review*, pp. 1–87. Chicago: University of Chicago Press. (267)

Baaklini, A. I. (1976). *Legislative and Political Development: Lebanon, 1842–1972*. Durham, NC: Duke University Press. (119)

Bagley, C. R. (1966). Does candidates' position on the ballot paper influence voters' choices? – A study of the 1959 and 1964 British general elections. *Parliamentary Affairs* 19: 162–174. (246)

Bain, H. M., and D. S. Hecock (1957). *Ballot Position and Voter's Choice*. Detroit: Wayne State University. (229, 230, 245, 246)

Baker, G. E. (1955). *Rural versus Urban Political Power*. New York: Doubleday. (259, 260)

Baker, G. E. (1966). *The Reapportionment Revolution*. New York: Random House. (258, 262)

Baker, G. E. (1971). Gerrymandering: privileged sanctuary or next judicial target? In Polsby (ed.), *Reapportionment in the 1970s*, pp. 121–124. (271)

Baker, G. E. (1972). Redistricting in the seventies: The political thicket deepens. *National Civic Review* 61: 277–285. (272)

Baker, G. E., and B. Teitelbaum (1959). An end to cross-filing. *National Civic Review* 48: 286–291. (250)

Balinski, M. L., and H. P. Young (1980). The Webster method of apportionment. *Proceedings of the National Academy of Sciences USA* 77: 1–4. (171)

Balinski, M. L., and H. P. Young (1982). Fair representation in the European parliament. *Journal of Common Market Studies* 20: 361–374. (190)

Balinski, M. L. and H. P. Young (1983). *Fair Representation: Meeting the Idea of One Man, One Vote*. New Haven: Yale University Press. (179, 190)

Banfield, E. C., and J. Q. Wilson (1963). *City Politics*, Cambridge, MA: Harvard University Press and MIT Press. (223)

Banzhaf, J. F., III (1966). Multi-member electoral districts: Do they violate the 'one man, one vote' principle? *Yale Law Journal* 75: 1310–1338. (268, 276)

Barnett, M. R. (1982). The congressional black caucus: Illusions and realities of power. In M. B. Preston, L. J. Henderson, Jr., and P. Puryear (eds.), *The New Black Politics: The Search for Political Power*, pp. 28–54. New York: Longman. (218)

Beck, N. (1975). The paradox of minimax regret. *American Political Science Review* 69: 918. (39)

Bensel, R. R., and E. Sanders (1979). The effect of electoral rules on voting behavior: The electoral college and shift voting. *Public Choice* 34(1): 69–85. (38, 40)

Berrington, H. (1975). Summary of electoral systems and formulae. In Finer (ed.), *Adversary Politics and Electoral Reform*, pp. 362–368. (172)

Bicker, W. H. (1971). The effects of malapportionment in the states: A mistrial. In Polsby (ed.), *Reapportionment in the 1970's*, pp. 151–201. (265)

Birke, W. (1961). *European Elections by Direct Suffrage.* London: Sythoff. (102)

Black, D. (1958). *The Theory of Committees and Elections.* Cambridge: Cambridge University Press. (202)

Black, J. H. (1978). The multicandidate calculus of voting: application to Canadian federal elections. *American Journal of Political Science* 22: 609–638. (37, 39)

Black, J. H. (1980). The probability-choice perspective in voter decision making models. *Public Choice* 35(5): 565–574. (37)

Blondel, J. (1969). *An Introduction to Comparative Government.* London: Weidenfeld and Nicolson. (123, 165, 170, 171)

Bogdanor, V. (1981). *The People and the Party System: The Referendum and Electoral Reform in British Politics.* Cambridge: Cambridge University Press. (155)

Bogdanor, V. (1983). Conclusion: Electoral Systems and Party Systems. In Bogdanor and Butler (eds.), *Democracy and Elections: Electoral Systems and Their Political Consequences.* Cambridge: Cambridge University Press. (45)

Bogdanor, V., and D. Butler (eds.) (1983). *Democracy and Elections: Electoral Systems and Their Political Consequences.* Cambridge: Cambridge University Press. (4, 45)

Bon, F. (1978). *Les Elections en France: Histoire et Sociologie.* Paris: Editions du Seuil. (172)

Brams, S. J. (1976). *Paradoxes in Politics: An Introduction to the Nonobvious in Political Science.* New York: Free Press. (178)

Brams, S. J., and M. D. Davis (1974). The 3/2's rule in presidential campaigning. *American Political Science Review* 68: 113–134. (197)

Brams, S. J. and P. C. Fishburn (1978). Approval voting, *American Political Science Review* 72: 831–847. (194, 196, 199)

Brams, S. J. and P. C. Fishburn (1982). Deducing preferences and choices in the 1980 presidential election. *Electoral Studies* 1: 333–346. (198)

Brams, S. J. and P. C. Fishburn (1983). *Approval Voting.* Boston: Birkhauser. (1, 15, 194, 196, 199, 202)

Brams, S. J. and P. C. Fishburn (1984a). Some logical defects of the single transferable vote. In Lijphart and Grofman (eds.), *Choosing an Electoral System: Issues and Alternatives*, pp. 238–250. (1)

Brams, S. J. and P. C. Fishburn (1984b). A variable-size legislature to achieve proportional representation. In Lijphart and Grofman (eds.), *Choosing an Electoral System: Issues and Alternatives*, pp. 270–275. (1)

Brew, D. E. (1981). Examples of methods of counting used in different systems of proportional representation. In C. Sasse et al. (eds.), *The European Parliament: Towards a Uniform Procedure for District Elections*, pp. 412–423. Florence: European University Institute. (176)

Brittan, S. (1975). The economic contradictions of democracy. *British Journal of Political Science*, 5: 129–159. (104)

Bromage, A. W. (1962). *Political Representation in Metropolitan Agencies.* Ann Arbor: Institute of Public Administration, University of Michigan. (152)

Bromage, A. W. (1964). *Manager Plan Abandonments.* New York: National Municipal League. (140, 151)

Buchanan, J. M., and G. Tullock (1962). *The Calculus of Consent.* Ann Arbor: The University of Michigan Press. (202)

Buchanan, J. M., and R. E. Wagner (1977). *Democracy in Deficit: The Political Legacy of Lord Keynes.* New York: Academic Press. (104)

Bullock, C. S. (1975). The election of blacks in the South: preconditions and consequences. *American Journal of Political Science* 19: 727–739. (217)

Bunge, W. (1966). Gerrymandering, geography and grouping. *Geographical Review* 56: 256–263. (183)

Burnham, W. D. (1965). The changing shape of the American political universe. *American Political Science Review* 59: 7–28. (245)

Butler, D. (1981). Electoral systems. In Butler et al. (eds.), *Democracy at the Polls: A Comparative Study of Competitive National Elections*, pp. 7–25. Washington, DC: American Enterprise Institute. (72)

Butler, D., H. R. Penniman, and A. Ranney, eds. (1981). *Democracy at the Polls: A Comparative Study of Competitive Elections.* Washington, DC: American Enterprise Institute. (4, 102)

Butler, D. E. (1955). The redistribution of seats. *Public Administration* 55: 125–147. (280)

Butler, D. E. (1963). *The Electoral System in Britain Since 1918.* Oxford: The Clarendon Press. (278, 280)

Cadart, J., ed. (1983). *Les Modes de Scrutin des Dix-Huit Pays Libres de l'Europe Occidentale: Leurs Resultats et Leurs Effets Compares.* Paris: Presses Universitaires de France. (4)

Cain, B. E. (1978). Strategic voting in Britain. *American Journal of Political Science* 22: 639–655. (36, 37, 39)

Campbell, A., and W. E. Miller (1957). The motivational basis of straight and split ticket voting. *American Political Science Review* 60: 293–312. (243, 244)

Campbell, A., et al. (1960). *The American Voter.* New York: Wiley. (202)

Campbell, J. S., et al. (1970). *A Staff Report to the National Commission on the Causes and Prevention of Violence.* Washington, DC: U.S. Government Printing Office. (Reprinted by Bantam.) (151)

Campbell, P. (1965). *French Electoral Systems.* London: Faber and Faber. (91)

Canon, B. C. (1978). Factionalism in the South: A test of theory and a revisitation of V. O. Key. *American Journal of Political Science* 22: 833–848. (28)

Cappon, Lester J., ed. (1971). *The Adams-Jefferson Letters.* New York: Simon & Schuster. (276)

Carstairs, A. M. (1980). *A Short History of Electoral Systems in Western Europe.* London: Allen & Unwin. (155, 177)

Casey, J. P. (1977). The development of electoral law in the republic of Ireland. *Northern Ireland Legal Quarterly* 28(4): 357–381. (307)

Cassel, C. A. (1985). Social background characteristics of nonpartisan city council members: A research note. *Western Political Quarterly* 38 (forthcoming). (227, 235)

Chappell, H. W., Jr., and W. R. Keech (1983). Welfare consequences of the six-year presidential term evaluated in the context of a model of the U.S. economy. *American Political Science Review*, 77: 75–91. (108)

Childs, R. S. (1952). *Civic Victories.* New York: Harper. (140)

Childs, R. S. (1965). *The First 50 Years of the Council-Manager Plan of Municipal Government.* New York: American Book-Stratford Press. (141)

Chubb, B. (1970). *The Government and Politics of Ireland.* Stanford, CA: Stanford University Press. (91)

Chubb, B. (1974). *Cabinet Government in Ireland.* Dublin: Institute of Public Administration. (307)

Chubb, B. (1978). Procedures for voting and counting the votes in force in 1977. In H. R. Penniman (ed.), *Ireland at the Polls,* pp. 175–177. Washington, DC: American Enterprise Institute. (307)

Claunch, R. G., and L. C. Hallman (1978). Ward elections in the South: Electoral change through federal court order. *GPSA Journal* 6: 3–15. (206)

Cohan, A. S., R. D. McKinlay, and A. Mughan (1975). The used vote and electoral outcomes. *British Journal of Political Science* 5(4): 363–383. (293, 307)

Cole, L. A. (1974). Electing blacks to municipal office: Structure and social determinants. *Urban Affairs Quarterly* 10: 17–39. (216)

Cole, L. A. (1976). *Blacks in Power: A Comparative Study of Black and White Elected Officials.* Princeton, NJ: Princeton University Press. (218)

Common Cause (1977). *Toward a System of Fair and Effective Representation.* (274, 276)

Congressional Quarterly (1975). Guide to U.S. Elections. (248)

Congressional Quarterly Weekly Report (1981). October 31. (276)

Congressional Quarterly Weekly Report (1982). June 26. (269)

Cope, C. R. (1971). Regionalization and the electoral districting problem. *Area* 3: 190–195. (183)

Craig, F.W.S., and T. T. Mackie (1980). Europe Votes 1: European Parliamentary Election Results 1979. Chichester: Parliamentary Research Services. (115, 122)

Craig, J. T. (1959). Parliament and boundary commissions. *Public Law* 24: 23–45. (280)

Crow, R. E. (1962). Religious sectarianism in the Lebanese political system. *Journal of Politics* 24: 489–520. (115)

Cummings, M. C. (1966). *Congressmen and the Electorate.* New York: Free Press. (243)

Curtis, G. L. (1971). *Election Campaigning Japanese Style.* New York: Columbia University Press. (102)

David, P., and R. Eisenberg (1961). *Devaluation of the Urban and Suburban Vote; Vol. 1.* Charlottesville: Bureau of Public Administration, University of Virginia. (258)

Davidson, C., and G. Korbel (1981). At-large elections and minority group representation: A re-examination of historical and contemporary evidence. *Journal of Politics* 43: 982–1005. (212)

Dixon, R. G. (1964). Recent developments in reapportionment: The constitutional struggle for fair representation. Address to Conference of Chief Justices, August 6. (267)

Dixon, R. G. (1968). *Democratic Representation and Reapportionment in Law and Politics.* New York: Oxford University Press. (263, 267, 272)

Dobrusin, H. M. (1955). Proportional Representation in Massachusetts. Unpublished manuscript. (149)

Downs, A. (1957). *An Economic Theory of Democracy.* New York: Harper & Row. (34, 39, 197, 202)

Dubois, P. L. (1979). Voter turnout in state judicial elections: An analysis of the tail on the electoral kite. *Journal of Politics* 41: 865–887. (244)

Duverger, M. (1946a). Les Partis Politique. In Universite de Bordeaux, Conferences du Lundi (1945–1946), pp. 21–32. Bordeaux: Ed. Delmas. (70)

Duverger, M. (1946b). Les partis politiques. *La Vie Intellectuelle* 20: 62–73. (70)

Duverger, M. (1951a). *Les Partis Politiques.* Paris: Le Seuil. (4, 5, 65, 71, 77)

Duverger, M. (1954a). *Les Partis Politiques* (2nd rev. ed.). Paris: Colin. (44, 47, 65, 67)

Duverger, M. (1954b, 1959, 1963). *Political Parties: Their Organization and Activity in the*

Modern State (B. North and R. North, Trans.). London: Methuen. New York: Wiley. (77, 103, 155)

Duverger, M. (1955). *Droit Constitutionnel et Institutions Politiques*. Paris: Presses Universitaires de France. (70)

Duverger, M. (1982). *La République des Citoyens*. Paris: Ed. Ramsay. (84)

Duverger, M. et al., eds. (1950). *L'Influence des Systèmes Electoraux sur la Vie Politique*. Paris: Colin. (70, 71, 65)

Dye, T. R. (1965). Malapportionment and public policy in the states. *Journal of Politics* 27: 586–601. (265)

Dye, T. R., and S. A. MacManus (1976). Predicting city government structure. *American Journal of Political Science* 20: 257–271. (205)

Dye, T. R., and J. Renick (1981). Political power and city jobs: Determinants of minority employment. *Social Science Quarterly* 62: 475–486. (220, 221, 223)

Eckstein, H., and D. E. Apter, eds. (1963). *Comparative Politics: A Reader*. New York: Free Press. (45)

Eisinger, Peter K. (1982). Black employment in municipal jobs: The impact of black political power. *American Political Science Review* 76: 380–392. (217, 219, 221)

Elder, N.C.M. (1975). The Scandinavian states. In S. E. Finer (ed.), *Adversary Politics and Electoral Reform*, pp. 185–202. London: Anthony Wigram. (175)

Engstrom, R. L. (forthcoming). The (new) Voting Rights Act: Continuity and change in black politics. In J. Lea (ed.), *Contemporary Southern Politics: Continuity and Change*. (205)

Engstrom, R. L., and M. D. McDonald (1981). The election of blacks to city councils: Clarifying the impact of electoral arrangements on the seats/population relationship. *American Political Science Review* 75: 344–354. (207, 208, 209, 216, 225)

Engstrom, R. L., and M. D. McDonald (1982). The underrepresentation of blacks on city councils: Comparing the structural and socioeconomic explanations for South/non-South differences. *Journal of Politics* 44: 1088–1099. (205, 212, 217)

Erikson, R. (1971). The partisan impact of state legislative representation. *Midwest Journal of Political Science* 15: 57–71. (263)

Farquharson, R. (1969). *Theory of Voting*. New Haven: Yale University Press. (197, 202)

The Federalist Papers. New York: Heritage Press, 1945; New American Library, 1961. (105, 106, 107, 109, 274)

Feld, R., and D. S. Lutz (1972). Recruitment to the Houston city council. *Journal of Politics* 34: 924–933. (234)

Ferejohn, J. A., and M. P. Fiorina (1974). The paradox of not voting: A decision theoretic analysis. *American Political Science Review* 68: 525–536. (39)

Ferejohn, J. A., and M. P. Fiorina (1975). Closeness counts only in horseshoes and dancing. *American Political Science Review* 69: 920–925. (39)

Fesler, J. W. (1967). *The 50 States and their Local Governments*. New York: Knopf. (261)

Findley, J. C. (1959). Cross-filing and the progressive movement in California politics. *Western Political Quarterly* 12: 699–711. (249, 250)

Finer, H. (1924, 1935). *The case against proportional representation*. Fabian Tract No. 211. London. (25)

Fishburn, P. C. (1973). *The Theory of Social Choice*. Princeton: Princeton University Press. (202)

Fishburn, P. C. (1983). Dimensions of election procedures: analyses and comparisons. *Theory and Decision* 15: 371–397. (2, 194, 196, 202)

Fishburn, P. C., and S. J. Brams (1981). Expected utility and approval voting. *Behavioral Science* 26: 136–142. (199, 201)

Fishburn, P. C., and S. J. Brams (1983). Paradoxes of preferential voting. *Mathematics Magazine* 56: 207–214. (195)

Fishburn, P. C., and W. V. Gehrlein (1982). Majority efficiencies for simple voting procedures: Summary and interpretation. *Theory and Decision* 14: 141–153. (200)

Fisher, S. L. (1974). A test of Anthony Downs' wasted vote thesis: West German evidence. Paper presented at the Public Choice Society, New Haven. (37)

Fisichella, D. (1982). *Elezioni e Democrazia*. Bologna: Il Mulino. (67, 68)

Freeman, J. L. (1958). Local party systems: Theoretical considerations and a case analysis. *American Journal of Sociology* 64: 282–289. (232)

Friedrich, C. J. (1937). *Constitutional Government and Politics*. New York: Harper. (26)

Gallagher, M. (1975). Disproportionality in a proportional representation system: The Irish experience. *Political Studies* 23(4): 501–513. (301, 302)

Garvin, Tom (1981). The growth of faction in the Fianna Fail party, 1966–1980. *Parliamentary Affairs* 34(1): 110–123. (307)

Gehrlein, W. V. (1983). Condorcet's paradox. *Theory and Decision* 15: 161–197. (200)

Gehrlein, W. V., and P. C. Fishburn (1979). Effects of abstentions on voting procedures in three-candidate elections. *Behavioral Science* 24: 346–354. (200, 201)

Georgel, J. (1981). The electoral systems of Greece, Portugal and Spain. In Sasse et al. (eds.), *The European Parliment: Towards a Uniform Procedure for Direct Elections*, pp. 315–336. (156)

Getter, R. W., and P. D. Schumaker (1978). Contextual bases of responsiveness to citizen preferences and group demands. *Policy and Politics* 6: 249–278. (220)

Gibbard, A. (1973). Manipulation of voting-schemes: A general result. *Econometrica* 41: 587–601. (198)

Gietzelt, A. (1981). *Proposals for Change in Our Electoral System*. Published by Senator Gietzelt at Parliament House, Canberra, ACT 2600. (129)

Gilbert, C. E., and C. Clague (1962). Electoral competition and electoral systems in large cities. *Journal of Politics* 24: 340–347. (232)

Gilsdorf, R. (1970). Factionalism in the Italian Christian Democratic Party, 1958, 1963. Ph.D. dissertation, Yale University. (102)

Ginsburgh, V., and P. Michel (1983). Random timing of elections and the political business cycle. *Public Choice* 40(2): 155–164. (109)

Graham, B. D. (1962). The choice of voting methods in federal politics, 1902–1918. *Australian Journal of Politics and History* 8: 164–181. (128)

Granberg, D., and E. Brent (1980). Perceptions of issue positions of presidential candidates. *American Scientist* 68: 617–625. (196, 202)

Greenstein, F. T. (1970). *The American Party System and the American People* (2d ed.). Englewood Cliffs, NJ: Prentice-Hall. (229, 232)

Gregory, M. (1981). Zimbabwe 1980: Politicisation through armed struggle and electoral mobilisation. *Journal of Commonwealth and Comparative Studies* 19: 62–94. (115, 117)

Grofman, B. (1975). A review of macro election systems. In R. Wildenmann (ed.), *Sozialwissenschaftliches Jahrbuch fur Politik: Vol. 4*, pp. 303–352. Munich: Günter Olzog Verlag. (2, 175, 176)

Grofman, B. (1982a). Alternatives to single-member plurality districts: Legal and empirical issues. In Grofman et al. (eds.), *Representation and Redistricting Issues*, pp. 107–128. (1, 204, 276)

Grofman, B. (1982b). The effect of ward vs. at-large elections on minority representation: Part II, A review and critique of twenty-three recent empirical studies. Unpublished manuscript. (207, 214)

Grofman, B. (1982c). Reformers, politicians and the courts: A preliminary look at U.S. redistricting. *Political Geography Quarterly* 1: 303–316. (285)

Grofman, B. (1982d). Book review: Political geography. *American Political Science Review* 76(4): 883–885. (1)

Grofman, B. (1983b). Measures of bias in seats-votes relationships. *Political Methodology* 9: 295–327. (213)

Grumm, J. (1958). Theories of electoral systems. *Midwest Journal of Political Science* 2: 357–376. (27, 33, 65)

Gudgin, G., and P. J. Taylor (1974). Electoral bias and the distribution of party voters. *Transactions,* Institute of British Geographers 63: 53–73. (184, 187)

Gudgin, G., and P. J. Taylor (1979). *Seats, Votes and the Spatial Organization of Elections.* London: Pion. (184, 186, 187, 188, 189, 190, 277, 286)

Gudgin, G., and P. J. Taylor (1981). The decomposition of electoral bias in a plurality election. *British Journal of Political Science* 11: 515–522. (187)

Hagensick, A. C. (1964). Influences of partisanship and incumbency on a nonpartisan election system, *Western Political Quarterly* 17: 117–124. (236)

Hamilton, H. D. (1969). Costs of reform: Structural change in city governments may not resolve alienation problems. *National Civic Review* 58: 469–475. (151)

Hamilton, H. D. (1971). The municipal voter: Voting and nonvoting in city elections. *American Political Science Review* 65: 1135–1140. (228)

Hand, G. (1979). Ireland. In Hand et al. (eds.), *European Electoral Systems Handbook,* pp. 121–139. London: Butterworths. (307)

Hansard Society (1976). *The report of the Hansard Society on electoral reform.* London: Hansard Society. (190)

Hansard's Parliamentary Debates (1867 and 1885). Third Series, 188 and 294. (22)

Hansen, S. B. (1975). Participation, political structure and concurrence. *American Political Science Review* 69: 1181–1199. (228, 238)

Hare, T. (1859). *The Election of Representatives, Parliamentary and Municipal.* London: Longman, Roberts, Green. (21)

Hare, T. (1861). *The Election of Representatives, Parliamentary and Municipal: A Treatise* (rev. ed.). London: Longman, Green. (195, 202)

Havard, W., and L. Beth (1962). *The Politics of Misrepresentation.* Baton Rouge, LA: Louisiana State Press. (260)

Hawley, W. D. (1973). *Nonpartisan Elections and the Case for Party Politics.* New York: Wiley. (227, 228, 231, 236)

Hearl, D. (1980). Belgium: Two into three will go. In V. Herman and M. Hagger (eds.), *The Legislation of Direct Elections to the European Parliament,* pp. 30–54. Westmead: Gower. (118)

Heilig, P. (1983). District representation and satisfaction with city government. Presented at the Annual Meeting of the American Political Science Association. (153)

Heilig, P., and R. J. Mundt (1983). Changes in representational equity: The effect of adopting districts. *Social Science Quarterly* 64: 393–397. (205, 206, 212, 213, 217)

Heisel, W. D. (1982). Abandonment of proportional representation and the impact of 9-X voting in Cincinnati. Presented at Annual Meeting of the American Political Science Association. (153)

Hermens, F. A. (1941). *Democracy or Anarchy: A Study of Proportional Representation.* Notre Dame, IN: University of Notre Dame Press. (25, 140, 152)

Hoag, C. G., and G. H. Hallett (1969). *Proportional Representation.* New York: Macmillan. (Originally published, 1926.) (202)

Hogan, J. (1945). *Election and Representation.* Cork: Cork University Press. (66, 178)

Holcombe, Arthur (1910). Direct primaries and the second ballot. *American Political Science Review* 5: 535–552. (25, 27)

Holler, M. J. (1982). Forming coalitions and measuring voting power. *Political Studies* 30: 262–271. (192)

Hudson, M. C. (1968). *The Precarious Republic: Political Modernization in Lebanon.* New York: Random House. (120)

Humphreys, J. H. (1911). *Proportional Representation: A Study in Methods of Election.* London: Methuen. (176)

Irvine, W. P. (1984). 'Additional member' electoral systems. In Lijphart and Grofman (eds.), *Choosing an Electoral System: Issues and Alternatives,* pp. 251–269. New York: Praeger. (190)

Jackson, J. E. (1974). *Constituencies and Leaders in Congress: Their Effects on Senate Voting Behavior.* Cambridge, MA: Harvard University Press. (105)

Jennings, M. K., and H. Zeigler (1966). Class, party and race in a city election. *Journal of Politics* 28: 148–163. (231)

Jewell, M. E. (1967). *Legislative Representation in the Contemporary South.* Durham, NC: Duke University Press. (262)

Jewell, M. E. (1982). *Representation in State Legislatures,* Lexington, KY: University Press of Kentucky. (224)

Johansen, L. N. (1979). Denmark. In Hand et al. (eds.), *European Electoral Systems Handbook,* pp. 29–57. London: Butterworths. (178)

Johnston, R. J. (1976a). Parliamentary seat redistribution: More opinions on the theme. *Area* 8: 30–34. (187, 286)

Johnston, R. J. (1977a). National sovereignty and national power in European institutions, *Environment and Planning A* 9: 569–577. (191)

Johnston, R. J. (1977c). Population distributions and electoral power: Preliminary investigation of class bias, *Regional Studies* 11: 309–321. (191, 192)

Johnston, R. J. (1979a). *Political, Electoral and Spatial Systems.* Oxford: The University Press. (155, 171, 277, 285, 286, 287)

Johnston, R. J. (1979b). Political geography and political power. *Munich Social Science Review* 1(3): 5–31. (191)

Johnston, R. J. (1982a). Political geography and political power. In M. J. Holler (ed.), *Power, Voting and Voting Power,* pp. 289–306. Vienna: Physica-Verlag. (191, 192)

Johnston, R. J. (1983a). An unresolved issue for electoral reformers. *Representation* 23: 6–10. (191)

Johnston, R. J. (1983b). Fair representation and power in the European Parliament. *Area* 15: 347–353. (191)

Johnston, R. J. (1983c). Texts, actors and higher managers: Judges, bureaucrats and the political organization of space. *Political Geography Quarterly* 2: 3–20. (285)

Johnston, R. J. (1984). Seats, votes, redistricting and the allocation of power in electoral systems. In Lijphart and Grofman (eds.), *Choosing an Electoral System: Issues and Alternatives,* pp. 86–107. New York: Praeger. (278)

Johnston, R. J., and A. J. Hunt (1977). Voting power in the EEC's Council of Ministers: An essay on method in political geography. *Geoforum* 8: 1–9. (191)

Johnston, R. J., and D. J. Rossiter (1981b). An approach to the delimitation of planning regions. *Applied Geography* 1: 55–69. (188)

Johnston, R. J., and D. J. Rossiter (1982). Constituency building, political representation and electoral bias in urban England. In D. T. Herbert and R. J. Johnston (eds.), *Geography and the Urban Environment: Volume 5,* pp. 113–156. Chichester: Wiley. (189, 287)

Jones, C. B. (1976). The impact of local election systems on black political representation. *Urban Affairs Quarterly* 11: 345–356. (205, 212)

Jones, M. H. (1978). Black political empowerment in Atlanta: Myth and reality. *Annals of the American Academy of Political and Social Science* 439: 90–117. (218, 220)

Judd, D. R. (1979). *The Politics of American Cities: Private Power and Public Policy.* Boston: Little, Brown. (204)

Kamin, L. J. (1958). Ethnic and party affiliations of candidates as determinants of voting. *Canadian Journal of Psychology* 12: 205–212. (229)

Karnig, A. K. (1975). "Private regarding" policy, civil rights groups, and the mediating impact of municipal reforms. *American Journal of Political Science* 19: 91–106. (222, 239)

Karnig, A. K., and B. O. Walter (1976). Election of women to city councils. *Social Science Quarterly* 56: 605–613. (205, 212, 216, 237)

Karnig, A. K., and B. O. Walter (1977). Municipal elections: Registration, incumbent success, and voter participation. *The Municipal Yearbook 1977,* pp. 65–72. Washington, DC: International City Management Association. (228, 232, 233)

Karnig, A. K., and B. O. Walter (1981). Joint electoral fate of incumbents. *Journal of Politics* 43: 889–898. (233)

Karnig, A. K., and S. Welch (1980). *Black Representation and Urban Policy.* Chicago: University of Chicago Press. (205, 217, 218, 219, 220, 222, 224, 225, 237)

Karnig, A. K., and S. Welch (1982). Electoral structure and black representation on city councils. *Social Science Quarterly* 63: 99–114. (209, 210, 211, 216)

Katz, R. S. (1980). *A Theory of Parties and Electoral Systems.* Baltimore: Johns Hopkins University Press. (21, 28, 42, 72, 86, 155)

Katz, R. S. (1981). But how many candidates should we have in Donegal? Numbers of nominees and electoral efficiency in Ireland. *British Journal of Political Science* 11(1): 117–122. (293)

Katz, R. S., and L. Bardi (1980). Preference voting and turnover in Italian parliamentary elections. *American Journal of Political Science* 24: 97–114. (89)

Keech, W. R. (1968). *The Impact of Negro Voting: The Role of the Vote in the Quest for Equality.* Chicago: Rand McNally. (217)

Keech, W. R., and C. P. Simon (1983). Inflation, unemployment, and electoral terms: When can reform of political institutions improve macroeconomic policy? In Kristen Monroe (ed.), *The Political Process and Economic Change,* pp. 77–107. New York: Agathon Press. (107)

Kelly, J. S. (1978). *Arrow Impossibility Theorems.* New York: Academic Press. (202)

Key, V. O. (1949). *Southern Politics.* New York: Knopf. (26, 28)

Key, V. O. (1956). *American State Politics.* New York: Knopf. (260, 264)

Key, V. O. (1958). *Politics, Parties and Pressure Groups.* New York: Thomas Y. Crowell. (247)

Key, V. O. (1966). *The Responsible Electorate.* Cambridge, MA: Harvard University Press. (202)

Kingdon, J. W. (1968). *Candidates for Office: Beliefs and Strategies.* New York: Random House. (102)

Koury, E. M. (1976). *The Crisis in the Lebanese System: Confessionalism and Chaos.* Washington, DC: American Enterprise Institute. (122)

Krakowski, M. (1975). Inflation, unemployment and presidential tenure. *Journal of Political Economy* 83: 867–872. (110)

Kramer, J. (1971). The election of blacks to city councils: A 1970 status report and a prolegomenon. *Journal of Black Studies* 1: 443–476. (212)

Kuklinski, J. H. (1978). Representativeness and elections: A policy analysis. *American Political Science Review* 72: 165–177. (105)

Kyriakides, S. (1968). *Cyprus: Constitutionalism and Crisis Government.* Philadelphia: University of Pennsylvania Press. (122)

Laakso, M. (1979). The maximum distortion and the problem of the first divisor of different P.R. systems. *Scandinavian Political Studies* 2: 161–169. (177, 178)

Lächler, U. (1982). On political business cycles with endogenous election dates. *Journal of Public Economics* 17: 111–117. (109)

Lakeman, E. (1970, 1974). *How Democracies Vote: A Study of Majority and Proportional Electoral Systems.* London: Faber and Faber. (154, 155, 157, 172)

Latimer, M. K. (1979). Black political representation in southern cities: Election systems and other causal variables. *Urban Affairs Quarterly* 15: 65–86. (212, 216)

Laver, M. (1981). *The Politics of Private Desires.* London: Penguin. (190, 192)

Laver, M., and J. Underhill (1982). The bargaining advantages of combining with others. *British Journal of Political Science* 12: 27–42. (192)

Lee, E. (1960). *The Politics of Nonpartisanship: A Study of California City Elections.* Berkely: University of California Press. (226, 227, 229, 230, 231, 234, 236)

Lee, E. (1963). City elections: A statistical profile. *The Municipal Yearbook 1963.* Chicago: International City Managers Association, pp. 74–84. (228, 232, 233)

Lemieux, P. (1977). The Liberal Party and British political change: 1955–1974. Ph.D. dissertation. Massachusetts Institute of Technology. (36)

Leuthold, D. A. (1968). *Electioneering in a Democracy.* New York: Wiley. (102)

Leys, C. (1959). Models, theories, and the theory of political parties. *Political Studies* 8: 127–146. (41)

Liebert, R. J. (1974). Municipal functions, structure, and expenditures: A reanalysis of recent research. *Social Science Quarterly* 54: 765–783. (222, 225, 238)

Lijphart, A. (1982). Comparative perspectives on fair representation: The plurality-majority rule, geographical districting, and alternative electoral arrangements. In Grofman et al. (eds.), *Representation and Redistricting Issues,* pp. 143–159. Lexington, MA: Lexington Books. (225)

Lijphart, A. (1984a). Advances in the comparative study of electoral systems. *World Politics* 36: 424–436. (1)

Lijphart, A., and R. W. Gibberd (1977). Thresholds and payoffs in list systems of proportional representation. *European Journal of Political Research* 5: 219–244. (157, 174)

Lijphart, A., and G. A. Irwin (1979). Nomination strategies in the Irish STV system: The Dail elections of 1969, 1973 and 1977. *British Journal of Political Science* 9(3): 362–369. (293)

Lineberry, R. L., and E. P. Fowler (1967). Reformism and public policies in American cities. *American Political Science Review* 61: 701–716. (223, 238)

Lipset, S. M. (1960). *Political Man.* New York: Doubleday. (202)

Lipson, L. (1948). *The Politics of Equality: New Zealand's Adventures in Democracy.* Chicago: University of Chicago Press. (122)

Loosemore, J., and V. J. Hanby (1971). The theoretical limits of maximum distortion: Some analytic expressions for electoral systems. *British Journal of Political Science* 1: 467–477. (171)

Lorinkas, R. A., B. W. Hawkins, and S. D. Edwards (1969). The persistence of ethnic voting in urban and rural areas: Results from a controlled election method. *Social Science Quarterly* 49: 891–899. (229)

Loveday, P., et al., eds. (1977). *The Emergence of the Australian Party System.* Sydney: Hale and Iremonger. (127)

Lowell, A. L. (1896). *Governments and Parties in Continental Europe* (2 vols.). Boston: Houghton Mifflin. (24, 27, 28)

Lyons, W. (1977). Urban structures and policy: Reassessing additive assumptions of reform. *Political Methodology* 4(2): 213–226. (238)

Lyons, W. (1978). Reform and response in American cities: Structure and policy reconsidered. *Social Science Quarterly* 59: 118–132. (222)

MacDonald, J. R. (1909). *Socialism and Government*, 2 vols. London. (24)

Mackenzie, W.J.M. (1957). The export of electoral systems, *Political Studies*, V: 240–257. Reprinted in Eckstein and Apter (1963). (65)

Mackenzie, W.J.M. (1958). *Free Elections: An Elementary Textbook*. London: Allen & Unwin. (102, 155, 172)

Mackie, T. T., and R. Rose (1974). *The International Almanac of Electoral History*. London: Macmillan. (115, 122)

Mackie, T. T. and R. Rose (1982). *The International Almanac of Electoral History* (2d ed.). New York: Facts on File. (155)

MacMahon, A. W. (1933). Political parties, United States. In A. Johnson (ed.). *Encyclopedia of the Social Sciences*, Vol. 6, pp. 596–601. New York: Macmillan. (26, 34)

MacManus, S. A. (1978). City council election procedures and minority representation: Are they related? *Social Science Quarterly* 59: 153–161. (215, 216)

Mair, P. (1981). Towards an available electorate? Parties, party loyalty and patterns of opposition in post-war Ireland. Unpublished paper, European University Institute, Florence. (304)

Mair, P. (1982). Muffling the swing: STV and the Irish general election of 1981. *West European Politics* 5(1): 76–91. (304)

Mair, P., and M. Laver (1975). Proportionality, P.R. and S.T.V. in Ireland. *Political Studies* 23(4): 491–500. (303, 307)

Mair, P., and M. Maguire (1978). The single transferable vote and the Irish general election of 1977. *Economic and Social Review* 9(1): 59–70. (303)

Maley B., and M. Maley (1980). A description of recent elections. In M. Mackerras (ed.), *Elections 1980*, pp. 252–279. Sydney: Angus and Robertson. (128, 129, 130)

Mayer, L., and I. J. Good (1975). Is minimax regret applicable to voting decision? *American Political Science Review* 69: 916–917. (39)

Mayhew, D. R. (1971). Congressional representation. In Polsby (ed.), *Reapportionment in the 1970s*, pp. 249–285. (245)

McHenry, D. E. (1950). Invitation to the masquerade. *National Municipal Review* 39: 228–232. (250)

McKay, R. (1965). *Reapportionment*. New York: The Twentieth Century Fund. (261)

McKay, R. (1968). Reapportionment: Success story of the Warren Court. *Michigan Law Review* 67: 223–236. (262, 264)

McNelly, T. (1982). Limited voting in Japanese parliamentary elections. Presented at the annual meeting of the American Political Science Association, Denver. (164)

McRobie, A. D. (1980). The electoral system and the 1978 election. In H. R. Penniman (ed.), *New Zealand at the Polls: The General Election of 1978*, pp. 64–98. Washington, DC: American Enterprise Institute. (115, 116, 118)

Meehl, P. E. (1977). The selfish voter paradox and the thrown-away vote argument. *American Political Science Review* 61: 11–30. (39)

Meier, K. J., and R. E. England (1982). *Black representation and educational policy*. Paper presented at the annual meeting of the American Political Science Association, Denver. (222)

Mellen, S.L.W. (1943). The German people and the post-war world. *American Political Science Review* 37: 607–625. (25)

Merrill, S., III (1979). Approval voting: A "best buy" method for multicandidate elections. *Mathematics Magazine* 52: 98–102. (199)

Mill, J. S. (1910). Considerations on representative government. In A. D. Lindsey (ed.), *Utilitarianism, Liberty, and Representative Government*. London: Everyman Library Editions. (Originally published, 1861.) (21)

Monro, W. B. (1919). *The Government of the United States.* New York. (26)

Morgan, D., and J. P. Pelissero (1980). Urban policy: Does political structure matter? *American Political Science Review* 74: 999–1006. (239)

Morrill, R. L. (1981). *Political Redistricting and Geographic Theory.* Washington, DC: Association of American Geographers. (192)

Morrissey, M. J., and R. J. Johnston (1984). The sources of electoral bias in Jamaica election returns 1967–1980. *Caribbean Geography* 2: 175–185. (187)

Motomura, H. (1983). Preclearance under section five of the Voting Rights Act. *North Carolina Law Review* 61: 189–246. (225)

Mueller, J. E. (1970). Choosing among 133 candidates. *Public Opinion Quarterly* 34: 395–402. (246)

Mundt, R. J., and P. Heilig (1982). District representation: Demands and effects in the urban South. *Journal of Politics* 44: 1035–1048. (206)

National Civic Review (1962). Consequences of decisions 51: 481. (261)

National Municipal League (1961). *Compendium on Legislative Apportionment.* New York. (258)

National Municipal Review (1915). "Notes," 4. Ibid. (1917). "Notes," 6. (151)

Neels, L. (1979). Preparations for direct elections in Belgium, Part II. *Common Market Law Review* 16: 243–249. (118)

Niemi, R., and J. Deegan (1978). A theory of political districting. *American Political Science Review* 72: 1304–1323. (274, 277)

Nohlen, D. (1978). *Wahlsysteme der Welt—Daten und Analysen: Ein Handbuch.* Munich: R. Piper. (115, 172, 177)

Nordhaus, W. D. (1975). The political business cycle. *Review of Economic Studies* 42: 169–190. (104, 106)

Nuscheler, F. (1969). Zypern. In D. Sternberger and B. Vogel (eds.), *Die Wahl der Parlamente und anderer Staatsorgane: Ein Handbuch,* pp. 1419–1427. Berlin: De Gruyter. (117)

Obler, J. (1973). The role of national party leaders in the selection of parliamentary candidates: The Belgian case. *Comparative Politics* 5: 157–184. (87)

O'Leary, C. (1961). *The Irish Republic: And Its Experiment with Proportional Representation.* Notre Dame, IN: University of Notre Dame Press. (28)

O'Leary, C. (1979). *Irish Elections, 1918–1977: Parties, Voters and Proportional Representation.* New York: St. Martin's. (28, 155, 290, 294, 296)

O'Loughlin, J. (1980). District size and party electoral strength: A comparison of sixteen democracies. *Environment and Planning A* 12: 247–262. (190)

O'Loughlin, J. (1982a). The identification and evaluation of racial gerrymandering. *Annals of the Association of American Geographers* 72: 165–184. (192)

O'Loughlin, J. O., and A. M. Taylor (1982). Choices in redistricting and electoral outcomes: The case of Mobile, Alabama. *Political Geography Quarterly* 1: 317–340. (189, 217)

Olson, M. (1965). *The Logic of Collective Action.* Cambridge, MA: Harvard University Press. (202)

Orleans, P. (1968). Urban politics and the nonpartisan ballot: A metropolitan case. In S. Greer et al. (eds.), *The New Urbanization.* New York: St. Martin's. (236)

O'Rourke, T. (1980). *The Impact of Reapportionment.* New Brunswick, NJ: Transaction Books. (265, 266, 276)

O'Rourke, T. G. (1982). Constitutional and statutory challenges to local at-large elections. Presented at the annual meeting of the American Political Science Association. (225)

Orr, D. M., Jr. (1969). The persistence of the gerrymander in North Carolina congressional redistricting. *Southeastern Geographer* 9: 39–54. (285)

Ostrogorski, M. (1908). *Democracy and the Organization of Political Parties,* (2 vols.). New York: Macmillan. (24)

Paddison, R. (1976). Spatial bias and redistricting in proportional representation systems: A case study of the republic of Ireland. *Tijdschrift voor Economische en Sociale Geografie* 67: 230–240. (190)

Pattanaik, P. K. (1978). *Strategy and Group Choice.* Amsterdam: North-Holland. (198, 202)

Pedersen, M. W. (1966). Preferential voting in Denmark. *Scandinavian Political Studies* 1: 167–187. (90)

Pitchell, R. J. (1959). The electoral system and voting behavior: The case of California's cross-filing. *Western Political Quarterly* 12: 459–484. (249, 250)

Pitkin, H. F. (1967). *The Concept of Representation.* Berkeley: University of California Press. (206)

Polyzoides, A. (1927). Greece's experiment with proportional representation. *American Political Science Review* 21: 123–128. (27)

Pomper, G. (1966). Ethnic and group voting in nonpartisan elections. *Public Opinion Quarterly* 30: 79–97. (229)

Preston, M. B. (1978). Black elected officials and public policy: Symbolic or substantive representation? *Policy Studies Journal* 7: 196–201. (218, 224)

Priesse, E. L. (1913). Bibliography of proportional representation in Tasmania. *Papers and Proceedings of the Royal Society of Tasmania,* pp. 39–75. (137)

Rae, D. W. (1967, 1971). *The Political Consequences of Electoral Laws.* New Haven: Yale University Press. (2, 15, 28, 31, 33, 40, 45, 46, 51, 52, 67, 72, 85, 102, 114, 116, 123, 155, 164, 166, 171, 175, 176, 177, 190, 202, 277, 294, 301, 302)

Rae, D. W., et al. (1971). Thresholds of representation and thresholds of exclusion. *Comparative Political Studies* 3: 479–488. (5, 95, 157)

Riker, W. (1962). *The Theory of Political Coalitions.* New Haven: Yale University Press. (202)

Riker, W. H. (1976). The number of political parties: A reexamination of Duverger's law. *Comparative Politics* 9: 93–106. (32)

Riker, W. H. (1982a). Two-party system and Duverger's law: An essay on the history of political science. *American Political Science Review* 76: 753–766. Excerpted with revisions, in this volume, chap. 1. (5, 15, 19, 45, 46, 47, 48, 65, 69, 72, 74)

Riker, W. H. (1982b). *Liberalism Against Populism.* San Francisco: Freeman. (10)

Riker, W. H., and P. C. Ordeshook (1968). A theory of the calculus of voting. *American Political Science Review* 62: 25–42. (39)

Roberts, G. K. (1975). The Federal Republic of Germany. In S. E. Finer (ed.), *Adversary Politics and Electoral Reform,* pp. 203–222. London: Anthony Wigram. (123)

Robinson, T. P., and T. R. Dye (1978). Reformism and black representation on city councils. *Social Science Quarterly* 59: 133–141. (212, 216, 225, 237)

Rogers, C., and H. D. Arman (1971). Nonpartisanship and election to city office. *Social Science Quarterly* 51: 941–945. (234)

Rokkan, S. (1968). Elections: Electoral Systems. In D. L. Sills (ed.), *International Encyclopedia of the Social Sciences,* Vol. 5, pp. 6–21. New York: Macmillan and Free Press. (2)

Römer, K. (1980). *Facts about Germany: The Federal Republic of Germany.* Gutersloh: Lexikothek Verlag. (121)

Rondot, P. (1966). The political institutions of Lebanese democracy. In L. Binder (ed.), *Politics in Lebanon,* pp. 127–141. New York: Wiley. (120)

Rose, R. (1983). Elections and electoral systems: choices and alternatives. In Bogdanor and Butler (eds.), *Democracy and Elections: Electoral Systems and Their Political Consequences*. Cambridge: Cambridge University Press, pp. 20–45. (66)

Rose, R. (1984). Electoral systems: A question of degree or of principle? In Lijphart and Grofman (eds.), *Choosing an Electoral System: Issues and Alternatives*, pp. 73–81. New York: Praeger. (66)

Rosensweig, J. A. (1981). Highest average methods of allocating seats under proportional representation: A clarification. *Political Studies* 29: 279–281. (175)

Rosenthal, A. (1981). *Legislative Life: People, Process and Performance in the States*. New York: Harper & Row. (232)

Royal Commission Appointed to Enquire into Electoral Systems (1910). Report. London. (25)

Rusk, G. (1970). The effect of the Australian ballot reform on split ticket voting. *American Political Science Review* 64: 1220–1238. (243, 245)

Sacks, P. M. (1970). Bailiwicks, locality and religion: Three elements in an Irish Dail Constituency election. *Economic and Social Review* 1: 531–554. (102, 292)

Saffell, D. (1982). Reapportionment and public policy. In Grofman et al. (eds.), *Representation and Redistricting Issues*, pp. 203–219. Lexington, MA: Lexington Books. (276)

Salisbury, R. H., and G. Black (1963). Class and party in nonpartisan elections: The case of Des Moines. *American Political Science Review* 57: 584–592. (228, 231, 236, 241)

Sanders, H. T. (1982). The government of American cities: continuity and change in structure. In *The Municipal Yearbook 1982*, pp. 178–186. Washington, DC: International City Management Association. (241)

Sani, G., and G. Sartori (1983). In H. Daalder and P. Mair (eds.), *Western European Party Systems*, pp. 307–340. Beverly Hills, CA: Sage. (56, 68)

Sartori, G. (1968a). Political development and political engineering. In J. D. Montgomery and A. O. Hirschman (eds.), *Public Policy*, Vol. 17, pp. 261–298. Cambridge, MA: Harvard University Press. (55, 56, 66, 68, 297)

Sartori, G. (1968b). Representational systems. *International Encyclopedia of the Social Sciences*, Vol. 13. New York: Macmillan/Free Press. (2, 68)

Sartori, G. (1976). *Parties and Party Systems: A Framework for Analysis*. New York: Cambridge University Press. (48, 55, 56, 57, 60, 66)

Satterthwaite, M. A. (1975). Strategy-proofness and arrow's conditions: Existence and correspondence theorems for voting procedures and social welfare functions. *Journal of Economic Theory* 10: 187–217. (198)

Sauer, C. O. (1918). Geography and the gerrymander. *American Political Science Review* 12: 403–426. (183)

Scarrow, H. A. (1983). *Parties, Elections, and Representation in the State of New York*. New York: New York University Press. (251, 254)

Schanberg, S. H. (1965). *New York Times*, August 17. (151)

Schattschneider, E. E. (1942). *Party Government*. Reprint. Westport, CT: Greenwood, 1977. (26)

Schumaker, P. D., and R. W. Getter (1977). Responsiveness bias in 51 American communities. *American Journal of Political Science* 21: 247–281. (220, 222)

Schwartzberg, J. J. (1966). Reapportionment, gerrymanders, and the notion of compactness. *Minnesota Law Review* 50: 443–452. (183)

Sen, A. K. (1970). *Collective Choice and Social Welfare*. San Francisco: Holden-Day. (202)

Seymour, S. (1915). *Electoral Reform in England and Wales*. London: Oxford University Press. (278)

Shane, H. D. (1977). Mathematical models for economic and political advertising campaigns. *Operations Research* 25: 1–14. (197)

Shank, A., and R. W. Conant (1975). *Urban Perspectives: Politics and Policies*. Holbrook Press. (140)

Shaw, F. (1966). *The Defense of the Manager Plan and PR in Cleveland: Too Little and Too Late*. Typescript. National Municipal League Archives, University of Cincinnati Library, Box 2, File 15. (144, 151, 152)

Shively, W. P. (1970). The elusive psychological factor: A test for the impact of electoral systems on voters' behavior. *Comparative Politics* 3: 115–125. (35)

Shively, W. P. (1980). *The Craft of Political Research* (2d ed.). Englewood Cliffs, NJ: Prentice-Hall. (213)

Simson, H. (1979). *Zimbabwe: A country study*. Research Report No. 53. Uppsala: Scandinavian Institute of African Studies. (122)

Smith, G. B. (1975). The failure of reapportionment: The effect of reapportionment on the election of blacks to legislative bodies. *Howard Law Journal* 18: 674. (262)

Smock, D. R., and A. C. Smock (1975). *The Politics of Pluralism: A Comparative Study of Lebanon and Ghana*. New York: Elsevier. (120)

Spafford, D. (1972). Electoral systems and voters' behavior: Comment and a further test. *Comparative Politics* 5: 129–134. (35)

Sprague, J. (1980). *On Duverger's Sociological Law: The Connection between Electoral Laws and Party Systems*. Political Science Paper 48. St. Louis: Washington University. (33, 40)

Spreafico, A., and F. Cazzola (1970). Correnti di partito e processi di identificazione. *Il Politico* 35. (102)

Stockwin, J.A.A. (1983). Japan. In Bogdanor and Butler (eds.), *Democracy and Elections: Electoral Systems and Their Political Consequences*, pp. 209–227. Cambridge: Cambridge University Press. (164)

Straetz, R. A. (1958). *PR Politics in Cincinnati*. New York: New York University Press. (153)

Stratmann, W. C. (1974). The calculus of rational choice. *Public Choice* 18: 93–105. (194)

Suleiman, M. W. (1967). *Political Parties in Lebanon: The Challenge of a Fragmented Political Culture*. Ithaca, NY: Cornell University Press. (120)

Svara, J. H. (1977). Unwrapping institutional packages in urban government: The combination of election institutions in American cities. *Journal of Politics* 39: 166–175. (204, 205, 225)

Taebel, D. A. (1975). The effect of ballot position on electoral success. *American Journal of Political Science* 19: 519–526. (246)

Taebel, D. A. (1978). Minority representation on city councils: The impact of structure on blacks and hispanics. *Social Science Quarterly* 59: 142–152. (205, 212)

Taylor, P. J. (1973). Some implications of the spatial organization of elections. *Transactions, Institute of British Geographers* 60: 121–136. (184)

Taylor, P. J., and G. Gudgin (1975). A fresh look at the parliamentary boundary commissions. *Parliamentary Affairs* 28: 405–415. (188, 280)

Taylor, P. J., and G. Gudgin (1976a). The myth of non-partisan cartography. *Urban Studies* 13: 13–25. (186, 187)

Taylor, P. J., and G. Gudgin (1976b). The statistical basis of decision making in electoral districting. *Environment and Planning A* 8: 43–58. (188, 189)

Taylor, P. J., and G. Gudgin (1977). Antipodean demises of Labour. In R. J. Johnston (ed.), *People, Places and Votes*, pp. 111–120. Armidale N.S.W.: University of New England. (189)

Taylor, P. J., and R. J. Johnston (1978). Population distribution and political power in the European Parliament. *Regional Studies* 12: 61–68. (191)

Taylor, P. J., and R. J. Johnston (1979). *Geography of Elections*. London: Penguin. (175, 186, 191, 278)

Thayer, N. (1969). *How the Conservatives Rule Japan.* Princeton, NJ: Princeton University Press. (102)

Tornudd, K. (1968). The Electoral System of Finland. London: Hugh Evelyn. (88)

Tufte, E. R. (1973). The relation between seats and votes in two-party systems. *American Political Science Review* 67: 540–554. (34)

Upton, G.J.G., and D. Brook (1975). The importance of positional voting bias in British elections. *Political Studies* 22: 178–190. (246)

Urwin, D. W. (1974). Germany: Continuity and change in electoral politics. In R. Rose (ed.), *Electoral Behavior: A Comparative Handbook,* pp. 109–170. New York: Free Press. (121)

Van den Bergh, G. (1955). *Unity in Diversity: A Systematic Critical Analysis of All Electoral Systems.* London: Batsford. (172, 177)

Van Valey, T. L., et al., (1977) "Trends in residential segregation: 1960–1970." *American Journal of Sociology* 82: 826–844. (217)

Vedlitz, A., and C. A. Johnson (1982). Community racial segregation, electoral structure, and minority representation. *Social Science Quarterly* 63: 727–736. (217)

Vogel, B. et al. (1971). *Wahlen in Deutschland: Theorie, Geschichte, Dokumente, 1848–1970.* Berlin: De Gruyter. (123)

Walker, J. L. (1966). Ballot forms and voter fatigue: An analysis of the office block and party column ballots. *Midwest Journal of Political Science* 10: 448–463. (244)

Walton, H., Jr. (1972). *Black Politics: A Theoretical and Structural Analysis.* Philadelphia: Lippincott. (218)

Weaver, L. (1971). Nonpartisan Elections in Local Government. Lansing, MI: Citizens Research Council of Michigan. (151, 226)

Weaver, L. (1982). *Two cheers for proportional representation in Cambridge, Massachusetts: A preliminary report on research in progress.* Presented at the annual meeting of the Conference Group on Representation and Electoral Systems, American Political Science Association. (144)

Weaver, L. (1984). Semi-proportional and proportional representation systems in the United States. In Lijphart and Grofman (eds.), *Choosing an Electoral System: Issues and Alternatives,* pp. 191–206. (144)

Weber, R. E. (1980). Gubernatorial coattails: A vanishing phenomenon? *State Government* 53: 153–156. (244)

Weber, R. J. (1979). Comparison of voting systems. Unpublished. (199, 201)

Weiner, M. (1957). *Party Politics in India: The Development of a Multi-Party System.* Princeton: Princeton University Press. (31)

Welch, S. (1978). Election to the legislature: Competition and turnout. In J. Comer and J. Johnson (eds.), *Nonpartisanship in the Legislative Process: Essays on the Nebraska Legislature.* Washington, DC: University Press of America. (232)

Welch, S., and A. K. Karnig (1979). Correlates of female office holding in city politics. *Journal of Politics* 59: 478–491. (237)

Wertman, D. (1977). The Italian electoral process: The elections of June 1976. In H. R. Penniman (ed.), *Italy at the Polls: The Parliamentary Elections of 1976,* pp. 41–79. Washington, DC: American Enterprise Institute. (176, 177)

Wildavsky, A. (1964). *Leadership in a Small Town.* Totowa, NJ: Bedminster Press. (236)

Williams, J. F. (1918). *The Reform of Representation.* London: J. Murray. (24, 28)

Williams, O., and C. Adrian (1959). The insulation of local politics under the nonpartisan ballot. *American Political Science Review* 53: 1052–1063. (228, 230, 231, 236, 241)

Winter, William O. (1982). The long, unhappy life of the Hare system in Boulder. Paper delivered at the annual meeting of the American Political Science Association. (144)

Wittman, D. (1983). Candidate motivation: A synthesis of alternative theories. *American Political Science Review* 77: 142–157. (110)

Wolfinger, R., and J. O. Field (1966). Political ethos and the structure of city government. *American Political Science Review* 56: 306–326. (205)

Wright, J.F.H. (1980). *Mirror of the Nation's Mind: Australia's Electoral Experiments.* Sydney: Hale and Iremonger. (128)

Xydis, S. G. (1973). *Cyprus: Reluctant Republic.* The Hague: Mouton. (117)

Young, H. P. (1978). The allocation of funds in lobbying and campaigning. *Behavioral Science* 23: 21–31. (197)

Zauderer, D. E. (1971). The rig of the game: An analysis of the political consequences resulting from an alteration in the Ohio ballot form. Doctoral dissertation, University of Indiana. (244)

Zeller, B., and H. A. Bone (1948). The repeal of P.R. in New York City—Ten years in retrospect. *American Political Science Review* 42: 1127. (143, 151, 152)

Zimmerman, J. F. (1971). Electoral reform needed to end political alienation. *National Civic Review* 60: 6–11, 21. (151)

Zuwiyya, J. (1972). *The Parliamentary Election of Lebanon, 1968.* Leiden: Brill. (120)

Court Cases

Baker v. Carr, 369 U.S. 186 (1962). (258, 259, 260, 271, 276)

Cintron–Garcia v. Romero–Barcelo, 671 F.2d 1 (1982). (139)

Colegrove v. Green, 328 U.S. 549 (1946). (259)

Connor v. Johnson, 402 U.S. 690, 692 (1971). (269)

Gaffney v. Cummings, 412 U.S. 735 (1972). (276)

Kirkpatrick v. Preisler, 394 U.S. 526 (1969). (276)

Mahan v. Howell, 410 U.S. 315 (1973). (276)

Reynolds v. Sims, 377 U.S. 533 (1964). (261, 262, 268, 271, 274)

United Jewish Organizations of Williamsburg v. Carey, 430 U.S. 144 (1977). (269)

Wells v. Rockefeller, 394 U.S. 542 (1969). (276)

White v. Weiser, 412 U.S. 783 (1973). (276)

Subject Index